National Parks and the Woman's Voice

Althea Roberson, the first African-American woman ranger at Yosemite National Park, tries her Park Service Stetson on a member of the next generation. *(Courtesy of Althea Roberson.)*

National Parks and the Woman's Voice

A HISTORY

Polly Welts Kaufman

University of New Mexico Press

ALBUQUERQUE

In memory of Dorothy Boyle Huyck and Katharine Harriman Welts, who both shared with many women their love of the natural world.

Library of Congress Cataloging-in-Publication Data

Kaufman, Polly Welts, 1929–
National parks and the woman's voice / Polly Welts Kaufman.—1st ed.   p. m.
Includes bibliographical references and index.
ISBN 0-8263-1870-3
1. United States. National Park Service—Officials and employees—Biography.
2. Women in conservation of natural resources—United States—Biography.
3. United States. National Park Service—History.
4. National parks and reserves—United States— History.
I. Title
SB481.5.K38   1996   305.9'3636—dc20   95-32469   CIP

Contents

Acknowledgments

*R*esearching the history of women and their influence on national parks has been like riding a storm wave to shore in a small boat. You think you have landed safely, but before you catch your balance, another wave is upon you. Eventually you must jump out into the unsettled sea, pull the boat in, and tie it up.

Despite continual changes in the national park story, the one factor that has been constant throughout the ten years of this project has been the steady support of people in the Park Service. No request for information was ever denied me, and many individuals reached into their files or memories to provide material they thought I should have. Although the story is still ongoing, it is time for me to jump out and tie it up.

This book had its genesis in the work of Dorothy Boyle Huyck, who was the first person to examine both the opportunities and problems women faced in their new roles. She conceived and designed a project to document the history of professional women in the National Park Service, gathering significant archival and manuscript resources, photographs and 140 taped oral history interviews before her untimely death in August 1979. I am grateful to her husband, Earl, and her daughter, Heather Huyck, who made it possible for me to continue the project by allowing me to use Dorothy Boyle Huyck's papers and arranging for me to listen to her interviews. While the scope and purpose of the book changed over time, I take this opportunity to honor Dorothy Boyle Huyck's groundbreaking contribution.

I also want to acknowledge the role individual Park Service women played in arousing my interest, unknowingly, in a series of events in June 1981. The first was at the Berkshire Conference on the History of Women at Vassar College, where two groups of Park Service women made what seemed to me then astounding presentations. They shared the news that in New York State two places of great significance in women's history were about to become national parks: the site at Seneca Falls of the first women's rights convention and Val-Kill, the retreat and home of Eleanor Roosevelt in nearby Hyde Park. Judy Hart and a team of women explained that, six months earlier, President Jimmy Carter had signed a bill creating Women's Rights National Historical Park. Later, Heather Huyck and other Park Service women took us through Val-Kill, which at that time had not yet been rehabilitated. The second group of events occurred the following week on a trip with my husband to the Four Corners Region in the Southwest. At Canyon de Chelly, Kayci Cook, who, as a uniformed volunteer, was beginning her now established Park Service career, took us on an extensive well-informed walk, explaining that although she was a fourth-generation Park Service daughter, she was the first woman in her family to hold an official position. A few days later, at the seventy-fifth anniversary of Mesa Verde National Park, Lorraine Mintzmyer, the first woman regional director, chaired the program. A commemorative newspaper reported that women had founded Mesa Verde. All these events convinced me that women's roles in national parks had a past as well as a present, and I knew I wanted to tell the story.

It was not until 1985 that I was able to begin the research, and by then Ed Bearss, Park Service chief historian, had found funding for my travel to each of the then ten regions where I taped interviews with 340 Park Service women employees and forty-three wives. Each region also arranged for me to meet with the women as a group and distribute questionnaires.

I am indebted to many other individuals in the Park Service, particularly to Barry Mackintosh, who read the manuscript, corrected mistakes in fact, and accepted my interpretation even when it did not concur with his, as long as I presented evidence; to Magaly Green, who kept me informed about relevant Park Service developments over the entire period of the project; to Dwight Pitcaithley, for his useful and continuing support for the project from its beginnings; to Terry Wood, who introduced me to Park Service alumni with significant stories; to Eleanor Pratt for her explanations of personnel policies and statistics; to Cynthia Kryston, who helped me find the Park Service units that interpreted women's history; to George Fischer, who shared a rare 1970 roster I used for comparisons; to Richard Cripe for his 1972 work-force study; to Tom DuRant who searched for photographs of Park Service women; to *Ranger* editor Bill Halainen and NPS *Courier* editor Mary Maruca, who provided a forum for my findings in their publications; to Loretta Schmidt, who helped trace Albright women graduates; to Noel Poe for offering the marvelous tapes of the anniversary of the saving of Florissant Fossil Beds; and to Mollie and David O'Kane, who looked out for the project from start to finish. I would like to thank all the Park Service women who talked with me or filled out questionnaires. I only wish I could have included many more of their stories.

Several historians outside the Park Service supplied sources I never would have found on my own. In particular my thanks go to Carolyn Merchant, whose research on women in the Progressive conservation movement was a critical aid to my interpretation; to Denise Vick, at Yellowstone, who uncovered and shared the correspondence between the inspector general and Horace Albright that forms a cornerstone of my thesis; to Shirley Sargent, for her pioneering work on Yosemite women; to Ronald Fields and Michael Panhorst, who, respectively, guided me to material on artist Abby Williams Hill and sculptor Theo Ruggles Kitson; to Stephen Fox, who led me to Peter Edge and the sources on Rosalie Edge; to Deborah Herbert, for her research on Genevieve Gillette; and to family historian Edna

Emerson, who shared with me the letters of her sister, Courtney Jones, an early Park Service wife.

Among librarians and archivists who were especially helpful were Wikje Feteris, of the Cary Memorial Library in Lexington, Massachusetts, who handled my inter-library loan requests with complete success; Sarah Pritchard, who guided me through the Library of Congress; Eva Moseley, at the Schlesinger Library at Radcliffe College, who led me to Rose Arnold Powell's story; to David Nathanson, Park Service librarian at Harpers Ferry; to Mary Vocelka at Yosemite; and to Tim Manns, at Yellowstone.

Many people, both inside and outside the Park Service, offered me a place to stay or took special care with my travel arrangements. They include in part: Judith Albert, Elizabeth Buehler, Heidi and Craig Bystrinski, Marilyn Davis, Judy Hart, Earl and Heather Huyck, Mary Jenkins, Sandy Kogl, Jo Ann Kyral, Jean and John Linehan, the O'Kanes, Shirley Thorn, Jean Trainor, Harriet and Arnold Truman, Marilyn Wandrus, and Peggy and Oliver Webb.

Special acknowledgements are due to editors Alice Ingerson, who published parts of chapter 3 in *Forest and Conservation History,* and Dixie Ehrenreich, who published parts of chapter 6 in *Women in Natural Resources.*

I would especially like to thank the persons who assisted me with the publication of this work: Ellen Nylen, Linda Morrison, and Ellen Purdom, who indexed the interview tapes; Charles Grench, Stephen Fox, and Jean Humez for their helpful editorial suggestions; and Barbara Guth, who efficiently carried the book through from submission to publication, combining thoughtfulness with high professional standards.

Finally, my debt to my family is enormous: Rog, for his insights and support; Katharine, for her interest and encouragement; Roger, not only for his editorial comments but for his unwavering faith in my ability to undertake and complete the project and for holding things together while it was in process.

Introduction

*I*f a family planning to visit a national park were to describe their expectations about how a park ranger looked and acted, they would undoubtedly project a traditional image. Their park ranger would be dressed in a neat uniform and wear the Stetson known as the Smokey Bear Hat. Their ranger would generally be a white male, but sometimes female, in good physical condition, well mannered, friendly, and somehow difficult to tell apart from the ranger they saw the day before. The image that would not immediately come to their minds would be that of a person of color, someone with gray hair, or short and chunky, a pregnant woman, or someone speaking with a regional accent; in a word, a person expressing difference.

Although chances are that when the family arrived in the park, they would actually observe many differences among park rangers, nevertheless, the image of a park ranger, carefully constructed over time by the National Park Service, persists in the public imagination. This image, a projection of the male-defined culture of the Park Service, has been the major factor influencing women's opportunities and their expectations for the roles they could fill in national parks. Park Service culture also affected women's efforts to make their voices heard.

The culture of the National Park Service developed out of two contrasting streams. The first major influence was the military. Early park rangers were former cavalrymen, holdovers from the years the U.S. Cavalry protected Yellowstone and Yosemite. Their primary goal was to prevent such threats to the parks as fire and poaching. Horace M. Albright, first civilian superintendent of Yellowstone, noted that at most only half of them were "good public contact men." Several so lacked the ability to meet the public that he assigned them to patrol the far regions of the park.[1] Many of these first rangers expected to remain single or live apart from their families while on duty. The military culture of the Park Service was reinforced by returning World War II veterans, men attracted to the security and camaraderie of Park Service careers.

The second, contrasting, stream contributing to the culture of the Park Service was public communications. It originated in the interpretation by its first two leaders of the 1916 organic act that brought the service into being. Stephen T. Mather, formerly a successful businessman, and Albright wanted to meet the needs of visitors and to educate them. Although the service's mandate specified protecting the natural and historic resources of national parks, it also included providing "for the enjoyment" of the parks in such a way as to leave them "unimpaired for the enjoyment of future generations." Park rangers selected by Mather and Albright, called "Mather men," were closer to the public's image than the cavalrymen were. To the role of protector of the parks, were added the qualities of cordiality, grace, and chivalry, reflecting the personality and social class of Mather himself. Because Mather believed that the survival of the parks depended on public acceptance, he encouraged Park Service staff to be welcoming to visitors and supported the development of elegant tourist facilities.[2] Albright added educational programs and hired ranger-naturalists to carry them out.

The conflict in the two streams of Park Service culture—the military ethos and the public communications approach—had serious ramifications for women. Many of the old-time rangers from the military tradition looked upon the new male ranger-naturalists as effeminate, calling them "pansy pickers" and "butterfly chasers." When Albright began to hire women as ranger-naturalists after World War I, male ranger-naturalists came to see women as a threat to their futures. A decade later, as the male naturalists struggled to develop a profession, they defined their positions as men's jobs and excluded women. If they believed their jobs were on the line because they and their work were not perceived as masculine, then hiring women seemed to confirm the effeminacy of the positions. Even though, nationwide, the pool of women educated in science continued to grow, the Park Service hired only a few highly qualified women as seasonal naturalists during the next three decades.

The masculinity issue appeared again with a different group of Park Service men in the 1960s, but this time it produced rather than eliminated jobs for women. Many male historians disliked conducting tours of historic sites. An official report said that some saw working as interpreters as "unprofessional; not something for the alert and ambitious." Drawing on contemporary perceptions of appropriate gender roles and the experience of tour directors at the United Nations and Rockefeller Center, the Park Service's solution was to hire women as historical interpreters.[3]

Earlier, it was Park Service wives who helped soften the military aspects of the service's culture; some would say they humanized the Park Service. Wives at Yellowstone began to join their husbands on winter assignments and create homes in remote locations. Soon families at park headquarters joined together to hire a teacher for their children. Park communities began to grow around national parks with many functions provided by wives. In the early 1950s, wives met to form a national park women's organization to press for adequate housing. Citing substandard living quarters, their leader, Herma Albertson Baggley, a former ranger-naturalist at Yellowstone, declared, "the day a [male] park employee's marriage license became his discharge paper is long past."[4] Park Service men respected the ability of women and depended on their wives to fulfill a variety of functions; the parks have always been understaffed and women's skills were needed. But even though wives performed virtually every function in a national park, demonstrating a range of talents, they were still considered surrogates without authority working under the direction of their husbands. They saw themselves as companion wives or assumed the service's clerical positions.

As the culture of the Park Service began to move away from its military roots, the door was opened to women as professional employees. The evolving culture placed less value on physical prowess and developed a more democratic management style. The Park Service began to utilize knowledge gained from scientific and historical research for protecting natural habitats and historic structures. Young women were prepared to accept challenges within the service. In addition to the visible examples of competent wives, women outside the service had long since proved their abilities as naturalists, nature guides, archeologists, and sportswomen. Several women, including Herma Albertson Baggley, even wrote the field guides to bird and plant identification used by the male ranger-naturalists and their wives. A final impetus came from federal equal opportunity incentives in place in the mid-1960s combined with the steady increases in the cost of living that prompted women to seek paid jobs.

The old Park Service culture, however, continued to influence how men viewed women's roles in the service. Even the chivalrous manner, no matter how cordial, implied that women were only helpmates needing protection, not full colleagues deserving to be heard. As they worked to gain acceptance, many of the first uniformed women, including the pioneer rangers, superintendents, and maintenance workers, came to believe that they must choose what translated to a male-defined model of behavior and appearance as opposed to a model that would reflect diversity. Some postponed marriage or having a family because they believed those actions would hinder their chances for promotion. One of their most frustrating battles was winning the right to wear the traditional Stetson and the gray and green uniform that conferred full authority on their positions in the eyes of the public. The pioneering Park Service women consciously expressed difference only in those roles where the Park Service expected them to be different, namely as wives and in clerical positions.

Another group of women who, although independent of the Park Service, had a profound influence on national parks, responded in a different way when they encountered a male-defined culture, this time in the conservation movement. As concerned citizens, they demanded that specific landscapes or historic sites be preserved as parks for the nation's future generations. At first these women supported the utilitarian conservation movement that emphasized managing natural resources for use and was spearheaded by Gifford Pinchot and the U.S. Forest Service. But women activists left mainstream conservation after they joined preservationist John Muir in a losing battle to keep Yosemite's Hetch-Hetchy Valley from being turned into a reservoir, a project supported by Pinchot and his allies. After helping to develop a constituency to support the establishment of the National Park Service, women advocates worked as outsiders to preserve national parks through their own women-run organizations. Whether their vehicle was the Garden Club of America or a grass-roots movement apart from existing male-directed conservation organizations, women environmentalists chose a separatist approach to their preservation campaigns. Not until the drive to save wild Alaska in the 1970s did women work as national leaders within established environmental groups for a major preservation cause.

The record of women in preservation, which includes protecting landscapes ranging from the shorelines of the Great Lakes to the Santa Monica Mountains of Los Angeles County, though impressive, has been overlooked by historians who documented environmentalists in male-directed organizations. Women—determined to protect pieces of the nation's heritage for their children and their children's children—also pioneered in the preservation of historic places, saving many sites that became part of the National Park System.

The actions of women who were motivated to speak for national parks either within the Park Service or from the outside illustrate two of the choices women have when they confront a male-defined culture. Either they can embrace it and try to hide their difference, or they can abandon the male-defined culture, create their own goals based on their own values, and work as outsiders to bring the desired change. Legal theorist Christine A. Littleton describes the former as *equality as assimilation,* a concept implying that the only way women can achieve equality is to accept the values and norms of the male-defined culture as the valid one and to make every effort to become part of it. The latter is the separatist approach chosen by the women preservationists.

What Littleton proposes is a third route, a model of *equality as acceptance.* In this approach, differences between men and women, whether biological or cultural, are accepted as equal norms complementing each other. Equality as acceptance opposes distinctions made to preserve the hegemony of white males. It recognizes similarities in the skills of women and men, refuses to restrict women (or men) to particular roles, and resists the devaluation of what has been defined as female.[5] Above all, this model values the diversity, including in gender, racial/ethnic backgrounds, and class, that so enriches national parks, whether it be in the makeup of the staff that is directly responsible for the parks or in the choice of participants making decisions about which historic or natural spaces should be preserved as national parks.

Women have made enormous contributions to the National Park System, both as outsiders and insiders. But their perspectives and values have often been divergent from men's; that is where their greatest contributions lie. The women who worked independently of the Park Service as preservationists valued the continuation of life most of all.[6] Women led drives to save Joshua trees and other desert plants in a national monument, to protect the natural succession of forests on the Olympic Peninsula, to keep inviolate fossils representing life as it was more than thirty million years ago, to save a wild sand dune habitat bordering an industrial lakeshore, to protect birds by opposing development of park lands on fragile Atlantic barrier islands, and to stop dams from being built on wild and scenic rivers. Above all, they valued the future of human life as they worked to heal the nation's differences and to open national recreation areas near urban centers for the spiritual and psychological restoration of the diverse peoples living in congested areas. For the purpose of sectional and racial reconciliation, they erected monuments to the Civil War soldiers who died at Shiloh, Vicksburg, or Andersonville and led the effort to make national historic sites for *Brown vs. Board of Education*, representing the legal end of African-American segregation, and Manzanar, a World War II internment camp for Japanese Americans.

Women provided essential support in the drives to save such national icons as Independence Hall, Valley Forge, and Bunker Hill Monument. Women's groups first identified such future national historical parks as the Anasazi cliff dwellings at Mesa Verde and the site of Virginia's first settlement at Jamestown. A strong sense of purpose in individual women resulted in national historic sites at Fort Vancouver, a center for the fur trade in Oregon Territory; Golden Spike in Utah, where a railroad united the continent; and Pipestone, a quarry in Minnesota where Native Americans mine material to craft ceremonial pipes and art objects.

With limited resources, African-American women kept the Frederick Douglass Home intact until the Park Service recognized its significance. Women were responsible for three of only a handful of parks that interpret the arts, and, beginning in the 1970s, for parks presenting the lives of individual women, and one telling the story of women's struggle for equal rights.

Women's socialization as nurturers and carriers of culture, their smaller size, and their outsider status contributed to changes they made as Park Service employees. Women brought new interpretation to battlefields, where they emphasize the cost, not the tactics of war; to visitor protection where they use "voice judo" as opposed to confrontation; to controversial historic space where they present "the other side." Women interpreters were instrumental in bringing the significance of their own racial and ethnic cultures to parks and in preserving cultural landscapes in natural parks. They introduced women's history in more than one hundred parks. Women maintenance workers mitigated development in parks by finding less intrusive methods than wholesale bulldozing in making landscape changes. Women trained in resource management reintroduced such lost species as Kemp's ridley sea turtle and the swift fox. A few Park Service women sacrificed their careers when they spoke out against outside interests whose goals threatened the integrity of existing national parks.

As the National Park Service enters the new century, the culture of the organization is visibly changed. Visitors are welcomed to parks incorporating women's roles in their exhibits and talks. Nearly one in three of the park rangers the visitor meets is a woman wearing the traditional uniform. One-third of the fifteen thousand Park Service employees are women and twenty percent of the women represent minorities.[7] Behind the scenes, women landscape architects, archeologists, scientists, historians, resource managers, and curators have achieved legitimacy; they help set the tone and determine the allocation of funding and personnel and the choice of projects and programs. Although men still dominate the top management positions, they no longer make decisions with advice from a cadre of persons who come from the same mold. It was women in the role of wives who began the process of changing the militaristic/chivalrous culture of the Park Service. It will be women speaking out as colleagues and citizens teamed with men open to diversity who will complete the task.

PART I

Speaking for Parks: The Pioneers

ONE

Travelers and Explorers

*W*omen with independent spirits in the last half of the nineteenth century were eager to share in the strenuous life and to experience nature's grandeur in America's wonderlands. Not only were they drawn to national parks, but they were also anxious to share their experiences in print or on canvas. They saw the parks as lands symbolizing an American Eden or places enshrining the schoolbook values of the nation. When they published books or articles in popular magazines about their journeys or exhibited paintings of park scenes, they were, in effect, urging other women to express their own self-determination by joining in the adventure.

Women took up the challenge: many went on "tramps" in national parks with the mountaineering clubs that were being founded around the turn of the century; some achieved early ascents of mountains in the parks; others saw the parks as resources for studying natural history. In park lands, white women confronted Native American culture and tried to interpret it in its many variations. Other women met the challenge from the parks in a different way; they provided the skills and hard work needed to pioneer the first park hostelries under primitive conditions.

Women were not completely unrestricted, however, while pursuing their new activities. Even though their explorations of the parks were accepted and even encouraged, they were expected to be accompanied by men. In addition, their adventures were inextricably tied up with what they wore. Although many of the women gave up sidesaddles quite purposefully in the 1870s, few dared give up their skirts. When skirts began to hinder their activities, women invented all kinds of devices, using buttons, hooks, and flaps in an effort to solve the problem of mobility while preserving the semblance of a skirt. The Yosemite suit, a skirt falling halfway to the ankle and covering bloomers that ended just below the knee, was an early compromise for women cross-saddle riders in Yosemite Valley. By masking the real meaning of their achievements at a time when conservatives believed women's rights and education would unsex women and lead to infertility, skirts provided a kind of cover under which women could participate fully in the outdoor world with a minimum of public scrutiny. Not until World War I and the final push for woman's suffrage could women climbers and riders wear jodhpurs or knickers without undue notice. Trousers would wait until another war.

Adventure and Epiphany at Yosemite

For women travelers, Yosemite Valley, carved by ancient glaciers out of California's Sierra Nevada, was an early destination. High-spirited adventure characterized the trip to Yosemite Valley in May 1857, more than thirty years before Yosemite became a national park, by Harriet Kirtland and Anna Park, two young teachers from San Francisco. One of the first white women to travel into the valley, Kirtland recorded in her diary that she rode sidesaddle and wore a long skirt. The party included two married couples, James Denman, principal of a San Francisco high school and his wife and L. A. Holmes, editor of the *Mariposa Gazette* and his wife. Denman's news stories about white women traveling safely to Yosemite paved the way for increasing numbers of women to make the trip.[1]

Harriet and Anna camped opposite Yosemite Falls in a "room" made of blankets. Kirtland's first attempt to see Vernal Falls was thwarted by the warning of a grizzly bear—a threat that was dealt with; they ate the bear that night—and high water. Her second try was successful after the men felled a tree for a bridge, although Kirtland was totally soaked. The young women celebrated, racing their horses on the meadow and performing skits around the campfire. Denman's published account was quite different from Kirtland's private one. In an attempt to prove that Yosemite was designed by a "special intelligence," he tried to quantify the magnificence of the cliffs and falls by calculating their heights. Kirtland's first view of the Sierras shining with snow made her feel "small and insignificant" and undeserving of the "goodness of Providence"; but she felt the view "would awe us, and give us grand ideas, and make us truly noble, generous, and good"—exhilaration that was not diminished by their forty-two mile return trip to Mariposa on horseback, taking eighteen hours and ending at midnight.[2]

Pomo Indian women and their families had occupied the valley they called Ahwahnee until the Mariposa Battalion drove them away six years before Harriet Kirtland's visit. Seventy-six years later, Maria Lebrado, a granddaughter of Chief Tenaya, returned to the valley for the first time since their flight and told their story. Known as To-tu-ya, or Foaming Water, she called the falls and cliffs by their Native American names: Chorlock, for Yosemite Falls, and Loya, for Sentinel Rock, where her family's village was located.

Around the time of Kirtland's visit, small groups of Native Americans had begun to filter back into the valley, fishing and working for the white settlers who had moved there to service the growing tourist trade. During the summers, indigenous people from Mono Lake lived in the valley, staying on to harvest the acorn crop. Among them was Ta-bu-ce, a young girl in the 1880s and 1890s, who later would share the culture of her people by demonstrating basket weaving and the process of making flour from black acorns.[3]

By the time Mary Elizabeth Phillips rode into Yosemite Valley in July 1870, the Yosemite suit was the standard dress for women visitors. The four women in Phillips's party made their suits of blue flannel. Phillips told her diary that the suits "look pretty frisky . . . quite the thing in the valley."[12] But she was not prepared for a cross-saddle. When she had to ride astride because of the lack of sidesaddles, she complained, "'Tis abominable. I would not be one bit tired if it were not for that abominable position."[4]

Their party stayed at the Hutchings Hotel, which had been opened by James Hutchings, his young wife, Elvira, and her mother, Florantha Sproat, in 1864, the year the U.S. Congress granted the oversight of Yosemite Valley to the State of California. James and Elvira's daughters, Florence (Floy) and Gertrude (Cosie), were the first white children to be born in Yosemite Valley.[5] Floy was almost six at the time of Phillips's visit, and Cosie almost three. John Muir, who had been in Yosemite for two years, was running Hutchings's sawmill, using blown-down trees. Staying at the Hutchings Hotel was an adventure for Phillips: the family living room (later known as the Big Tree room) had at one end a large fireplace and at the other a live, growing cedar; the partitions between the bedrooms did not reach the ceiling—and the mattresses were stuffed with dried ferns.

Although still steep, the trail to the falls of the Merced River had been improved since Kirtland's visit. Phillips rode to Nevada Falls (the upper falls) and walked down steps beside Vernal Falls; there she found herself in the midst of a complete, circular, rainbow and felt she was one with it. Returning to the valley, she, too, celebrated with a horse race beside the river, beating a male companion. Challenged to race again, as her horse was jumping a ditch Phillips flew off into a sand pit. Her friends, Fannie and Min, rolled off their horses into the water. "Quite a day," Phillips wrote. "Such sound sleeping and such an appetite I never had before. The air is so charming that one cannot but feel in good health."[6]

Phillips noted that one of her favorite authors, Sara Jane Lippincott, was also a guest at the Hutchings Hotel. Lippincott, whose pen name was Grace Greenwood, publicized her Yosemite experiences in a book that revealed the reason so many women authors traveled to Yosemite during the 1870s. They appeared almost to compete with each other in publishing their discoveries. Each presented the journey as a woman's pilgrimage, including elements of both women's emancipation and spiritual freedom. The special clothing of the female initiate was a Yosemite suit. Lippincott believed the best saddle was the Mexican, with a "high pommel" and "long, roomy stirrups" that required women riders to sit astride. Nature probably intended it, she wrote, "otherwise we should have been a sort of land variety of the mermaid." The trials included a tough night stagecoach ride followed by fifteen miles the first day and twenty-six the second on horseback.

Lippincott warned her readers that the trip would be difficult and that it was not to be undertaken by "mere lovers of pleasure . . . dainty . . . aged, timid and feeble people" and "all people without a disciplined imagination." But women were as able as men to pass the trials. For those who did, she said, the reward was to see "what Nature, high-priestess of God, has prepared for them who love her." For the eyes of the nineteenth-century women authors who journeyed to Yosemite, the deserving woman pilgrim would experience an epiphany, a sublime feeling of oneness with God. Where James Denman tried to use statistics to prove Yosemite's grandeur, the women writers described their emotions. The view from Inspiration Point was to Lippincott "a sight that appalled, while it attracted: a sublime terror; a beautiful abyss; the valley of the shadow of God!"[7]

For Helen Hunt [Jackson], an essential component of the pilgrim's experience was having a connection with Yosemite's Native American heritage. Her account of her 1872 visit to Yosemite (published seven years before she launched her campaign for American Indian rights) reveals her sensitivity toward the original settlers of Yosemite. She called them by their chosen name, the Ah-wah-nee-chee, and scolded Lafayette Bunnell not only for "killing off Indians in the great Merced River Valley" but for trying to remove them from history by changing the place names. In her writings, she restored the Native American names. In the very sound of Ah-wah-nee, she said, was "the same subtle blending of solemnity, tenderness, and ineffable joy with which the valley's atmosphere is filled." The Ah-wah-ne-chee "always spoke the truth," she wrote. *Pi-wy-ack*, their name for the lower falls of the Merced River, meant *white water* or "shower of shining crystals" and *Yo-wi-he*, the name for the upper falls, meant "the twisting" or "the meandering." When she climbed to the falls on horseback, she understood the old names: "How well they told the truth!" she exclaimed. The white men were "liars . . . they called the upper fall 'Nevada,' and the lower one 'Vernal;' and the lies prevailed." With regard to human ability to calculate the height of Yosemite's cliffs, Hunt found that "the figures had lost their meaning . . . obliterated by what seemed to be immeasurable height."[8]

By their example and through their writings, each of the women challenged other women to replicate her Yosemite experiences. Mary Cone and the three women in her party, traveling both by horseback and on foot, climbed to Cloud's Rest, four thousand feet above the valley, where they felt "nearer heaven" than ever before. Cone added to the list of initiation rites: being "swept down" with a broom after each ride, so heavy was the dust. The Yosemite pilgrims also included women from England. Constance Gordon-Cumming, an artist, and Maria Theresa Longworth Yelverton, a novelist, each stayed several months. Gordon-Cumming produced a collection of water colors and drawings depicting Yosemite as a place where Native American people could still make a home. Yelverton wrote a novel, *Zanita*, using Floy Hutchings and John Muir as models for characters. Floy was portrayed as an untameable child of nature. Both the artist and the novelist found the monuments of Europe to be wanting, when compared with the walls of Yosemite. Yelverton rode astride on principle, "convinced that side-saddles were diabolical inventions of the tyrant man, to drag woman lopsided through the world." She left the valley on horseback, alone, and nearly perished in an unexpected snowstorm.[9]

The opportunity to use the Yosemite setting as a showcase for women's emancipation was not lost on women's rights leaders. In 1871, Elizabeth Cady Stanton and Susan B. Anthony concluded their California suffrage campaign with a trip to Yosemite. Deciding ahead of time to ride astride, they prepared by purchasing

Yosemite suits. When the mule provided for Stanton for the descent into the valley was "so broad" that she could not reach the stirrups, she decided to walk. Fortunately for her, that very day the first carriage ever to enter the valley had arrived and it was sent to pick her up. Anthony, who, according to Stanton, "made the descent with grace and dignity," welcomed her and "laughed immoderately" at her "helpless plight." Stanton was the center of attention at Hutchings and although she listened to anyone's adventures, she thought none equaled her own. At the Calaveras Grove of Big Trees, she lectured on suffrage in a chapel built on top of a sequoia stump, commenting that "these majestic trees that had battled with the winds two thousand years . . . have probably never before listened to such rebellion as we preached to the daughters of the earth that day." When the women noticed that many trees were named for men, they proceeded to write the names of "a dozen leading women" on cards and tack them to unnamed trees.[10]

Not every woman traveler to Yosemite in those times was vitalized by her experience. At least one disagreed strongly in print. Olive Logan, a well-known actress, writer, and lecturer, recoiled at having to wear the Yosemite suit and suffered over the initial crowded stagecoach ride that covered passengers with dust. When she arrived in the valley on horseback, the experience fell flat. She wrote: "And what do we see? Tall rocks, a few tall trees, a high and narrow waterfall, a pretty little river! No more. . . . Was it for this we had so suffered! In truth and very truth, it does not pay." Logan left after three days, ending her article with the admonition: "don't go to Yo Semite . . . never ride of your own free will in a California stage."[11]

The first serious woman botanist at Yosemite was Jeanne Carr, who is best known as John Muir's mentor. The wife of horticulture professor Ezra Carr, she saw plants as evidence of God's handiwork. In 1869, on her first visit to Yosemite, she collected a snow plant from a root of the Grizzly Giant sequoia tree in Mariposa Grove and carried it home, packed in moss and cradled in the crown of her hat. Four summers later, in her mid-forties, she botanized, camped, and hiked for three months in Yosemite's high country with John Muir, artist William Keith, botanist Albert Kellogg, and her son, Al. She became the first white woman known to have explored the rugged Tuolumne Canyon to Hetch-Hetchy Valley. A newspaper approved of her activities, saying that she "scales the highest summits of the Sierra Mountains on botanical expeditions, and practically asserts woman's rights by carrying her portion of the tent and provisions over heights that only the feet of Indians have trod."[12]

Although the Hutchings family left the valley in 1875, they returned in 1880 after James was appointed Guardian of Yosemite. Tragedy struck within the year. Floy, then sixteen, an expert horsewoman, was eager to guide visitors and answer their questions, often with Cosie close behind. Floy had pulled herself up Half Dome when she was only thirteen, the year after a fixed cable was installed. They explored Yosemite with the four Crippen sisters, daughters of the family who had taken over the hotel. While wading in Mirror Lake, the youngest daughter, twelve-year-old Effie, died after severing an artery on a broken wine bottle. Three weeks later, Floy was killed in a climbing accident. Mount Florence, a peak twelve thousand feet high, was named for her. By the time she was sixteen, Cosie Hutchings was virtually on her own. During college and until her marriage, in her thirties, she worked for the concessions at Yosemite and as a teacher at Wawona, near Mariposa Grove. Soon after her marriage, to William Mills, she left Yosemite for the mountains of Vermont but returned when she was in her seventies to spend eight years camping and again climbing the mountains of Yosemite's high country, often alone.[13]

Women continued to provide the labor for Yosemite's growing tourist trade. Among them was Bridget Degnan, who moved to the United States from Ireland with her husband John and infant son, pioneering at Yosemite in 1884. They raised seven children, John working as a laborer for the state while Bridget built up a successful bakery. She began with a wood stove that held only a few loaves, expanding until she had an oven that baked one hundred loaves at a time. John transformed the bakery into a successful restaurant. The Degnan children, who all graduated from college, attended the Yosemite Valley School, opened in 1875 for fourteen pupils. A string of single women teachers at the Yosemite school were noted for presenting student work in annual exhibitions and dramatic programs for the community.[14]

At the turn of the century, a new kind of hostelry was being pioneered by Jennie and David Curry. Graduates of the University of Indiana, both of the Currys were teachers and both loved the outdoor life. For three summers, they took teachers on camping trips through Yellowstone, using horses and wagons and providing meals. When David became a principal in a California high school (where Jennie taught math) they decided to run a stationary tent camp in Yosemite Valley. Their three children, Foster, Mary, and Marjorie, ranging in age from eleven to four, helped as they were able. From being a business of 240 guests in seven tents in 1899, the Curry venture had grown by 1922 to 650 tents, 60 rooms in cottages, a cafeteria, and a post office and store. From providing room and board in exchange for work for a few Stanford University students, they then employed 107 students from all over the country; from one paid cook, they expanded to twenty-two cooks. Guests who in 1899 came by horse-drawn stage now arrived in private cars. By then Mother Curry, as Jennie had come to be known, had been widowed for five years and was assisted by her grown children, especially her daughter Mary Curry Tresidder, who gradually took over the management of Camp Curry. An ardent hiker and skier and an accomplished horsewoman, Mary helped develop the High Sierra camps and increase the winter business. After the death of her husband, Dr. Don Tresidder, president of Stanford and a former president of the Yosemite Park and Curry Company, Mary assumed the presidency of the company.[15]

Yosemite also figured in publicity gained by sportswomen at the turn of the century. In 1896, when the three Sweet sisters and Maybel Davis climbed Yosemite's highest peak, Mount Lyell, in deep snow, they were featured in the *San Francisco*

Chronicle. The highlight of their two-week camping trip was sliding a mile down a glacier in less than a minute. However, the woman whose 1900 photograph most equates women's emancipation with Yosemite was Kitty Tatch, head waitress at the Sentinel Hotel. Tatch loved to pose for photographers on Overhanging Rock, at Glacier Point, three thousand feet above the valley. The photographers turned the pictures into best-selling postcards, autographed by Tatch. Wearing a long wide skirt, she danced and did high kicks, her tiny figure dwarfed by the sheer cliffs, announcing by her clothes that it was a woman who performed those feats. Alone or with her friend Katherine Hazelston, who worked at Glacier Point, Tatch liked to get as close to the edge as possible.[16]

Wonders and Dangers at Yellowstone

Women travelers to Wonderland or the Geysers, as Yellowstone was called, survived holdups, bear scares, dust, overcrowded stagecoaches, and, in one case, an attack by American Indians. Emma Stone, of Bozeman, Montana, is thought to have been the first white woman to make the trip. She traveled with her husband and two sons in July 1872, four months after Yellowstone became America's first national park administered by the federal government. Created out of more than two million acres of Rocky Mountain wilderness in the northwestern corner of Wyoming and containing ten thousand thermal features, Yellowstone caught the public's imagination. E. S. Topping, fresh from exploring the Norris Geyser Basin, guided them from Mammoth Hot Springs to the Old Faithful area. Emma Stone liked to tell about the trip's hardships. They followed animal trails and river beds, often dismounting to bushwack through thick timber.[17]

The following summer, six-year-old Mabel Cross, became the first white child to visit Yellowstone. Her father, Robert Cross, a U.S. Army captain, wanted the family to visit the park before he left his assignment as post trader for the Crow Indian Agency. The party also included two young men and a camp cook. A string of pack mules carried their tents, bedding, and staples. While riding on a pony named Dolly in a saddle especially fashioned for her by a blacksmith, Mabel climbed steep trails, jumped over logs, rode through streams, and swam the Yellowstone River. The party lived on game, and fish that were so plentiful they could sometimes be caught with bare hands. Because he wanted Mabel to see the falls of the Yellowstone River, Cross fastened himself by rope to a tree so he could carry her out on a ledge for a view of the lower falls (while her mother closed her eyes). They spent twenty-four days in the saddle and rode about 350 miles.[18]

Three years later, Emma Carpenter Cowan made what was for her a second and ill-fated trip to the park. The party included other members of her family and four male friends from Helena, Montana. They were equipped with a double-seated carriage, a baggage wagon, four saddle horses, tents, provisions, and musical instruments for entertainment around the campfire. Emma sensed the primordial quality of the park; she felt she was in a new land, "fresh from the Maker's hand."

One night, they pitched a tent close to the Castle Geyser; when its eruption awakened them, she was "sure the earth would be rent asunder and we would be swallowed up. . . . One seemed," she said, "in close proximity to Dante's Inferno." But the events that were to follow were real, not imagined.

Soon after they broke camp to head for home, the Cowans met a band of Nez Perce warriors, in flight with their families from the tribe's forced removal to a reservation. Relations at first seemed friendly, but when the whites were forced to exchange their horses for the Nez Perce's worn-out mounts, the Cowans realized that they were powerless. Emma Cowan understood, at least in retrospect, that the trade was "a fair reflection of the lesson taught by the whites," who many times convinced the government to move Native Americans off lands white settlers wanted, giving the indigenous people less desirable lands. Feelings began to get tense, and two of the Nez Perce men fired shots at and seriously wounded Emma's husband, George, who was left for dead. The Nez Perce took Emma, her brother, and young sister captive. Still believing George was dead, Emma, her sister, and brother were released after a few days and the brother led them on an arduous journey via Mammoth Hot Springs to Bozeman, then to her father's home in Virginia City, Montana. A week later, she received word that her husband was alive. He had crawled to safety and was found by cavalry scouts. She traveled back to Bozeman to take him home, where he took the winter to recuperate. Thinking back on the experience later, Emma Cowan believed that the Nez Perce showed "a quality of mercy . . . that a Christian might emulate, and at a time when they must have hated the very name of the white race."[19]

Sarah and George Marshall were the first people to run a hotel at Yellowstone. Their log hotel was located near the lower geyser basin. In October 1880, George drove their first visitors, Carrie and Robert Strahorn, by stagecoach the 120 miles from Virginia City to the hotel, and took them on a tour of the park. During the Marshalls' first winter, when the living section was separated from the unchinked upstairs by only a canvas wagon-cover, their fourth child, Rosa Park, was born— the first white child to be born in Yellowstone. When George Marshall visited the Strahorns in Omaha the following spring, he left Sarah and the children alone for a month. Soon after he left, she discovered two bears trying to break into the storehouse. She wounded one with a rifle; when he charged, she slammed the door shut, just in time. She followed him up the mountain behind their house and killed him. That summer, Marshall completed the hotel. The Marshalls offered guests the use of a bathhouse and a washhouse supplied with water from the hot springs and fed them domestic fowl and six kinds of wild meat: blacktail deer, whitetail deer, bear, two kinds of grouse, and squirrel.[20]

By 1883, with the opening of the massive National Hotel at Mammoth Hot Springs and heavy promotion by its sponsor, the Northern Pacific Railway, hotels became an option to "sage brushing," as camping was called. A five-day tour by stagecoach included stops at accommodations ranging from the new hotel, which one English woman described as having "an air of general discomfort," to Marshalls' and tent camps at the Norris and the upper geyser basins. The roads were so dusty that women in stagecoaches draped their large hats with veiling and rented long linen dusters; for "dudes," camping outfits complete with guides were available. Englishwoman Georgina Synge shared with her country the geyser games that became the standard Wonderland experience. She dropped her handkerchief into the "Cubs" so it would be thrown up "snowy white" and she "soaped" the Beehive so it would play two days ahead of time. But Synge saw the new "stage houses" as "too 'civilized'" and warned travelers not to delay, but visit while the Park was still "unspoilt."[21]

Not all visitors to Yellowstone took the packaged tour. Twenty-five years after Emma Stone's pioneering visit to the park, three generations of the Stone family toured the Geysers. Each family traveled in its own covered wagon, carrying tents for sleeping in and camp stoves for cooking. They ate well. In the morning one of the mothers mixed bread dough, letting it rise during the day for baking as soon as they made camp. A crate of live chickens, for butchering, was attached to the side of one wagon; they also carried home-cured hams and bacon, eggs, a crock of homemade butter, and dried fruit. They depended on the park's resources for trout, range-grass feed for their horses, and hot water, the latter coming from the pools. They poured the geyser water into tubs and used it for washing both clothes and children. By the 1890s, thousands of people toured the park each summer. As wagons and stages met, the occupants would yell out the names of their home states or native countries.[22]

Many women visitors saw their adventures in the park as an opportunity to relive the excitement of the Old West—or at least to live it as they imagined it to have been. In an article in *Harper's*, Alice Wellington Rollins, an Easterner, urged tourists to choose a summer trip to Yellowstone instead of to the Alps for patriotic reasons; the park, she said, was the "one place left in the United States where it is still possible to 'rough it.'" Visitors sometimes met Calamity Jane selling her picture and her life story at the Mammoth Hotel. That the Old West lived on could be confirmed: five holdups for the period are documented, notably one in 1908 that involved seventeen stagecoaches.[23]

When the hotels at Yellowstone Lake, the Grand Canyon of the Yellowstone River, and Old Faithful opened, young women, many from the East, traveled to work in them in the summer, looking for adventure. They reported to old-timers like Willie Frances Bronner, a single parent who brought her eight-year-old daughter, Jean, with her for the first of their nearly ten seasons in 1908. Bronner's day began with kneading a dozen loaves of bread and ended with organizing singing and storytelling for guests around a campfire. Jean remembers her mother growing into "a self-confident, independent person." For Jean and her mother, the entrance of the automobile into Yellowstone in 1915, signaled the end of the park's frontier days.[24]

Army Officers' Wives at Fort Yellowstone

In 1886, women with a different role from that of traveler or hostelry worker arrived in Yellowstone. They were the wives of officers of U.S. Cavalry units assigned to protect the park's wildlife from poaching, its thermal features from vandalism, and to regulate the concessioners. Wives of enlisted men were not allowed to live in army posts and if they followed their husbands, they had to find housing and employment in nearby towns. One unconfirmed, but widely-held, belief is that in the summer, some of the wives of enlisted men camped to be near their husbands who were housed in barracks in various park locations.

Letitia Follett Bradley, wife of Dr. Alfred E. Bradley, post surgeon at Yellowstone from 1895 to 1898, has provided a picture of family life at Fort Yellowstone, the army post established at Mammoth Hot Springs. She also tells of an unusual reenactment of the Battle of the Little Bighorn, near Fort Custer, her husband's previous assignment. "At least a thousand" Sioux and Crow Indian people staged the reenactment of what she called "the Custer Massacre." Along with twenty of the officers and their wives, the Bradleys rode on horseback to the battlefield, ten miles from the post, to witness the event. The Sioux and Crow men were dressed in "war paint and feathers," their wives in "beautiful deerskin and buckskin clothes, decorated with rows and rows of elk teeth." Letitia described the event: "The Indians divided themselves in two groups, one representing Custer and his troops. An old chief would ride out in front of the crowd and chant the story . . . then there would be a wild swirl of ponies (all ridden bareback) while the action was demonstrated." Because the participants got "so excited and worked up," Letitia explained, the fort authorities decided not to allow a performance the following year. Among the regulations for the reenactment was one stating that officers' wives were not to be taken captive. Letitia wrote: "One bullet in each officer's revolver was to be saved to prevent that."

The Bradleys hired a boxcar to take their family goods to Yellowstone from Fort Custer. Into one end of the boxcar went a cow, two horses, a crate of chickens, and a crate of houseplants; into the other end went the family's household goods, all crated; into the center went their open buggy. The family, including Harriett, who was almost three, and Follett, who was almost five, rode in passenger coaches. During their first Yellowstone winter, the Bradleys sent to Chicago for two sleds, and soon everyone on the post was coasting down the one plowed road. Since there was no school, Letitia, a former teacher, taught Follett. She also did all the family's sewing, and, when her husband came down with Rocky Mountain Spotted Fever, Letitia served as his nurse.[25]

The Bradleys bequeathed to Yellowstone a special human legacy: Marguerite Lindsley [Arnold], who became one of the first woman rangers in the Park Service and whose life spanned both Yellowstone's military and civilian administrations. She was the daughter of Alfred Bradley's sister Maude, who visited the park and met and married Chester Lindsley, a civilian who was the park's chief clerk. From her childhood, Marguerite remembered the pageantry of the cavalry: "bugle calls, sunrise and sunset guns, regimental bands, post flags at half mast for Decoration Day, . . . sabre drills, polo matches, pistol and rifle range practice."[26]

In letters, a close friend of Marguerite's mother's, Bessie Haynes Arnold, wife of Major Frederick Arnold, describes the lively and strenuous social life at Fort Yellowstone: horseback riding, bowling, basketball, skating, skiing, sleigh rides, and a weekly silent movie, all preceded or followed by teas or suppers rotating among households. The Park Service bought and exhibited Bessie Arnold's wildflower drawings.[27]

The Arnolds left when the cavalry abandoned Fort Yellowstone in 1918, but the Lindsleys remained. Chester Lindsley became acting superintendent of the park, and later, postmaster. Marguerite Lindsley's extensive knowledge of the natural history of the park, including its wildlife, and her personal identification with Yellowstone's wildness, impelled her to jump the fences—in jodphurs, astride an English saddle—that kept women confined to the roles of travelers, concessioners, or park wives. In 1921, while still a college student, Marguerite began a ten-year career as a Park Service ranger. The cavalry also left behind a cadre of men who stayed on as Park Service rangers, as well as a legacy of policies and procedures that imprinted the service with many military practices and terms. It would be expectations established by the military culture that would eventually cost Marguerite Lindsley her job.

The Abyss and the Summit

The Grand Canyon, a mile-deep gash cut by the Colorado River in northern Arizona, revealing rock two billion years old; Longs Peak, rising 14,255 feet out of the Front Range of the Colorado Rockies; Mount Whitney, topping the crest of the Sierra Nevadas in California at 14,495 feet, all produced strong emotions in late nineteenth-century women. They met the challenge to encounter these places even before they were designated national parks.

For Hopi people, the Grand Canyon of the Colorado River has always been sacred space—its walls, springs, and side canyons all infused with the essence of spirituality. For white women travelers, it was the abyss itself that aroused their deepest feelings. "It was like sudden death," wrote poet Harriet Monroe, who first stood on the canyon's edge in May 1899. "We stood at the end of the world. . . . The earth lay stricken to the heart, her masks and draperies torn away, confessing her eternal passion to the absolving sun." Monroe, fighting an impulse to fling herself into the canyon, was saved by the song of an oriole, with which she felt a oneness: it "seemed to welcome me to the infinite . . . and gave me healing and solace." Mary Wager Fisher felt she had arrived at the beginning, not the end, of time—"the place where the foundations of the earth were laid."[28]

When Harriet Monroe wondered how Grand Canyon innkeepers and guides could live with its awesomeness, she might have found an answer from Ada Bass, wife of William Bass, for whom the canyon became home. As Ada Diefendorf, a music teacher from New York, she met Bass while a guest at Bass Camp, located on the South Rim, about twenty miles from Grand Canyon Village. Three years later, in 1895, Ada married Bass and found plenty of work awaiting her. Guests expected to be conducted into the canyon with full meals and camping outfits. Because her husband was so often in the field, Ada learned to be self-sufficient. She furnished their home with crafts made by local Indian people, made quilts for their guests, baked, kept track of supplies, supervised the camps, and canned, filling 144 jars during one peach harvest. When their four children were old enough to begin school, Ada taught them at home, including music played on her piano. She also built up a library. William was so conscious of Ada's role that when they sold the business in the early 1920s, they divided the proceeds evenly. The Bass's older daughter, Edith, was a true child of the canyon. When she was only three, she rode her own horse down to the river. By the time she was ten, she could respond to the signal fire on the North Rim indicating that a guided group of riders was about to descend and needed her to lead fresh horses down to the river to meet them. She became skilled at hunting and roping horses and driving wagons. Edith married and began to raise her own family on a homestead near Bass Camp. A year after her parents left the canyon, Edith Bass died unexpectedly from appendicitis complications, aged twenty-eight.[29]

Mountains, too, were unsettling experiences for nineteenth-century women. For English traveler Isabella Bird, it was the ascent of Longs Peak, in the future Rocky Mountain National Park, that gave rise to her deepest feelings. Bird's feat, in 1873, is the most famous ascent of a mountain by a woman in nineteenth-century America. Climbing with Rocky Mountain Jim Nugent—a man considered by some to be a desperado—only five years after the first white man had reached the top, Bird was so overwhelmed by her trials that she hesitated to describe them. The experience linked her with the sublime. Fascinated by an "unspeakable awfulness," she saw the mountain as a personality letting loose "storms of snow and wind . . . in its fury"; "forked lightnings play round its head like a glory." She would not have made the last few hundred feet, she said, had not Jim "dragged me up, like a bale of goods, by sheer force of muscle." So exhilarated was she when she achieved the summit, she lost her giddiness. As she descended, she "faced the precipice of 3,500 feet without a shiver."[30]

But Bird was actually preceded by a few weeks by Anna Dickinson, a young lecturer on the lyceum circuit and suffragist. After riding to the tops of several of Colorado's "fourteeners" (as the mountains over fourteen thousand feet are called) she decided she was ready for Longs Peak. The only woman in a party of thirteen, Dickinson climbed with the editor of Rocky Mountain News, assuring publicity for the feat. A companion, Ferdinand Hayden, of the U.S. Geological Survey, accepted her designation of a nearby peak as Lady Washington. This established a female counterpart to Mount Washington, the highest mountain in the northeast, which Dickinson had ascended twenty-seven times. To Dickinson it was the talk around the campfire that made her climb worth the great effort—the talk about "all things, in fact, that touch the brain and soul, the heart and life, of mortals who really live, and do not merely exist." At the summit, she left her name on a yard-long tape measure, found, along with her cape, neatly folded, in a crevice, the following year.[31]

Before climbing Longs Peak became a popular goal for women climbers, the mountain took the life of one woman aspirant. Arriving at the foot of Longs Peak in September 1884, Carrie Welton was determined to climb it. She rented a cabin owned by Elkanah Lamb, engaged his son Carlyle as a guide, and dressed in a man's suit, underneath a dress. By the time they reached the Keyhole, more than a thousand feet below the summit and well above timberline, a storm had come up and Lamb suggested they turn back. Because of her insistence, they struggled to the summit. She used up all her energy in descending to the Keyhole and could go no further. Lamb gave her all the clothing he could spare and hastened for help. By the time Elkanah and Carlyle Lamb arrived, Carrie had died, probably of hypothermia. Elkanah Lamb continued to rent cabins and encourage Longs Peak climbers, including his wife, Jane, who celebrated her seventieth birthday by climbing the mountain with him. He later sold his cabins to his nephew Enos Mills.[32]

The drive to establish new women's records was apparent among many early mountain climbers, men as well as women. Nowhere was this goal as evident as in the first white women's ascent, in 1849, of Mount Katahdin in Maine, now the northern terminus of the Appalachian Trail. Hannah Taylor Keep and Esther Jones were the two of a group of five Maine women, guided by Marcus Keep, who reached the true summit. They climbed Pamola, the lower eastern peak, and crossed the Knife Edge "like children walking upon a crooked rail or stone fence . . . where," according to Keep "no foot of better halves had been." But before their ascent, a rival of Keep's heard about the plan and organized a group of two women and two men to make the climb a week earlier. They stopped short of the Knife Edge, however, but left a note on Pamola that read: "Top of Mount Katahdin" for the Keep climbers to find. Six young women accompanied woman's rights supporter Thomas Wentworth Higginson to the top of Pamola in 1855. Advocating both dress reform and healthful exercise for women, they wore bloomers and announced: "Our moral is that there is more real peril to bodily health in a week of ballroom than in a month of bivouacs."[33]

Two California peaks in future national parks tempted early women climbers: Lassen, then the country's only active volcano, and Mount Whitney, the highest mountain in the continental United States. When, in 1864, Helen Brodt became the first woman to climb Lassen, the party accompanying her discovered a lake and named it for her. They compared the mountain's clouds of sulphur to "an immense steam-engine blowing off steam."[34] Whitney, in the future Sequoia National Park, was first climbed by women—four of them—in 1878. Teacher Anna Mills published the story almost twenty-five years later in the journal of the new Mount Whitney Club, of which she was the first vice president. Although Mills had been lame since childhood, she believed her "surplus of determination" made up for what she "lacked in the power of locomotion." Because much of the journey was made on horseback and the final ascent required the use of both hands and feet, Mills was successful.

Mills and her companions spent more than a month camping in the Kern River Valley, heading for Whitney. They met mountaineer William Crapo, who offered to guide them, wanting, Anna Mills reported, "to have the honor of leading the first party of ladies to the top of the United States." Just before they reached the final camp, Mills was thrown from her horse and injured her back. Although everyone discouraged her from continuing, she walked to "an obscure place, away up there so near heaven" and prayed, facing the mountain. "When I had finished," she wrote, "the mountaintop seemed closer, and I returned to camp with a much lighter heart." She made the ascent the following day with little trouble and the climbers "planted the Stars and Stripes on its topmost point" and sang the "Star-Spangled Banner" and "Nearer, My God to Thee." Looking back on the climb after twenty-five years, Mills concluded that in none of the mountains she later visited in Alaska, Hawaii, or Europe had she ever seen "a picture so varied, so sublime, so awe-inspiring." When Crapo told her story to a group of men camping on the peak three years after her ascent, they arranged to have an unnamed peak south of Whitney named Mount Mills in honor of her perseverance.[35]

Botanizing also took adventurous women into the mountains and canyons of future national parks. An authentic "Shakespeare's sister," botanist Ellen Powell Thompson joined the second expedition of the Colorado River led by her brother, the famous explorer John Wesley Powell, in 1871–72. She discovered and collected several new species.[36] As a young teacher in the 1880s, Alice Eastwood, who later became the curator for the herbarium at the California Academy of Sciences, collected plants, many of them new species, all over her native Colorado. She joined the Wetherill brothers in their first explorations of the Mesa Verde cliff-dweller sites. She knew that the living plants she observed, like the pots they found, connected her with the daily life of the prehistoric cliff dwellers, and figured out the multiple uses of such plants as the yucca. She traveled by stage, buckboard, train, foot, and horseback, giving up her sidesaddle forever after a strenuous trip with the Wetherills in the San Juan River Valley. "Getting on and off the tall horse was hard on me," she said, "and a side-saddle on a long trip in a hot country is *very* hard on a horse." Al Wetherill attested to her independence. "She roamed around collecting plants and once was lost for a time," he said, "but we found her by the smoke from her campfire."[37]

Ice and Fire

Even though the setting was the coastal glaciers of Alaska, far north of the Rocky Mountains, High Sierra peaks, or the Granite Gorge of the Colorado River, the emotions aroused in Eliza Scidmore were the same: she felt she was present at the beginning, or the end, of time. The only woman on the National Geographic

Society's board of managers, Scidmore was a passenger on the ship *Idaho* when, in 1883, the first group of tourists entered Glacier Bay, on the mountainous coast of southeast Alaska. As they neared the Muir Glacier, she felt a "strange fascination" for the wall of ice: "The crash of the falling fragments, and a steady undertone like the boom of the great Yosemite Fall," she wrote, "added to the inspiration and excitement. There was something, too, in the consciousness that so few had ever gazed upon the scene before us, and there were neither guides nor guide books to tell us which way to go, and what emotions to feel."

The party climbed into lifeboats and landed on the Muir Glacier where, as "high-booted pilgrims," they walked for two miles over ice and debris that arched over the river emerging from the retreating glacier. They discovered a remnant of a cedar forest covered by the glacier during an earlier advance. On a second expedition, the arrival of trading Hooniah Indians in canoes made Scidmore keenly aware that her group was not the first to explore the area. Scidmore kept abreast of Alaskan exploration and brought its news to the public in guidebooks and articles.[38]

The coast of Alaska had been familiar to American women from the time sea captain's wives had joined their husbands—the only women allowed on extended whaling voyages in the mid-nineteenth century.[39] But not many women travelers visited Alaska until 1884, when a territorial government was established. Soon, visiting southeast Alaska became the thing to do and how-to books about the far north found an audience. Septima Collis's recommendations for women hinted at adventures to come: pack "broad-soled, low-heeled shoes . . . with a few nails in sole and heel protruding just enough to impress the smooth surface of glacial ice; a pair of smoked glasses," and "powerful field-glasses." Sitka, later the site of Alaska's first national park, was a favorite steamer stop. In 1889, Abby Johnson Woodman described Mount Vestovia with "its great silver firs and cedars" as "a fine relief for the quaintness of the old Russian castle, the Greek church and the low rambling architecture of the Russian regime." Its "sharp, white crest" shining with "constant light like a silver star" made "a benediction on the little city."[40]

Women botanists and anthropologists were particularly attracted to southeast Alaska's differentness from the continental United States and wanted to share their findings. At Glacier Bay, in 1891, botanists Grace Cooley and Clara Cummings studied the order in which once "exiled plants" reappeared to follow the retreat of the glaciers. Cooley identified a new buttercup species, which later was named for her.[41] In 1896, anthropologists Frances Knapp and Rheta Louise Childe decried the tourists' cursory view of Sitka from a steamer. As a corrective, they presented a study of the Tlingit Indians, partly based on interviews with elders conducted over three years in Sitka. Although they presented the Tlingits as having "artistic genius" and worked to record Tlingit culture, they also supported "the civilizing influence" of the mission schools which had the potential to destroy that culture.[42]

Klondike gold first attracted white women to interior Alaska. A conservative estimate by the Northwest Mounted Police was that 631 women climbed over the Chilkoot or White passes to the Klondike between 1897 and 1898. Women, single and married, found that their skills as cooks, laundresses, entertainers, and even fortune tellers translated into the most remunerative work. In the winter, the Chilkoot Pass, approached by fifteen miles of rough terrain, was a steep stairway hacked out of snow and ice over which gold-seekers had to drag their outfits.[43] Fannie Quigley followed the gold trail to the Klondike, in 1898. She set up an eating place wherever she found hungry miners and moved her outfit, which included a tent, a Yukon stove, bacon, beans, and flour, from strike to strike. In 1906, Fannie joined the Kantishna strike on the northwest side of Mount McKinley, where she met and married miner Joe Quigley and settled permanently, living with Joe at subsistence level. The Quigleys fed not only miners but also climbers (among them Peter Anderson and William Taylor, prospectors who, in 1910, made the first ascent of Mount McKinley) and, later, Park Service personnel. They served wild game, berries, and vegetables from Fannie's garden. Her favorite pastime was her exquisite embroidery, a skill she had brought with her from her childhood home in a Bohemian settlement in Nebraska.[44]

In 1913, of Alaska's peaks over 14,000 feet, only McKinley and Mount St. Elias had been climbed. The challenge of making a first ascent attracted woman alpinist Dora Keen, of Philadelphia. She chose Mount Blackburn, now part of the Wrangell–St. Elias National Park and Preserve. After failing in 1912, she succeeded the following year. She was "determined," she said, "to get to the top . . . to go where no one had ever tried to go before, to see ice-fields and glaciers more extensive than any others outside the Antarctic, to have an experience altogether wonderful, all for a comparatively moderate expenditure of time and money." Her expedition included seven men, all Alaskan prospectors who, she said, gave her "a new spirit, a new optimism, a new standard of courage, and a new inspiration for life." The expedition took four weeks and followed the Kennicott Glacier from 2,000 feet to the 16,390 foot summit. Virtually all the time was spent on snow and ice, with the threat of avalanches and widening crevasses increasing as the Alaskan spring progressed. They relayed supplies from camp to camp, using dog sleds as far as the base camp, thirty-one miles up the glacier. At their fourth camp, at 8,700 feet, a snowstorm kept Keen and the two prospectors who continued beyond the base camp in a snow cave for nine days. Keen and G. W. Handy reached the summit on May 19 at 8:30 A.M. met by a six-degree temperature and an icy gale. But nothing, she said, blocked "a view upon which our eyes were the first that had ever looked. . . . Probably nowhere except in Alaska could mortal man attain to the centre of so vast and imposing a stretch of unbroken snow over great glaciers and high snow peaks."[45]

In contrast to Alaska's ice was Hawaii's fire. Isabella Bird's ride down into the Kilauea caldera, Halemaumau, at the time a lake of molten lava, and up to the rim of Mauna Loa, nearly fourteen thousand feet high, took place the year before her more famous ascent of Longs Peak. On the side of Mauna Loa, the Kilauea crater, known as Madame Pele's home and now Hawaii Volcanoes National Park, was to her a "Plutonic region of blackness and awful desolation." Yet Bird discovered three "exquisite" ferns, "heralds of the great forest of vegetation" that spoke "of the love of God." When she reached Halemaumau, she wept, believing "a new glory and terror had been added to the earth." It was the "'fire which is not quenched' . . . the 'everlasting burnings.'"

Bird was fascinated by activity she noticed on top of Mauna Loa—an illumination that at night seemed to "flare up and take the form of a fiery palm tree." When she could find no one to give an explanation, she decided to arrange an expedition herself. After a difficult ride, a climb of more than seven thousand feet, her group reached the rim and looked down nearly a thousand feet into the crater. The mystery of the light was solved by a "perfect fountain of pure yellow fire . . . throwing up its glorious incandescence" to a height of six hundred feet. They camped overnight on the rim, watching the "fiery masses" that were "the colour of a mixture of blood and fire . . . burn[ing] for the Creator's eye alone."[46]

Bird's publications about her travels were widely read, but she was viewed as an explorer, a woman whose adventures in exotic places could not be emulated. By contrast, Emma Shaw, a Providence teacher, described her Hawaiian and Alaskan experiences in lectures to women's clubs in such a way as to bring the mysteries of her adventures and encounters with the native peoples into her listeners' living rooms. Shaw also wrote articles for the *Boston Transcript*, and the *Journal of Education*. By the time she visited Hawaii, she had visited Alaska three times (the first time in 1884) as well as exploring Yellowstone and sub-Arctic Canada. She made her descent into the Kilauea crater on horseback up to a point three miles from the destination. There, the horses were tethered and a lighted lantern was fastened to a pole as a beacon for their return. As she neared the "lake of fire . . . jagged walls . . . shut . . . out the whole outer world." The lava seemed to be "a squirming nest of serpents" that "might at any moment be warmed to life." When Shaw reached the lake, it burst into fire. Like Bird, she watched transfixed, overpowered by the "mystery of mysteries, the bottomless pit." At midnight, each person in the party, depending on a staff and carrying a lantern, climbed back up to the horses, guided by the fixed light. Shaw was certain she had climbed out of hell itself.[47]

Margaret Howard's journey to the rim of the Mauna Loa was so traumatic that she said, "To write an accurate account of the trip to the fiery furnace near heaven would require a pen dipped in red hot liquid lava." When her party arrived at the summit after a ride of nearly two days, their fuel supply was exhausted. Howard and her female companion, determined to see the crater at night, convinced the party to remain, despite below-freezing temperatures. Suffering from the cold and lack of hot food, they left at dawn. Howard reported that within a few days their guide died of the effects of the exposure.[48]

Mountaineering Clubs Legitimize Women's Place in the Wilderness

The organization of Western mountaineering clubs to explore the Sierra, Cascade, Olympic, and Rocky Mountain ranges encouraged groups of women to encounter wilderness areas and snow-covered peaks. Their model was the Appalachian Mountain Club founded in Boston in 1876, a club encouraging women to join from its beginning. Soon after the founding of the clubs (the Sierra Club in 1892, the Mazamas in Oregon in 1894, the Mountaineers in Seattle in 1907, and the Colorado Mountain Club in 1912) women made up nearly half of the memberships. Women interested in adventure no longer needed to hire private guides or organize small expeditions; instead, they could join club "outings." Although they still described some of their experiences as sublime, the paramount goal was to enjoy strenuous outdoor recreation and companionship with like-minded women and men. The more that women club members came to accept their legitimate place in the wilderness, the more they supported moves to protect those spaces as national parks.

"Marching" up peaks in large groups, in quasi military order, women often comprised a third of the successful climbers. One by one, peaks toppled to the "first ascent by a woman," all reported in club journals and popular magazines, the accomplishments serving to inspire other women. But early club women were not looking for a change in their primary roles; men always led the expeditions, and Sierra Club outings, in particular, produced many marriages. Early photographs show long lines of women hikers tramping up glaciers in long skirts, but they gradually traded their skirts for knickers.[49]

It was in the field that Fay Fuller earned her post as first historian and first woman vice president of the Mazamas: in August 1890 she became the first woman to conquer Mount Rainier, then called Mount Tahoma, a 14,410-foot, glaciered volcanic peak in Washington's Cascade Mountains. Fuller climbed with four men, none of whom had made the attempt before, only two years after John Muir's ascent. Originally from New England, Fuller was a twenty-year-old teacher in Yelm when she made the climb. Two weeks later, she published a lively account in her father's Tacoma newspaper, encouraging other women to follow in her bootsteps. Fuller and her father continued to publicize the mountain, urging their congressman to support the establishment of Mount Rainier National Park in 1899.

Again, the major problem was not whether a woman was able to make the climb, but what she would wear. She later said that her costume "was considered quite immodest." She wore a thick, blue flannel bloomer suit and "the strongest shoes . . . sold to boys," carried an alpenstock made from a shovel handle, and wore a ribboned straw hat. With some friends, she rode her own horse, astride, to Paradise Camp, taking three days and hoping "some opportunity would present itself." When the party of male climbers invited her to join them, Fuller was prepared: "I donned . . . warm mittens and goggles, blacked my face with charcoal, . . . drove long caulks and brads into my shoes, rolled two single blankets containing provisions for three days and strapped them from the shoulder under the arm to the waist . . . grasped my alpenstock and was resolved to climb until exhausted."

A thousand-foot cliff, known as Gibraltar, blocked the party's way to the summit. Fuller and two of the men, roped together, had nearly traversed the narrow shelf around Gibraltar when they encountered a slide of solid ice: the leader had to cut steps with a hatchet before they could continue. Still roped, Fuller climbed along an ice aisle, thinking it a "peculiar situation of walking on the backbone where two glaciers met and that two feet either way would precipitate one thousands of feet below." There seemed to be no bridge over one crevasse: as each one was tested, it would crash "down to the bottomless depths with loud sounds." Finally, one bridge held and a climber moved ahead, throwing the others a rope. Fuller "followed hand over hand" up an almost perpendicular cliff with crevasses on either side.

At 4:30 P.M. on August 10, 1890, Fuller proudly stood on the "tip top of Mount Tahoma." The experience was sublime: "Words cannot describe the beauty, how could they speak for the soul!" They camped in an ice cave near the edge of the steaming crater, spread their blankets, and bathed their feet in whiskey. All night she heard "God's music": avalanches "roaring down the mountain sides." "After enjoying some delightful slides down the steep hills," she said, they reached camp that afternoon. The next group to reach the top found their names in a sardine can, with hairpins proving to them that a woman had been to the summit. For Fay Fuller, climbing Mt. Rainier was like a religious conversion experience. It was for anyone who wanted "to begin life anew" and "fall in love with the world again."[50]

Women continued to climb the mountain annually. On Fuller's second ascent seven years later—with a group of fifty-eight Mazamas, one-third of them women—one man fell to his death and two others were rescued from a fall into a crevasse. In 1905, two hundred women and men from the Mazamas, the Sierra Club, and the Appalachian Mountain Club joined together for an outing on Mount Rainier from a base camp at Camp Muir. Twenty-two colleges were represented. Of the 112 successful climbers, 46 were women.[51] Other records, toppled and reported in articles written by women for both club and national magazines gave new legitimacy to women campers and climbers. In 1892, Helen Gompertz and Isabel Miller were the first Sierra Club women to climb Yosemite's Mount Lyell. Gompertz, a teacher in Berkeley, was a charter member of the Sierra Club. Her future husband, Joseph Le Conte, who followed John Muir as Sierra Club president, led the climb. In 1901, twenty men and women climbed Lyell; in 1903, 143 climbers reached the top of Mount Whitney, one hundred on the same day. Having founder and guiding spirit of the Sierra Club, John Muir, present on a club outing was long remembered.[52]

In Colorado, climbing Longs Peak was no longer a rarity for women. During 1915 and 1916, one-quarter, or 220, of the successful climbers were women, more than half from outside the state. A Colorado woman led efforts to use Native American words and understandings in the naming of landscape features. Harriet Vaille, director of the Colorado Mountain Club project, Edna Hendrie, and two male friends, took two Arapaho elders and a young Arapaho interpreter on a tour of the proposed Rocky Mountain National Park. Vaille's carefully recorded descriptive phrases yielded such names now in use as Big Meadow, Tonahutu Creek, Lumpy Ridge, and Never Summer Range, and preserved the information that for generations Native Americans had climbed Longs Peak to trap eagles.[53]

In the Olympic Mountains, the coastal range of Washington state, Anna Hubert, of the Johns Hopkins University, made a first ascent of West Peak on Mount Olympus; Dr. Cora Smith Eaton made a similar conquest of East Peak. Both these ascents came during the Mountaineers' first excursion to the area, in 1907, two years before Olympic National Monument was proclaimed. Base camp was reached by a four-day tramp over a new route opened up by an advance party through sixty miles of forest. Eaton served as one of the doctors for the expedition. In 1913, a combined expedition of the Sierra and Appalachian Mountain clubs, the Mazamas, and the Mountaineers, put seventy-seven climbers, half of them women, on top of the East Peak and eleven women and eight men on the peak of Mount Seattle.[54]

A favorite activity on club outings was botanizing. Club journals published field notes, generally written by women. Botanist Alice Eastwood shared her knowledge when she joined the Sierra Club's climb of Mount Whitney in 1903. Sierra Club women assisted Carlotta Case Hall and her husband, Harvey Monroe Hall, of the University of California, in preparing a key to the flowers, ferns, and trees of Yosemite in 1912. The list of ferns was prepared by Sara Plummer Lemmon, the widow of John Gill Lemmon, who in the early 1880s had pioneered with her husband as a collector of new plants all over the mountains of Arizona.[55]

A sense of ownership of the landscape developed in the club women as they learned and even helped name plants, mountains, and lakes. A few Sierra Club men named physical features after their wives, following the traditional gendered symbolism of naming lakes with women's first names and mountains with men's last names.[56] The landscape seemed secure; a feeling of immutability was expressed by Marion Randall Parsons after the 1913 expedition to the Olympic Mountains. A writer, painter, photographer, and musician, Parsons would soon begin a long term as a Sierra Club director. After climbing Mount Olympus, the expedition crossed the Olympic range and headed for the Pacific. Quinault Indian families took them in twenty-three dugout canoes the thirty-five miles down the Quinault River to the ocean. For Parsons, the combination of a month of camaraderie in the wilderness, the connection with the indigenous people, and the view from Mount Olympus aroused oceanic feelings within her: the landscape revealed a "borderland of the spirit . . . where earth's beauty met the tides of things infinite and divine"; the outing was "a summer world of light and laughter where seasons never change nor flowers die."[57]

Commissions for Women Artists

The publicity campaigns of the Western railroads early in the new century not only enticed women tourists to national parks, but also offered women opportunities for unusual careers in the arts. Railroad advertisements, posters, and booklets showed women happily and easily climbing mountains, riding horseback, and viewing scenery from open touring cars or railroad observation cars. The ads featured such new national parks as Glacier in the Northern Rockies, where the Great

Northern Railway was a major supporter and developer of the park, and Crater Lake, in Oregon's Cascade Mountains, where the Southern Pacific Railroad played a similar role. Women were shown at the rim of the Grand Canyon, accompanied by attentive park rangers. The portrayal of an exuberant woman as a mountain climber in a park setting implied that the park adventure was not too strenuous and that it was safe. The railroads were both acknowledging the role of women as decision makers about the destinations of family vacations and encouraging single women to travel in parks. Women artists and writers were among the first to respond to the call of the railroads to explore each "romantic terminus." Unwittingly, some would also contribute to the making of nature and Native American culture into commodities.[58] Anxious to paint park landscapes, several women artists accepted free travel from railroads in exchange for their canvases.[59]

Abby Williams Hill was one painter to receive commissions, from both the Great Northern and the Northern Pacific Railways. Her assignments were to produce paintings of remote locations reached by company trains. A professional painter and member of the Art Students' League in New York, she married Dr. Frank Hill and moved to Tacoma about the same time that Fay Fuller first climbed Mt. Rainier. The Hills' son was born with a partially paralyzed left arm and leg. Believing in the efficacy of the outdoor life, Abby Hill taught her son and their adopted daughters at home, spending five summers with them in a tent camp on Vashon Island. Hill said of herself: "I was cut out for the wilds,"—a statement that would challenge her when, in 1903, the Great Northern Railway offered her a contract to produce a series of landscapes in the North Cascades. In exchange for the use of her paintings to advertise the beauty of the Northwest at the St. Louis Fair, she was given four tickets, each worth a thousand miles, and ownership of her canvases after the exhibit. She was required to depict some of the most inaccessible scenery in the region, carrying only a letter of introduction to the employees of the railroad company. On each of five painting trips, Hill took two of the four children—a different pair each time. Hill and the children, who ranged in age from eleven to fifteen, traveled by train, stagecoach, steamboat (on Lake Chelan), and pack train before setting up camp at Hill's chosen sites.[60]

Hill's paintings were so successful that she earned a second contract, this time with the Northern Pacific, and it, in turn, was renewed twice. In 1904, she camped with her children at Eunice Lake on the northeast side of Mount Rainier to paint the mountain. They melted snow for water, and, confined to tents on rainy days, read aloud to each other. At Yellowstone in 1905 and 1906, Hill and the children became a tourist attraction. They bathed in the warm springs, cooked in the hot springs, and prepared water for afternoon tea over a small geyser. The family enjoyed the wildlife, particularly twin bear cubs that Hill attracted with bacon fat. She spent many hours painting the Yellowstone falls perched on a cliff four hundred feet above the canyon. When the painting was nearly finished, "a big twister" struck. While the canvas was being blown about halfway down the canyon, Hill and one of her daughters "attended strictly to keeping ourselves flat down on the cliff and hanging on." A guide they had befriended lowered himself into the canyon by rope and rescued the painting, wet and spotted with dirt, but intact.[61]

For Hill, nature revealed God's presence. "Art," she said, "ought to teach people to love nature better, ought to lift them, cheer them." Perhaps because she was always surrounded by the curiosity of children, her paintings project a sense of fresh discovery. Hill, too, was attracted to the otherness of Native American people. She became friendly with the Flathead Indians of Montana, exchanging English lessons for dancing lessons and, at their request, wrote to Washington, D.C., to air their grievances. She also interpreted their legal correspondence. An outsider herself because of her unconventional lifestyle, she identified with Native American people and had her portrait taken in Yakima Indian dress, with her hair braided with otter fur by the indigenous women.[62]

The Great Northern Railroad also capitalized on the interest of such women writers as Mary Roberts Rinehart. Rinehart's three-hundred-mile horseback tour in 1915 of the new Glacier National Park restored her spirits after a stint as a European war correspondent. Already a celebrity for her serialized crime fiction, she was the spark of the riding party of forty-two people, half of them women. The railroad hired her to write a pamphlet after she publicized the park in articles and two books. "If you are willing to learn how little you count in the eternal scheme of things," she wrote, "go ride in the Rocky Mountains and save your soul."[63]

Rinehart became a supporter of the Blackfeet Indians, who lived in the vicinity of the park. Members of the tribe were enlisted to entertain her party and when they learned Rinehart had been to the war, they took her into the tribe, naming her Pitamakin, for their traditional woman warrior. After the Blackfeet people told her about their problems with the Bureau of Indian Affairs, she visited their reservation. Shocked by her findings, she presented the evidence in person to Franklin Lane, secretary of the interior. Like Helen Hunt [Jackson] in Yosemite and Harriet Vaille in Colorado, Rinehart also urged the use of Native American place names in the park, rather than having "obscure Government officials" and "unimportant people . . . memorialize themselves on Government maps." She wrote, "The white man came, and not content with eliminating the Indians he went farther and wiped out their history."[64]

Rinehart especially appealed to women, noting that the women who were "helped into their saddles at the beginning of the trip swung into them easily" as the trip progressed and with each day "the feeling of achievement grew." Although the women rode astride, even then they wore divided skirts, which they buttoned back into a single skirt as soon as they dismounted. In one of her popular stories about a young woman named Tish, who believed skirts were "badges of servitude," Tish and her two women companions captured bandits at Glacier's Piegan Pass, thinking the men were actors in a movie company. When, in the story, Tish and her friends led the captured men into the Great Northern's grand hotel at Many Glacier, one of them remarked, "I can stand up as well under trouble as any one. It's being led in by a crowd of women that makes it so painful"; only then did the women learn they had captured real bandits. The story's heroines took it in stride, demanding steak and potatoes and a cocktail instead of tea.[65]

Another woman with a sense of connection to the land and people of a national park was architect and interior designer Mary Jane Colter. Her identification with the Grand Canyon and the native peoples of the Southwest was expressed in the buildings she designed at the canyon over a period of thirty years for the Fred Harvey Company, operators of the Santa Fe Railroad's hotels and restaurants. Her goal for her first building, Hopi House, in 1905, was to provide an authentic setting on the South Rim where Hopi people could create and sell their crafts, albeit as Harvey Company employees. Constructed by Hopi builders, Hopi House reflected the indigenous Hopi dwellings at Oraibi, Arizona.

A graduate of the California School of Design, Colter was first attracted to Sioux Indian art in St. Paul, Minnesota, where for fifteen years she taught manual arts in the boys' mechanic arts high school. Her exposure to the Spanish and Native American culture of California and the Southwest awakened in her the desire to create buildings that harmonized with the landscape and drew on its oldest human history. She was influenced by the arts and crafts movement, which was a reaction against mass production and its concomitant loss of cultural roots. The movement hoped that craftsmanship would restore the moral value of art and the dignity of labor threatened by materialism and industrialization.[66]

Colter's buildings still give character to the South Rim, where seven of them survive. She also designed Phantom Ranch, a collection of native stone and wood buildings on the floor of the canyon, a vertical mile below. She marked the west and east ends of the South Rim with Hermit's Rest (1914) and the Watchtower (1932) as romantic representations of Pueblo Indian culture, and in between, designed the Lookout to rise out of the Kaibab limestone in such a way as to be almost indistinguishable from the canyon wall. Both on the inside and outside of her buildings, she placed artifacts from the Old West and Native American crafts, symbols, and legends. Before designing the Watchtower, she flew in a small plane over Pueblo ruins to locate the remains of prehistoric towers and then was driven by a Harvey car to sketch them. She modeled the ground floor on a kiva, with a stairway leading up to the Hopi Room representing the *sipapu*, the spiritual entrance place of the Hopis into the world. Hopi artist Fred Kabotie painted the Snake Legend on the walls of the Hopi Room. After she retired, by then almost eighty, Colter gave her collection of Navajo and Pueblo jewelry and Mimbres pottery to the Mesa Verde National Park Museum. Although future critics would say she contributed to the turning of Native American spirituality into a commodity, her goal was to help the public appreciate American Indian culture as she interpreted it.[67]

At the same time that Hill and Colter were beginning their fine arts careers in national parks, a young woman sculptor from Massachusetts, Theo Ruggles Kitson, was starting her nearly twenty years of work for Vicksburg National Military Park in Mississippi. Kitson created sixty-nine pieces of statuary, but her best known memorial was *The Volunteer,* the first monument to be erected at Vicksburg. *The*

Volunteer honored the Massachusetts men who were among the thirteen thousand unidentified Union soldiers buried in the national cemetery adjoining the battlefield. The statue was praised for its representation of a jaunty, confident young soldier. When critic Lorado Taft viewed the statue, he said, "One is almost compelled to qualify the somewhat sweeping assertion that no woman has as yet modelled the male figure to look like a man." The shipping and unveiling of the statue in 1903 caused quite a stir, both in Massachusetts and Mississippi. Kitson insisted that the statue stand on a granite boulder from the Quincy quarries. Shipped by train from Massachusetts, the boulder weighed twelve tons and required ten yoke of oxen to pull it from the Vicksburg train station to its location in the park, across five miles of marshland and up a five-hundred foot rise.[68]

Theo Kitson saw her Civil War sculptures as providing an opportunity for reconciliation and healing, not for the commemoration of heroism. Kitson herself was chosen to unveil the statue, but she insisted that a Confederate woman assist her in the unveiling. Alice Cole, the daughter of a Confederate soldier, joined her. Only twenty-nine at the time, already the mother of three, Kitson brought along her three-month-old baby. None of Kitson's statues present their subjects in heroic poses. Two of them are notable for presenting a scene of healing after tragedy. Although her submission for a statue of General George McClellan was not selected, her model depicts him, on horseback, sympathetically leaning down to talk with two wounded soldiers. In 1906, Kitson's statue of Civil War nurse Mother Mary Bickerdyke, the first Civil War monument commemorating a woman, was dedicated in Galesburg, Illinois, by Illinois veterans. Kitson depicted a kneeling woman raising up a wounded soldier to drink from the cup she offers. Inspired by the same motives, other women, from both the North and the South, soon organized to promote the healing of the wounds of war by establishing memorials in national parks.[69]

In the early twentieth century, women moved beyond the role of observer to that of protector when they believed places defining the nation's history or landscapes inspiring the country's spiritual well-being were in danger. Many women identified with the heritage of Native Americans. Among the first places they worked to protect were the Anasazi cliff dwellings at Mesa Verde, Colorado. The mystery and romance that surrounded their early visits soon gave way to a sense of urgency as Colorado women organized to rescue the sites from pothunters and curiosity seekers. Women in the Sierra Club were also inspired to action, as they joined John Muir in his fight to save Hetch Hetchy Valley in Yosemite's high country from being dammed as a reservoir. When women spoke out in struggles to preserve land and history, they were no longer only travelers, seeking personal inspiration and spiritual renewal from the landscape; they had become activists who were ready to demand the preservation of spaces they had come to claim as their own.

Early Park Founders and Advocates

The response of Colorado women to the need to protect the Mesa Verde cliff dwellings and of California women to John Muir's call to save Yosemite's Hetch Hetchy Valley galvanized both groups to organize locally and nationally. They strengthened and formed local support groups and linked them with existing national women's club networks to create a constituency that could move their causes from the local to the national level. The growing numbers of women who became activists in the national park movement wanted to turn the country's natural and historic landscapes into great natural classrooms, where moral, spiritual, and patriotic values would be passed on to future generations "forever."

As women honed their skills on the early struggles to protect wild and historic places, they also changed their perspective from that of amateur conservationists to citizen preservationists; they stepped out of their private roles into the politics of public advocacy. The collective backing by thousands of women in the General Federation of Women's Clubs brought major support to the bill establishing the National Park Service itself in 1916. The women-run Garden Club of America monitored national parks and spoke out against threats to the integrity of the parks. In historic preservation, local and national women's groups used the commemoration of historic sites both to instill patriotic values in the coming generation and to promote healing of the losses from the nation's wars.

Mesa Verde: The Issue of a Woman's Park

Although two pioneer women anthropologists, Alice Fletcher and Matilda Coxe Stevenson, made the first move to preserve archeological sites in the southwest, it was a woman's club, the Colorado Cliff Dwellings Association, that, to use their own slogan, *Dux Femina Facti*, led the way in the drive to preserve Mesa Verde. In 1887, Fletcher and Stevenson appealed to the anthropology section of the American Association for the Advancement of Science (AAAS) to ask Congress to designate southwestern ruins as "national reserves." At the request of the AAAS, they surveyed potential sites and found more than forty isolated ruins "which demand preservation." The list included Chaco Canyon, Canyon de Chelly, Walnut Canyon, and the future Mesa Verde. Their goal did not reach fruition until the 1906 Antiquities Act allowed the president to set aside archeological sites without congressional approval.[1]

Meanwhile, Virginia Donaghe McClurg, who would devote most of her adult life to both publicizing and protecting the Mesa Verde cliff dwellings, was launched on a parallel effort. Her first trip to the cliff dwellings was in 1882, on an assignment to write about the "buried cities" for the *New York Daily Graphic*. She visited the Mancos ranch of the Wetherills, early Mesa Verde explorers, and saw only a few minor ruins, but her interest was aroused. In 1886 she outfitted an expedition that included a guide, photographer, and housekeeper. Traveling on horseback, with pack mules, they discovered the remnants of a loom in a ruin she named Brownstone Front, probably the present Balcony House. Although they camped a mile from Cliff Palace, its discovery by white people would wait two more years, when the Wetherills stumbled upon it while looking for lost cattle on the mesa top.[2]

McClurg began to lecture widely on the ruins, anxious to preserve them from vandals and pothunters. In 1889, she had married Gilbert McClurg, who was also a writer and lecturer. At the 1892 Columbian Exposition, she was the only woman to lecture in the Anthropological Building. She also repeated her talk twice in the Woman's Building. After a lecture series in Denver the following year, she inspired listeners to circulate a petition to preserve Mesa Verde as a national park. It was signed by prominent Coloradans and presented to Congress by Senator Edward Wolcott, without success. In Paris, McClurg gave her Mesa Verde lecture to the Ethnological Congress at the 1900 Exposition and was presented to Madame and President Loubet, who awarded her the Gold Palm.[3]

After a decade without progress toward rescuing the ruins, McClurg decided to enlist the help of the Colorado Federation of Women's Clubs. They appointed her to head a committee charged to "save the Cliff Dwellings" at Mesa Verde. Incorporated as the Colorado Cliff Dwellings Association, with chapters in Colorado, New York, and California, the committee provided lectures and public information and paid for mapping the area and for the first wagon road to the ruins. McClurg consciously modeled the organization on the Mount Vernon Ladies' Association that had preserved George Washington's home under the leadership of Ann Pamela Cunningham. McClurg adopted Cunningham's title of regent.[4]

The club's plan allowed the Ute Indians to remain on their land, adding to the "ethnological and artistic values of the proposed park" and providing a place "where the red man finds himself safe." The dilemma of how to preserve the ruins without becoming "party to another [American Indian] removal" was solved by asking Ute elder, Chief Ignacio, and Acowitz, his designated successor, to lease Mesa Verde to the women's committee. McClurg worked out an initial agreement at the Wetherill Ranch that allowed the Utes to retain their grazing rights. In a ten-year lease signed in 1901, the Weeminuche Utes received three hundred dollars a year in return for giving up control of the cliff dwellings. The Colorado Cliff

Dwellings Association received water rights and permission to construct a toll road. They saw the treaty as a step along the way toward government protection of the ruins.[5]

When the anthropology section of the AAAS held its annual meeting in Denver in 1901, McClurg arranged to bring J. Walter Fewkes, of the Bureau of Ethnology, and other anthropologists and scientists on an overnight tour of Mesa Verde that was guided by members of the Cliff Dwellings Association. Their new road was completed to within two miles of Cliff Canyon where they camped. The journey to the ruins, made on horseback and foot, was such a success that it encouraged the effort to make Mesa Verde a national park.[6]

As the reality of a national park came closer, McClurg shifted her stand. It appears that the more vested she became in the creation of the park, the less she wanted to relinquish control of it to the federal government. She pressed for a state park, to be run by the women of the Colorado Cliff Dwellings Association—again using Mount Vernon as her model. The cliff dwellings would be safer as a woman's park, McClurg stated. Reflecting the woman's rights movement that won the right to vote for Colorado women in 1893, McClurg said that women in Colorado "cast 52 percent of the state vote" and were prominent in public affairs. She could not see why Mesa Verde "should not be under the protective care of a body of 125 women, with hereditary membership, who know more about the matter and care more about the matter than anyone else." In that way, Mesa Verde would be kept "out of politics" and its treasures reserved for the state of Colorado. Federal control, she maintained, leaving disposition of the artifacts to the discretion of the secretary of the interior, would put the Colorado cliff dwellings in danger because the secretary would allow museums and universities to "indulge in 'excavations and gatherings.'" McClurg's fears about artifacts being taken out of the state were confirmed when a bill was introduced in Congress giving the Smithsonian Institution the sole right to excavate the ruins.[7]

The strongest opponent to the women's park plan was Lucy Peabody, vice regent of the Colorado Cliff Dwellings Association. A former secretary in the Bureau of Ethnology in Washington, D.C., who had married William Sloane Peabody, a retired officer of the U.S. Geological Survey, and moved to Denver, Peabody led the support for a national park. In the years when the park bill was before Congress, she became its staunch supporter and traveled to Washington to testify for it. When the disagreement between Peabody and McClurg became public, Peabody left the association, taking several members with her. The General Federation of Women's Clubs sided with Peabody and endorsed the national park at its biennial convention in St. Louis in 1904.[8]

The *Denver Post* appealed to McClurg and the women of the Cliff Dwellings Association to support the national park bill, but McClurg responded with a letter outlining her reasons for continuing to oppose it. The bill for federal control of the ruins passed in June 1906, and the American Anthropology Association extended a vote of thanks to Lucy Peabody for her "exceptionally noteworthy service to science" in "the securing of this national measure for the preservation of the great monuments of ancient culture in southern Colorado." Virginia McClurg was not mentioned: it was Lucy Peabody who became known as the "Mother of Mesa Verde National Park."[9]

The denouement for Virginia McClurg came with her sponsorship of the building of a replica of cliff dwellings at Manitou Springs, duplicating portions of Spruce Tree House, Cliff Palace, Balcony House, and Square Tower House. These actions were too much for many association members and forty resigned in protest. McClurg, however, remained in control of the association itself, which lasted until her death. A few years after the establishment of the park, the association provided funds to repair Balcony House. In 1917 they staged a pageant, *The Marriage of the Dawn and the Moon*, at Spruce Tree House. McClurg continued to write and lecture about Mesa Verde with a new goal in mind: the desire to have her own role in preserving Mesa Verde acknowledged.[10]

When the park bill was in Congress, a cartoon in the *Denver Post* showed a young Colorado women, wearing a long skirt and a Stetson. She is handing over a model of the cliff dwellings to Uncle Sam saying, "They'll be safer in your care, Uncle!" Although hindsight tells us that Mesa Verde deserved national park status, it is also clear that no one, except the women of the Cliff Dwellings Association, was ready to have women run a park. When Mesa Verde was finally perceived as valuable enough for it to be granted park status, women were viewed as having fulfilled their maternal role: they were expected to send their child, a new park, into the world.[11]

From Conservationists to Preservationists: Losing Hetch Hetchy

The battle to defeat a proposal to make a reservoir for San Francisco in Hetch Hetchy Valley, an area in Yosemite's high country considered by many to be comparable to Yosemite Valley, transformed women all over the country from conservationists into preservationists. Inspired by John Muir, for whom Hetch Hetchy would be a final struggle, the women of the Sierra Club rallied the California Federation of Women's Clubs, who in turn garnered support from the General Federation of Women's Clubs, estimated at 800,000 women nationwide.[12]

When the General Federation organized its Forestry Division in 1902, it was forest preservation that concerned them most, although they generally used the term *conservation*. At their own meetings and at those of the American Forestry Association, women used the language of preservation and restoration, referring only infrequently to the utilitarian management of natural resources that underlay the concept of conservation. "Like a prairie fire," Lydia Phillips Williams, chair of the General Federation's Forestry Committee, reported at the 1905 American Forest Congress, women's involvement in movements "for the preservation of large blocks of forest is spreading . . . from the cypress groves of California to the spruce clad slopes of New Hampshire." The committee congratulated themselves on extensive tree planting projects and for having saved not only Mesa Verde but the Calaveras Grove of Big Trees in California as a state park and the Palisades of New Jersey: Calaveras had been "in danger of extinction through private greed"; the Palisades was "a beauty spot" in danger of being "despoiled."[13]

Conservationist Gifford Pinchot, who became the first Chief Forester of the U.S. Forest Service in 1905, valued the support of the women's clubs for the "patriotism" they demonstrated. He sent Enos Mills, who would soon be part of the successful effort to create Rocky Mountain National Park, on a tour to lecture to women's clubs in forty-two states on forest and bird protection. But when the General Federation sided with John Muir on the Hetch Hetchy controversy at their 1908 and 1910 biennial conventions, they aligned themselves solidly on the preservation side of the issue. They broke with Pinchot and the American Forestry Association who strongly supported using the valley as a reservoir.[14]

John Muir had begun leading Sierra Club women on tramps down the Tuolumne River Canyon into Hetch Hetchy Valley in the late 1890s, but when the valley was threatened, the club focused on the area still more, organizing its annual outing to explore Hetch Hetchy in 1908. Providing national publicity for the cause by describing the tour for *Putnam's Magazine,* poet Harriet Munroe called Hetch Hetchy, "a little garden of paradise . . . where the gods have had their way." Converting it into a reservoir, she said, would set "a vicious precedent" and destroy it "forever." As the controversy grew more intense, Sierra Club member Cora Calvert Foy used stronger language in *Out West.* In an article subtitled, "A Story of San Francisco's Vandalism," she echoed Muir and called Hetch Hetchy a place "where the Maker of all things did some of His most perfect work." San Francisco chose it without investigating more expensive privately owned possibilities because it was the "cheapest," she said, because "it belongs to all of the people, instead of some of the people."[15]

At a hearing of the U.S. House Committee on Public Lands in January 1909, more than fifty women individually went on record with letters demanding the preservation of Hetch Hetchy. Among those airing their views were the Sierra Club's first women leaders, Marion Randall Parsons and Aurelia Harwood, who pointed out that San Francisco did not need the reservoir: "Competent engineers" had identified at least fourteen other sources of water. Parsons called for a congressional investigation. Other women used arguments that would be used again and again in preservation struggles. Florence Keen of Philadelphia, sister of alpinist Dora Keen, said that San Francisco had "no right to deprive future generations" of "one of our fine national recreation grounds"; Martha Walker, of Los Angeles, called the scheme a "glittering example of our 'commercial spirit.'"[16]

The controversy continued for more than five years. In 1910 the General Federation ran a picture of Hetch Hetchy Valley on the cover of their *Bulletin,* opposing "the spoilation of this national reserve." Their frustration over their inability to be heard made them question the validity of representative government. "The annual raid of the spoilers is once more derailed," the editor reported, "And yet . . .

there is no certainty that it may not be thrown away by the very men who are supposed to be its guardians. What wonder that the people have so little confidence in their representatives and are so often in despair as to the possibility of representative government." The women *had* been heard, however; California Congressman William Kent wired Pinchot that the reservoir plan was in danger because of a conspiracy "engineered by misinformed nature lovers and power interests who are working through the women's clubs." By equating "misinformed nature lovers" with "women's clubs," the dam's proponents tried to discredit the preservationists, making them appear to be unscientific, effeminate, and sentimental. Without suffrage, women's voices could easily be ignored because women did not have the power ultimately to turn their opponents out of office.[17]

The final loss of Hetch Hetchy Valley came with a Senate vote in December 1913. It was followed by John Muir's death a year later. The Sierra Club organized an outing down the Tuolumne Canyon to take a last look at the valley. Among the "trampers" was Ellen Emerson, granddaughter of Ralph Waldo Emerson, visiting from the East. She said it was "impossible to reconcile ourselves to the thought of drowning that beautiful meadowland under many fathoms of water." Bertha Gorham Pope added that "much of this glory is soon to be 'erased like an error and cancelled,' offered up [as] a living sacrifice on Utility's already prosperous altars."[18]

The conclusion of the Hetch-Hetchy controversy, coupled with the increasing professionalization of the management of natural resources for utilitarian use in organizations like the U.S. Forest Service, made activist women withdraw from their brief foray into male-run conservation organizations. Although their enthusiasm for the preservation of natural landscapes was in no way diminished, women returned to their traditional women's club networks, where they could choose, and support, their own campaigns. When the creation of a National Park Service came before Congress in 1916, the General Federation of Women's Clubs, still saddened by the Hetch Hetchy outcome, did not hesitate to put their membership behind the move to create a new organization with the goal of preserving parks "unimpaired for the enjoyment of future generations."[19]

Clubwomen Support New Parks and a National Park Service

Mary Belle King Sherman, who led the General Federation of Women's Clubs during the founding years of the National Park Service, was so dedicated to the cause that she became known as the National Park Lady. She changed the focus of the federation's Conservation Department from that of emphasizing conserving natural resources to one of protecting scenic landscapes, a concept she termed "the conservation of natural scenery." In the past, she stated, "no one thought of natural scenery as having anything to do with conservation. It was not looked upon as a natural resource, and even less as an asset."[20] Sherman was recording secretary of the Chicago Women's Club and of the General Federation of Women's Clubs until she was forced to withdraw because of an accident to her shoulder. Immobilized in a cumbersome cast, during her long convalescence at her summer home in Estes Park, Colorado, she spent many hours looking out of her window at Longs Peak and became "obsessed with a longing to stand on the highest peak and look over the vast range on the other side." When she did succeed in climbing Longs Peak, by horse and on foot, accompanied by her son, she became a convert to preserving nature. She vowed that she would devote the rest of her life "to helping others to see and feel" what she had experienced—"the vast beauty of the world"—and pledged herself "to help save such scenes as this for that purpose."[21]

Sherman's first opportunity arose in her own back yard. In 1915 she became chairman of the General Federation's Conservation Committee and joined Enos Mills in the successful drive to create Rocky Mountain National Park. Testifying before the House Committee on Public Lands, she explained that the park would benefit its millions of visitors "physically, mentally, and morally." She cited support from the ten thousand members of the Colorado State Federation and the Denver Daughters of the American Revolution.[22]

Sherman next led the General Federation on a campaign to develop more national parks. In 1915 she instituted "a natural scenic area survey" of the whole country, asking each state conservation chair to name the parks in her state and suggest areas that should be protected. Sherman presented her findings to the National Park Conference in Berkeley, California, where she and Marion Randall Parsons, by then a director of the Sierra Club, were the only women delegates. Sherman pledged the support of the federation's two million members in their new work in the "conservation of natural scenery" and the development of national parks. "Outside of home influences," she said, "the intimate acquaintance with nature is one of the strongest and greatest that can be brought into the life of a child." Every community, she said, needs a place where people will make "direct contact with things of beauty and interest in the outdoor world."[23]

Sherman found that state federations were active in nine national park campaigns. California clubwomen, who after the loss of Hetch Hetchy Valley were even more determined than before, supported the addition of Mount Whitney and the valleys of the Kings and Kern rivers to Sequoia National Park. The Washington State Federation wanted to create a national park by adding the adjoining high peaks to Mount Olympus National Monument, and Arizona clubwomen were working to change the status of the Grand Canyon from a national monument to a park.

Sherman singled out the Florida Federation of Women's Clubs as the only club to have "actually . . . secured" a state park.[24] The full significance of the Florida achievement would not be recognized for several decades, but by creating Royal Palm State Park on Paradise Key, they created the nucleus of Everglades National Park. For more than thirty years until the national park was authorized, Florida clubwomen owned and managed the 4,000-acre park.

In 1905, the Florida Federation of Women's Clubs endorsed a resolution to preserve the unique groves of royal palms standing on a hammock on Paradise Key.

When highway development and poaching threatened the palms in 1914, members Mary Barr Munroe and Edith Gifford asked the federation to renew their efforts. As Florida Audubon Society members they had worked with their husbands in an unsuccessful campaign to preserve Paradise Key. They convinced the new Florida federation president, May Mann Jennings, wife of a former governor, to make the rescue of the area a major goal of her administration. When Mary Kenan Flagler, widow of a Florida developer, offered to donate 960 acres on the key and surrounding land, Jennings asked the state to match the offer with state land to create a park managed by the federation. Jennings's strategy depended on the women's club network. Instead of contacting an official or legislator directly to ask for his support, she first interested the official's wife in the project; if the wife was not already a clubwoman, although many of them were, Jennings found another clubwoman who could introduce her to the wife.

In 1915, the legislature matched the Flagler gift and established Royal Palm State Park under the care of the federation. Even when news of the possibility of a park increased the poaching of rare plants, the legislature did not appropriate any money to protect it. Undaunted, Jennings wrote federation members that plans for trails, pavilions, and a lodge could still become a reality if they raised the funds. Jennings began a campaign to publicize and fund the park with only moderate support from the federation. She found a family willing to serve as wardens and live there in a tent until a lodge was built. A one-year appropriation of $1,200 from the Dade County Commissioners provided funds to construct the lodge, paths, and picnic tables the next year.

Mary Belle King Sherman joined the Florida Federation of Women's Clubs as their keynote speaker at the dedication of Royal Palm Park in November 1916, during their annual convention. For Sherman, the park demonstrated the power of the clubwomen's network to preserve "national scenic areas." A motorcade of 168 cars, full of Florida clubwomen traveled forty miles from Miami to the park. Jennings, by then known as the Mother of Forestry, dedicated the park "to the people of Florida and their children forever."[25]

Scarce funds continued to plague the Florida clubwomen's efforts until 1921. Then, after years of lobbying by Jennings and the clubwomen, the Florida legislature approved a $2,500 annual appropriation and added 2,080 acres. Jennings called the park God's Own Garden, with "over 250 kinds of plant life, including stately royal palms and rare orchids" and "between two and three thousand water-fowls of many kinds." She called it the "only jungle of its kind in the United States and the only one owned by a Federation of Women's Clubs," noting that it "set an entirely new precedent in the matter of conservation work for women." Another twenty-five years passed before Jennings, who was then seventy-five, and the federation turned the park over to the federal government as the core of new Everglades National Park. Appropriately, Royal Palm Lodge served as the new national park's first visitor center.[26]

Meanwhile the campaign to establish a National Park Service under the Department of the Interior was underway with the introduction of a bill to Congress in January 1916. Sherman kept clubwomen informed of its progress through the federation magazine. In order to justify two administrations, she differentiated between national forests and national parks. Managed by the Forest Service under the Department of Agriculture, a forest reserve, she explained, "has an important place in the material part of our life" and was "a place where most beauty must be sacrificed." But a national park, she said, "supplies the better, the greater things of life." A park has "some of the characteristics of the museum, the library, the fine arts hall, of the public school, the zoo, and the home."[27]

The General Federation passed a resolution supporting a National Park Service at its biennial convention held that May in New York. Sherman presented Stephen T. Mather, soon to become first director of the Park Service, then assistant to the secretary of the interior. Mather praised the clubwomen for helping to crystallize opinion in favor of the service. In addition to lobbying congressmen, members produced a mailing list of 275,000 names for the *National Parks Portfolio*, the Department of the Interior's major publicity effort in support of the bill. Clubwomen combed lists, culling out duplicates, of women's and men's clubs, college alumni groups, social registers, and scientific and professional societies. The *Portfolio*, a series of pamphlets on individual parks bound together, was written by Robert Sterling Yard, former editor of *Century* magazine. The Park Service bill became law on August 25, 1916, incorporating within its mission a basic tension between the use and the preservation of park lands.[28]

In her speech at the 1917 National Parks Conference, Sherman described national park projects supported by the federation.[29] One park she particularly endorsed was the state park that later developed into Indiana Dunes National Lakeshore, across Lake Michigan from Chicago, where she lived. The "wonderful Dune[s]," she said, "are in constant danger of being used for commercial purposes." She designated November 1919 as "Save the Dunes Month" and asked each club to devote a program to the Indiana Dunes: "Women of the East, let us join together to secure the first National Park east of the Mississippi River! Women of the West, who realize the advantages of the preservation of Natural Scenery, help us to save the finest specimens of Dune formation in the world!" Although national park status took nearly fifty more years, Bess Sheehan organized women in the six hundred clubs of the Indiana Federation to secure Indiana Dunes State Park in 1923, saving land essential to the future national lakeshore.[30]

For the next five years, Sherman guided the federation in national park issues. She was appointed a trustee of the National Parks Association. But by the time she became president of the General Federation in 1924 for a four-year term, her interests were divided. Still an ardent advocate of nature study for children, she put her energy into adding natural science to the public school curriculum. It appears that her hope for parks to serve as classrooms for young people had not materialized, and she had adopted a more direct approach. As the Park Service developed a male-oriented culture, clubwomen had less influence than when it was a new agency anxious for public support. Without Sherman's strong leadership for park projects, the federation turned to other goals. Only on the local level, where an issue was close to home, did state federations continue to work for national parks.[31]

A Park for the PEO Sisterhood: The Great Sand Dunes

In Colorado in the early 1930s, chapters of the PEO Sisterhood, a service organization of college women in the United States and Canada, protected the Great Sand Dunes in the south central part of the state. Lying on the eastern edge of the San Luis Valley and creeping up the Sangre de Cristo Mountains, the dunes cover nearly 40,000 acres and rise to almost a thousand feet. Elizabeth Spencer, wife of a local historian, called on the Monte Vista PEO chapter to save the dunes. They were called the "Desert of Hissing Sands" and she described them as giving off a ghostlike sound of "longing and sorrow" from constantly moving sand particles. She urged club members to protect the dunes—a unique landscape "of mystery and enchantment"—and as a site that honored the area's heroes, historic forts, and early Native Americans.[32]

The Del Norte and Alamosa PEO chapters, the two others in the valley, joined the drive, which was conducted on two levels: constituency building and political action. The clubwomen spurred citizens to write letters to the Colorado congressional delegation urging them to protect the dunes. Lieutenant Governor George Corlett, an attorney whose wife, Jean, was active in the campaign, convinced the Colorado legislature to pass a memorial supporting the project and prepared petitions for the women to sign and send to Congress. In a letter to Senator Edward Costigan, enclosing the petitions, the women were careful to point out that his mother was a past PEO state president.

Representative George Hardy suggested that the women write Horace Albright, Park Service director. Hardy had recently entertained Albright at dinner and wrote that he had "some inside dope" that "the prospect is very good." Albright thanked the women for their subsequent letter and photographs with a characteristically personal touch. The article on "skiing on sand," he said was especially interesting and "a fine way to travel over these enormous sand dunes." In March 1932, Arthur Demaray, the service's assistant director, told the proud women that President Herbert Hoover had signed the proclamation. It was one of only three successful national monument campaigns in that year, out of ninety proposals.[33]

The Garden Club and a Park for Desert Plants

When Minerva Hamilton Hoyt started her crusade to preserve desert landscapes in Southern California in a national park, her first ally was the Garden Club of America. The club was organized nationally in 1913 to exchange information among amateur women gardeners and to pull together support from member state and local garden clubs to protect native plants and birds and to sponsor beautification projects. The club's experiences in protecting the desert and a redwood grove led them into the field of preservation. Unlike the varied goals of the General Federation of Women's Clubs, nearly twenty years older, the Garden Club's mission was from the start limited to environmental concerns.[34]

When the Garden Club held its annual meeting in April 1926, in Santa Barbara, California, Eastern members traveled west in their own train, the Garden Club of America Special. Among the eleven railroad cars was an observation car stocked with books about the natural history of California. Their train took the spur to the Grand Canyon, and, despite a snowstorm at the rim, several members rode mules down the Bright Angel Trail to the Colorado River and back in one day, noting the changing wildflowers as they progressed from winter at the rim to summer at the bottom.[35]

Their first stop in California was Pasadena, where members of the Garden Club vied with one another to show off their gardens. Minerva Hamilton Hoyt, soon to become the California club's conservation chair, provided a luncheon in her gardens at her home, Hillcrest. Groves of palm, live oak, and eucalyptus trees, flowering acacias, and bougainvilleas grew in a garden smaller than a city block that had taken six months and twenty workers to create. Hoyt was about to launch her campaign to preserve desert plants and would look to the Garden Club for support.[36]

Hoyt, called the Apostle of the Cacti for her crusade to protect desert plants, eventually moved beyond the Garden Club's original mission: from the role of gardener who manipulated the environment to create pleasing and even exotic landscapes to the stance of preservationist who wanted to protect the desert in its natural state. Yet Hoyt would use the creation of desert gardens as a method to garner support to protect the wildness of the desert. In the late 1890s, when she first arrived in the undeveloped town of Pasadena, newly married to A. Sherman Hoyt, a physician and financier from New York City, she felt "the call of the desert." To Hoyt, it was a "world of strange and inexpressible beauty, of mystery and singular aloofness which is yet so filled with peace." Although she was active in building her community, she always found time for the desert, "invading it on horseback or in a buckboard." After the death of an infant son and, in 1918, of her husband, she turned to the desert for solace. Accompanied by her African-American maid, she slept in the open in a sleeping bag, soothed by the "primeval and erie" night wind in the Joshua trees and the "pungent odor" of the juniper. The desert "possessed me," she said, "and I constantly wished that I might find some way to preserve its natural beauty."[37]

Hoyt decided that the only way to convince people the desert was in as much danger of exploitation as forest lands were was to bring the desert to them. The Garden Club's exhibit space at the 1928 International Flower Show at the Grand Central Palace in New York was her first opportunity. Hoyt used her skill as a gardener to press home her preservation message. Employing collectors, taxidermists, and a scene painter to bring cactus, flowers, birds, and animals from the Mojave Desert to life in a naturalized setting, Hoyt sent the materials east in a refrigerator car, supplemented by daily air shipments of desert flowers. After the show, she donated the exhibit to the New York Botanic Garden, a showcase where it would reach the most children. It earned her a Gold Medal from the Garden Club and supporters for her cause.[38]

The following year, the Massachusetts Horticultural Society invited Hoyt to expand her exhibit at their centennial exhibition in Boston. She divided the space into three arched areas: a desert habitat; examples of Death Valley's reptiles, animals, plants, insects, rocks, and soil, viewed against a backdrop showing Devil's Golf Course (below sea level), with Mt. Whitney in the distance; and a redwood exhibit that contained a tree section 1,500 years old, young redwoods, and native plants. For this show, Hoyt used both a refrigerator car and a freight car; airplanes flew in fresh plants twice a day. A few months later, the exhibits were on ships, headed for the Chelsea Spring Flower Show in London, by invitation of the Royal Horticultural Society. Later donated to Kew Gardens, the exhibits caused a sensation in London. The *Times* headlined its account, "Two Coyotes Have Taken London," and the Royal Horticultural Society gave her their highest honor, the Lawrence Gold Medal.[39]

A year later, at the World's Botanic Congress in Cambridge, England, Hoyt announced the formation of the International Deserts Conservation League. Its membership made up of garden club members and botanists, the league was an international society for scientific research, the protection of desert plants, and the establishment of desert parks. Mexico was the first country to respond: President Ortiz Rubio set aside a 10,000-acre cactus forest in the Tehuacan region as a monument to her work and the National University of Mexico titled her Professor Extraordinary of Botany and arranged a tour of Mexican desert landscapes for her party. But although Hoyt was recognized abroad, her struggle to preserve desert landcapes in the United States would take more time.[40]

Hoyt began to focus on a specific area for a national park after Frederick Law Olmsted Jr., who was surveying potential California parks for the state park commission, chose her to report on desert landscapes. She recommended an area of a million acres east of Palm Springs, running between the Salton Sea to the south and Twentynine Palms to the north. The area encompassed the arid Colorado Desert in the east and the higher, cooler, and wetter Mojave Desert in the west—the habitat of the Joshua tree. Hoyt was particularly anxious to protect the Joshua tree because it had become popular with plant collectors and as a source of lightweight wood. Preferring a national park to one run by the state, she presented her proposal in 1930 to Horace Albright. He turned her down, citing the problem of conflicting land titles and the need to secure Death Valley and Saguaro national monuments first.[41]

With the creation of the two desert parks and the election of President Franklin D. Roosevelt, Hoyt's chances improved. Raised on a Mississippi cotton plantation, Hoyt not only knew the role of hospitality but, as the daughter of a prominent Mississippi Democrat, she also understood the usefulness of connections. Harold Ickes, secretary of the interior, supported proposals for parks as a way of combatting the Depression and because he knew that Roosevelt favored parks. Hoyt had to move quickly when a bill for a California desert park, including many of the areas she proposed as a national park, passed the California legislature. She convinced Governor James Rolph, Jr., to veto the bill to give her time to pursue the national park plan. After Rolph gave her an introduction to Roosevelt, she sat on the White House steps until the president would see her. He summoned Ickes, who told her: "The President is for this and I am for it." With the aid of Desert Conservation League members, she prepared two volumes of photographs of desert plants and landscapes.

Hoyt still had to convince Park Service officials of the value of the park. Roger W. Toll, superintendent of Yellowstone, recommended that protection only be given to the stand of Joshua trees, a reduction from more than 1,000,000 acres to about 140,000 acres. When Hoyt protested, naturalist Harold C. Bryant, who headed research and education for the Park Service, made a field visit. At a reception held at Hillcrest, Bryant announced his support of a nearly 800,000-acre national monument. Land title issues, involving unused Southern Pacific Railroad land and California school lands, complicated the process. Each problem was solved by land exchanges. When the Park Service suggested that Hoyt buy the Southern Pacific land for the park, she had to refuse; by then she had used up all her resources in her campaign.[42]

Hoyt's dream of a desert park was finally achieved on August 10, 1936, when Roosevelt established Joshua Tree National Monument by proclamation, preserving 825,340 acres. In 1955, ten years after her death, the Joshua Tree Women's Club placed a plaque, honoring her work, on a native boulder at Keys View, locally called Inspiration Point, the highest point in the monument, looking across the desert to San Jacinto and San Gorgonio peaks. The plaque quoted her feelings about the desert: "I stood and looked. Everything was peaceful, and it rested me."[43]

Joshua Tree lost one-third of its acreage in 1950 because of pressure from mining interests, but the efforts of other women fifty years after the monument was first created restored a majority of the withdrawn lands and upgraded Joshua Tree to a national park. Senator Dianne Feinstein of California steered the Desert Protection Act through Congress late in 1994 after it had been blocked in committee for seven years. Feinstein built on the work of Judith Anderson, who chaired the first meeting of the Desert Protection League in 1984. Kathryn Lacey, legislative aide to Senator Alan Cranston, drafted the original bill in 1986 and provided staff support through to passage. Anderson, a Sierra Club activist, compiled the maps for the entire act and brought four hundred letters of support to the 1992 Senate hearing.[44]

Meanwhile, the Garden Club continued to support park projects and to protest vigorously any incursions on national park lands. After 1930, when the club began to raise funds to protect a redwood grove in California's Humboldt Redwoods State Park, a large part of the members' political work was devoted to preserving park lands. When they decided not to build a permanent steel bridge to reach their grove because it would "defeat the very purpose" they had in "preserving the primitive forest," they realized that similar issues applied to national parks. In 1934, the Garden Club organized its National Parks Committee "to throw our influence toward the preservation of that for which the parks had been dedicated."[45]

When Garden Club members testified before Congress, they spoke as a separate group of women in tandem with but not as part of the male-directed preservation associations. Like the first conservation associations, such new organizations as the Wilderness Society, founded in 1935, had become professionalized. Although the National Audubon Society evolved from state societies—the first, Massachusetts, founded by Harriet Lawrence Hemenway and Minna Hall in 1896—no woman has ever held the post of president. By the early 1930s, even the Sierra Club had moved away from its early promise of including women in its management to male-dominated boards.[46]

In 1941, the Garden Club put their eight thousand members against a proposal to allow mining in Organ Pipe Cactus National Monument. In the 1940s, the club supported the creation of Kings Canyon National Park, opposed abolishing Jackson Hole National Monument, and testified against a bill to reduce the size of Olympic National Park designed to permit lumbering of virgin timber. Between 1950 and 1956, club members testified and instituted a letter-writing campaign to protest the Interior Department's approval of the Bureau of Reclamation's plan to build Echo Park and Split Mountain Dams in Dinosaur National Monument. It would be, they said, "an entering wedge and an official precedent for the invasion of other park areas." Still, the Garden Club did not entirely neglect its original purpose: in 1959 they dedicated a garden featuring thirteen white magnolia trees, one for each of the original colonies, around a landscaped park at Independence National Historical Park.[47]

Rosalie Edge and the Emergency Conservation Committee

Rosalie Barrow Edge's love of bird life impelled her into battles to protect national parks in much the same way that Hoyt and the Garden Club were inspired to broad-based action on national park issues. Like Hoyt, Edge formed her own organization to achieve her goals, and like the garden clubs, she became a watchdog over virtually every controversial national park issue over a period of thirty years. But Edge's tactics were different: they reflected a militancy that presaged the methods of environmental activitists to come.

Edge's passions were working for woman suffrage and birdwatching. Well schooled in the methods of the New York City suffrage campaign, she transferred her militancy into bird protection after women got the vote. Preservation campaigns also filled her life after a failed marriage.

For Edge, birds were "the handiwork of the Creator." Man could not compete with the "motor power" of such creatures as the ruby-throated hummingbird, which is able to migrate three thousand miles south and return. In 1919, she learned through a pamphlet that the governing board of the National Association of Audubon Societies, of which she was a life member, was connected to commercial duck hunters whose practices threatened the survival of thirty-five species of birds. The pamphlet, *A Crisis in Conservation*, was sent to her by its author, Willard Van Name, an independently minded biologist with the American Museum of Natural History. He was told by the museum directors, who were also Audubon directors, that he could not publish such criticism under his name. "Aroused to indignation," Edge decided to apply suffrage tactics to the Audubon Society, hoping to return it to its original conservation stance.[48]

At the Audubon annual meeting, Edge demanded an explanation of the association's alliance with hunters in two areas: opposing a federal bag limit on migratory birds and accepting the practice of baiting ducks to make them easy targets. She got no satisfaction. At the suggestion of Van Name, she set up the ad hoc Emergency Conservation Committee (ECC) to publish and circulate pamphlets exposing anti-conservation actions, especially, she said, those of "powerful organizations" with "misleading names" who sought "not protection of wild life, but profit from the so-called 'sport.'" Edge and Van Name were joined by Irving Brant, a journalist and lover of the outdoors. Together they became the main pamphlet writers for the ECC.[49]

Edge operated the ECC for nearly thirty years out of a minimally-funded one-room office in New York City. Beginning with names given her by Van Name and William L. Hornaday, retired curator of the New York Zoological Garden, Edge developed a mailing list of sixteen thousand names sympathetic to wildlife preservation. ECC annual reports list a board of about forty "consulting biologists and conservationists," but in fact the ECC was virtually a one-woman show. Edge pulled out all the stops in her efforts to reform the Audubon association. She republished Van Name's pamphlet and a new one by Brant and sought and gained national publicity. Hornaday supplied records proving Audubon's financial dependence on the waterfowl hunting lobby and joined her in asking direct questions at the annual meeting. Edge sued Audubon for its mailing list and led two proxy fights. In 1934, the campaign forced T. Gilbert Pearson to resign as Audubon president, but Edge did not trust the association again until late in life.[50]

The fight established the ECC as a permanent preservation organization and soon the committee began to take on national park issues. One of Edge's first pamphlets published official correspondence sent her by a former park naturalist revealing that rangers were controlling the white pelican population in Yellowstone Lake by destroying eggs and young birds. Her pamphlet brought results and the practice was stopped.[51]

The ECC's first major national park battle was protecting a grove of sugar pines, two hundred feet in height, on Forest Service land bordering Yosemite. Van Name learned that the Forest Service planned to sell the trees to lumber companies because the new Big Oak Flat Road made the grove accessible. In 1932, the ECC published two pamphlets exposing the plan, and Edge convinced Senator Gerald Nye of North Dakota to introduce a bill to protect the pines. Because there was not yet enough public interest to pass the bill, she went to see the Yosemite superintendent, Charles G. Thomson. "I have come from New York," she said, "to ask you one question. *Do you want to save these Sugar Pines?*" His reply: *"With all my heart."* Thomson rallied local advocates for the trees in opposition to the local congressman, Harry Englebright, who supported the plan to cut them.

A new unpaid ECC agent, William Schulz, built a constituency for the trees in California, particularly among the women in the Federation of Women's Clubs, garden clubs, and the Daughters of the American Revolution, urging them to get "right into the fight." Brant garnered the support of Secretary Ickes and President Roosevelt, who pledged unused public works funds to eliminate the need for an appropriation. Edge admitted that she played the role of "picador to Englebright" at the subsequent congressional hearings: she asked him to show the two thousand letters he said he had received from Californians anxious to acquire the pines. The bill passed in August 1937, and the pines were saved.[52]

For Edge, a major part of the ECC's work was the "business of defending and creating National Parks." She believed that a basic issue cut across all the national park issues of the era: the protection of virgin forests. Forests had been cut out of national parks "on the pleas that they added nothing to Park scenery," she said, wryly adding that the "great talk of holding 'National Park standards' high" only included "the height of scenery that lay above tree-line." The ECC's work for national parks, she said, was "all one battle, a contest with the Forest Service in defense of the Park Service." Although she had no quarrel with the Forest Service's proper functions, she strongly opposed their cutting "the few remaining remnants of age-old wonders," because they were "not renewable."[53]

Edge believed the ECC's greatest achievement was in rescuing old-growth forests by helping to create Olympic National Park on Washington's Olympic Peninsula, in 1938. In 1915, as a wartime measure to open up logging, the Forest Service had convinced President Woodrow Wilson to reduce Olympic National Monument (established in 1909 as a sanctuary for the Roosevelt elk) to include only the high mountains. In 1933, the spark that created a move to upgrade the monument to a national park was the taking of 230 elk by hunters in a four-day open season. Already angry that "primeval forests" were being lumbered, Edge and the ECC joined the Mountaineers to convince the local congressman, Monrad C. Wallgren, to introduce a bill creating a park out of the existing monument and the surrounding Forest Service lands. The opposition included the regional office of the Forest Service and the Grays Harbor sawmills to the south. Edge traveled to the area to build support and when she testified before Congress, she explained that although local people supported the park in private, they would not speak out in public because they were intimidated by lumber interests. A national park in this "historic forest of the Northwest," she declared, would give more dependable employment than harvesting timber, because once the forests were logged in three to five years, lumbering jobs would be gone.[54]

The battle to create Olympic National Park continued for five years and was fought on many fronts. The ECC built a constituency in the Pacific Northwest and published five pamphlets, circulated to thousands of people. When Wallgren, in a second bill, omitted substantial areas of rain forest that had been included in a first bill, Edge minced no words. In a new pamphlet, *Double-Crossing the Project for the Proposed Mount Olympus National Park,* her rallying cry was: "No economic need, but only commercial greed." Brant inspired President Roosevelt to make a personal inspection of the area and when the president promised a park to Seattle school children, his support became clear. Wallgren's third bill restored the original areas to the park. Edge testified again during the eleven days of final hearings. Ickes countered the claims of the lumbermen in a speech written by Brant and broadcast in Seattle and Tacoma. In Congress, quick action by Representative René De Rouen, chairman of the House Public Lands Committee, working with Brant, brought the necessary votes minutes before Congress adjourned in June 1938. Congress authorized the president to proclaim additional acreage later.[55]

Threats to the Olympic forests were not over. As Edge later wrote, "No conservation effort can ever be written off as safely finished." In 1947, Edge published yet another pamphlet when the Interior Department endorsed bills cutting forested acres out of the park. *The Raid on the Nation's Olympic Forests*, ECC's ninety-third publication and the last to be written by Edge, had the largest distribution of any ECC pamphlet. It provoked a flood of mail to the Interior Department. Bearing the written results of the outcry in his hands, Brant convinced President Truman to withdraw the bills.[56]

In the late 1930s, ECC pamphlets aroused support to establish Kings Canyon National Park, adjoining Sequoia National Park in the high Sierras. When a new highway made the area accessible, protection became more urgent. Edge watched over the bill, sending out mailings after each new threat. The bill passed in 1940.[57]

Rosalie Edge never retired. In her mid-seventies she urged President Truman to complete Olympic National Park. Interior Secretary Oscar L. Chapman explained that the areas had just been saved and told her "how important" her efforts had been in "defense of this great Park." Two years later, when Truman supported the plan to build Echo Park Dam in Dinosaur National Monument, she fired off a letter to him in the name of the ECC, urging him to "put right an ill advised recommendation acting as you must have done on very bad advice" and conducted a letter-writing campaign against the dam. In her typewritten autobiography, briefly revised in handwriting at a later date, the large word, DEFEATED, triumphantly covers her paragraph condemning the dam.[58]

Edge believed that women had a special responsibility to speak out to preserve natural resources. Because most preservation measures were "so closely related to business," she said, it was "sometimes difficult for men to take a strong stand on the side of public interest. But women can do it, and they should." "An implacable widow" was Edge's choice for the subtitle of her autobiography. *New Yorker* reporter Robert Lewis Taylor had bestowed the title on her in a 1948 profile. Edge was proudest, however, of Van Name's calling her the "only honest, unselfish, indomitable hellcat in the history of conservation."[59]

Women Promote Patriotism by Preserving Historic Sites

For more than one and a half centuries, women in the United States have banded together to promote patriotic values by preserving historic sites or by commemorating events of national importance. Whether they named their organizations the Daughters of the American Revolution, the United Daughters of the Confederacy, or the Native Daughters of the Golden West, their goals were the same. They did not want the country to forget the sacrifices of its citizens, and they deemed it essential that newcomers learn and respect the values of the republic. As women, they assumed responsibility for passing those values to the next generation.[60]

With the stroke of a pen in 1933, President Roosevelt changed the Park Service from an agency primarily concerned with protecting America's scenic landscapes and natural wonders, mostly in the West, to one equally responsible for preserving the country's historic battlegrounds and memorials, mainly in the East and South. In addition to the War Department's military parks, the Park Service was assigned the care of the Forest Service's national monuments. Women's groups not only had already left their marks on many of the Park Service's new units, but they continued to play a role in saving additional places symbolizing the nation's heritage.

Honoring Boston's Patriots

Its "jagged top" looking like "a giant's tooth spewed up from the sea," the Bunker Hill Monument stood unfinished on the Charlestown hill that rises out of Boston Harbor where the British charged the American patriots on June 17, 1775. Although General Lafayette laid the cornerstone and Daniel Webster gave an address in 1825 before thousands of people, the building of the obelisk came to a standstill at eighty feet after nearly ten years. Sarah Josepha Hale decided that it was up to women to complete the monument. In 1830, as editor of the Boston-based *Ladies Magazine*, she tried to collect money directly from women, suggesting that they emulate Roman women who gave up their jewelry to pay their city's ransom, but she raised only three thousand dollars from as many women.

Realizing that even if women had little control over cash, they could produce handicrafts and food to sell, Hale moved to a second plan ten years later. By then she was editor of *Godey's Lady's Book* and could give the project national publicity. An executive committee of six women hired Quincy Hall in the center of Boston's market district for a huge women's fair during fall harvest week. For seven days, hundreds of women staffed forty-three tables and sold goods made and sent by women from all over the East coast and virtually every New England town. They kept expenses to a minimum. When the women submitted their proceeds of $30,035.53 to the Bunker Hill Monument Association, they admonished the men: "Having done what we could, it only remains for us to hope that our days may yet see the completion of a Monument which shall stand to tell of our Fathers to coming generations." Eighteen months later, the monument was completed.[61]

The women of Boston rallied again in 1876, this time to save the Old South Meeting House from destruction. Noted as the site of the fiery gathering of the Sons of Liberty that produced the Boston Tea Party in 1773, the church was abandoned by its congregation for a new building in the newly fashionable Back Bay section of the city. When litigation to save Old South failed, its destruction began with the removal of the clock from the tower. An emergency meeting filled the church and won a two-month reprieve, but despite the oratory from the men who were present, the meeting failed to raise anywhere near the $400,000 required for the land on which the building stood.

Again it was women who saw a practical solution. Twenty Boston women worked behind the scenes to buy the building itself for $3,500, announcing that the only question left was whether it should "remain where it belonged" or be moved to another site. Next, Mary Tileston Hemenway, the recently widowed wife of one of Boston's most successful merchants, came forward, anonymously at first, with the $100,000 needed to secure a mortgage on the land; the building, safe on its original site, was taken over by the Old South Association. Another great Boston fair, a ball, and lectures eventually paid off the mortgage. Hemenway and the Old South Committee used the meeting house as a museum to develop patriotism by encouraging the study of American history through lectures, pamphlets, and public school programs and essay contests.[62]

Antebellum Sites in the South

Both Bunker Hill Monument and Old South Meeting House would eventually come under the protection of the National Park Service, but the women who controlled another site, considered by some to be the nation's most revered shrine, successfully resisted federal control. Mount Vernon, George Washington's home in Virginia, was rescued, restored, and operated by the Mount Vernon Ladies' Association (chartered by the State of Virginia in 1856) in a truly nationwide women's campaign directed by Ann Pamela Cunningham. An expert at building support, Cunningham constructed a network of women from both the South and the North. Assuming the title of regent, she selected vice regents in thirty states, and they, in turn, selected local lady managers, as they were called. When a congressman proposed transferring Mount Vernon to the Park Service in 1932, the Park Service's chief historian, Verne Chatelain, urged Director Horace Albright to support the action, saying he believed that "no one single historic spot in the east has so much interest for the American people"; he expected "every step" to be taken to enable the Park Service to "acquire this shrine." Albright agreed to support the bill, but the women of the Mount Vernon Ladies' Association, backed by the State of Virginia, held firm in their opposition and remain the independent managers of Mount Vernon to this day.[63]

It was two other women's groups, each modeled on the Mount Vernon Ladies' Association, that took the first steps to preserve the Virginia sites that in 1930 became the Park Service's first two historic sites in the East: Jamestown and George Washington's birthplace. The first group, the Association for the Preservation of Virginia Antiquities (APVA), was founded in 1888 by Mary Jeffrey Galt to preserve Jamestown; the second was the Wakefield National Memorial Association, founded in 1923 by Josephine Wheelwright Rust to create a park using a reconstruction of George Washington's birthplace as the centerpiece. Both women pursued their work with missionary fervor, anxious to restore pride in Virginia's antebellum past.

Although the APVA was a women's organization, a Gentlemen's Advisory Board, as they called it, spoke for them in public. They hoped to restore the precedence of Jamestown over Plymouth as the country's first permanent English settlement and to claim the honor for the Virginia assembly of being the nation's first seat of representative government. After the APVA acquired the part of Jamestown Island containing the ruins of the seventeenth-century church and graveyard in 1893, Mary Jeffrey Galt took charge of the excavations and the process of stabilizing the ruins. She was particularly moved when, digging with her hands, she discovered the foundation of the church where she believed "our beloved Pocahontas was married."[64]

A professional artist, Galt wanted to alter the site as little as possible, but the APVA allowed the Colonial Dames to sponsor the church's reconstruction for the 1907 tercentennial, using a hypothetical design. The APVA continued to hold pilgrimages for adults and schoolchildren. When the Park Service included the remaining portion of Jamestown Island in Colonial National Monument in 1930, they worked out the plan currently in effect for joint Park Service/APVA administration of Jamestown. In the mid-1990s, the APVA sponsored an archeological dig focused on identifying the site of the 1607 fort that protected the settlement.[65]

When Josephine Wheelwright Rust announced her plan to reconstruct George Washington's birthplace at Wakefield in tidewater Virginia at the first meeting of the Wakefield National Memorial Association, she had already arranged to purchase fifty acres surrounding the War Department's monument marking the site. Even though she knew that the evidence describing the design of the house and its exact location was conflicting, Rust and her group were determined to meet the 1932 deadline of the bicentennial of George Washington's birth. In 1926, Congress granted the Wakefield Association permission to build a replica, subject to the approval of the Fine Arts Commission and the War Department. With the help of volunteer historian Charles Arthur Hoppin, historic architect Edward Donn drew up plans of a characteristic house of the place and period, changing the building material to brick because Rust thought it would reduce maintenance costs. Although the Fine Arts Commission and the War Department gave their approval, each recommended that the real foundation be undisturbed so that visitors would realize that the reconstruction was not the actual house of Washington's birth. The association was determined, however, to reconstruct the house on what they believed was the exact site.[66]

Rust announced the fund-raising campaign in 1928 in *The New York Times*. John

D. Rockefeller Jr. agreed to match the amount the Wakefield Association raised to build the house with funds to buy four hundred acres surrounding it; he also influenced them to allow the site to be transferred to the Park Service. A subsequent congressional appropriation helped meet the stipulations of Rockefeller's gift. When new excavations revealed that the site chosen for the replica was probably not the original location, Rust disagreed, saying that the newly unearthed foundations probably represented outbuildings, and the association continued with their plans. Rust urged vice regents in each state to ask donors to buy parts of the replica: "a memorial brick" for $5, a chimney for $2,000, or a room for $5,000.

Rust died before the memorial was completed and Louise du Pont Crowninshield took Rust's place and continued to raise funds to make the birthplace as accurate a portrayal of a mid-eighteenth century Virginia plantation as possible. In the end, both the association and the skeptics were satisfied: excavations determined the actual site to be one hundred feet southwest of the replica, allowing both the original foundation to be exhibited and the replica to exist nearby as the Memorial Mansion.[67]

As early as 1904, the Georgia Society of Colonial Dames began its efforts to restore Fort Frederica, a colonial fort founded on St. Simons Island in 1736 by James Oglethorpe as a buffer between Spanish Florida and the English Carolinas. Belle Stevens Taylor deeded the ruin to the Colonial Dames, whose goal is to preserve "the records and relics" of the original thirteen colonies to teach "lessons of patriotism." They restored the fort and cared for it for forty years. After many attempts to get state or federal aid to keep the fort from washing into the river, in 1942 they transferred it to the Park Service. When no congressional appropriation was forthcoming, they organized the Fort Frederica Association to find the necessary funds, raising $100,000. The woman credited with acting as a spark plug to the association was local historian Margaret Davis Cate.[68]

Monuments for Healing and Reconciliation

Both the Daughters of the American Revolution (DAR) and the United Daughters of the Confederacy (UDC) worked to heal the psychological wounds caused by the tragedies of the Civil War. To help in this work, they took care of Civil War sites and erected memorials, now included in the National Park System.

In 1896, the Women's Relief Corps, a DAR auxiliary, took over the care of the Civil War prison at Andersonville, Georgia, from the Georgia Grand Army of the Republic. The women landscaped the grounds, built a caretaker's house, and in the interests of national healing, planted a rose bush from every state. They transferred the site to the War Department in 1910, but in 1915 they dedicated a sundial there to Clara Barton, who in 1865 had directed the work of identifying and marking the graves of the thirteen thousand Union prisoners who died there.[69]

Remembering a time "when every Southern home was a house of mourning," the UDC grew out of organizations formed during and immediately after the Civil

War to meet the daily needs of Southern people. Like the DAR, the UDC saw in their mothers an example "too deeply rooted to fade away with the clouds of war." As acts of healing and reconciliation, they constructed monuments on the site of the battle of Shiloh, where there were twenty thousand casualties, and at Arlington National Cemetery, site of the UDC's Confederate monument, unveiled in 1914.[70]

The Shiloh project took seventeen years to complete. Tennessee women first formed the UDC's Shiloh Chapter in 1900 with the erection of a monument as their purpose. In 1905, they convinced the national UDC to take on the project as a memorial to all Confederate soldiers. Determined to raise enough money to erect a work of art, UDC state chapters took twelve years to raise the necessary $50,000. The sculptor they chose for the work, in a national competition, was Frederick C. Hibbard. On May 17, 1917, the monument, piled with flowers from every state, was unveiled with thirty thousand people in attendance. Female figures express the theme and title of the work: *Victory Defeated by Death.* The symbolism is both general, to the war, showing the Confederacy's ultimate defeat, and specific, to the battle of Shiloh, in which the Confederate Army won on the first day but lost General Albert Sydney Johnston before being defeated on the second day. The central figure is a young woman with bowed head, representing the Confederacy. She holds a laurel wreath, which is being taken from her by a hooded woman, Death, on her right; the defeat is made final by a second hooded woman, Night, on her left. On one side, a group of soldiers marches with heads high; on the other side, their heads are bowed and one of the soldiers is missing.[71]

Post–Civil War Presidential Sites

The commemoration of presidents by preserving sites sometimes fell to local groups. For both Andrew Johnson and Theodore Roosevelt, the groups included women relatives. Three generations of Johnson women worked to restore President Andrew Johnson's place in history by preserving the elements of the present Andrew Johnson National Historic Site. Johnson was always known as the president who was impeached, although, because of one vote, in 1869, Congress did not remove him from office. His eldest daughter, Martha Johnson Patterson, who often replaced her invalid mother as the White House hostess, wanted to see him "vindicated" and "come into the honor he justly deserved." She began the drive to memorialize her father by willing the family cemetery in Greenville, Tennessee, where Johnson was buried, to the federal government.[72]

Two more generations cared for the other Johnson sites before the Park Service took them over. Patterson had willed to her daughter-in-law and son, Mattie and Andrew Johnson Patterson, the family homestead, carefully kept the way it was during Johnson's lifetime, and her interest in the tailor shop where Johnson practiced his trade. They, in turn, convinced the State of Tennessee to buy the tailor shop as a memorial to be cared for by Mattie and the Andrew Johnson Women's Club. Mattie's only child, Margaret Johnson Patterson, and her mother were successful in lobbying Congress to create a national monument that combined the homestead and the tailor shop with the cemetery. As part of an agreement in 1935, the Park Service hired Margaret Patterson [Bartlett] as a museum technician, a position she held from 1942 until 1976. Born in the homestead, she was a unique interpreter, trained, even as a little girl, to guide visitors through the home of her great-grandfather, the president.[73]

Another women's group working to commemorate a president was the Woman's Roosevelt Memorial Association. Dedicated to imbuing the next generation with the ideals of President Theodore Roosevelt, the association was determined to reconstruct his birthplace in New York City near Gramercy Park soon after his unexpected death in 1919. Emily Vanderbilt Hammon headed the committee of New York society women that included Roosevelt's sisters, Corinne Roosevelt Robinson and Anna Roosevelt Cowles.[74]

The women hoped to make the birthplace "a centre of Americanism" following the period of heavy immigration from Eastern and Southern Europe and preserve it "as a shrine for American youth," presenting Roosevelt's life as an inspirational example of how a "frail, delicate boy" overcame his handicaps by hard work and physical exercise. They chose a woman architect, Theodate Pope Riddle, and launched a campaign to raise $250,000. With women chairing the effort in twenty-four states and the motto, "There must be no sagging back in the fight for Americanism," the women raised half of the total and purchased the site.[75]

Substantial financial aid from the Roosevelt Memorial Association, a men's group, helped the women fund the reconstruction. They installed the Roosevelt Memorial Association's collection of Roosevelt memorabilia in their exhibit rooms and embarked on public school projects, holding student assemblies at the birthplace, where they awarded prizes for winners of essay and oratorical contests based on Roosevelt themes. Perhaps because the leadership of the woman's group remained unchanged and enthusiasm for Americanization programs waned, by 1956 the remaining members merged with the men's group, renamed the Theodore Roosevelt Association. Seven years later the association donated the site to the National Park system, to be administered in cooperation with the association.[76]

DAR Memorials Become Catalysts for National Parks

Meanwhile, the Daughters of the American Revolution was at work at the local level. While women's groups dedicated to memorializing a particular historic site set up networks to concentrate support for their chosen project, the DAR encouraged each chapter to work separately to promote patriotism by commemorating local historic sites. As a result, thousands of memorial markers and hundreds of historic buildings dedicated or restored by local DAR chapters are spread throughout the country. Local chapters have been so diligent in marking sites for the past hundred years that even the DAR Office of the Historian General does not know where they all are. By its commemoration of a forgotten historic site with a marker and a dedication ceremony, or by accepting for perpetual care a piece of historic land or a building, the DAR often played the role of catalyst in preserving a site that eventually became part of the National Park System.[77]

Five years after its founding in 1890, the DAR won its first major preservation victory. In Philadelphia, the local DAR chapter moved to gain custody of none other than Independence Hall, the historic site most meaningful to them, soon after city offices left the second floor. When the city awarded the Sons of the Revolution the use of the second floor, the DAR asked them if they could hold meetings there as well. When the Sons referred them to the city for permission, the women obtained an ordinance granting the DAR and the Sons equal use of the space. It was the DAR's entering wedge. The Sons refused to join them in a restoration project and petitioned for sole custody of the entire building. When the city turned the Sons down, they retreated, leaving the DAR in charge. The DAR not only proceeded to direct and pay for the restoration of the second floor, but convinced the city to restore the whole building in time for the Fourth of July in 1898.[78]

When the national DAR held its annual convention in Philadelphia the next spring, no doubt to admire Independence Hall, they included a pilgrimage to Valley Forge, site of Washington's encampment in the winter of 1777–78, where more than two thousand soldiers died of disease. Their guide, Major I. Heston Todd, showed the women a field of unmarked graves on his land identified by a single gravestone that had been placed there for one of the victims. Moved emotionally, the women accepted his gift of the grave, some adjoining land, and an access road in return for their pledge to erect a memorial and care for it. Two years later, after a national campaign, the DAR dedicated a memorial shaft, the first monument at Valley Forge, as a tribute "to constancy unto death."[79]

The DAR was the second group of women to begin the effort to preserve Valley Forge. The first were women who helped organize the celebration of the centennial of the encampment. They were encouraged by its success to start a campaign to raise money to purchase the Isaac Potts house, Washington's Valley Forge headquarters. Led by Anna M. Holstein, they fell short, by half, of their goal of $6,000, but bought the building anyway, carrying a mortgage for eight years until it was retired by the Patriotic Order Sons of America. Both Anna Holstein and, a decade later, the DAR, urged the federal government to protect Valley Forge. Although the DAR did convince Pennsylvania congressmen to introduce a bill in 1901, protection of the site did not become a reality until seventy-five years later, when bicentennial fervor propelled the park into the care of the Park Service.[80]

In North and South Carolina, DAR chapters provided the nucleus for two Revolutionary War parks. The first was Kings Mountain. After the centennial of the battle in 1880, forty acres and a monument were transferred to the protection of the local DAR chapter. They cared for it for fifty years until the impetus of sesquicentennial celebrations led to the creation of a park.[81]

The second of these sites was Moores Creek. The bill to create a national military park there languished until the DAR decided to give it their full support. In

1926, after guiding a resolution to establish the park through the North Carolina DAR and the national DAR, Margaret Overman Gregory, North Carolina state regent, and national DAR leaders testified for the bill before the House Committee on Military Affairs. Tradition says that the committee recommended passage just to humor the women, expecting the House to reject the bill. It passed, however, and when it reached the Senate it was in safe hands. Senator Lee Slater Overman, who was both a historian and Gregory's father, guided it through. At elaborate ceremonies celebrating the bill and commemorating the anniversary of the Moores Creek battle, Grace Lincoln Brosseau, DAR president general, echoed DAR women before her when she said that the DAR was carrying on for "our mothers," keeping "intact that for which they paid so great a price." By connecting themselves with their grandmothers and great-grandmothers, DAR women were consciously carrying on the role of Republican Mother, assigned to women after the Revolution, of taking responsibility for educating the country's future citizens.[82]

DAR women, who in order to qualify for membership had to prove descent from a Revolutionary War soldier, also wanted to honor Revolutionary War heroines. At the Moores Creek celebration, the DAR especially noted Mary Slocumb, whose statue in the park now symbolizes the women who spontaneously nursed soldiers wounded in Revolutionary War battles near their homes.[83]

In the West, DAR chapters anxious to remember the sacrifices of pioneers, particularly travelers on the overland trail, also were the first to commemorate sites that later became national parks. In 1912, the Missouri, Kansas, New Mexico, and Colorado chapters erected markers along the Santa Fe Trail. When the Colorado chapter unveiled the stone marker on the site of Bent's Old Fort, Albert E. Reynolds, the owner of the land, offered to deed the four-and-one-half acre site to the adjoining counties for a park. But it was not until the La Junta Chapter of the DAR was founded that Reynolds found a suitable recipient. He regaled the women with stories about Bent's Old Fort and they dreamed of reconstructing it. Although the DAR's material contributions were small—a graded entrance road, the planting of two hundred trees, and the construction of a cobblestone gateway arch—it was the women who first protected and memorialized the site. In 1953, they deeded it to the State Historical Society of Colorado. Two more decades passed before the reconstruction took place, by then under the aegis of the National Park Service.[84]

The DAR first identified several other pioneer sites that later became national parks. The Daniel and Agnes Freeman homestead, now Homestead National Monument in Beatrice, Nebraska, was marked by the DAR in 1925. Ten years later the chapter contacted thirty-six state chapters for support in a successful campaign to establish the park. It includes a monument to Agnes Freeman, who earned a physician's license in order to serve her community and started the local school, calling her "A True Pioneer Mother." In 1923, the Idaho DAR marked the site of the 1836 Lapwai Mission to the Nez Perce nation established by the Rev. Henry Harmon Spalding and Eliza Hart Spalding, one of the first white women to cross the Mississippi. The site is now included in Nez Perce National Historical Park. DAR chapters in the South first revived interest in the Natchez Trace, a wilderness trail of four hundred miles between Nashville and Natchez traveled by Indians and hunters. Between 1909 and 1933, DAR chapters in Mississippi, Alabama, and Tennessee marked the trace in fourteen different locations creating the interest from which the Natchez Trace Parkway grew.[85]

Preservation of Native American culture was the goal of the DAR in Pipestone, Minnesota, the location of a quarry of red stone that is sacred to Native Americans, who believe the stone acts as a conduit between humans and a divine spirit. In 1925, the DAR laid a plaque on a rock near the pipestone quarry and purchased land around the legendary Three Maidens, three granite boulders where Native Americans place offerings before mining the stone. The area also became the site of an annual Hiawatha pageant. The DAR transferred the land to the city of Pipestone and, in 1929, passed a resolution that the pipestone quarries should become a national park.

Spearheading the DAR's efforts was Winifred Bartlett, the first woman county clerk in Minnesota. She went to the American Indian elders to establish the need before joining with other citizens interested in federal protection of the quarries. "It was our duty to support the Indians," she said. "We should help protect it on their behalf because they couldn't do it." In 1932, they set up the Pipestone Indian Shrine Association, with the aim of developing a park. As president, Bartlett developed support in the beginning by speaking to the local all-male Kiwanis Club.[86]

When the first representative from the Department of the Interior to survey the site was not enthusiastic about a park, Bartlett went to Washington to generate interest in the project. Commissioner of Indian Affairs John Collier found some emergency funds and telegraphed the superintendent of the American Indian school near the site to put up a fence to protect the quarry. Bartlett and her committee showed Minnesota Senator Henrik Shipstead the site and convinced him to introduce legislation. The positive report from a new Park Service investigator, support from Dakota and Chippewa tribes, and the Pipestone Association's pamphlet pushed the bill through Congress in 1937. The act created Pipestone National Monument, but without funding. The superintendent of the American Indian school served as custodian until 1940, when Congress appropriated funds for a seasonal custodian.[87]

Bartlett's second goal was still not met. She hoped not only to protect the quarries but also wanted to perpetuate the pipestone craft, believing, she said, that "we should keep to the traditions and legends just as nearly true to the Indian story as possible." Only Native Americans were allowed to quarry the rock, but use declined during World War II. In 1954, Bartlett and a local doctor decided to revive the Pipestone Indian Shrine Association as an association cooperating with the Park Service to provide an incentive for pipestone crafts by providing a sales outlet. Progress was slow at first, but sales generated interest among Native Americans and after twenty years, their annual sales exceeded $100,000. By working with the DAR as the first step in her effort to preserve Native American culture, Bartlett was able to take the subsequent steps that led to the creation of a national monument.[88]

Claiming National Icons in the Name of Women's Rights

Eager to demonstrate the inconsistency of many of America's symbols when measured against the lack of equal rights for women, women's rights activists claimed for themselves several national icons in national parks: the Bunker Hill and Washington monuments, Independence Hall, the Statue of Liberty, the presidential heads on Mount Rushmore, and a giant sequoia tree.

Writing for the *Woman's Journal* in 1875, on the centennial of the Battle of Bunker Hill, editor Lucy Stone claimed its memory: "[It] belongs especially to the Woman Suffragists. They are contending for the very same principles, and carry success with every defeat." But, she continued, the centennial "was made by men who refuse to women the rights for which men died on that memorable battle-field." Again, ten years later, at the dedication of the Washington Monument, Stone said that neither the ceremonies "nor the shaft itself, could make women forget that they are still a subject class, 'taxed without representation and governed without consent.'" She hoped for a day when "no class shall be mocked by the empty sound of respect for equal rights."[89]

Susan B. Anthony, Matilda Joslyn Gage, and three other woman's suffrage leaders chose the celebration at Independence Hall of the one hundredth anniversary of the signing of the Declaration of Independence to make a public statement. They asked to present the women's Declaration of Sentiments, modeled on the Declaration of Independence, so that it would become part of the official record—not even asking to have it read. When General Joseph Hawley of the Centennial Commission not only denied them a spot on the program but refused to give them places in the audience, they took things into their own hands and secured seats in the press section. During the pause between the reading of the original declaration and an anthem, Anthony and Gage proceeded to the speaker's stand, where unsuspecting foreign guests and military officers let them through. Anthony handed their declaration, "handsomely engrossed" on a three-foot scroll tied with red, white, and blue ribbons, to the startled presiding officer, Senator Thomas Ferry. His face paled as he bowed and took the declaration, thereby making it an official part of the proceedings. As they left the stand, the women handed out printed copies of their declaration. Remembering the event later, Stanton wrote that "on every side eager hands were outstretched, men stood on seats and asked for them, while General Hawley thus defied and beaten in his audacious denial to women of their right to present their Declaration, shouted, 'Order, Order!'" The women moved to an outside platform, where Anthony read the declaration "to a listening, applauding crowd. . . . And thus, "Stanton said," in the same hour, on opposite sides of Old Independence Hall, did the men and women express their opinions on the great principles proclaimed on the natal day of the Republic."[90]

The Statue of Liberty was the suffragists' next target. In the same centennial year, the New York Woman Suffrage Convention resolved that the plan to erect the Statue of Liberty on an island in New York Harbor "points afresh to the cruelty of woman's present position, since it is proposed to represent Freedom as a majestic female form in a State where not one woman is free." When the statue was dedicated ten years later, the New York women acted out their dissent by renting the steamer *John Lenox*. They flew protest banners as the ship took its place between two battleships near the front of the three-mile nautical parade circling the island. On board, Matilda Joslyn Gage ended her protest speech by dedicating it to "the daughters of 1986," saying that the Statue of Liberty "is set in our harbor, not to show what the nation has already attained, but as the ideal toward which all the righteous women and men of the Nation do constantly strive." The women of 1986 kept the faith. One hundred years later, to the hour, they too rented a ship, circled the island, and delivered Matilda Joslyn Gage's protests, adding new ones, once again.[91]

After women's suffrage was achieved, one effort to rename a feature in a national park for Susan B. Anthony was successful and one was not. Unsuccessful was the attempt to include Susan B. Anthony as one of the gigantic figures on Mount Rushmore in the Black Hills of South Dakota. In 1933, Rose Arnold Powell began a one-woman, seven-year-long campaign. Developing support from women's groups, including the League of Women Voters, and from such prominent women as historian Mary Beard, she came close to achieving a partial victory when, shortly before his death in 1941, Mount Rushmore sculptor Gutzon Borglum, who was sympathetic to women's rights, agreed to carve Anthony's portrait on the west side of the mountain if funds could be found. After Borglum's death, all efforts focused on completing the original design and Borglum's pledge was forgotten.

Powell's goal echoed those of all the women who preserved and memorialized national landscapes and historic sites: she wanted to pass her values on to the country's youth. But like Stone, Anthony, Gage, and Stanton, Powell gave the highest rating to the republic's value of equality. "Our greatest heroines," she said, "should be honored with our much-lauded heroes. . . . Many a thrilling story of feminine heroism lies buried, which if resurrected would inject an element in American life which is missing, and it would deflate masculine superiority; at the same time inflating feminine inferiority. Result—one standard."[92]

In 1938, a giant sequoia was named for Anthony in Sequoia National Park's Giant Forest, after a campaign by southern California women in business and the professions. The women were pleased with the park's selection of a tree they said was "a memorial to all womanhood." The tree, 20 feet in diameter and 262 feet high, was estimated to be three thousand years old. A thousand people gathered for the tree ceremony and a luncheon decorated with old suffrage banners. Tulare County clubwomen performed a pageant portraying historic American women.[93]

In the first half of the twentieth century, women park advocates were most successful when they organized their preservation campaigns themselves and set their own goals. Their separatism was reinforced when organizations more committed to preservation than the early male-run conservation associations became professionalized, and male-dominated. These included the Sierra Club and the National Park Service, organizations women had helped to found.

Although the women activists lived in different regions of the country and supported national park projects that ranged from erecting historic markers to rescuing nearly a million acres of desert habitat, these disparate women—unknown to each other—spoke with one voice. For them, the public interest did not lie in the management of resources for the present generation or even the next. Their goal was to preserve the natural and historic landscapes they thought best represented the country's core values, both to teach and enrich the lives of all generations to come.

As women in significant numbers began to earn college degrees and enter the work force, they sought careers in the natural sciences, archeology, and history. Some women found they could promote the values they hoped to preserve in national parks by attaining professional positions in the Park Service—the first women to do so. Some of them would begin careers in the growing number of national parks that women activists had expended so much energy and care to create.

Katherine Tatch and Katherine Hazelston, waitresses at Yosemite National Park, dance on Overhanging Rock at Glacier Point in 1900. *(Photo by George Fiske, Yosemite National Park.)*

Fay Fuller, who in August 1890 became the first woman to climb Mount Rainier, begins her historic ascent with, *from left:* W. O. Amsden, Leonard Longmire, and E. C. Smith. *(Courtesy of National Park Service, Mount Rainier National Park.)*

Right: A wife of a U.S. Cavalry officer rides astride at Yellowstone National Park in the early 1900s when the Cavalry protected the park. *(Courtesy of National Park Service, Yellowstone National Park.)*

Above: Assisted by Alice Cole, daughter of a Confederate soldier, Theo Ruggles Kitson, *right of statue,* unveils her sculpture, "The Volunteer," at Vicksburg National Military Park in 1903. The statue honors Massachusetts men who died in the Civil War battle. *(Courtesy of Henry Hudson and Theo Alice Ruggles Kitson papers, Archives of American Art, Smithsonian Institution.)*

Right: At Yosemite in 1933, Lucy Telles displays the largest basket she created. *(Courtesy of National Park Service, Yosemite National Park.)*

Minerva Hamilton Hoyt, founder of Joshua Tree National Monument, at the desert garden exhibit she prepared for the New York International Flower Show in 1926, pictured in *Western Woman*, 6 (December 1929). *(Courtesy of The Library of the New York Botanical Garden, Bronx, New York.)*

Mary Belle King Sherman, who organized the General Federation of Women's Clubs to support the bill establishing the National Park Service in 1916, attends the dedication of Rocky Mountain National Park in 1915. *From left:* Enos Mills, F. O. Stanley, Ed Taylor, Sherman, Governor George Carlson. *(Courtesy of National Park Service, Rocky Mountain National Park.)*

Right: Women members of the Moun-
taineers join their male colleagues to climb
Mount Seattle in the Olympic Mountains
in 1913. *(Photo by H. V. Abel, Mountaineers
Club Collection, #12989, University of
Washington Libraries.)*

Left: Elizabeth Burnell, licensed as a nature
guide by Rocky Mountain National Park in
1917, directed Enos Mills's Trail School for
twelve summers. *(Courtesy of Enda Mills Kiley,
Enos Mills Cabin, Estes Park, Colorado.)*

Right: Clare Marie Hodges,
the first woman park ranger
in the National Park Service,
was appointed at Yosemite in
1918. *(Courtesy of National
Park Service.)*

Left: Marguerite Lindsley [Arnold] was selected as a ranger-naturalist at Yellowstone in 1921 and served for ten years. *(Courtesy of National Park Service.)*

Above: Enid Reeves Michael, a seasonal naturalist at Yosemite from 1921 to 1942, with the ranger-naturalist staff in 1916. *From left:* E. Rett, R. D. Harwood, George C. Ruhle, Michael, D. D. McLean, Carl P. Russell, and Harold C. Bryant. *(Courtesy of National Park Service.)*

Right: Herma Albertson [Baggley], who in 1931 was the first woman the Park Service selected as a ranger-naturalist from the Civil Service register, wore a standard uniform during her appointment at Yellowstone from 1929 to 1933. *(Courtesy of National Park Service, Yellowstone National Park.)*

Pauline Mead [Patraw], a seasonal ranger-naturalist at the Grand Canyon from 1929–1931, wore a standard uniform except for a hat adapted from the Fred Harvey Company's Courier guides. *(Courtesy of National Park Service.)*

The Park Service career of Jean McWhirt Pinkley, who began as an archeologist at Mesa Verde in 1939, lasted thirty years. She is shown introducing Mug House to visitors in the late 1950s. *(Courtesy of National Park Service.)*

Park wife Amy Bryant and her husband, Harold C. Bryant, later chief naturalist for the Park Service, in their Yosemite tent home in the 1920s. *(Courtesy of National Park Service.)*

Hap Dodge, wife of Natt Dodge, Southwest chief naturalist, and children Nattalie and Griffin, at their adobe duplex at Casa Grande National Monument in Arizona in 1938. *(Courtesy of Nattalie Dodge Bradley.)*

Sallie Pierce Brewer [Harris], leads a pack mule on the trail from Rainbow Bridge back to Navajo National Monument where her husband, Jim, was custodian in 1939 and she was an "Honorary Custodian Without Pay" or an "HCWP." *(Courtesy of National Park Service.)*

Courtney Reeder Jones, an "HCWP," and David Jones, custodian, at the doorway to their 1939 quarters inside the prehistoric Pueblo ruin at Wupatki National Monument. *(Courtesy Edna R. Emerson and Courtney R. Jones.)*

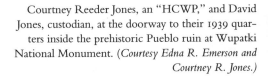

Frances and Charles Sharp pulled their house trailer from Southwest monument to monument when Charles served as a relief ranger during the late 1930s to mid-1940s. *(Courtesy of Frances and Charles Sharp.)*

Mollie O'Kane assists her husband, David O'Kane, Park Service engineer, in 1973 with surveying at Virgin Islands National Park, one of their many park locations. *(Courtesy of Mollie and David O'Kane.)*

First Women
Ranger-Naturalists

*I*sabel Bassett [Wasson] shared her news in the Wellesley College alumnae newsletter: "Next summer I am to be a government ranger in Yellowstone Park. You
never heard of a woman ranger? Well, neither have I." Bassett seemed to be as surprised herself as she expected her classmates to be. Her report continued: "I am to
be a general informant on the park, give talks at the hotels, train the guides and auto
drivers, and start a museum."[1]

During the summer of 1919, Bassett had joined her parents on a *Brooklyn Daily
Eagle* tour to witness the dedication of a new highway joining Glacier and Yellowstone national parks. A native of Brooklyn, New York, and a recent graduate in geology, Bassett was "tremendously excited about seeing geological phenomena" that
she had studied, "but had never seen." It was her first trip West, and the tour leader,
radio commentator H. V. Kaltenborn, took advantage of her enthusiasm by asking
her to lecture to the group after dinner. Her descriptions of the origins of Yellowstone's geological features so impressed Horace Albright, then park superintendent,
that he asked her to return the following summer as Yellowstone's second, and first
woman, naturalist. By the time she took up the position, she was married and held
a master's degree in geology from Columbia.[2]

Although Albright inherited Yellowstone's military culture, he was also committed to developing positive communications with the public. He saw Bassett's
talents as an opportunity to strengthen his fledgling education program. But in the
1920s and early 1930s, the conflict between the military culture and the goal of
public communications would have a serious effect on the careers of the first young
women naturalists as they challenged the all-male tradition of the National Park
Service.

Finding a niche for their skills and training in the service's new educational
programs, Isabel Bassett Wasson and the women who followed her represented a
growing group of women eager to enter careers as naturalists. Stemming from
the long tradition of women's amateur study of natural history, by 1920 enough
women had become professional naturalists to serve as models and raise expectations for other women. They served on faculties of women's colleges and as nature-

study teachers in public schools. They published popular handbooks identifying wildflowers and birds and they created herbariums. Like the women who worked to preserve the nation's premier landscapes, trees, and plants in national parks, women naturalists hoped to generate moral and spiritual values in young people and adults by connecting them with nature.

The year after her three months in Yellowstone, Isabel Wasson explained her title of ranger to her college classmates. "It was a matter of new work under an old name. I didn't 'range,' I talked." She worked at the information desk in the morning and gave lectures at three different locations daily, one in the afternoon, one in the early evening, and a third around an evening campfire, making certain that each lecture was different because she had developed a following. Once a week she worked with the park naturalist, Milton Skinner, to collect information on park animals, birds, and geological features.

Wasson was enthusiastic about the new educational program. The conditions at Yellowstone were, she said, "ideal for teaching. People were on vacation with the time to explore, observe, and grope for explanations of the natural wonders around them." Although Albright asked her to return a second summer to perform work described as "more important" even than before, she had to decline: she was both planning to join her husband and work as an oil geologist in Oklahoma and she was expecting a baby. When she asked to return in 1922, Albright wrote that a cut in funding would prohibit it.[3]

Albright, who became director of the Park Service in 1929, throughout his tenure continued to support the employment of women as ranger-naturalists. In 1931, two years before he left the service, a report on educational activities in national parks listed several women ranger-naturalists. At Yellowstone were Marguerite Lindsley [Arnold], employed as a ranger-naturalist for ten years, and Herma Albertson [Baggley], who served nearly five years. At the Grand Canyon was ranger-naturalist Pauline Mead [Patraw] and at Yosemite, Enid Michael. Not listed but working as a naturalist was Ruth Ashton at Rocky Mountain National Park.[4]

Each of these women, except for Michael, held a master's degree in botany or biology. Three of them published classic guides to plants in parks. But after Herma Baggley resigned in 1933, virtually no women naturalists worked in any national park, except for Michael at Yosemite. Amid some controversy, Michael survived as a summer naturalist for more than twenty years.

Women Forerunners of Park Service Naturalists

When the Park Service began to hire and train naturalists in 1920, there was already a significant group of women with the potential for successful careers in the service's new educational programs. Adventurous women botanists and ornithologists had long experience in leading nature walks and were already contributing to the knowledge of plants and birds in specific parks by writing the field guides the new Park Service naturalists needed. Women school teachers were so attracted to national parks that Albright noticed that they and "other feminine vacationists in the parks are so numerous that they far outnumber the men."[5] Other young women, often college students, found jobs in the concessions in the parks and doubled as nature guides for hotel visitors.

The best-known woman botanist in the West was Alice Eastwood, curator of the California Academy of Sciences's herbarium for half a century. Her wildflower exhibits were models for Enid Michael's displays at Yosemite; it was Eastwood who helped Michael classify Yosemite's plants. Eastwood's keys to Rocky Mountain and Pacific Coast flowers were invaluable to naturalists and she published descriptions of plants at Yosemite, Kings Canyon, and Grand Canyon national parks. Her extensive field experience, coupled with her large correspondence, helped scores of naturalists classify plants native to Alaska and the West. She also called out to the public to protect plant habitats.[6]

Florence Merriam Bailey's guides to bird life in individual national parks were highly valued by the Park Service. Her last guide done for a national park, *Among the Birds in the Grand Canyon Country,* was published in 1939, based on earlier research. In the foreword, Arno B. Cammerer, director of the Park Service, explained that she saw the birds "as a visitor might see them" and answered "the questions a visitor might ask should he have the good fortune to meet her along the trail." Her first bird guide for a national park was for Glacier, published in 1918 with a study of the park's mammals by her husband, Vernon Bailey, a naturalist for the U.S. Biological Survey. Ten years later came *Birds of New Mexico*, used by the custodians of the Park Service's Southwestern Monuments and their wives to help them with their bird counts. She again joined her husband for a study of Mammoth Cave National Park in 1933.[7]

Bailey transcended the role of naturalist: she became an environmentalist dedicated to protecting habitats in advance of male ornithologists caught up in collecting trophies. Unlike botany, a field long open to women, ornithology began as a male occupation: bird identification was competitive and depended on shooting birds and collecting skins. When binoculars replaced the gun as the accepted tool for bird study late in the nineteenth century, women quickly entered the field. Birdwatchers called "snapshooters" used cameras instead of guns. Women birdwatchers became bird protectors as they joined the campaign, often as leaders, to outlaw killing birds for their feathers, used to decorate women's hats. Bailey's guides were detailed descriptions of a bird's habitat and behavior over a period of time and not designed simply for quick bird identification. She drew the reader into the pleasures of bird study and the need to preserve habitats.[8]

In botany, Frances Theodora Dana's *How to Know the Wild Flowers* filled such a need that its first edition in 1893 was sold out in five days. Dana's friend and, later, illustrator, Marion Satterlee, had urged her to take up a challenge put forth by nature writer John Burroughs for someone to give us "a handbook of our wild flowers . . . arranged according to color with place of growth and time of blooming." By the time of the tenth anniversary edition, 66,000 copies had already been sold. Mary

Elizabeth Parsons, acknowledging both Alice Eastwood's help and Frances Dana's model, brought out *The Wild Flowers of California* in 1897, illustrated by Margaret Warriner Buck, to present "the flowers peculiarly Californian."[9]

It was the nature study movement, spreading from its beginnings in New York State in 1895 to the entire country, that first offered wide-scale employment to women naturalists as nature study teachers in public schools. The movement presented many women role models. Katherine Chandler's *Habits of California Plants,* written in 1903 especially for children, began as articles on the *San Francisco Chronicle* children's page. Chandler credited Alice Eastwood as her teacher and stressed observation, urging children to notice how each plant had "its own individual way of doing its life work." She urged children to take up her life work. "Right here in California," she wrote, "where there are so many new plants as yet unstudied . . . is a very good place for a boy or girl to plan to become a famous naturalist."[10]

The publication of Anna Botsford Comstock's *Handbook of Nature Study* in 1911 made Comstock the most widely-recognized leader of the nature study movement. Her massive compendium, including sections on birds, mammals, fishes, insects, amphibians, rocks, plants, climate, weather, and stars, went through twenty-four editions between 1911 and 1939. It began as leaflets, many written by women, published as a correspondence course for nature study teachers and as articles published in the *Nature Study Review,* founded in 1906. That her influence was nationwide was demonstrated by a poll conducted by the League of Women Voters in 1923 that selected her as one of America's twelve greatest living women.

The nature study movement coincided with the professionalization of the natural sciences, a trend that soon separated amateurs from professionals—the professionals valuing experimentation over observation and the study of physiology over building a taxonomy. Although the nature study movement encouraged "investigation" and used simple scientific equipment, it also ascribed a moral value to nature study. Beginning as a way of interesting farm children in nature as a step toward improving agriculture, it soon spread to being perceived as a cure for urban problems. As the "thought-core" for the entire school curriculum, nature study was an antidote for poor health and "nerve exhaustion" among children and teachers.[11]

Although nature study provided careers for women, it channeled women naturalists into public school teaching with the added implication that their science was not rigorous. The year after the American Nature Association began to publish *Nature Magazine* in 1923, devoted to interesting the public in natural history, the *Nature Study Review* became a department in the new magazine. Women nature study supervisors wrote articles on teaching methods and the General Federation of Womens' Clubs presented a nature study curriculum, one grade at a time. Except for Anna Botsford Comstock, then in her seventies, the editorial board was composed of men. When Comstock gave up the position, the department was discontinued and the specific goal of improving children's lives by leading them to nature was abandoned by the magazine.[12]

Meanwhile, the women of the West Coast mountain clubs—the Sierra Club,

Mazamas, and the Mountaineers—continued to publish field notes. Winona Bailey listed flowers in Olympic National Park, finding species that normally lived in arctic zones flourishing at low altitudes. The Sierran Puffball intrigued Elizabeth Morse, secretary of the California Mycological Society, who unexpectedly discovered the puffball throughout the Cascade Mountains. Mount Rainier National Park reported in its *Nature Notes* that her visits "literally made this Park 'fungi-minded.'" She found and named a new species after the park and created an exhibit of fungi for the park museum.[13]

Women Nature Guides

Even before the Park Service developed its educational programs, women found positions as nature guides in inns and hotels in Glacier, Yellowstone, and Rocky Mountain national parks. Herma Albertson got the exposure as a naturalist that led to her employment by the Park Service in 1929 through nature guiding at Old Faithful Lodge, where she also worked as a chambermaid.[14]

Nature guiding had been developed into a fine art several decades before at Rocky Mountain National Park by Enos Mills, a founder of the park in 1915 and the naturalist chosen by Gifford Pinchot to lecture to women's clubs. For six months of the year, Mills operated Longs Peak Inn where he opened a nature museum, trained nature guides, and ran a trail school for visitors. He put nature instead of the nature guide's knowledge on stage. Mills encouraged women to be nature guides and predicted that many women would enter the field, believing that their work "was identical with that of men guides."[15]

In 1916, Esther and Elizabeth Burnell went to Longs Peak Inn as visitors. Both had attended Lake Erie College. Elizabeth was a teacher of college mathematics, who earned her master's degree from the University of Michigan the next year. Esther had studied at Pratt Institute and worked as an interior decorator. Before the summer was over, Esther decided to fulfill a lifelong dream: she would homestead in Estes Park, in a claim four miles from the village, near MacGregor Pass. She survived her first winter still enthusiastic about her new life and became a legend for her thirty-mile trip by snowshoe alone across the Continental Divide.[16]

With the encouragement of Mills, the sisters took and passed an examination as "nature teachers" and became licensed by Rocky Mountain National Park as nature guides in the summer of 1917; they thus can be considered to be the first women designated as naturalists by the Park Service. Superintendent Claude Way called the women nature guides "a new attraction," calling them "young ladies versed in flowers, birds, animals and trees who teach men, women and children nature lore." He was satisfied with his experiment, saying, "They have been highly successful and popular this season and fill a long felt need." Way reported that he restricted women nature guides to one-day trips below timberline, but the Burnell sisters apparently never accepted such boundaries. Elizabeth became the first woman guide on Longs Peak.[17]

Much sought after by visitors, Elizabeth headed Mills's trail school for twelve summers. She led groups up Longs Peak and on week-long camping expeditions, and
gave evening talks. She left her mathematics career to help initiate nature study in the
Los Angeles schools. In 1925, she coauthored a popular field guide to the birds of the
Southwest. Reflecting Enos Mills's philosophy, she cautioned her readers: "There is
keener pleasure as well as greater scientific value in knowing a few birds well than in
habitually striving for long lists and seeking rarities and doubtful records."[18]

Esther spent another winter in her homestead, this time joined by her sister Elizabeth, but at the end of the summer of 1918, Esther married Enos Mills. Together
they operated the inn and pursued many writing projects. After Mills died unexpectedly in 1922, Esther continued to operate Longs Peak Inn for more than twenty
years. For a time, she and Elizabeth also ran the trail school.[19]

Yosemite Field School Women

When the Yosemite School of Field Natural History opened in 1925, women
responded immediately. The first class, a six-week session held in the summer, was
attended by more women than men. But although Enid Michael lectured on plant
life, the staff members were men. Students learned about the school from their college professors, the Sierra Club, or from notices in natural history journals. Park
Service personnel interviewed prospective candidates at Yosemite or in Park Service areas near their homes. Students paid twenty-five dollars for the course and
lived in tents in Camp Number 19, the staff campground. Activities were the same
for men and women, including practice in guiding hikes and giving campfire talks.
In 1933, the sessions were expanded to seven weeks, to include a research project
and a two-week expedition in the high country.[20]

The Yosemite Field School was designed by its founder, Harold C. Bryant, who
headed research and education for the Park Service, to train naturalists for the service. But women students soon learned that only male trainees would be considered for positions. The reason given was that women "couldn't fight fires, rescue injured rock climbers, bury dead animals, or carry out police duties."[21] Apparently Park
Service naturalists were still considered to be rangers first and naturalists second.

Nevertheless, some women persisted in viewing the field school as an entree to
naturalist positions. In 1924, a few years after her graduation from Mount Holyoke
College, Ruth Ashton [Nelson] returned to Estes Park, where she had stayed at
Mills's Longs Peak Inn with her family as a child. After working as a camp coun-
selor in nature study and horseback riding, she bought a homestead in Estes Park.
She found an information desk position at Rocky Mountain National Park in 1925
and enrolled as a graduate student at Colorado State College. Her master's thesis,
published as *Plants of Rocky Mountain National Park*, became so popular as a guide
that she revised and republished it over a period of fifty years.[22]

Ruth Ashton's ambition was to become a full-fledged Park Service naturalist.
She knew she was qualified and already successful in her naturalist activities for the

park. In the spring of 1928, she took two steps. She applied to the Yosemite Field School, and she wrote Roger Toll, Rocky Mountain superintendent, asking for a permanent position of ranger-naturalist. Toll offered her the old position at the information desk. Although he praised her work, he discouraged her from seeking the professional position. "It has always been my feeling," he said, "that a man was preferable for the position of park naturalist." He added that if the park ever found itself in a position to hire a number of ranger-naturalists "it might work out very well to have one of them a woman and the others men."[23]

Ashton did attend the Yosemite Field School and the following winter she tried again to seek a naturalist position. This time she wrote to Ansel Hall, chief naturalist for the Park Service, requesting information about the park naturalist exam. He, too, was discouraging. "Although your technical preparation in the sciences must have given you excellent preparation in the field of natural history," he said, "I feel that I cannot encourage your taking the Park Naturalist examination." He blamed it on "administrative reasons which have been imposed upon us by Washington making it necessary for us to secure men as candidates." Unsuccessful in her efforts, Ashton returned as an information clerk for three more summers until her marriage to Aven Nelson, professor of botany at the University of Wyoming.[24]

Women dominated classes at the field school for the first four years; the classes of 1927 and 1928 each had thirteen women—to four men in 1927 and to six men in 1928. Soon Bert Harwell, assistant director of the school and Yosemite chief naturalist (and a field school graduate), began to argue that there were too many women. Originally, the school took the first twenty applicants. "Naturally," Harwell argued, "more women teachers could plan for a summer well in advance than men, so the first classes were mostly women." In 1929, a new application form helped him "get the number of women whittled down to ten—one-half of the number to be admitted in each session." In 1931, an all-male class was tried, but it was abandoned after one year. Around 1937, Harwell remembered, the "Inspectors from Washington" tried again to limit the school to men because the school was supported to train naturalists and men were "needed . . . for that work." Harwell had argued back. "*Some* women do find places in the Naturalist field," he had said, "and then it does something to the School to have women attend. They keep the men from dropping down to a level of no shirts and plenty of whiskers." Women, he, by then, believed, "tone up the organization during the sessions and later as alumni."[25]

Women continued to attend the Yosemite Field School, to be active in its alumni organization, and to hope that some day they would be accepted as Park Service naturalists. Mildred Ericson, from Minneapolis, remembered her first day at the school in 1939. By then the classes had settled down to a ratio of four women to sixteen men. Harwell greeted them all and proceeded to give the men a pep talk about becoming Park Service naturalists, "and then he turned to us four girls, smiled at us and said, 'Nice to have you here in the school, girls, but of course there's no jobs for you in the National Park Service.'" None of the women argued back, but Ericson "was so provoked" that she decided she was going to find a job as a naturalist. She persuaded the Works Progress Administration program in Minnesota to start a nature guide service in their state parks under her direction. After World War II, she convinced the naturalist at the National Capital Parks Region of the Park Service in Washington, D.C., to hire her as a guide because he needed help with his popular nature walks. The next year, Yellowstone accepted her as a seasonal naturalist, a career that lasted for nearly twenty summers. During the winter, she taught science and published more than fifty articles on natural history in national magazines, illustrated with her own photographs.[26]

The Yosemite Field School was discontinued during World War II, but revived between 1948 and 1953. The ratio of four women to sixteen men was resumed. After Bettie Willard finished the course in 1948, she told John Doerr, Park Service chief naturalist, that she wanted to be a naturalist for the service. He was gracious but said, "Did you realize we never hire women?" Dorr Yeager, naturalist for the Western Region, was also at the meeting. He escorted her out of earshot and offered to survey superintendents in his region to see if any was willing to hire a woman naturalist. Four agreed, and Willard became one of the first uniformed women naturalists to have worked for the national parks since the 1930s. She worked for one summer at Lava Beds and another at Crater Lake, performing a full range of naturalist duties. Willard later earned her doctorate at the University of Colorado, and in the mid-1990s was still teaching field study courses and doing extensive research and publishing on alpine tundra at Rocky Mountain National Park. Initially she drew on the work of her friend, Ruth Ashton Nelson.[27]

Because the editors of the *Yosemite Field School Alumni Newsletter,* Beth and Margaret Byrkit, became concerned about women's future in the field school, they published a Women's Number in 1936. Noting that the ratio of women to men, once three to one, had been reversed, they asked women to respond to the question, "How have Field School experiences helped you?" The answers, they emphasized, showed that "surely the women merit their place in the School." More than half of the 120 women graduates were teachers, including many at the college level. Nine were Girls' Club or Girl Scout leaders, seventeen were nature counselors in camps, and four were naturalists in state parks. Eleven were studying for advanced degrees and five had married rangers, naturalists, or biologists. All, they concluded, were "exerting their influences . . . for park-mindedness and conservation, and understanding of the world of nature."[28]

Even though the field school did not open up opportunities for them in the Park Service, many of the women graduates saw the school as a turning point in their lives. Alice Goen, who worked in a California state redwoods park the summer after attending, said she "proved that there is a demand by the public for such nature guide work, and that a girl can do it." She was then a junior forester for the Forest Service, working on a survey of the effect of drought on plant life. In a section on news from national parks, the editors listed more than thirty male field school graduates who were currently seasonal or permanent ranger-naturalists, demonstrating that for many of their male classmates, the field school did indeed produce the intended result of employment in the Park Service.[29]

Pioneering Positions for Women at Mt. Rainier and Yosemite

Despite the discouragement met by Yosemite Field School women when they tried to become Park Service naturalists, several women like Isabel Wasson at Yellowstone had already succeeded in pioneering ranger and ranger-naturalist positions. The first two women rangers in the National Park Service served in the summer of 1918: filling in for male rangers who had left for military service were Clare Marie Hodges at Yosemite and Helene Wilson at Mount Rainier. Wilson worked at the main entrance to Mount Rainier, taking down the engine number of each car, its license, and each occupant's name and address. She alternated with a male ranger. In the month of August, they issued permits for more than three thousand cars, in addition to stages and horse-drawn vehicles, making a total of more than eighteen thousand people.[30]

Because she was hired at Yosemite six weeks before Wilson began at Mount Rainier, however, the distinction of being the first woman ranger in the Park Service goes to Clare Marie Hodges. In 1904, when she was fourteen, she rode four days on horseback with her family to reach Yosemite Valley. On a later trip, her party rode up Tenaya Canyon from the valley to Tuolumne Meadows. A graduate of San José Normal School, where she contributed to the herbarium, Hodges began teaching in the Yosemite Valley School in 1916. She rode horseback and hiked all over Yosemite's trails. "The Valley," she said, "became like an open book to me." She and a ranger friend once cooked their lunch of bacon and eggs in an ice cake under a frozen waterfall. "It was quite a feather in my cap," she commented, "because they told us no woman would dare attempt it."[31]

In the spring of 1918, Hodges heard some rangers talking about the difficulty of filling in for men who had been drafted into the army. Believing that she had "two years of unconscious preparation," she "plucked up [her] courage" and applied to Washington B. Lewis, the superintendent. She told him: "Probably you'll laugh at me, but I want to be a ranger." He didn't even smile, she remembered. "I beat you to it, young lady. It's been in my mind for some time to put a woman on one of these patrols—only I couldn't find the right one before." Her application was sent to Washington, accepted, and she was given a badge. Thus Hodges became a ranger, mounted on a horse, riding patrol, reporting to the chief ranger, with a Stetson on her head—but a ranger who also wore a middy blouse and a divided skirt. Although the other rangers suggested she carry a gun when she took the gate receipts from Tuolumne Meadows down to park headquarters, an overnight ride, she decided against it.[32]

Superintendent Lewis tried another experiment using women as rangers between 1923 and 1928: he allowed rangers' wives to be compensated for their work at their husbands' stations. For two years, Beatrice and Edward Freeland received equal pay for checking in cars at the Bridalveil Falls and Alder Creek entrance stations. Working in tandem, they were on duty seven days a week from 6 A.M. to 10 P.M. John and Martha Bingaman followed the Freelands at Alder Creek for three seasons, including a winter.[33]

Eva and Charles McNally shared positions as park rangers on Tioga Road ranger stations with equal pay in the summers of 1926 and 1927. Eva believed the park hired the wives "so the husbands would be more content." Although Charles purchased a uniform, Eva wore her own knickers; but for a $5 deposit she was issued a badge. She collected fees and sealed guns with a wire so visitors couldn't shoot the wildlife and checked to make sure dogs were leashed. Visitors and staff accepted her with good humor. She remembered going over the old Tioga Road to a dance at Mono Lake with other staff, leaving her husband behind on his shift. She borrowed Charles's gun and holster to impress the proprietor of the Stockton drug store where she had worked in the winter who came for a visit. When asked how the public reacted to having a woman ranger, Charles replied, "Surprised!" adding, "She could make a decision of her own, and not have to wait for her husband!"[34]

When Superintendent Lewis hired Enid Reeves Michael as a temporary ranger-naturalist in June 1921, he probably did not expect that her appointment would outlast his. Michael served in the temporary position for more than twenty years, becoming a mainstay at Yosemite, kept in her position by the support of a large public following. In addition to leading nature walks and maintaining a wildflower display and garden, she contributed 172 articles, on a variety of subjects, to Yosemite *Nature Notes*. Michael always knew she was an anomaly at Yosemite. Unlike the pioneer women naturalists in other parks, she was never issued a uniform. A teacher in Pasadena, she met Charles Michael, assistant postmaster at Yosemite and an ardent birdwatcher, on a Sierra Club hike. They married, and Enid, then thirty-eight, moved to Yosemite in 1919. Soon after she arrived, she offered to help Ansel Hall with a wildflower, shrub, and tree display on the porch of the administration building. Surprised that so many plants grew in the park, Superintendent Lewis and the chief ranger, Forrest Townsley, ordered a set of shelves to be built to improve the display. When the naturalist service was started by Harold Bryant the following year, Lewis offered to put Enid Michael on the payroll as a seasonal ranger-naturalist. Bryant believed that the positions should be filled by men and "did not approve of women taking part," Michael remembered, "but, I was there and I guess in time he concluded to make the best of an unfortunate situation."[35]

By 1929, Enid Michael had collected and mounted a thousand plant specimens as well as recording visits by one hundred and thirty species of birds. She and Charles also trained black bears to take sugar cubes from their hands and drink syrup from a hand-held bottle. During the winter, she took rare plant specimens, many located by her in the high country, to Alice Eastwood for identification. Except for three months in the summer, she prepared the exhibits on her own time, but she never let the opportunity pass to suggest that she should be hired full time.[36]

Michael's appeal to friends to pressure the Park Service to hire her as a permanent naturalist in 1923 almost cost her even the seasonal position. Bess Hayne Fisher, state chair of conservation for the California Federation of Women's Clubs, forwarded several letters to the Park Service director, Stephen Mather, requesting the permanent appointment of Michael as a year-round botanist at Yosemite. Fisher asked if the federation, "some sixty thousand strong," could help him secure the necessary appropriation for a Nature Guide Service. Fisher's support was initially enlisted by C. H. Adams, secretary of the Merchants' Exchange in San Francisco, a friend of Michael's, possibly from the Sierra Club. Adams also wrote to Mather directly.[37]

Superintendent Lewis responded to Mather's follow-up inquiries with some feeling. He told Mather that he was "very sorry" that Michael had "propagandize[d]" the federation and others "to secure influence in her behalf." He said "that in itself would be sufficient to deny recommendation for [the] appointment she seeks." He had tried to compensate her with the summer position and by furnishing her "wood, lights and water without charge." Her full-time employment was not necessary, because the park naturalist could handle the educational work during the off-season. Lewis responded in a similar vein to Fisher and Adams. To smooth over the superintendent's anger, Adams took full responsibility for having contacted the federation. Lewis remained unconvinced, but he did continue Michael's seasonal positions.[38]

A gift of $4,000 from philanthropist Marjorie Montgomery Ward in 1931 helped Michael achieve a more permanent position for a time. After Michael showed Ward unused space behind the museum, Ward offered to support a wildflower garden there. Calling her "the best botanist in this park," the new superintendent, Charles G. Thomson, put Michael on a temporary year-round appointment that lasted more than three years. But she reverted to her seasonal status after she ran into another conflict, this time with Bert Harwell, the park naturalist.[39]

Two strong personalities were at odds. Michael, believing that the superintendent had put her in charge of the garden, did not see why she should submit to Harwell's supervision. Harwell, who had the authority of his position, found her independent attitude difficult to work with and had his own plans for the garden. Shortly before Michael left for a winter vacation in 1934, Thomson and Harwell told her she must comply with Harwell's instructions. Superintendent Thomson was clearly caught in the middle. Although Harwell asked him to write Michael that she would not be hired for the next summer, what Thomson did suggest to Michael was that she convince Harwell "that you and he can work shoulder to shoulder" and praised her for her past work. Michael responded with a long letter to Harwell, pledging "to work in harmony" with him, but he did not change his mind. The impasse was broken when Thomson asked for advice from Harold Bryant. Thomson called Enid Michael "a vivid personality," part of the ranger-naturalist effort so long that "she is something of an institution." He spoke of her intimate knowledge of the park. "She is unique in her place here," he explained, with many visitors coming just to spend days in the field with her. Bryant agreed that Michael be given a trial year, and Harwell finally agreed to have her return, though he stipulated that "everything concerning the garden" would have to "clear" through his office.[40]

Harwell left for another park in 1940, and Michael continued in a seasonal position until 1943, when the Park Service reduced naturalist positions because of the war. In one of her last reports, Michael noted that about a thousand visitors came to the garden each day. The termination of her appointment as a summer seasonal signified the end of women's opportunities to be naturalists at Yosemite for more than two decades.[41]

The First Women Naturalists at Rocky Mountain and Grand Canyon

At the end of the 1920s, both Rocky Mountain and Grand Canyon national parks experimented with individual women ranger-naturalists who had special qualifications. Rocky Mountain superintendent, Roger Toll, found he could not pass up an opportunity to hire Margaret Fuller Boos as a seasonal ranger-naturalist for the summers of 1928 and 1929. Boos had recently completed her Ph.D. in geology at the University of Chicago and researched and published articles on the physical geology of the Front Range in and near Rocky Mountain National Park. Although he wrote Boos that he "should prefer a man for the work," he wanted to hire her both because of her experience in public speaking and teaching and because she had "several hundred dollars worth of lantern slides." The park's own slide collection was poor, he said, and if Boos were hired, he would like her to take slides for the park.[42]

As Rocky Mountain's first ranger-naturalist, Boos led the park's interpretive program for two summers. She wore the same uniform as the male rangers, including breeches, high boots, a white shirt, tie, and Stetson. During her second summer, she gave twenty-two evening lectures to more than fifteen hundred people, on geology, glaciology, birds, trees, and wildlife, and led nearly four hundred visitors on fourteen field trips, eight lasting all day. She contributed twenty articles to the park's *Nature Notes* and wrote a guide to the geology of the park. At the end of her second summer the park offered Boos a permanent position, but she turned it down to join her husband to work for Phillips Petroleum. Among her later achievements was establishing the geology department at the University of Denver.[43]

The first woman ranger-naturalist at the Grand Canyon, Pauline Mead [Patraw], fell in love with the canyon when she was a graduate student in botany at the University of Chicago. While on a field trip to the North Rim, she decided to study the ecology of the Kaibab Plateau for her master's thesis. Years later, she still remembered her feeling when she stood by herself at the edge of the canyon for the first time: "I just felt as if I'd discovered it!" It took Mead two years to collect the material and make the observations for her thesis. When she decided to compare notes with the ranger-naturalist on the South Rim, she walked by herself the nearly twenty-five miles down one rim and up the other. Because the Forest Service was interested in her research, she applied to that agency first, but was turned down because the Forest Service did not hire women. When she applied to the Park Service, she was accepted. Mead was not only well qualified, she was also well connected. She became close friends with Bertha Mather, Stephen Mather's daughter, at the University of Chicago High School. While Mead was working on her research, Mather invited her to be his guest at the dedication of the new North Rim Lodge. When she saw her application some years later, she noticed a handwritten note scribbled on it saying, "It will be remembered that Miss Mead was Steve Mather's guest at the dedication." Mead later remembered: "I'm sure that helped me, because women were not employed at that time very much."[44]

Pauline Mead served for the two summer seasons of 1929 and 1930 and continued on for the second winter until the spring of 1931 when she married Preston Patraw, the assistant superintendent. "It was a lovely job, just lovely!" she recalled. She lectured at Yavapai Point and led nature walks and motorcades along the rim during the day. At first she wore a riding habit, but as she became more accepted in her position, she adopted a man's uniform, but with a difference that seemed to reflect the superintendent's ambivalence about having a woman naturalist on his staff. Instead of the traditional Stetson, he preferred her to wear a soft-brimmed felt hat like the hats worn by the women couriers hired by Fred Harvey to guide visitors to sites in the Southwest. In the evening she gave campfire talks on botany and geology. "It was so wonderful to be able to lecture on the edge of the Canyon and talk about the Canyon (with) the Canyon in front of you. There was no feeling of self-consciousness," she remembered. After her marriage, Pauline Patraw continued to study botany. She published more than twenty articles in *Nature Notes* and made plant lists for Grand Canyon, Pecos, Zion, and Bryce. Her book, *Flowers of the Southwest Mesas*, came out in 1952, with a sixth edition published in 1977.[45]

The "Woman-Ranger Question" at Yellowstone

It was at Yellowstone, under Superintendent Horace Albright, that the Park Service hired the most women naturalists. There the visibility of women attracted the attention of Washington officials, with servicewide repercussions that eventually discouraged all but the most secure superintendents from hiring women—even as seasonal ranger-naturalists—until the 1960s. Beginning with Isabel Wasson in 1920, Yellowstone hired ten women as rangers or ranger-naturalists. After Herma Albertson Baggley resigned in 1933, the park hired only men as ranger-naturalists. The chief exception was a brief period during World War II when Yellowstone paid rangers' wives to perform essential services.

The second woman appointee at Yellowstone was Marguerite Lindsley [Arnold]. Daughter of the acting (and first under the Department of the Interior) superintendent of Yellowstone for the three years before Albright's appointment in 1919, Lindsley was born in the park and lived there almost her entire life. It was only logical that Albright would appoint her in 1921, the year following his successful experiment with Isabel Wasson as a ranger-naturalist. At the time, Lindsley was a student at Montana State College. She worked at the new information office and guided visitors over the formations at Mammoth Hot Springs, joined during one season by another woman, Mary Rolfe, a teacher and writer.[46] Lindsley continued in her position for ten years. She was a spirited sportswoman; no one knew the park better, and she recorded its wildlife, vegetation, and weather in more than fifty articles in *Nature Notes*. She was so closely associated with the park that when she died at the age of fifty-one, many of her pieces were collected in a memorial issue of the *Notes* and a poem calling her a "breath of Yellowstone," was widely circulated.[47]

During Lindsley's childhood in the park, it was still Fort Yellowstone, protected by the U.S. Cavalry. Her mother taught her at home until she was fourteen. Intending to become a doctor, she majored in bacteriology and applied to the School of Medicine at the University of Pennsylvania. Because she lacked the prerequisites, she entered the university as a master's candidate. After receiving her degree in 1923, she worked in a biological laboratory outside Philadelphia. In telling her story in 1927 to a writer who was collecting short biographies of women, Lindsley explained why she returned to Yellowstone. Her job in the laboratory was "most interesting and instructive," and, she said, "if there had been no spring that year I might still have been there, somewhat of a bacteriologist by this time." Using her earnings to buy a secondhand Harley Davidson motorcycle and sidecar, Lindsley and a woman she met at work disguised themselves as men and rode across the country in "hail, sleet, mud and washouts," camping along the way. She considered her journey home only the "next to greatest escapade" in her life "so far." What she deemed the greatest was when she made the 143-mile loop of Yellowstone on skis in March 1925. She and the wife of the Mammoth couple who accompanied her were the first women to accomplish the feat. Lindsley was also a skilled horsewoman. Her son said she "rode the biggest and fastest horse in the park on an English low-cant saddle."[48]

Late in December 1925, Albright named Lindsley a permanent park ranger, a position she held until she resigned to marry ranger Ben Arnold in the fall of 1928. She continued her summer seasonal positions until five months before the birth of her son in 1932. During the summer she was in charge of the information office at Mammoth Hot Springs. It was open from 7 A.M. to 10 P.M. and two seasonal male rangers assisted her in handling from two to six hundred visitors a day. She saw Milton Skinner, the park naturalist, as a mentor and worked with him to develop the park museum. On her sleeve she wore a full pine cone, the symbol of a permanent ranger; the seasonal men who reported to her wore twigs on their sleeves and were called ninety-day wonders. During the winter months, Lindsley wrote articles for *Nature Notes*, prepared exhibits, and checked on scientific work in progress.

Although Lindsley enjoyed her museum work, she told the writer of women's biographies, "I love the outofdoor work most of all and always have my own horse. Water gauges in the rivers are to be read weekly, trails inspected, fire patrols. . . . A systematic animal count, antelope or elk, requires everyone to mount and count at once." But she cautioned, "Do not stress the outside work too much—many still think that women's work should be inside and it is a problem sometimes to satisfy everyone even tho I may be qualified for the work in the field."[49]

Lindsley identified closely with nature, observing "the intimate family life" of otters, bear, buffalo, deer, elk, and antelope. The "red letter day" of her life was when, alone on snowshoes at dusk on a high hill, she watched two timber wolves demolish an elk carcass. Another evening, as she stood by herself in the dark, she said, "some primitive instinct of loneliness . . . made me throw back my head and howl at the stillness. . . . I repeated the cry, trying to imitate the weird and fascinating note of a coyote. My efforts were rewarded. . . . I called again and another group joined the first and this time the echoes chased each other around the hills for nearly two minutes before they all died away and quiet reigned."[50]

When Chief Inspector J. F. Gartland from the Department of the Interior visited to examine Yellowstone in the late summer of 1926, four women in addition to Lindsley were on the ranger staff. Two of them served on entrance gates. On the east gate, on duty twenty-four hours a day in tandem with her husband, was Irene Wisdom, the wife of Ranger Roby "Tex" Wisdom. She served for seven summer seasons, beginning in 1924.[51] On the north gate at Mammoth, the main entrance to the park, serving with her father, who was a ranger, was Frances Pound, working her first of four seasons. She was brought up in Yellowstone, and, as a child, sometimes joined her father to patrol the park in the winter on horseback and to help out at the ranger station. Because she collected gate receipts, she carried a gun while on duty and once helped her father arrest two bank robbers; on another occasion, by herself, she arrested a man smuggling in eight gallons of home-brewed alcohol.[52]

The third woman on duty during Gartland's visit was Frieda Nelson, who was working in the chief ranger's office for her second summer. She also patrolled campgrounds on horseback, wearing a full uniform, the same as that worn by men. That she knew her position was unusual for a woman is demonstrated by a comic photograph of her laughing while displaying suspenders that held up oversized breeches. Elizabeth Conard, daughter of Henry Conard, professor of botany at Grinnell College, was the fourth woman on duty that summer. Henry Conard's summer position was training park naturalists and Elizabeth worked as a ranger-naturalist at Camp Roosevelt, substituting for her father when his duties took him to sections of the park.[53]

When Chief Inspector Gartland reported to the secretary of the interior after his survey of Yellowstone, he voiced his strong disapproval of women serving as rangers. He asked that the women on duty at entrance stations hold titles other than ranger and found fault with the park for assigning Elizabeth Conard as a ranger-naturalist at Camp Roosevelt. Gartland praised the "ranger guide nature service carried on by the regular rangers" but criticized the naturalists' interpretive activities, especially a nature trail installed at Old Faithful by Ansel Hall, chief naturalist, calling it "of doubtful interest to any great number of people." Park visitors have "little time to saunter through the woods," he said, "and follow a trail to find peewee's nests, water lilies and the like." Noting that Hall's forte appeared to be collecting for museum exhibits, he saw little to indicate "that he is bringing practical benefits to the National Park Service." What Gartland applauded was a lecture by an "old-time" ranger who gave "his talk from horseback, recounting his experiences with bears and describing their habits, a number of which came out from the woods and could be plainly seen by the audience."[54]

Embedded in Gartland's remarks was the root of the opposition to employing women—criticism that soon grew stronger in the Park Service. His report signified an attack on both the new naturalist service and women's expanding roles in the Park Service. The two areas were connected. Behind them both was the fear of feminization of the image of park rangers. The division between traditional rangers and new rangers was strong from the beginning and reflected the two arms of Park Service culture: the military and the public communications traditions. Many early rangers, who were often "backwoods types," some even holdovers from the U.S. Cavalry, looked upon the new rangers, particularly the ranger-naturalists, as effeminate, calling them "nature fakers," "posy pickers," and "tree huggers." Allowing women to be called rangers threatened the masculine image of Park Service staff.[55]

Albright took the offensive diplomatically. Perhaps the chief inspector would see the "points . . . differently with additional information," he told Mather. "The woman ranger question is the first one to discuss." He explained that no women in the park did ranger work, but under civil service rules there was no other title he could use. He detailed Marguerite Lindsley's work, stating that she had done "a remarkable job" with the information office that summer. Elizabeth Conard helped her father with naturalist work when he was away, and the only ranger work she did was to "take shifts at the station to answer inquiries." She stayed in a cabin near her father's tent next to the road camp where she "was always chaperoned" by the road foreman's wife.

Following with a plea to be able to continue to hire women as ranger-naturalists, Albright asked: "If Miss Conard is not eligible for reemployment then how can we continue the services of Enid Michael in Yosemite Park? Personally, I believe that in certain phases of our educational work women can do just as well or better than men." He explained that Irene Wisdom was assisting her husband and Frances Pound, her father, a policy "to save [living] quarters" that had "other advantages."

Albright tried to reason with Gartland's point of view. He admitted that he did "not like the idea of having a woman on what everyone likes to think of as a 'he man' force. There is a certain romance and glamour to the title 'ranger' which seems to be lost when a woman occupies the position." But, he continued, "we have never been able to get a man to take an interest in the information office, we have had many failures on the part of temporary rangers at the gates, we have found that most male rangers are more or less useless in the Chief Ranger's office and I think that if we are going to keep our organization at the highest efficiency we may have to employ a few women in the organization."

In answer to Gartland's favorable remark about the lecture by the "old-time" ranger, Albright was firm. With the exception of the ranger who Gartland heard speak and possibly one other, he said, "there is not a member of the permanent force at the present time who could give a lecture if he had to—not even if his life depended on it. . . . Of course," he added wryly, "I should have excepted Miss Lindsley from what I said above because she can lecture." He then went on to praise the lectures given by the ranger-naturalists. He said he was proud of his ranger force but "out of 31 permanent rangers not over half of them are good public contact men and several of these men we would not put in contact with the public at all. We keep them in outlying sections on fire patrol, and protection work." As for Ansel Hall's nature trail, Albright found it "had been [so] extensively used" that "it had been practically worn out."[56]

When Henry Conard, by then back at his college position, heard about the order from Washington not to hire women as rangers, he wrote Albright: "I am still 'suffering from shock' in relation to the lady-rangers." Albright encouraged Conard to write to Mather and explained that he did want to select women "where their qualifications make them particularly desirable" but "owing to the difficulties of housing women rangers, I shall always pursue the policy I have followed in the past, that women will not be selected for rangers when men possessing approximately the same qualifications are available."[57]

Mather immediately received letters from several of Conard's colleagues in botany. From the University of Chicago, George Fuller praised the work of women nature guides at Rocky Mountain and Yellowstone. Answering for Mather, Arno Cammerer, associate director, made it clear that the real issue—whether or not women could do the job—was going to be sidestepped from then on. Although "the high ability of women . . . has been amply demonstrated . . . certain physical conditions make it desirable . . . not to extend further the opportunities of employment to women." The lack of suitable living quarters was again given as the reason. Conard's subsequent letter to H. C. Work, secretary of the interior, included a strong protest about the new policy and his resignation from his summer position at Yellowstone. He said, "I sincerely petition you to so arrange that this anti-woman order may be withheld for one year so that the injustice and stupidity of this order may become evident." Work gave the answer about living quarters that would become the stock answer. He hoped it would "not be necessary to employ women in this activity until some way can be found to give them a different designation than that of ranger . . . a term associated with vigorous and courageous men of the West."[58]

Lucy Braun, botany professor at the University of Cincinnati, who started the Wild Flower Preservation Society in 1924, also protested. Not only were "women as well equipped as men," she said, but they understood the woman visitor better than men and some women would go on park trips only with a woman guide. "Women *are* capable of leading parties, either of women, or of men and women, and of meeting successfully the emergencies of the trail." Her conclusion was clear:

"I know it, for I have done it, and expect to continue to do it." Nevertheless, Cammerer's response to Braun was what by then had become a form letter.[59]

Ironically, it was that winter that Marguerite Lindsley's work as a park ranger received widespread publicity in *Sunset* magazine. She received many letters from women who saw her as a role model and asked how they could become rangers. She not only discouraged them, but she also revealed she did not want women to be rangers unless they were accepted with full status. Lindsley told one correspondent that she would rather lose her job "than see women employed where they are at a disadvantage." To the daughter of a Forest Service ranger in Colorado, she said she could well understand her "ambition for a life work which will keep you out of doors." But, she added, "it is probable that the Park Service may discontinue their [women's] employment and . . . the ranger staff will be made up entirely of men."[60]

Opposition to hiring women as naturalists continued to grow within the Park Service. If hiring women as ranger-naturalists confirmed the effeminacy of the post, then allowing women to be naturalists, no matter how qualified or successful, might damage the chances of the survival of the fledgling and vulnerable naturalist service in the parks. The naturalists were anxious to increase their status in the scientific community outside the service and to gain respect and support from inside the service. At the first Park Naturalists' Conference in 1929, where they began to develop professional standards, one naturalist publicly challenged the position of women as nature guides. Speaking on the qualifications of a nature guide, he stated categorically: "Public attitude seems to register against female guides. Even though a woman possess a wealth of information . . . she will not be as well received, will not be as successful, as the male guide."[61]

In the same year as the first naturalists' conference, Herma Albertson began her position as a ranger-naturalist at Yellowstone. Three years before, she had decided to "work into the naturalist work" by becoming a "pillow puncher" on the domestic staff at Old Faithful Lodge, working as a nature guide in the afternoons. In her first year she helped to lay out the nature trail so disapproved of by the chief inspector. The only guide on the trail for three years, she increased her following from three to three hundred hikers. She also acted as a relief lecturer in two other places and created a wildflower display at the lodge. In the fall of her third year, Albertson said later, "My reward came." Albright called her into his office and asked her if she could come the next summer and work full time as a ranger-naturalist. "I have never been more thrilled over a position," she said, "and think I never shall be. It was the one thing I had dreamed and struggled to attain."[62]

Herma Albertson earned a master's degree in botany from the University of Idaho in 1929, the year she began to work for the Park Service. She hoped to attend the School of Forestry but when she learned that the school did not admit women, she became an instructor in the university's botany department. When she passed the junior park naturalist examination in 1931, Yellowstone offered her a permanent post. Albertson was the first woman ever selected by a park from the civil service register for a park naturalist position. She took over Marguerite Lindsley Arnold's responsibilities for the information office at Mammoth and developed the herbarium begun by Henry Conard. Albertson remembered that she was treated the same as the male professionals and had no trouble supervising men. Her uniform was identical to that worn by men, even buttoning left over right. On the other hand, she did remember being constantly photographed by visitors.[63]

Roger Toll, the new Yellowstone superintendent, however, did not use Albertson as a naturalist at first. When Albright found out, he reprimanded Toll: "I did not realize that she had been used as a stenographer since her employment last spring," he said in a letter. "It never occurred to me that during the summer this highly capable girl, one of our very best speakers in the Naturalist service and one of the most enthusiastic public contact workers that we have in the Service, would be kept at a desk doing stenographic work." He asked Toll to release Albertson for naturalist duties immediately and secure a temporary stenographer.[64]

After marrying George Baggley, the chief ranger, Herma worked until December 1933, when her resignation virtually ended the first period of women professional field workers in the Park Service. Even after her paid employment ended, she continued to offer her services. She collaborated with William McDougall, a plant ecologist, to write a needed guide to the wildflowers in the park. They published the book in 1936, dedicating a revised edition in 1956 to the memory of Marguerite Lindsley Arnold.[65]

The First Women Anthropologists in the Park Service

By the time Albright resigned from the Park Service in 1933, the service had lost its will to hire women in professional field positions; not until the 1960s did the service again discover women to be an essential resource for naturalist and ranger positions in national parks. Almost the only exception to this practice was Mesa Verde National Park and a few Southwestern monuments, where a few women trained in anthropology were hired during the 1930s. One of them, Jean McWhirt Pinkley, began a career at Mesa Verde in 1939 that lasted for thirty years. Another, Sallie Pierce [Harris], first hired in the winter of 1934 at Montezuma Castle to classify artifacts from a recent dig, resumed her paid career at the start of World War II. She continued working for the Park Service in the Southwest until the late 1960s. These two women archeologists, both raised in the Southwest and trained at the University of Arizona, would be among the very few women in the Park Service to hold professional field positions in this interim period, from the time women pioneered Park Service field positions to the beginning of the modern movement for equal opportunity.

The Park Service's acceptance of a few women in the 1930s for positions interpreting archeological sites was supported by examples of prominent women ethnologists and archeologists doing research in the Southwest, several in Park Service sites. The first group of women were students of Franz Boas at Columbia University. They included Ruth Bunzel, whose classic study of Pueblo pottery had already been published; Gladys Reichard, who was then studying Navajo language and religion while she learned how to weave Navajo rugs; and Ruth Underhill, who was preparing a life history of Chona, a Papago woman.[66]

Universities in the Southwest had trained women archeologists since the 1920s, and women who studied at the University of Arizona under Byron Cummings and the University of New Mexico under Edgar Hewett undertook archeological research in national monuments. Hewett encouraged women to attend the field school at Chaco Canyon National Monument. Among them was Florence Hawley [Ellis], who pioneered new research methods at Chaco Canyon before becoming a professor at the University of New Mexico. An early student of A. E. Douglass, who developed tree-ring dating, Hawley collected and analyzed wood samples, making Chetro Ketl the best dated ruin at Chaco. She analyzed layers of a dump, using the statistical frequency of potsherds dated by associated bits of charcoal to create a chronological sequence of Chaco pottery. Her 1936 field manual of Southwestern pottery types was a classic for several decades.[67] Bertha Dutton, later curator of ethnology at the Museum of New Mexico, completed a study of Leyit Kin at Chaco. She excavated and dated four kivas and seventeen rooms.[68]

Through writing, teaching, and museum curatorship, these women were among the significant number of women anthropologists in the Southwest who helped create public interest and demonstrate women's competency in the field, not only during the second quarter of the twentieth century but also beyond. Park Service families in the Southwest read with interest Ann Axtell Morris's popular book, *Digging in the Southwest*. It chronicled her field experiences with her husband Earle at Pueblo Bonito in Chaco Canyon and Canyon de Chelly National Monuments.[69] Bertha Dutton fostered an interest in archeology among young women by organizing an archeological mobile camp for senior Girl Scouts. They excavated sites and visited national monuments. Dutton became a member of the Park Service Southwest Region's advisory board.[70] Kate Peck Kent shared her studies of prehistoric textiles in many publications. While working at the Denver Art Museum, Kent got a start in her specialty when she analyzed fragments of materials made from cotton discovered at Montezuma Castle and Tonto national monuments.[71]

Mesa Verde hired four women professionals in the field of anthropology during the 1930s. The typical photograph of the Mesa Verde seasonal staff in that period shows a sole woman, dressed like the men except that she wears a skirt, in the center of the front row, with a row of men behind her. Betty Yelm [Kingman], Jean Pinkley, who followed her at Mesa Verde, and Sallie Pierce at Montezuma Castle first passed civil service examinations and were selected from the list of eligibles after being interviewed. The two other women hired at Mesa Verde were from Washington, D.C., where they had Park Service connections, but they, too, were qualified, having majored in anthropology in college.

The first woman hired as a seasonal at Mesa Verde was Caroline Thompson [Simmons]. Her father was an early member of the National Parks Association and had traveled with Albright and Mather. Because she majored in anthropology at Bryn Mawr, her father thought she would enjoy a summer working at Mesa Verde. Hired as a museum assistant for the summer of 1932, she was the only woman on the seasonal staff, with a dozen men. Remembering it as the "happiest summer" of her life, Thompson explored the park on horseback with another seasonal on her days off and on some nights would join the Ute people at their summer encampment on the mesa. She demonstrated that women could fit in with an all-male interpretive staff. The problem of where a woman would have her living quarters was solved by having Thompson and the women who followed her stay in the park hospital, but they ate with the men.[72]

When Betty Yelm [Kingman], a senior in anthropology at the University of Denver in 1933, noticed that the announcement for the civil service examination for junior park archeologist did not say "for men only," she decided to take it. She knew the Park Service well, having spent her summers in her family's cabin in Estes Park, surrounded by Rocky Mountain National Park. She was selected as a museum assistant at Mesa Verde on a permanent basis, working for five months at a time, with furloughs in the winter. Because she knew more about archeology than most of the seasonal men, she was able to expand her duties to include leading car caravans and giving campfire talks. One of the reasons a woman may have been hired, she later said, was that male seasonals did not like to work in the museum. She published articles in both the Rocky Mountain and Mesa Verde *Nature Notes*. Yelm, who left to be married at the end of her fifth season, later worked with her husband, Eugene Kingman, director of the Jocelyn Museum in Omaha, to create exhibits displaying American Indian crafts as art objects.[73]

By the time Virginia Sutton [Harrington] received her seasonal appointment at Mesa Verde for the summers of 1935 and 1936, the chief naturalist, Don Watson, was used to having women lead car caravans and give campfire talks. Sutton, whose family knew Arthur Demaray, Park Service associate director, was appointed as a ranger. Unlike the two women before her, she adopted the men's uniform entirely, including pants. A history graduate of Swarthmore College, Sutton completed a master's in anthropology at the University of Chicago, between her two seasons at Mesa Verde. After she decided to change from prehistoric to historic sites, she became a seasonal historian-ranger at Colonial National Historical Park in Virginia. Utilizing her experience at Mesa Verde, she initiated a program to interpret the excavations at Jamestown. Sutton passed the junior archeologist examination with the second highest grade and was selected as a permanent archeologist at Colonial. She served for two years, until her marriage, but continued to work with her husband, Jean Harrington, who pioneered the field of historic archeology for the Park Service.[74]

Sallie Pierce [Harris] and Jean McWhirt [Pinkley], the two women archeologists who held lifelong professional careers in the Park Service, grew up in frontier situations in Arizona. Their early lives prepared them for Park Service careers in the Southwest. Pierce's father was a mining engineer. Before her family moved to Patagonia, near the Mexican border, where there was a school, she lived at Mansfield Mining Encampment in the Santa Rita Mountains of southeast Arizona. She had her own horse and learned to drive a car as early as she could. Pierce could not remember a time when she didn't know "how to find my way some place and find my way back." Jean McWhirt's father was a doctor for the Old Dominion Copper Company, and they lived near the San Carlos Apache Reservation before moving to Prescott, where she went to high school. Both women knew Nancy Pinkley, daughter of Frank Pinkley, who supervised the Southwestern monuments from Casa Grande National Monument. McWhirt completed a master's degree, studying with Florence Hawley Ellis. Pierce, who preceded McWhirt at the University of Arizona, spent two summers excavating at the Chaco Canyon Field School.[75]

After Pierce passed the Civil Service exam in archeology, she believed she was qualified for a new traveling position in the Southwestern monuments. Dean Byron Cummings had recommended her for her first job, the Civil Works Administration position at Montezuma Castle. Her father and Horace Albright worked for the same mining company after Albright left the Park Service and she enlisted his support. Although he called her "a very capable girl," he recommended that she be hired at a single location because he did not approve of her traveling between the monuments and raised his old objection, "the lack of suitable quarters." By the time Sallie Pierce's name was reached on the eligible list for the Mesa Verde museum position, which continued as a slot for a well-qualified woman, she had married Jim Brewer, who was himself a traveling custodian for several Southwestern monuments. During the next eight years she gained the experiences she sought: she lived and worked in eight different areas—but not for pay. She held the essential position of Honorary Custodian Without Pay, the name Frank Pinkley gave to the wives living in monuments staffed by one full or part-time male custodian.[76]

Meanwhile, Jean McWhirt also passed the junior park archeologist exam. She followed Betty Yelm as the permanent museum assistant at Mesa Verde in 1939, working for five months and furloughed each winter. Near the beginning of World War II, she married Pinkley's son Addison, a navy commander, and left her position. After he was lost at sea the following year, she returned to her Mesa Verde position under a war service appointment. When Sallie Pierce Brewer's husband entered the navy, she took a war service appointment as a park ranger at Casa Grande. Although these positions were designed to last only through the duration of the war, both women found ways to continue in the Park Service.[77]

Woman's Place in the Park Service

Throughout this period, the nature of the position of park naturalist was being established and refined. At the Second Naturalists' Conference, in 1940, park naturalists spelled out professional standards and practices. The number of naturalists attending increased to about fifty from the ten present in 1929, still all men. In forty lectures, they presented themselves as masculine rangers with added qualifications in natural history. They hoped this image would overcome the persisting perception of naturalists as effeminate. In one lecture, a naturalist from Yellowstone asked that seasonal rangers and ranger-naturalists be trained together "to cut down that ridicule of the naturalists being 'pansy pickers and butterfly chasers.'" In another, a Rocky Mountain naturalist described the importance of the park's junior nature program as a way to train children to associate nature study with masculinity. "In the parks," he explained, "the child can associate with a man, who to him is a ranger, the embodiment of Kit Carson, Buffalo Bill, Daniel Boone, the Texas Rangers, and General Pershing; and learn from this man that even flowers, trees, birds . . . are not objects of contempt, but are matters for manly interest."[78]

Park Service naturalists had come to define their profession as men's work, implicitly denying the participation of women. That the exclusion of women was not based on rational standards of qualifications and commitment to service is best illustrated by a comment of the Park Service's supervisory naturalist, Carl Russell, in 1945. In recommending that Jean Pinkley continue her position in the Mesa Verde museum instead of being granted the title of naturalist, Russell explained: "There is no good reason why women should not hold park naturalist jobs," but, he added, "we have simply said, rather arbitrarily, that we do not favor the placement of women in these positions. As a general rule I think we are right in this."[79]

The first professional women in National Park Service field positions did not bring lasting change to the status of women in the Park Service. They did demonstrate that women could do the job, however, and when the movement for equal opportunity took hold in the service in the 1960s, many Park Service people could picture women in uniform because they recalled the early women pioneers. In 1939, Martelle Trager, wife of a Park Service naturalist, summed up the situation in her book, *National Parks of the Pacific Northwest.* "The ranger naturalists are usually men," she wrote, "but a few girls have been able to crash the gates."[80]

The Park Service needed the skills and energy of women naturalists and rangers, but after the mid-1930s, with rare exceptions, the male-oriented culture of the service would accept these talents from a woman only if she assumed her traditional role as a wife and performed essential duties as a surrogate for her husband. Women who wanted to join in the adventure of living and working in national parks, helping to protect them and educating the public about their goals, were left with one choice. Ruth Ashton Nelson, who had tried unsuccessfully for so many years to become a ranger-naturalist at Rocky Mountain National Park, eventually concluded: "The best way to get into the Park Service is to marry a ranger."[81] Despite nearly two decades of women's accomplishments outside conventional expectations, the concept of "woman's place" remained intact in the National Park Service.

F O U R

Park Service Wives

*A*lthough Margaret Becker Merrill's *Bears in My Kitchen,* published in 1952, was ostensibly a story about her husband Bill's experiences as a park ranger, her fan mail came mostly from young women. "How did you happen to meet Ranger Merrill?" several wrote. Some went even further and asked: "How can I marry a ranger?" The writers of the fan letters, like Bill Merrill himself, had no problem understanding that Margaret also performed ranger duties and was, as Bill Merrill put it, "a real ranger," too. He knew that without his wife's support, he would not have been able to perform his duties. And young women were ready. They knew that if they wanted to live a park ranger's life, they should marry one.

For young women like Margaret Becker, working for the concessioners in national parks in the 1920s offered freedom and adventure—a return to the pioneer period of the Old West with a special dose of fun. Becker was the daughter of a traveling civil engineer; her mother could make a home anywhere. The family settled down in Bozeman, Montana, during the high school and college years of the four daughters. Yellowstone and Jackson Hole at the foot of the Grand Tetons became the family's playground.

As the Becker sisters hiked, camped, and rode horseback, they became fascinated with national parks and the life of a ranger. They made $15 a month with room and board as "savages" for Wylie Permanent Camps, working as waitresses, chambermaids, and dishwashers. Traditionally the savages lined up to greet buses filled with visitors by singing "Welcome to Yellowstone" and put on skits and led singing in the evening. Margaret sang to Meda's ukelele or played the piano. The Becker sisters dated park rangers and three of them married rangers. As a team, Margaret and Bill Merrill pioneered for thirty-two years in remote ranger stations in Yosemite, Sequoia, and the Olympics.[1]

Bears in My Kitchen was written in the tradition of the *I Married Adventure* accounts, popular with women readers from the 1930s to the 1950s. In this genre, women who shared adventurous lives with their husbands recounted their experiences for women who sought a vicarious life of adventure. Presenting themselves as women who met the challenges of outdoor life while still fulfilling traditional roles of wives, these authors described their lives as companion-wives of world and arctic explorers, aviators, archeologists, and naturalists. The tradition of this genre stretched back into the nineteenth century, when officers' wives chronicled their lives in military posts all over the West. The accounts presented role models for young women, who believed that the freedom and adventure they craved could best be satisfied by marrying men with adventurous careers.[2]

In the early years, the Park Service did not recognize the essential role of wives of field personnel. Administrators reflected the inherited military tradition and hired single men as park rangers. After the ban was lifted on hiring married men at Yellowstone, rangers were expected to live apart from their families during winters when they were stationed in snowed-in stations. Because the staff at the central headquarters at Mammoth Hot Springs was small, the superintendent and chief clerk might be the only men allowed to bring their families to the park; their wives were comparable to military officers' wives and the status of rangers and maintenance men was more like that of enlisted men, whose wives were not provided quarters at army forts or camps. Stories of park rangers smuggling in their wives to live with them in remote ranger stations at Yellowstone are part of the lore of the Park Service.[3]

In the pioneering years of the Park Service, wives like Margaret Merrill took on many important roles informally. After the founding of the service in 1916, there was an increased emphasis on enhancing the visitors' appreciation of the parks and providing for their safety. By making homes in remote areas, wives brought stability to parks. They filled the role of helpmate, offering information, first aid, meals, and comfort to visitors and staff and served as centers of communication. By bringing families to live in parks, wives also began the process of mitigating the Park Service's military culture.

Park Service Companion-Wives of the 1920s

In the early 1920s, three self-sufficient women were among those who saw marrying into the Park Service as a way to encounter adventure and explore a fascination with the lives and art of Native American people. Representing the companion-wife who expected to be a full partner in her husband's work, each published books related to her experiences in national parks.

Dama Margaret Smith was the first Park Service wife to publish an account of her adventures. Her 1930 book, *I Married a Ranger*, describes life at the Grand Canyon when it was a new national park. In 1921, Smith (then Dama Margaret Griffee) transferred from a clerical position in Washington, D.C., to the post of field clerk at the park. The first woman federal employee at the new park, Griffee lived in a cabin amid the tents of the rangers and road crew and took her meals with them. She soon met and married the chief ranger, "White Mountain" Charles J. Smith, a former government scout at Yellowstone and one of the first Park Service rangers.

The mix of Park Service staff and employees of the Fred Harvey Company produced an active social life at the Grand Canyon and included the Harvey waitresses, who were often young women from the East or Midwest looking for new lives. Dama Smith helped entertain special visitors, ranging from Tom Mix and Eva Novak (who were making a movie) to Marshal Foch of France. The Smiths also hosted a Christmas dinner for the rangers, offering exotic specialties chosen ahead of time by the guests, like fresh oysters. Their house survived a fire, flood, and an explosion, stories she relished to tell.

Smith developed a market for her Grand Canyon stories in popular magazines, providing publicity for the park, that encouraged other women to participate in similar adventures. When her husband became superintendent at Petrified Forest National Monument, she published word portraits of individual Hopi and Navajo people for the new *Desert* Magazine, later developing them into her *Indian Tribes of the Southwest* and *Hopi Girl*. When her husband's move to the superintendency of the Grand Tetons took her away from Arizona, she apparently felt isolated. She returned to Washington, D.C., leaving him and their adopted American Indian daughter behind, remarried, and continued her writing career.[4]

The initial preparation for Elizabeth Compton Hegemann's career as the joint owner of a Navajo trading post came during her years in the mid-1920s as a Park Service wife. A native of Cincinnati, Elizabeth Compton made annual trips to the Grand Canyon with her family, where she met and married Mike Harrison, a ranger on the South Rim. They became friends with the Supai, Navajo, Hopi, and Paiute peoples, attending their ceremonies and collecting examples of their art. She apprenticed in the Harvey Company's Hopi House, an American Indian arts and craft shop. After three years, she left her husband and the Park Service, married again, and operated the Shonto Canyon Trading Post in northern Arizona.[5]

A third park wife who strongly identified with Native American people and filled the role of companion-wife in the 1920s was Aileen O'Bryan Nusbaum, wife of archeologist Jesse Nusbaum, during his first superintendency of Mesa Verde National Park, from 1921 to 1931. Intrigued by the ancient culture of the Pueblo and Navajo people, she poured her enormous energies into designing park buildings and programs. A native of the Southwest, O'Bryan returned as a single parent to a New Mexico ranch with her son after World War I, after spending twelve years in Paris. There she studied art and drama at the Sorbonne and served as a nurse in an American hospital during the war.[6]

After marrying Nusbaum, Aileen worked closely with him to design Pueblo-style buildings for the park. Because of the park's remote location, medical emergencies needed to be handled on the spot. She helped install a ward in an army field tent, staffed by a medical student in the summer season; she assisted with nursing and pressed for a hospital building. A congressional party visiting the park was so impressed with her plans for the building and her work that they added $7,500 to the Interior Department's budget to build and equip what was called the Aileen Nusbaum Hospital.[7]

Aileen Nusbaum also collected myths from Navajo chief Sandoval (Hastin Tlo tsi hee), using his nephew Sam Ahkeah, head of the Window Rock Navajo Council, as his interpreter. She eventually published the collection for the Smithsonian. She used the Navajo Fire Ceremony as the basis for a play she directed with Spruce Tree House as a stage. Navajos who worked in the park were the performers. Produced after dark, the play presented Native American ceremonies and dances with dramatic lighting and an off-stage narration. Photographer Laura Gilpin said that the audience who viewed the play from above the ruin was given "the sensation of looking down on forgotten ages from some far off star."[8]

Soon after Jesse Nusbaum became director of the New Mexico Museum of Anthropology in Santa Fe, the Nusbaums separated. Aileen resumed her maiden name and worked on the New Mexico guide for the Federal Writers' Project. For O'Bryan, Hegemann, and Smith, the helpmate role the Park Service offered to wives in national parks in the 1920s proved to be too confining. Lack of choice over where they lived and what they could do eventually came in conflict with their strong needs for personal autonomy.[9]

Yellowstone Wives Gain Acceptance

Not all women who married into the Park Service in the 1920s and 1930s were young women from the East looking for personal fulfillment. Many of the first women to marry rangers or maintenance men at Yellowstone were women who grew up on farms or ranches in the Rocky Mountain states. They met their husbands in college or at Yellowstone, where they held summer jobs with the concessioners. They were prepared for lives as park wives by their backgrounds and they were ready to take on the role of helpmate to their husbands and raise families in the park well before the park was ready for them to assume those roles.

The tradition of expecting field personnel to be single men continued into the Park Service's early years at Yellowstone. In part, this was because the condition of ranger stations, as one wife recalled, was "not adequate for anyone but those of pioneer spirit." Potbellied stoves for heat, old large army woodstoves for cooking, water obtained from streams or lakes, and melted from ice in the winter, no inside refrigeration, and Coleman lamps for light were the rule. The ranger station at Old Faithful Geyser had electricity only in the summer, when the generator at the lodge was operating. Ranger stations varied from small log cabins with outside privies to old army buildings. Even so, by the early 1930s the new young rangers began to demand that their wives and soon their children be allowed to join them in the park.[10]

Irene and Leon Evans met in college and, during winters, both taught school in Idaho, where Irene had been raised on a small ranch. With their small children, they spent four summers in the early 1930s at the Cooke City Entrance Station in the northeast corner of the park, where Leon worked as a seasonal. Because single men were still preferred as rangers, new men, even if married, were often treated as if they were single when hired permanently. Winter assignments meant being snowed in for the season. When Leon received a permanent appointment at the beginning of the winter of 1933–34, he was assigned to Yellowstone Lake ranger station in the park's interior. His family was sent home to Idaho. After that winter, however, the Evanses joined a few other families who were beginning to pioneer family ranger stations. The family spent the next winter at West Yellowstone, where the children went to a one-room schoolhouse, but for the next few winters they lived in snowed-in ranger stations where Irene taught the children until the oldest reached sixth grade.[11]

Meanwhile, Icel and Bill Wright, who lived at park headquarters at Mammoth Hot Springs, near Gardiner, Montana, where Bill was the park's supply officer, needed a school for their boys. Even at Mammoth, the park did not hire people with children, but the Wrights' first son was born four years after they arrived. Because the Wrights did not pay taxes to the state of Montana, the town of Gardiner would not accept their children in school. The Wrights had to take things into their own hands. They hired Mae White, a summer employee for the concession, as a teacher, paying her $50 a month, plus quarters for the winter. When Irene and Bill Evans transferred to Mammoth, they worked with Montana Congressman Wesley D'Ewart to introduce a bill to Congress allotting funds from gate receipts to maintain the school. The school they started is still open for park children.[12]

Yellowstone wives not only became useful to the park, they also began to change its military culture. Lois Kowski, who lived in ranger stations throughout the park with her husband, Frank, in the early 1940s, had been a teacher who worked summers as a "savage" at Yellowstone Lake Hotel. She believes that the Park Service would not have survived without families, because they "humanized" the service by creating homes. Without consciously meaning to, she herself demilitarized radio communications with headquarters: Lois closed with "Goodbye," instead of "Roger, over and out."[13]

With the coming of World War II, the Yellowstone administration forgot they were ever reluctant to include wives in daily operations. Wives were pressed into service to run entrance stations and to serve on fire lookouts. In the summer of 1942, a period of high fire danger, Lois Kowski and Louise Chapman, whose husband, Scotty, was a ranger, took turns alternating between the lookout above Tower Junction and West Yellowstone entrance station. Later, Louise Chapman registered visitors and sealed guns on the northeast gate. Icel Wright and Ethel Skinner, whose husband Curt was a ranger at Mammoth, alternated handling Bunsen Peak Lookout, walking six miles each day. Icel remembers being so frightened by a severe lightning storm, with rain blowing in the tower, that she rolled herself up in a tarp on the floor. Later the same day, she located strikes and reported them to the chief ranger. The next day she reported three major fires that subsequently were put out by smoke jumpers. In order to warn bears of her approach, she blew a whistle when walking up the trail.[14]

Irene Evans, whose family was stationed at Canyon Ranger Station that summer, rode horseback eight miles each way to Observation Peak every day. One morning when she reached the steep ascent just below the top of the mountain, a huge black grizzly bear with silvery guard hairs in his coat lurched up onto a fallen log beside the trail. She and her horse were both badly startled. She recalled: "My horse . . . shied off the trail, went over the edge, and straight down the steep incline falling to his knees on his front legs; rearing up immediately and took off down the hillside at a gallop." Irene managed to stay in the saddle and finally brought the horse under control; she made it to the lookout, where she unlocked the door and, she said, "woman-like threw myself onto the cot and burst into tears." A few days later, her horse was startled by a bull moose. This time she told her husband she would not go back up the mountain, but by morning she was ready to return and made it through the rest of the season with no further incidents. At the end of the season, she watched five major fires burn until snowfall.[15]

Throughout World War II, wives filled in where needed, demonstrating that they were indeed legitimate members of the park community. In an interview about his past, Lon Garrison, a postwar Yellowstone superintendent, commented that during the war when women "were put out in the job market" they saw that they "were not as limited as they had seemed." To which his wife, Inger, who was also being interviewed, replied: "Well, *men* saw that they [women] were not as limited. It had to be that way," because men "were still in charge."[16]

Honorary Custodians Without Pay in the Southwestern Monuments

Among the Park Service locations where wives lived in the most rustic conditions were those in the Southwestern monuments. There, Frank (Boss) Pinkley, superintendent from 1923 until his death in 1940, never doubted that the active partnership of wives and their custodian husbands was essential to the survival of the monuments in his charge. Growing from fourteen to twenty-seven in number, the monuments were staffed by lone custodians; in the early years, this meant men with only nominal pay who earned their livelihoods in another way. During the 1930s, public service projects designed to combat the Depression increased the activity and staffing in the monuments. The custodians communicated with each other through monthly reports assembled and printed with comments by Pinkley, who tended the monuments like a father out of his base at Casa Grande National Monument in central Arizona. By then, Pinkley was a widower. Married in 1906 when Casa Grande was a lone frontier post, he revered the memory of his partnership with his wife, Edna. He continued to recognize the importance of the wives' roles by calling them Honorary Custodians Without Pay, or HCWP for short.[17]

When Pinkley learned that Sallie Pierce, who had recently worked as an archeologist at Montezuma Castle, had married Jim Brewer in July 1934 he was delighted. After he "bargained" for Jim to staff Wupatki National Monument, he found he had won Sallie, too: "We think we're doing well when we can angle for one archeologist and get two!"[18]

Sallie Brewer treated her position as an HCWP as seriously as if she were still paid. During her nearly eight years as an HCWP, Sallie and Jim Brewer pioneered in eight Southwestern monuments, including a summer when Jim was a "roving ranger." Until their last two years, none of the places included housing: they lived in tents, a log cabin, a hogan, or used the ranger pickup truck with a chuck box at the tailgate, sleeping on the ground. Their longest assignments were at Wupatki and Navajo national monuments, the latter the location of the remote Betatakin, Keet Seel, and Inscription House ruins. But none of their homes was more unusual than the twelfth-century Wupatki pueblo where they lived in Room 36 of the one hundred-room ruin—perhaps the first residents in five hundred years. Jim Brewer had been on the team from the Museum of Northern Arizona that reconstructed the room. For the twenty-five dollars that Pinkley allotted to them to furnish a residence, they built shelves and a bedstead, bought a Coleman stove for cooking, borrowed a Franklin stove for heat, and used gasoline lamps for light. For running water, they buried a 55-gallon drum in the fill of an unexcavated room behind the kitchen wall, a faucet projecting into the room. Once a week, they filled another drum from a pipeline running from Wupatki Spring to a stock tank below the pueblo and carried it in their pickup truck to a high point. There they connected a hose to the drum in the pueblo and let gravity do the rest. They wrapped their few perishables in a damp cloth and placed them in a ventilation hole where moving air kept butter from melting. To reach Room 36, they climbed a twelve-foot ladder and entered through a prehistoric, T-shaped doorway.

Wupatki was fourteen miles from the nearest telephone and forty miles north of Flagstaff, with more than half of the distance by unimproved road. Until the Brewers made signs, the best way to find the monument was to follow the most heavily used car tracks. Because the first road ran through deep volcanic cinders that acted like sand traps for most vehicles, Jim spent a good deal of time on road work and rescuing visitors, leaving Sallie to type reports and greet the visitors who did get through. Visitors included archeologist Byron Cummings, Sallie's former dean at the University of Arizona; A. E. Douglass, who developed tree-ring dating; photographer Laura Gilpin; and a New York radio personality, Alexander Woollcott, who made the trip after they invited him to Wupatki to find the peace and quiet he announced on a radio program he desired.[19]

The Brewers made many positive connections with the Navajos living in the Wupatki Basin, especially with their nearest neighbors, the Peshlakai family. On two Christmases they held two-day parties for more than thirty members of local Navajo families, complete with a tree and an exchange of presents that included a box of contributed clothes and a crate of oranges and candy. The day before, on the woodstove in the cook shack remaining from the museum excavation crew, Sallie counted seven pots cooking at once, filled with rice, beans, mutton, and coffee.[20]

Sallie Brewer was particularly interested in helping the Navajo families upgrade their crafts to make them more marketable. Working with their Navajo neighbors and the Museum of Northern Arizona, in June 1936 the Brewers sponsored an exhibit of the best local Navajo crafts. The Navajo men constructed a hogan and four ramadas for 110 exhibits and demonstrations. Weavers worked in one ramada on four looms along with carders and spinners, and a silversmith worked in another. Heirloom rugs from the museum and new vegetal-dyed rugs were displayed as models. About four hundred visitors, evenly divided between whites and Navajos, came to the exhibit. Mary-Russell Colton, cofounder with her husband, Harold, of the museum and curator of art, and the highly respected Navajo elder, Peshlakai Etsedi, Clyde Peshlakai's father, judged rugs for prizes. Twenty-one of the thirty-one Navajos exhibiting either won prize money or sold their crafts. Katharine Bartlett, the museum's curator for anthropology, led a discussion on the characteristics of the prize-winning rugs. Sallie Brewer held a "pow-wow" in the hogan with Peshlakai Etsedi and Clyde to promote improved weaving, spinning, and the use of vegetal dyes.[21]

After the exhibit, the Brewers took Clyde Peshlakai and his first wife, Sally, to visit Bob Budlong, custodian at Canyon de Chelly, and his wife, Betty, so they could see vegetal-dyed rugs at Chinle. There Betty was working with the Home Economics Department at the American Indian school to encourage Navajo girls to weave traditional rugs using natural dyes. Betty was also developing an exhibit for the monument on the processes involved in rug weaving, including specimens of plants used for vegetable dyeing. At their last Christmas party, Sallie gave Clyde and Sarah mounted pictures of early blanket and silver designs supplied by the museum so that the Peshlakais could lend them to weavers and silversmiths.[22]

While at Wukpatki, Sallie Brewer "lived by" the writings of anthropologist Gladys Reichard. With the aid of Navajo interpreters, she interviewed Peshlakai Etsedi for his boyhood memories of the Long Walk, the forced exile of the Navajos to Bosque Redondo near Fort Sumner between 1864 and 1868. They shared immediate sorrows with the Peshlakai family as well. Family members asked Jim Brewer to help bury their dead and the Brewers tried to help Navajo families whose custom was to vacate the hogan where the death had occurred even if they had no other place to live.[23]

Sallie Brewer's last post as an HCWP, Navajo National Monument, allowed her to help protect Rainbow Bridge and the beautiful Anasazi ruins, sheltered by arched overhanging cliffs in side canyons of the Tsegi Canyon in the high country of northeastern Arizona. At Navajo, the Brewers supervised the building of a Park Service house, the first traditional house they had lived in in their six years of marriage.[24] John Wetherill, one of the brothers who first explored Mesa Verde, then in his seventies, was the nominal custodian, assisted by his wife, Louisa. Fluent in the Navajo language, the Wetherills operated a trading post in nearby Kayenta, and the Navajos called John, Hosteen John, and Louisa, Asthon Sosi, or "slim woman."[25] The Brewers were appointed because the Wetherills were ready to give up the responsibility, but it was they who showed the Brewers the way.

In May 1938, a second Park Service couple found themselves stationed in the Wupatki pueblo for their honeymoon. When Davy Jones, a recent University of Arizona graduate in archeology, got his Park Service appointment, he and Courtney Reeder decided they could get married. They had met three years before on a University of Arizona dig at the Kinishba Ruin on the Apache Reservation, where Davy was a graduate assistant to Dean Cummings. Clyde Peshlakai was there for lunch on their first day at Wupatki. He felt, Courtney said, that "Wupatki was his property and that the Custodians . . . were sent there to do the paperwork and intervene with the Government . . . while he supervised everything else."[26]

Courtney developed a deep friendship with Clyde's older wife, Sally, who was an expert weaver, and who spoke only Navajo. An accomplished seamstress and dress designer, Courtney decided she wanted to learn how to make a rug all the way from carding, spinning, and dyeing through to weaving a finished product. As often as she could, she would go to the Peshlakai hogan, where Sally helped her build a loom next to hers under a juniper tree, with a view down a small canyon. When her rug was about four inches high, Courtney wrote her family, "They are very patient with me, and I am beginning to understand what is going on—they weave so fast that one has no idea how many little processes they must go through to weave one thread." Courtney developed a "most profound respect for a vegetable dyed rug." After spinning the wool for her rug, she dyed some of it with rabbit brush. It came out a "hideous sage green" at first, but by morning it had turned to a "cheery sunny yellow," making her conclude: "Rugmaking has its uplifting moments." By Christmas, she proudly showed her completed rug to Boss Pinkley. Sally Pesklakai returned Courtney's visits and, although each spoke a different language as they sat on top of the huge boulder outside Wupatki's prehistoric door doing handwork, they had no trouble communicating.[27]

Like Sallie Brewer, Courtney Jones shared her husband's duties with him at Wupatki. She guided visitors and remembered few lunchtimes without a guest, although they had to rely on canned food until they acquired a refrigerator run on bottled gas. The Joneses banded birds and they participated in the Museum of Northern Arizona's weekly seminars. Courtney kept the monument's wildlife observation files. The Joneses made Wupatki famous for its scorpions. They collected, fed, and mailed live scorpions to a scientist who was developing an antivenom serum. After he identified two of the species as new, he named one for the monument (vejovis wupatkiensis) and one for the Joneses (vejovis jonesii). When Courtney discovered that a female had given birth to twenty-four young in one of their bureau drawers, they spent an hour carefully picking them up with tweezers.[28]

Both the Brewers and the Joneses felt a strong sense of the spirit of the place at Wupatki. It was not difficult to feel a historic presence. Courtney knew that many Navajos believed the ruins were inhabited by chindis, or ghosts, and Navajo visitors sometimes asked them if they had seen any chindis. She also knew that some prehistoric people played flutes and had even found a petroglyph of a flute player. "One day when I was here alone," she said, "I heard a delicate, faint, piping sound, . . . and I enjoyed listening to it. When I had heard it enough to recognize the tune, I whistled it for Davy. It has a fine primitive rhythm, and is not unlike what Indian songs I have heard." Although Davy thought he heard it once too, he decided it was a wind song. But Courtney wasn't sure that she had not heard the songs "of the long departed builders of Wupatki . . . gathered in one of the rooms to reminisce about the good old days."[29]

By 1938, Betty and Bob Budlong had moved from Canyon de Chelly to El Morro National Monument, where they were fourteen miles from the nearest phone and could be reached only by an adobe road, slick when wet and impassable for days during heavy snows. The monument, also called Inscription Rock for the seventeenth-century Spanish carvings on its prominent sandstone mesa-point, is located sixty miles south of Gallup, New Mexico.

While Bob Budlong struggled to meet the communication problem by trying to build a radio-telephone system, Betty decided to remedy the need for human contact by starting a library. Many local residents were farmers who had been driven away from Texas and Oklahoma by the dustbowls during the Depression; they lived in widely scattered log cabins, growing pinto beans and corn, and were particularly isolated in the winter. The need for a library became clear at the first meeting of a club organized by local women: one mother said she was so desperate for material to read to her children that she was using detective stories. Betty asked for donations through Pinkley's monthly reports. Books arrived not only from all over the Southwest, including a library extension service, but also from the Park Service's Washington office, where Isabelle Story, chief of information, collected and sent 390 pounds of books at Christmas.

At first people checked the books in and out at the El Morro store on mail day, but soon people were arriving at the Budlong's two-room cabin, traveling by horseback, and in wagons, sleds, and Model T Fords. As the collection grew, storage became a problem. Betty said, "We slept over books, we ate over books, we sat over books, we stepped and stumbled over books." A strong circulation helped solve the space problem. By 1940, the collection had grown to 1,000 books, 341 of which were in circulation: 75 on loan to an isolated community sixty miles away, 100 at three small schools, and the rest in general circulation. A year later, the collection doubled in size and ten schools and six other communities, including a logging camp, were using the books.[30]

Not all the custodians in Pinkley's outfit, as he called the staff of the southwestern monuments, wives included, were young professionals starting careers in the Park Service. Like the Wetherills, some of the custodians came with the territory. They were a diverse group of highly independent individuals, and Pinkley was happy to make whatever arrangements he could to secure their services in restoring and protecting the monuments.

Prime examples of local people who volunteered were Leonard and Edna Heaton. Soon after the Heatons were married in 1926, they offered to look after the fort at Pipe Spring for a dollar a month if Leonard could put a service station there. The sandstone fort, completed in 1872 and sited near a reliable spring in the dry northern Arizona strip close to the Utah border, was built to protect a cattle ranch developed by the Mormon Church. At first Edna and Leonard lived in the fort, where pioneering conditions still prevailed. Because there was no hospital nearby, the first two of their ten children were born in the fort. The Heatons worked to restore the fort for forty years: Edna, assisted by the children, guided visitors, supervised the campground, grew much of their food, fixed broken machinery, and served as a communications center.

But even before the Heatons were established at Pipe Spring, the Park Service was already well known in the area. In 1923, while a party of people with Stephen Mather was traveling between Zion National Park and the Grand Canyon, Mather's touring car got mired in deep sand in the general area of the fort. After several hours of building up the tracks with brush and branches in the hot August sun, Mather's party made their way to Pipe Spring, where they met Leonard Heaton's father, Charles, who was on horseback, looking after his cattle. Heaton offered them lunch at his home in nearby Moccasin. He rode on ahead, and by the time the party arrived, the Heatons and two of their daughters had prepared a spread of their own freshly grown and baked food: eggplant, melons, tomatoes, and homemade bread and butter. Mather decided on the spot to make the Pipe Spring fort a national monument portraying pioneer life, and to repay the young Mormon women of the area, by treating eighteen of them to a trip to Yellowstone.

Mather chose women because he was aware that, while their brothers' horizons had been expanded during service in World War I, the local young women had never been more than a half a day's ride from their homes. To get to Yellowstone, the women rode in trucks that looked like motorized covered wagons, taking three days for the journey—sleeping on the ground in their own blankets and doing their own cooking. But once they reached the park, "everything was free," Jenny Heaton Brown, one of the sisters who had fed Mather's party, remembered, "food, our sleeping quarters, the buses that took us around to the different points in Yellowstone." They spent three days touring. The young women never forgot the expedition. Annie McAllister Heaton, who saw her first train on the trip, later became a teacher in Kanab and believed that the girls "really learned a lot on that trip. And it helped us for years later in school."[31]

Another of the self-supporting custodian couples was Martin Jackson and his wife Ada. They became interested in Montezuma Castle after they homesteaded in the Verde Valley in central Arizona. Jackson worked with Pinkley to stabilize the ruin and became custodian in 1921 for the nominal fee of $10 a month. They cleaned out and cribbed a well and installed a hand pump with the help of their teenaged son, Earl. Using the $500 allotted to them by Pinkley for a "shelter cabin," they combined boulders from the creek bottom, mortar, and lumber to build a two-room cabin to live in and display the monument's artifacts. The Jacksons eventually built a combination store and museum, where Ada sold rugs and baskets she purchased on buying trips through different American Indian reservations.[32]

About a year after he selected Earl Jackson to be custodian for Bandelier National Monument, in Frijoles Canyon, fifty miles west of Santa Fe, Pinkley acquired another talented HCWP. "No man is much good until he is married and thus obtains a balance wheel," he wrote Jackson, "and then a lot depends on the girl, but in your case . . . you picked a winner." Betty Morris, a recent Vassar College graduate with experience at a University of New Mexico archeological field school at Jemez Springs, was teaching science and Spanish in Santa Fe when she met Jackson. Not long after they were married, Betty received her permit from the U.S. Biological Survey to band birds and add to the region's contribution to a federal study of bird migration routes. Florence Merriam Bailey's *Birds of New Mexico* was her guide. Pinkley published Betty Jackson's bird lists in his monthly reports. During the five years after 1937 when they succeeded Earl's parents at Montezuma Castle, Betty sighted more than one hundred species in the square mile around their residence, banding many birds. She published a Christmas census in *Bird Lore* and shared her findings at a Museum of Northern Arizona seminar.

Teaching the two sons who were born while they served at Montezuma Castle to be young naturalists was as important for their survival as it was for their general knowledge. Although the children needed to know which snakes and spiders could hurt them, the Jacksons didn't want them to develop a fear of the monument's creatures. Once, when Martin was little more than a toddler, he summoned his mother to see a "hommless snake out there on the porch" because he wanted her to admire it. Sure enough, it was a harmless, medium-sized king snake, resplendent in red and black bands, alternating with white. When Earl became seriously ill with tuberculosis, Betty's role became that of an equal partner. In addition to nursing him, she took over some of his duties. During two of their years at Tumacacori Mission, in Arizona near the Mexican border, Betty guided visitors every afternoon. She made a skirt of official material by cutting out the parts from the pants of one of Earl's uniforms. After he recovered, Betty chaired a Red Cross home nursing program, grateful for what the program had taught her.[33]

The necessity of having the support of a wife in the Southwestern monuments was poignantly illustrated at Chaco Canyon. In July 1937, Lena McKinney, the wife of custodian Lewis McKinney, died suddenly after complications resulting from an operation, leaving three children ranging in age from four to ten. In the December monthly report, McKinney described his attempts to meet his children's Christmas expectations, wishing everyone "a better New Year." In the April monthly report, his marriage to Carolie was announced, and by May, her first bird list appeared, along with her thanks to the staff of the monuments for welcoming her as an HCWP.[34]

As travel to the Southwestern monuments increased, permanent staff replaced the volunteer custodians and the need for adequate park housing began to be demonstrated. Living in a tent month after month was difficult for young families. Marge and John Peavy lived in a tent for about two years during his time as custodian at Tonto National Monument near Roosevelt Lake, about thirty miles from Globe, Arizona. Marge did not see much romance in tent life. "A tent isn't the most pleasant place in the world to live," she said. "If it was, I'm sure that more people would live in them." In the summer, their tent was too hot for them to stay inside; in the rain, everything in the tent got wet. Although they did have a refrigerator and washing machine, the family had to keep their canned goods in a shed and use the public toilet. Marge was philosophical about her situation. Although she "would love to have a house," she was "sure that someday" they would "look back on this experience of living in a tent among the scorpions, centipedes, rattlesnakes, . . . and laugh and remember it as one of the most interesting parts of our lives." Their first relief ranger and his wife, Charles and Frances Sharp, arrived pulling a trailer for living quarters, about the time the Peavys left for Saquaro National Monument, where they finally lived in a house.[35]

After three years in the ancient Wupatki pueblo, the Joneses also moved into a new house at Wupatki, but it still doubled as a visitor center. In 1939, Courtney carried out an extensive survey for Pinkley on the housing needs of the monuments. It was a precursor of the national survey conducted by Park Service wives in the 1950s. As Courtney listed the suggestions from the twenty-eight wives in the Southwestern monuments, two differences between life in the monuments and life in the outside world emerged. Each she knew from personal experience. First was "the isolation of most areas." She noted that, although for some monuments it was possible to shop once a week, there were several posts where supplies must last two weeks or even a month in the winter. The second, seeming to be almost the antithesis of the first, was the need for privacy. When they lived in the ruin, the monument's office and their living space were the same. She had to be up and about, with the floors swept and the dishes done, early every morning before visitors arrived. Visitors often appeared without knocking, and she remembered a time when a child poked his head into their space during a meal and exclaimed, "Somebody lives here!"[36]

End of an Era in the Southwestern Monuments

Two events had a major impact on Park Service life in the Southwestern monuments in the early 1940s. The first was the sudden death of Frank Pinkley; the second was World War II. It was only logical that Park Service wives, so used to their roles as full partners with their husbands, would take on the responsibility of trying to hold things together.

After years of planning, Pinkley had finally achieved his goal of holding a three-day field school for the custodians and wives in February 1940. After welcoming his staff, including eighteen wives, whose attendance, he said, was "well earned by the excellent service . . . donated to us in your field work," Pinkley sat down, filled with emotion brought on by a moment he had long envisioned. He slumped in his chair and died of a massive heart attack, even as his followers paid tribute with their warm applause.[37]

Although the meetings continued as planned, there was a new urgency to continue the spirit Pinkley had infused throughout the Southwestern monuments, partly via the medium of his monthly reports. Meeting as a group for the first time, the wives decided to share their problems and observations through a newsletter, first called *The Roundtable*. Following the demise of the monthly reports, it took on the function of publishing staff news and was renamed *The Grapevine*. The editors praised the projects of the monument's wives and encouraged them to publicize their monuments by following the example of Polly Tovrea, wife of a park engineer who published articles about the monuments in local newspapers. Solutions to such problems as storage in small spaces and handling disgruntled visitors were exchanged, and new babies were welcomed.[38]

As the war began to affect the wives' lives, first with shortages and then with the enlistment of many of their husbands into military service, *The Grapevine* noted that "a ripple of unrest is passing among us" because "the future is uncertain." In the fall of 1942, the editors conducted a "woman-power" survey. Stating that "the Boss considered the HCWP a partner in her husband's job," they asked: "Are we good enough partners to be any help to the Park Service now?" A list followed, asking the wives to spell out their training and experiences in guiding, protection, naturalist activities, and paperwork. Recognizing their roles as surrogate custodians, they also asked the HCWP's to describe emergencies when they had "to take charge, and had some or all of the responsibility for running the Monument." They noted wryly that that was "a good place for an example!" *The Grapevine*'s publication of the results of the survey coincided with a memorandum from the director of the Park Service urging that women replace men in situations where they "can perform the required duties." *The Grapevine* found that two-thirds of the women answering were qualified to fill park jobs and possessed clerical or scientific training, or both. Most of the wives had experience as volunteers in interpretation, protection, museum work, and research.[39]

Several of the HCWP's did take jobs. Sallie Brewer became the first permanent woman ranger in the Southwestern monuments, working at Casa Grande for more than a year before she transferred to Tumacacari Mission. She served there for six years. Betty Jackson worked as the executive secretary of the Southwestern Monuments Association. Courtney Jones accepted an invitation to become a curator at the Museum of Northern Arizona, with part of her salary being room and board with the Coltons.[40]

During the first postwar years, it looked as if life in the Southwestern monuments would return to the 1930s norm. Anne Supernaugh and her husband Bill pioneered at Organ Pipe Cactus National Monument in the Sonoran desert on the Mexican border. They built a two-room house themselves, cooling water by hanging sweating canvas bags from the crossbeams, and had no telephone, but the development of roads, communications, and increased staffing in the 1950s brought more modern living conditions. Frances and Charles Sharp returned to Charles's position as a relief ranger, pulling their trailer from Tonto to White Sands, Montezuma Castle, Bandelier, and Casa Grande, until new staffing eliminated the need for a roving ranger. In 1947, they found themselves back at Tonto as superintendent and wife in a new cabin. In the mid-1950s, the building of two three-bedroom houses, away from the visitor center, enabled the family to have more of a personal life.[41]

The Joneses returned to Wupatki, but soon took on a new challenge in Puerto Rico where Davy became the first superintendent of San Juan National Historic Site. They again valued intimate contacts with community people, choosing to live in neighborhoods where they were the only Continentals, as they were called, and sending their daughter to a local school. Davy conducted park business in Spanish, and their neighbors taught Courtney how to read the Spanish-language newspaper and included them in neighborhood get-togethers.[42]

Although Park Service wives in the monuments would continue to pitch in for their husbands and represent the service to the community, the era when the Park Service was dependent on the services of the custodians' wives to keep the monuments functioning was passing. It lingered into the 1950s, in places like Canyon de Chelly, where Emma Guillet served as the postmistress and acted as deputy for her husband, Meredith, in his absence, and where their daughter, Dani, attended a one-room schoolhouse containing all eight grades.[43] Pinkley's HCWPs, whose work as surrogates for their husbands was willingly volunteered and enthusiastically accepted, however, had proved beyond a doubt that women were capable of undertaking any job the Park Service had to offer.

Park Wives Nationwide: Providing Schools and Community Services

The support of park wives nationwide raised the entire Park Service's expectations for their contributions. The early attitude at Yellowstone that wives were not welcome was replaced by an assumption that, when the Park Service hired a married man, it secured the services of "two for the price of one." Superintendents often looked at a candidate's wife before the man was hired. Former superintendent Lon Garrison explained that the service "justified rangers many times on the basis that they could provide twenty-four hour protection because they [the families] lived there."[44]

The dedication of park wives to the mission of the Park Service often matched their husbands' and the public services they performed, at least one wife believed, were not unlike those expected of a minister's wife of the same era. As wives began to meet the basic needs of their own families, they often found they were solving problems for the park community.[45]

The inevitable step after the Park Service became used to wives was the arrival of children and the need for schools. The experiences of the Yellowstone women in providing schooling for their children was repeated in other parks in remote locations. In the mid-1930s, Mildred "Hap" Dodge's husband, Natt, began his long career by serving as a "buck" ranger on the North Rim of the Grand Canyon. They lived about eighty miles from the nearest store, with their two children, in a wall tent, staying until the first snow. The only school-aged children were their daughter, Nattalie, and Amber and Zorro Bradley, children of a park engineer, Willard Bradley, and his wife, Blanche. Hap Dodge, a graduate of the University of Colorado and a former teacher at a junior high school, had once taught eight grades in a one-room school in Eastern Colorado. She was well prepared to set up a one-table school for the three children. Their learning, as for all park families, did not stop with formal schooling. The Dodge's refrigerator always contained jars labeled *Scorpion* or *Snake* to indicate the jar's contents, especially after they moved to the desert environment of Casa Grande National Monument, where Natt Dodge became a well-known Southwestern park naturalist. Blanche Bradley was an expert in high altitude woodstove cooking and in making gunnysack ice boxes, and she knew how to crust a side of beef, skills she passed on to other families. In the winter, on the South Rim, the children attended a three-room log schoolhouse. There Hap Dodge wrote the narrative for a pageant on the history of the Grand Canyon, with each student performing a historic role. She also ran a library, staffed with volunteers.[46]

Other Park Service wives pitched in to either start schools or to teach in local schools. Stationed at Lassen Volcanic National Park in the Cascade Mountains of Northern California, where they were once snowed in for forty days, were Beverly and William Holloman and their son, Mark. When Mark turned six, since there was no school near the park, Beverly, a qualified teacher, got permission from school district headquarters at Redding, in the valley fifty miles west, to set up a school in an unused service station building near the park entrance. The only pupils were Mark and two other children. When the Hollomans were transferred to Sequoia, Bill was stationed at Giant Forest, twenty-four miles and 5,000 feet above the park headquarters at Three Rivers, and the school problem arose again. For four years, Beverly taught at the Three Rivers school during the week, living in a trailer with their school age sons and joining her husband at Giant Forest for weekends. Each time they moved—to Greeneville, Tennessee, and Richmond and Fredericksburg, Virginia, where Bill took on park superintendencies—a teacher was needed in a local school and she took the job. At the Three Rivers school, as recently as the mid-1980s, one-third of the staff of nineteen were spouses of park employees, even though only 15 percent of the students were park children.[47]

A teaching degree was considered by some wives to be insurance that they could get a job wherever their husbands were transferred, although moving from park to park often meant having to get certified again to meet local regulations. One wife completed work for a teaching certificate in one state on the day her husband received notice of a transfer to another. In several cases where a park couple decided to become or remain "homesteaders" and not accept transfers to other parks, wives had long teaching careers and created important connections between the park and the community. In Shenandoah National Park, in Virginia's Blue Ridge Mountains, Stella Johnson's double role as a ranger's wife and a local teacher helped develop positive relations between the Park Service and the local communities. Operating on an informal basis, she both handled complaints about the parks and taught new park staff regional terms, traditions, and natural history. She helped introduce local crafts into park programs, including making baskets out of white oak strips and weaving rag rugs on a loom. Ray Schaffner, who moved to Shenandoah as a naturalist from the totally different environment of the Petrified Forest in Arizona, remembered the help Stella Johnson gave him by sharing her knowledge of the local flora and fauna. His wife, Vera, who had taught Mexican Americans in the Southwest, transferred her skills to Luray High School at the edge of the park, where she taught Spanish for nearly twenty years. Because of her salary, the Schaffners were able to become homesteaders, turning down the offer of a higher paying job in Washington, D.C.[48]

Wives served on school boards and as presidents of local Parent Teacher Associations. In the 1930s, Barbara McKee, wife of park naturalist Edwin McKee, was appointed to the Grand Canyon school board for three years. The board selected teachers, ordered books, and maintained the teachers' residence. Later, park wife Kay Shevlin became president of the Canyon PTA, raising money for playground equipment, sponsoring programs, and substituting for absent teachers. Early in the 1970s, Margot Schmidt Haertel became the first woman elected to the school board in the small town of Tulelake, California, near the Oregon border. The wife of Paul Haertel, superintendent of Lava Beds National Monument, Margot ran for office at the request of the teachers. She successfully negotiated a teachers' pay raise, averting a strike, and was eventually elected president of the board. For many years, Yosemite and Crater Lake wives helped run a ski school as part of school physical education programs.[49]

Solutions to the schooling of park children could work both ways. Sharon and Bruce Paige think their two boys were the reason that Bruce was selected as naturalist at Glacier Bay in southeast Alaska, near the bush community of Gustavus. The elementary school needed two more students before it could qualify for a resident teacher. When the boys were ready for high school, Sharon taught them through the state correspondence system for two years, then lived with them in San Diego during school sessions for their last two years. For the lower grades, some wives used the Calvert System, which provided graded materials and workbooks for home teaching. Other families turned down transfers to parks where there were no schools. Some had no choice but to send their children away to private school for their high school years.[50]

Wives filled in to provide needed services for communities near parks. When the summer postmistress at Isle Royale, an island in Lake Superior, left suddenly, Phelma "Phil" Jacobsen, a new ranger's wife, was sworn into the position after a morning's training. In Asheville, NC, near the Blue Ridge Parkway, Doris Howe kept the branch library from closing for six months. She developed libraries wherever her husband Bob was stationed. At Yellowstone, she opened the community library to schoolchildren. It was so popular that, when the new school was built in the park, she organized a library in the new building and trained park wives to run it. When the Howes transferred to Glacier Bay, she organized the park's research library, a volunteer job she continued for nearly twenty years following her husband's retirement. When Gustavus residents acquired funds for a library but not for staff, they wasted no time asking her to catalog their books.[51]

Adjusting to New Places and Building Morale

The almost inevitable transfers to a different park brought a set of problems for park wives. Putting up curtains was a symbol of establishing a home in a new place.

Helen Fry moved her draperies with her to fifteen different parks. When she hung new curtains in her retirement home, she couldn't part with the old ones: "I still think someday I'll be able to use them again. They don't look worn at all." Of the moves made by her husband, George, including to the superintendencies of the Great Smokies and Isle Royale, she said, "I was with him all the way." Like other wives of Park Service engineers, Mollie O'Kane moved so often that she found out how to make a home in tents, trailers, shacks, and apartments. She chased bears out of the garbage, moose out of the tent, and chipmunks out of the kitchen. She helped her husband, David, survey more than a dozen construction sites, sighting the transit, locating survey markers, and serving as a rodman.[52]

For a Park Service husband, his career was continuous within the same agency in a new setting, but a move was different for a wife. Mitzi Chandler, whose husband, Bob, has served in several challenging superintendencies, observed: "The wife is plopped down in a new circumstance and must make new inroads each time." The challenge, she believes, "forces growth." Helga Raftery always hated to leave any assignment. Moves were time-consuming and used up "a circle of time where you devoted yourself entirely to getting the family reorganized and reestablished." One young wife was afraid to make close friends because she knew she would leave in a few years and couldn't face the pain of leaving friends.[53]

Mollie O'Kane decided she needed to send her children to private school because they moved so much, but that required her to work to earn the tuition. She wrote advertising copy for department stores and newspapers; her career survived because she had a skill that withstood leaves of absences and moves to new jobs, but each time she had to start over again at the entry level. One wife's greatest frustration was not being able to find satisfying work related to her college training; others found it "next to impossible" to have a career or complete an education because of frequent moves to isolated parks.[54]

For new wives, introduction to Park Service living could be traumatic, especially when there were no other wives to offer support. As a new bride from Minneapolis, Leila Miller was not well prepared for her honeymoon experiences as wife of a winter ranger in Glacier National Park. Because their cabin was twelve miles from the nearest plowed road, necessity taught her how to bake bread in a woodstove, snowshoe, ski, and make friends with the wildlife. In her second spring, they were relocated to Lake McDonald Ranger Station. There she experienced an event similar to ones reported by other ranger wives in remote stations: she was alone in the cabin when a black bear attempted to enter, trying the door and windows. Her message on a shortwave radio brought a nearby fireguard who scared the bear away. Another experience of Miller's that is familiar to other park wives was having a long wait for her husband: he was five days overdue from a ski-patrol, after being snowbound in a snowshoe cabin without a radio.[55]

One of the essential jobs of a superintendent's wife has been to help make new employees feel welcome and in some cases to help resolve family problems. During one year when her husband, Boyd, was director of the Albright Training Center, Barbara Evison had guests for 365 meals. When she entertained the trainees and their wives, she would watch to see if someone looked uncomfortable; by active listening, she often kept small problems from growing bigger. Annie Neasham Freeland, who was raised in the Park Service, found the assignment of her husband, Dixon, to urban Yorktown after the rural mountains of the Great Smokies such a contrast that she had a difficult time adjusting. She did not share her feelings because she thought she should just "be big and brave and not ever complain." But from then on, when she sensed that young wives were having problems, "just from a sentence here and there," she talked with them to let them know that their feelings were ones held in common with other wives.[56]

In parks where living conditions were particularly difficult, employee morale could dip to a low ebb. When Amy and Fred Binnewies arrived at Death Valley in the mid-1950s as superintendent and wife, families traditionally moved up to Wildrose, elevation 6,000 feet, in the summer to escape the intense heat, often 120 degrees in the shade. After their first summer, Fred found it to be an inefficient way to operate the park and decided to spend the next summer in the valley and give other employees a choice. When most of them chose to stay in the valley, it was up to Amy to organize the wives to make the new arrangement work. They organized evening parties around the swimming pool, playing water volleyball, and joining in pot-luck meals. At first the houses were not cooled and they had to resort to such methods as hanging wet towels over their heads. With the first evaporative coolers, the heat in the houses dropped down to a tolerable 90 degrees. Because visitors to Death Valley were a long way from gas stations or other help, wives often took them in just to help them cool off. Rosemary Ryan, who lived with her husband, Matt, in an isolated ranger station, became an expert at cooling down overheated car engines, administering first aid, and serving iced lemonade.[57]

Responding to Emergencies and Isolation

Dealing with park emergencies has been a way of life for district rangers and park engineers and their wives. About her life in the parks, Ruth Kirk wished she "had taken time to enjoy it more and worry less." For her husband, Louie, his first emergency was a fire at Wind Cave National Park in the Black Hills of South Dakota, three weeks after they entered the Park Service. Although he responded to many emergencies after that, and the flurry of preparation after the call, followed by hours of waiting, became a familiar pattern, Ruth never got used to it. Roberta Davis did not forget the long night at Grand Teton when her husband Jack and another ranger were held at gunpoint all night by two men wanted by the FBI. A particularly tense time for the wives of engineers was the construction of the Grand Canyon's transcanyon water line. Park engineer David O'Kane remembers the wives who "waited with crossed fingers" while their husbands flew in and out of the canyon in helicopters subject to treacherous air drafts.[58]

One of the jobs assumed by park wives was breaking the news about a death to the families of victims. At the Grand Tetons, Frances Judge was the one chosen to tell a young woman that her boyfriend had just been killed in a climbing accident. When Nancy Dayton was a young ranger's wife at Sequoia, a teenager drowned in the river behind the house. It was Nancy's task to notify the nearest relative, who fainted on hearing the news and had to be revived. While they lived at Glacier, Nancy received a report on the park radio that a grizzly bear was attacking a young man on a mountain across from their station. She found her husband, got his rifle ready, and served as the communications center throughout the emergency. Margaret Merrill found the first aid course she took at Yosemite during World War II especially useful when they lived in the isolated Lake Crescent ranger station in the Olympics. She equipped an emergency room in their log cabin. Like several other wives, Merrill reported finding ways to handle drunks and, in one case, an escaped convict, while waiting for help. Her most useful tool was a cup of fresh coffee.[59]

A knock in the night could mean anything. A Civil War mansion at Richmond National Battlefield in Virginia, park housing for Maureen and husband Jim Cutler, and their family, was an unsettling place to live in. There were bloodstains on the floors, bullet holes in the walls, rumors of ghosts, and a trench in the yard that revealed bone chips from amputated limbs when it rained. Jim was on duty away from the house several nights a week. When four men came looking for "the ranger" late one night, Maureen did not want to admit she was alone. They left after she told them her husband was very sick and could not come downstairs.[60]

When a park wife living in an isolated station was expecting a baby, she generally planned to move outside the park to await the event, but stories of emergency helicopter rides are not uncommon. Annie Freeland's husband, Dixon, was caving at Carlsbad Caverns when her labor began. Something told him it was time to go home—and it was: they made it to the hospital with twenty-three minutes to spare. Six weeks later, their new son's stomach closed up. A surgeon flown in from El Paso saved his life.[61]

The greatest problem in isolated parks has been psychological. Loneliness and the constant care of small children have been particularly wearisome. Wives worked together to organize support systems for park families. When the community was small, shared meals followed by "yarning" or storytelling and spelling one another for trips to town have been the main methods. When the park community was large enough, wives organized lending libraries, newsletters, pot-luck suppers, craft classes, and entertainment. At the Grand Canyon, wives ran a library and published a newspaper, *The Canyon Calliope*, containing news, classifieds, letters to the editor, and discussions of local issues. Professional singer Ann Parks, a park wife, played the lead in the park's production of *The Fantasticks*. In the winter, weekly square dances at Glacier and the Grand Tetons helped bolster morale.[62]

Wives who have taken an active interest in the park's natural resources have been the most satisfied. At Mount Rainier, Esther Macy learned to ski when the sport was in its infancy in the United States. In the same park, ranger wives Ruth Kirk and Carolyn Miller joined three other wives to hike the one-hundred-mile

Wonderland Trail encircling the mountain. Using outdoor skills learned in remote ranger stations, Phil Jacobson proved her competence by climbing Mount Whitney with another park wife during six-days of backpacking; they covered seventy-four miles.[63]

Winterkeeping provided a spiritual experience for the park wives who chose that life. In 1922, Ranger George Magly and his wife, who is known only by his name for her, the Rangeress, kept the Giant Forest Ranger Station at Sequoia open all winter for the first time. Access was by snowshoe from Hospital Rock 3,700 feet below. Although a few visitors made the ascent to marvel at the giant sequoias covered with snow, their joint patrols looking for signs of poaching were usually solitary. They did run into flocks of quail, a golden eagle, and deer—birds and animals they were "teaching . . . to trust man." For three years in the early 1930s, Fern Bernard and her husband were winterkeepers in a cottage near the Old Faithful geyser at Yellowstone. Not only was their cottage heated by geyser water, but so was a small greenhouse, a short snowshoe away. She grew lettuce, radishes, carrots, beets, new potatoes, and geraniums, even when the thermometer dropped to forty below zero.[64]

Park wildlife fascinated park wives. Because families were not allowed to have domesticated animals as pets, they found some unusual substitutes. At Mount Rainier, Ione Gunderson made a pet out of a whistling marmot called Little Coot; at Tonto, Frances Sharp nursed a baby javelina back to health. Dorothy James stored their dry food in a barrel in a concessioner's building at Rocky Mountain. When it was time to use it, they found packrats had substituted soda and sundae spoons for the family's rice and tapioca. The list of animals revived by Iva Campbell at Hot Springs in Arkansas included opossums, owls, alligators, mice, raccoons, snakes, flying squirrels, and rabbits.[65]

Every park wife became used to entertaining visitors, including visiting Park Service officials, scientists, and celebrities, often because there was no other place for them to eat. Nancy Doerr arrived at Hawaii Volcanoes National Park as a bride early in 1932; her husband, John, was the first naturalist. Her first instructions were to be able to provide, in fifteen minutes, food for five men for five days should "Madame Pele speak." When the volcano did erupt, Nancy was ready. Jane Sullivan, as superintendent's wife at Colonial National Historical Park, near several Virginia military bases, was expected to serve a cocktail buffet in military style. Because she had to entertain within the family budget, she began to plan a month in advance and prepared and froze all the food, beginning two weeks ahead. Visitors at Lassen Volcanic National Park could expect fresh fish caught by Mary Ellen Rutter. When her father learned she was going to marry a ranger, he taught her how to tie flies to attract trout.[66]

In large parks, wives joined together to entertain visitors, but plans sometimes went awry. Inger Garrison, wife of the Yellowstone superintendent in the early 1960s, took pride in organizing park women to put on gourmet meals for important guests. On the morning before a reception for Park Service Director Conrad

Wirth, her kitchen was full of contributions of fruit, vegetables, and hors d'oeuvres, and she was making cinnamon rolls and bread. She left for a few minutes to pick up her mail, but as soon as she returned, she knew something had happened. The fruit and vegetables were gone, the refrigerator had been opened and emptied, and bread was scattered all over the kitchen. Large tracks in the flour led upstairs to the Garrisons' bedroom and identified the culprit—a 400-pound black bear. Reversing the plot line of the Goldilocks story, the rangers she called tranquilized the bear and removed it. By evening the wives had replaced the food and cleaned the kitchen.[67]

Wives have found that women's clubs, church and school activities, scouts, Red Cross work, and even local bridge groups have provided them with an entree into the communities near the parks. Because local people often find it easier to approach wives than official park personnel, wives have picked up helpful information about park problems. In new areas where parks are controversial, the role of a park family has been particularly important. When Zorro Bradley toured native villages for the Alaska Task Force, he took Nattalie and their children with him to demonstrate that Park Service people were real people, too. The children proved to be especially important as icebreakers.[68]

Speaking-out and Contributing Special Skills

In some cases when a park was threatened by development, wives have been able to speak out in ways their husbands were not able to do: as park officials, their husbands could provide information but not offer personal opinions. Park wives, on the other hand, have joined or even established organizations taking a definite stand. When Lois Dalle-Molle was president of the Denali Conservation Association in Alaska, an organization formed to protect the park from development, she felt free to voice opinions opposite to the park's, using information from her husband, who was the park's resource manager. During the construction of the coal-fired Navajo power plant at Page, Arizona, wives at the Glen Canyon National Recreation Area marched to try to mitigate the adverse effects on the environment that would be caused by the plant. Organized by park wife Sue Christianson, they introduced information about new technology, like wet scrubbers for the stacks, and prepared statistics proving that the plant would put eleven tons of particulate matter into the air a day if the plans were not changed.[69]

Like the park wives in the Southwestern monuments, many wives showed empathy for Native American people. When Maxine Dickenson's husband, Russell, was director of the Park Service, a Hopi elder approached him for assistance in preserving their traditional way of life. Maxine became one of the service's informal ambassadors to the Hopi people, and they named her Ho Mana, or Arrow Girl, the one who carries messages. She learned all she could about the Hopi culture and worked to influence the service to help preserve native lifeways and not just artifacts. Through her personal work as a potter, Inger Garrison developed a keen appreciation of American Indian art. She organized traveling shows for the Arizona Commission on Arts and Humanities and became an authority on constructing "living interpretation" programs based on human life experience. She urged the Park Service to recognize the value of the work of American Indian people hired to demonstrate their art by offering respect as well as "premium pay" for their services.[70]

Some park wives have contributed special skills to solving major park problems. Phyllis Freeland Broyles was a ranger's wife on the Mexican border at Big Bend for seven years in the 1950s. Her ability to speak Spanish led her to play an important role. Mexican people were illegally using the pasture within park boundaries for livestock and picking candelilla (used for making industrial waxes) and peyote. With Phyllis acting as translator, the Broyleses often took their two small children and crossed the border to meet with the sheriff of Boquillas to work on the abuses. While they met, their children played with their Mexican counterparts. Phyllis also represented the park on a team that inoculated three hundred children in Boquillas with DPT and polio vaccines. She sterilized the needles in distilled water boiled in her pressure cooker on the wood-burning stove at the Mexican customs station. Marilyne Mabery contributed her skill as a nurse with emergency medical training to each park where she and her ranger husband were stationed. She also organized the archeological collections at Canyonlands and Theodore Roosevelt national parks and updated the museum at El Morro.[71]

In historical parks, wives enhanced interpretative programs. For her work at Morristown National Historical Park in New Jersey, the Company of Military Historians awarded Henrietta Rixon their highest honor. The wife of the maintenance supervisor, she researched the lives of families living in Revolutionary army camps and demonstrated period arts and crafts to schools and community groups. When Susan Overton's husband was a ranger at Richmond National Battlefield, she made dozens of reproductions of uniforms for Civil War parks: the costumes were worn in cannon-firing demonstrations. Overton used authentic materials and avoided permanent press so the uniforms would look rumpled.[72]

At least two wives served in uniform as deputies for their husbands and held formal appointments in isolated parks. Paid on a "when actually employed" basis, Laura Joyner at Devils Tower National Monument and Evelyn Luce at Custer National Battlefield each filled their double roles for fifteen years. Laura Joyner, whose husband, Newell, became superintendent in 1932, functioned as a fire and traffic control person and hostess. Evelyn Luce, whose husband Major Edward Luce became superintendent in 1941, met visitors, helped plan the new museum, and cataloged artifacts; she researched the park's history in the National Archives. During World War II, she helped maintain the cemetery lawns. Evelyn took charge of the new museum acting as curator and meeting visitors. She also filled the traditional wife's role of providing meals and lodging to visiting Park Service personnel and historical researchers.[73]

Florence Stupka gave up the possibility of an independent career as a Park Service naturalist after she and her husband, Arthur, both passed the park naturalist ex-

amination in 1933. She refused a position offered her in the West and went with him
to Acadia National Park on the Maine coast. There they worked as a team, only
she was not paid. Together they edited and wrote for Acadia's *Nature Notes*. Margaret also took and developed slides to accompany Arthur's talks on natural history
and helped organize a museum. For his book on the birds of the Great Smokies,
she indexed and tabulated twelve years of his journals and other sighting records in
addition to typing the manuscript.[74]

Perhaps the most telling story revealing the importance of wives in remote parks
was an incident that happened to Zorro and Nattalie Bradley on their honeymoon.
On a late January afternoon, they drove up to the superintendent's house in a remote park. Although there was fresh snow on the ground, there were no footprints.
They knocked on the door several times and were finally let in by a despondent superintendent. His wife had left him for a seasonal employee and he was alone with
no staff. When Nattalie went to look for some food in the refrigerator, she found it
was empty. They staffed the park for several days so he could leave and get back in
touch with reality and believe they saved his life by bringing him human contact.[75]

Finding a Personal Identity

It was not uncommon, however, for a wife to think as Nancy Doerr did that she
was married to the Park Service as much as to her husband. "I didn't marry Mr.
Doerr," she said. "He married the Park Service and I married him, so I married
the Park Service." In Hawaii, Nancy was hostess to many exciting visitors, but later
in Washington, D.C., she resumed her own career in interior design. While her
husband was away on a supervisory trip, she found a job as a designer connected
with a furniture store. The year she planned the president's suite at Walter Reed
Hospital she was paid more than her husband.[76]

After years of immersing themselves in Park Service activities, other wives
found the careers they put on hold were no longer available to them. As an active
park wife, Gene Scovill moved eight times, raised three children, hosted visitors,
and trained in structural fire fighting and first aid. When her husband was transferred to Washington, D.C., she was unable to resume her full professional career
in early childhood education. She had to settle for teaching in a day care center for
low pay. She was not only disappointed, she said, in being "excluded from my chosen field," but "as important, was that my self-esteem was bruised for I was still dependent upon my husband's income and could not contribute in financially significant ways to our marriage." She wanted a "partnership" not a "dependency."[77]

After the first adventurous years of their marriages, many park wives found indeed that the key to survival was developing their own identities through fostering
their own interests. Artist Helga Raftery painted what was around her, including
scenes in many parks. Although she taught art classes and painted with groups, it
was not until she exhibited and began to sell paintings in a community gallery near
Sequoia that she defined herself as a serious painter. Inger Garrison was a skilled

potter and sculptor who used native silts and muds from the parks where she lived. During her eleven years as superintendent's wife at Chaco Canyon, Elinore Herriman became fascinated by the park's petroglyphs. Because rubbing was not allowed, she sketched and transformed them into prints and notecards by carving sandstone blocks or creating silk screens for printing.[78]

Park wives who have tuned into their surroundings have found that writing about a park's natural or cultural history can be a career in itself. Ruth Kirk began a writing and filmmaking career that resulted in more than twenty-five books, in addition to articles and film narrations. She organized a group of park wives to publish an issue of *Westways*.[79] Geologist Ann Livesay Sutton, one of the few women to serve as a seasonal naturalist after the mid-1930s, worked at the Grand Canyon during the summers of 1949 and 1950. She married park naturalist Myron Sutton and became his partner in publishing more than thirty books on natural history. Shirley Moore's interest in her children's education in the sciences, mostly learned in the parks, qualified her as youth editor for *Science News* and to publish young adult science books.[80]

Some wives did not find keys to survival in the Park Service. One wife believed she lost her entire sense of self in the service. She felt pressure to conform and to be always pleasant and positive. She saw herself as defined only in terms of the organization, not in ways that described her as an individual with particular strengths, talents, and needs. The expectation was for her entire destiny to be lived out through her husband, the parks, and their children. When another wife in a remote park told her husband that it was her turn to make a career choice and she could only do it by moving near a city, he refused. They were divorced: he, in effect, chose the Park Service over his wife, and she chose personal fulfillment over his career. On the other hand, parks were known to offer jobs to park wives who wanted to stay after their husbands abandoned them for other women.[81]

Between the mid-1930s and the mid-1960s, positions for women in national parks were defined as wives or secretaries. The lack of uniformed women as role models made it difficult for a young woman to picture herself as other than a support person. Margot Schmidt Haertel, a Park Service daughter, demonstrated her potential for a park position by serving as a Peace Corps volunteer in Ghana and as a Student Conservation Corps worker at Cedar Breaks National Monument, but she identified with her mother, Marguerite, an active park wife, rather than with her father, Hank, a superintendent. Another park wife and second generation Park Service person, Karen Garrison Reyer, daughter of Lon and Inger Garrison, was an accomplished outdoorswoman and had a lifelong knowledge of the parks. When she was growing up, her goal was not to be a ranger or a cowboy but to marry one. Dani Cook, another Park Service daughter, thought about becoming a ranger until she observed hostility from some of the male staff toward the early women rangers.[82]

If women who fell in love with men who happened to work for the Park Service accepted marriage, they also were committed to the park lifestyle. Phil Jacobsen believed marriage to a Park Service career man was a more exciting option for the wives of her generation than "living in a little town or being swallowed up in a city." She saw the "excitement and adventure" as liberating, "even though what you were doing was domestic." She felt a "sense of importance or belonging" because the wife "was really a necessary person in the park. Without the wives in the isolated parks," she said, "I think it would have been a three-legged dog." Speaking of their eleven years at Fort Laramie in an isolated corner of Wyoming, Gertrude Hieb echoed Phil Jacobsen. Without the family, she said, "It wouldn't have gone."[83]

Even after they became park wives and served as surrogates for their husbands in isolated ranger stations, neither Karen Reyer, Beverly Holloman, Margot Haertel, nor Phil Jacobsen took the step of visualizing themselves as paid field personnel. Because their work took place in a ranger station or superintendent's house, space that often doubled as a home and a park office, they moved naturally between their private and public roles. The construction of private park residences and separate visitor centers during the Mission 66 development program took park families out of the public space. Except in isolated parks and ranger stations where the old style lingered, Mission 66 marked the end of the pioneer period for park families. Now a wife made a conscious choice between living a private life or continuing her public role. Her public work even received a new name—VIP, Volunteer in the Parks—with specific duties, further separating her public and private selves, an essential step before a woman could see herself and other women in the image of ranger, naturalist, or even superintendent. Moreover, it was the wives themselves, whose demand for the tangible improvement of better housing was actually a latent desire for the recognition of the importance of their work, that set this major change in motion.

Park Wives Define Their Roles

In 1952, at the Superintendents' Conference at Glacier National Park, Park Service wives met to legitimize their function. Naming themselves the National Park Service Women's Organization, they had been "happily surprised" when the new director, Conrad Wirth, asked them to help him plan Mission 66, his ten-year program for capital improvements, to be completed by the service's fiftieth anniversary in 1966. Although park wives had long since known what was expected of them as individuals, this was the first time they had been asked to organize and assume tasks as a group on a national level. As they set about to determine their goals, they defined their roles: wives were the centers of Park Service family and community life; it was their responsibility to promote "friendship and understanding" in order to solve "common problems." But their most immediate problem, they said, was park housing.

Conrad Wirth asked Herma Albertson Baggley to organize the wives. Herma Baggley had been the first woman to achieve permanent status as a naturalist and was then the superintendent's wife at Lake Mead National Recreation Area. She asked Beatrice Freeland to call the meeting to order. Then superintendent's wife at Grand Teton National Park, Freeland had been paid as part of a team with her husband to collect gate receipts at Yosemite in the 1920s. The women wasted no time in using their new authority to attack the housing problem. They elected Herma Baggley national chair and, breaking with the Park Service's regional divisions, designated their own areas, basing their system on location, because they believed that geography, not administrative divisions, determined housing needs. After appointing a chair for each of five areas, the wives passed a resolution requesting "adequate housing . . . [to] assure a minimum decent standard of living."[84]

With the command of a field marshal, Herma Baggley rallied her troops, the park wives, to provide the figures on substandard housing. Although housing was only a piece of Mission 66, the statistics produced by the wives helped provide the rationale for the entire construction program: they were used to convince the Bureau of the Budget and the Congressional Subcommittee on Interior Appropriations to fund the program. The urgency of the need helped produce the first appropriation in 1955, a year before Mission 66's projected opening.

Although the price of park development was an acceleration of the impact on park resources—more than 2,500 miles of new or reconstructed roads, in addition to parking areas and drive-in campsites—the need for improved housing for park personnel was real. Even though wives agreed that the new housing should be "unobtrusive" and "styled to become a part of the individual area," they faced a dilemma: they also wanted the convenience of standard plans, so curtains and furniture would fit as families moved from park to park. One wife warned that a "standard outside appearance [would] create the atmosphere of a slum clearance project;" another that "most people did not want exactly the same type of house in every park." In the end, government economy prevailed; the official tally when Mission 66 concluded early in 1964 was 1,200 residences for 2,000 families, including single, double, and multiple houses. Many were constructed using the basic plans that have come to be known in the Park Service as the "Mission 66" style.[85]

In marshaling the facts to show the need for new housing, Herma Baggley revealed that she and the other wives were ready to identify Park Service problems and anxious to provide solutions. Their survey of one thousand employees with two thousand dependents confirmed the wives' own informal observations: parks were losing qualified personnel because of poor housing. "From one area comes this significant statement, which can be multiplied many times," Baggley wrote: "'Larger than average turnover in positions due to lack of adequate housing.'" The survey found that 10 percent of field employees lived in tents. While "camping and living in tents" was "a popular summer vacation experience" for both visitors and employees in the early years of the Park Service, she said, "today tent housing is definitely outmoded and undesirable to John Q. Public." It was no longer a "'lark'" to serve in a tent. Only the "enthusiasm and devotion" of seasonals, she said, citing Yellowstone, made them return "after the miserable experiences of cold winds, rain and often snow at Lake, or the intense heat at Mammoth." What is more, Baggley noted, the future of the Park Service was being undermined because limited quarters influenced the service to select single men as seasonals, even though 75 percent of the applicants were married. "The day when the park employee's marriage license became his discharge paper is long past," she said. "The proven stability of the married over the single employee is lost by the want of a place to live."[86]

It is no wonder that Baggley's summaries and statistics gave an impetus to Mission 66. Comparisons of park and local housing revealed that nearly half of the service's housing was below community norms; only 3 percent was above. Half of the housing lacked one or more of the basic utilities of electricity, inside running water, or inside toilets. Where families lived in one or two bedroom houses, overcrowding was the rule. Living was no better in historic structures: even though there might be more space, families were housed in former forts, CCC barracks, bunkhouses, barns, stables, or summer homes. Among the many specific recommendations was an urgent cry for family privacy: the wives requested that housing be separated from public areas. In conclusion, Baggley asked that the women be heard. They were concerned with the "need, not theory." Lest their findings be seen as too harsh, she ended with one wife's disclaimer and plea: "May I point out that I have absolutely no qualifications to justify my criticism of structures designed and planned by men who are professionals in their work. However, I do think the women's viewpoint is essential."[87]

The progress of housing construction was slow but steady and the women kept close watch on the issue. In 1955, they resolved that "sub-standard, obsolete structures must be demolished and removed from the residential area" when new housing was ready. Succeeding housing chairs surveyed wives for suggestions on how to improve new housing. When Congress imposed a $20,000 limit with standards planned to eliminate "frills" in 1960, only minor design changes could be expected. After George Hartzog became director in 1964, the women's organization decided to convince him that housing should be one of his priorities by conducting a new survey. Phil Jacobsen, who as vice chair wrote and submitted the 1966 housing report, explained that the women were not asking for "more elaborate houses," but for more "liveable" ones, "better suited to the mission" of the service. They "were aware of their definite responsibility to the Service as partners in employment as well as their role as social ambassadors." Jacobsen and Carolyn Shaw, another officer, and their husbands took their suggestions to Hartzog and his design staff in Washington.[88]

Hartzog and his assistants encouraged the women to take "a positive part in solving the problems that concern the National Park Service family." One of their responses was to publish an orientation booklet for new wives. Although by the time the booklet was published, in 1969, a few women had become park rangers, the booklet spoke only to women as wives serving a joint career with their Park Service husbands. It discussed the problems of moving, housing, schools, and park and community relations. The authors warned wives not to intrude into their husband's official duties, to keep their husbands uniforms "clean and neatly pressed," and to realize that their actions "color the community's impression of the NPS."[89]

Women's organizations in each region developed a systematic way to communicate among themselves. One by one they started newsletters, beginning in the Southwest with *Smoke Signal* in 1967. News from individual members and parks, reports of quilt raffles and other benefits for the education fund of the Park Services Employee and Alumni Association, craft shows, and housing progress reports made up the news.[90]

Even as park wives began to institutionalize their roles by building a national organization, the place of park women was changing. Their successful campaign for new housing spearheaded Mission 66, which in turn removed families from public space, reducing their isolation by the provision of new roads and communication systems. The Park Service began to professionalize some of the functions previously performed by wives. The doubling of park use by the public in the 1950s and the addition of nearly one hundred parks between 1933 and 1963 increased staff and changed the service from a small family-like organization to a large federal system.

As surrogates and helpmates for their husbands, wives had demonstrated their competencies for a long time, but before they could take the step toward independent careers, they had to develop a new view of themselves. The action of creating a national organization with servicewide goals made them see their work as professional, albeit unpaid. In the orientation booklets they wrote to initiate new wives into the service, they presented the work of a park wife as a career in itself.[91] Combined with their new ability to separate their public from their private lives, this attitude helped wives and the women who followed to view themselves as capable of holding independent careers.

The societal and economic pressures of the 1960s and 1970s did the rest: the Park Service was irrevocably changed. The family team consisting of an unpaid wife as backup for the ranger, maintenance man, or superintendent was replaced by a working couple. As wives became park employees or sought outside careers, problems of dual-career marriages, unheard of in previous decades, arose. Yet it was the park wife, in so unselfconsciously demonstrating that women could perform field and administrative duties, who had paved the way for the modern Park Service professional woman. Indeed, some of the first women to hold field positions were park daughters, widows, or women divorced from Park Service men.

There were losses, too. The most common complaint from wives who watched the service grow and become professionalized was: "The Park Service is not a family any more." As wives began to hold paid positions, they had less time to foster the social well-being of the park and neighboring communities. In 1976, when the Park Service Women's Organization seemed to languish, the national board met to reaffirm their primary purpose as one of communication and friendship. The next year they renamed themselves National Park Women, to include all park women, employees as well as wives. The Pacific Northwest's publication, *Breeze,* became a national newsletter in 1981, edited by Park Service wife Thelma Warnock and filled with personal news from parks and park families. The National Park Women continued to work to keep the Park Service family spirit intact. In 1992, National

Park Women celebrated their fortieth anniversary by publishing *Living in National Parks,* a book of stories of life in more than seventy national parks written by nearly ninety women, most of them wives.[92]

Even as they worked to preserve the Park Service as a family, the wives of the women's organization supported the personal progress of women. Their scrapbook of clippings from the 1970s reveals their attitudes. After noting that only two women had up to that time served as superintendents, one of the first clippings, headlined "Let the Record Show," announced that Evelyn Carlson was acting superintendent of Homestead National Monument. "So it's a red letter day when we can report the assignment of a woman even as 'acting superintendent'," the article states. Records of each new advance for women were duly pasted into the scrapbook: such important volunteer efforts as staffing the information kiosk in Washington in the spring and fall when seasonals were not on duty; the organization of recycling centers; the appointment of Carol Martin, a young Park Service widow, as the first woman superintendent to be chosen from the ranks, in 1971; road-crew flag women being added to Yellowstone construction teams; an all-woman trail crew at Glacier; women on horseback at Point Reyes, California, and Gettysburg; and women rangers wearing Stetsons in 1973.[93]

To the roles of visitor and explorer, founder and protector, pioneer naturalist and wife, women were ready to add the position of mainstream professional. As women's roles were transformed from one to another, sometimes to prevent them from assuming authority, their goals, and often their actual activities, remained the same. They wanted to add their voices to those of the women before them who fostered the survival of the nation's heritage, its landscapes, and places of history. By contributing their social and professional skills to the parks, wives began the process of breaking down the military culture of the Park Service, thereby opening up career possibilities for women. The new task was to convince the Park Service that woman's place was on the payroll, with full authority to supervise ranger walks, prepare a budget, monitor plants and wildlife, administer a maintenance schedule, or lead a search-and-rescue team.

PART II

Speaking for Parks: Modern Sisters

Women in Uniformed Field Positions

*I*n the early 1960s, the Park Service rediscovered the talents of women for uniformed field positions. A committee made up of a new generation of male park historians and interpreters, pressured by increased public use of historic parks and anxious to develop programs for visitors, spent two years researching and experimenting with the desirability of hiring women as guides before they came to a conclusion in May 1962: "The Service must make up for *lost* time and an *unperceptive* attitude by initiating a strong program of recruiting young women for some types of interpretive work." The final report of the Committee on Interpretive Standards, circulated throughout the service, noted that superintendents and regional directors were "generally favorable" to the plan and concluded: "The time seems ripe for an expansion in the employment of women. *It is overdue.*"[1]

Although the men who framed the report, cautiously limiting women to guiding visitors in busy historical parks, did not intend it, their actions, combined with a series of presidential executive orders and acts of Congress, gave a revived women's movement the tools to start women on their way toward achieving full participation in all functions of the Park Service. Try as Park Service leaders might to limit women to particular positions with specific duties, and to set women in field positions apart by having them wear a uniform distinctive for its differences from men's, once the process of change had begun, they could not stop it. By the 1970s, women in the field were becoming full-fledged park rangers and had entered law enforcement training, as well. Women on administrative levels of the Park Service were moving up into the higher grades, and, what is most significant, the first women park superintendents were in place.

Women Interpreters Rediscovered

The first evidence presented servicewide that women were an untapped resource for park guides did not come from within the Park Service. Neither the example of the collective work of years of guiding visitors by Park Service wives nor the precedent of uniformed women ranger-naturalists at Yellowstone, Rocky

Mountain, and Grand Canyon national parks in the 1920s and early 1930s provided the impetus for the new policy. Rather, it came from the discovery in late 1960 by historian Roy Appleman, chair of the Committee on Interpretive Standards, that women were successful guides at the United Nations and Rockefeller Center.

Appleman's report explained that women could solve the Park Service's problem with male "historian-interpreters." Some men found the job "boring, unrewarding," and reflected their attitudes in their talks. Such men were not good communicators: they spoke in "scholarly language" or emphasized their "own specialized interest[s]." Some ranger-historians were deemed "unsuited by temperament and personality to deal with the general public" and looked upon interpretation "as of lesser importance." Others saw the work as "unglamorous and unprofessional; not something for the alert and ambitious."[2]

An underlying reason for the reluctance of uniformed Park Service men to work as guides in historic areas is disclosed in Appleman's detailed report of his interview with the person in charge of guided tours at Rockefeller Center, a woman who had undertaken similar work at the United Nations. Her attitudes revealed what were then prevailing assumptions about gender characteristics. At first she chose young men as guides; but, she explained, they "were hard to control" and "did not receive instruction gracefully." The best male guides had "homosexual tendencies," something she concluded was "rather a natural thing because of the feminine traits required in good tour and guide leaders." Those men "had to be discharged."[3]

The problem of the perception of male interpreters as effeminate was not a new issue in the Park Service. In the 1930s, the ranger-naturalists' desire to forestall the feminization of their positions and to prevent ridicule from rangers from the military tradition was a major reason the Park Service stopped hiring permanent women naturalists. This time it was male historian-guides who were labeled as unmanly. Now, ironically in a reverse of the earlier solution, women were hired, not rejected, to solve the problem of preserving ranger masculinity, seen as especially acute in historical parks. If women worked as guides, male historians would be spared from work perceived as effeminate and be free to pursue scholarly research and tasks they considered more professional.

As Appleman outlined the reasons that Rockefeller Center found women to be the best tour guides, he constructed a stereotypical image of *woman*. A woman was "a natural hostess" and liked being "the center of a show." Women were "better at any task which is of a repetitive nature" than men and "more obedient." Appleman noted that "nearly everywhere outside the Service," women were used as guides in historic houses, noting in particular Colonial Williamsburg. His recommendation to the committee was that men should no longer be employed as guides; the Park Service should "institute a new policy of employing only women for it whenever the conditions will warrant a woman holding the job."[4]

Encouraged by Appleman's report, Independence National Historical Park in Philadelphia conducted a well-publicized experiment with women guides, beginning in June 1961. The park's interpretive program was being developed and it quickly grew, on peak days, to receiving 15,000 visitors. The park hired three women, all recent college graduates, and followed with the addition of two more in the fall.[5]

Instead of choosing the outfit worn by the few uniformed women in the service, officials again went outside for advice and adapted an airline stewardess uniform. In the 1940s and 1950s, when the Park Service saw women interpreters as temporary or surrogate, the women's uniform was similar to the Women's Army Corps (WAC) uniform and had many of the same features as the men's. Women wore the standard gray shirt, black tie, and badge; only a skirt and a generic overseas cap set them off as different from the men. But in 1961, when the service saw uniformed women as permanent, they formalized women's difference and reduced their status with the new uniform. A skirt was topped by a fitted green jacket and a white blouse with open collar and no tie. A pillbox hat was worn "two fingers above the eyebrows." Instead of a badge, women were issued a small metal arrowhead, the size of a tie tack. "USNPS" insignia on the lapels, a "USNPS" patch on the hat, and an arrowhead on the left sleeve made them official. The new women's uniform was adopted throughout the service and remained official for nearly ten years.[6]

After an intensive training program in all aspects of the park and its history, voice counseling, and advice on hairstyle and makeup, the women guides at Independence were ready for duty. They not only met a need; they also brought favorable publicity to the service, and the program grew. Lady Bird Johnson, then First Lady, was so impressed by their work that she asked two of them to serve as summer guides at the White House.[7]

When the Park Service directorate circulated Independence's report claiming primacy in employing women guides, however, reaction came from all over the service. "The most amazing thing about this material," Melvin Weig, superintendent at Morristown National Historical Park, wrote, "is the impression conveyed that the value of women as interpreters may be a somewhat recent discovery by the National Park Service." Weig was surprised that it was necessary to survey institutions outside the service to learn "how really effective women can be in the performance of educational functions." Since 1933, when his park opened, it had employed women as guides, historians, archeologists, curators, and naturalists; in 1963, the park was employing five women, each of whom had handled as many as a thousand visitors in a single day.[8]

Yellowstone had already responded to the Appleman report with a summary of its history of hiring women ranger-naturalists. The list was notable because, except for the temporary appointments given to wives during World War II, Yellowstone listed only two women after Herma Albertson Baggley's resignation in 1933. They were Mildred Ericson, who served as a summer seasonal, beginning in 1946, for nearly twenty years, and Mary Meagher, who began her long career at Yellowstone in 1959 under the title of museum curator. Meagher soon became a well-known authority on the bison of the park, the subject of her Ph.D. dissertation. From Scotts Bluff, Superintendent John Henneberger, whose memory was also longer than the committee's, recalled past "rangerettes" at Glacier, Mount Rainier, Yosemite, and Wind Cave. Superintendents at Vanderbilt Mansion, Adams, and Edison national historic sites responded that they, too, had used women guides. Throughout the service, the responses revealed that women had been called upon in the 1950s and early 1960s to serve as paid park guides to meet the increased park use by the public following World War II. They were hired as seasonal employees or in positions designated "when actually employed," working during peak visitor times, or as needed.[9]

By 1962, the second wave of feminism was just beginning. When, in 1961, President John F. Kennedy established the President's Commission on the Status of Women, with Eleanor Roosevelt as chair, he directed the Civil Service Commission to make the government, as the largest single employer of women, "a showcase . . . of equality of opportunity." He asked the commission to review policies affecting women's employment and "to assure that selection for any career position is hereafter made solely on the basis of individual merit and fitness, without regard to sex." Within six months, Attorney General Robert Kennedy had handed down his decision invalidating an 1870 law allowing federal appointments to specify sex. Congress repealed the 1870 law in 1965.[10]

The Park Service could not help but sense that change was coming. Until 1962, qualifying examinations for park rangers specified male applicants. Hundreds of rangers who received permanent status in 1949 after taking a well-publicized nationwide examination were working their way up the organizational ladder. Many of the men were veterans who had received five extra points (ten if they were disabled). Some had been serving in temporary positions since the war and had eagerly awaited permanent status. When, in the early 1960s, the service awakened to the need to hire women guides and hurried to claim a past with uniformed women, the organization was recognizing the shift in women's opportunities that—sooner than anyone could have expected—would bring a major change to the Park Service.[11]

In 1962, the Park Service pulled together its hiring record on uniformed women in a widely-circulated article in *Planning and Civic Comment,* showing photographs of uniformed Park Service women educating the public. Cautiously limiting women to guiding and museum work, the service stated its policy as "employ[ing] in its uniformed positions the best qualified men and women available," noting, however, that "women cannot be employed in certain jobs such as Park Ranger . . . in which the employee is subject to be called to fight fires, take part in rescue operations, or do other strenuous or hazardous work."[12]

A seasonal naturalist at the Everglades pictured in the 1962 article, Gail Zimmer [Belinky], believed that during her eight years the roles of women in uniform were too restricted. "There were a lot of people in the Park Service who wanted the women in the Park Service to be ornaments," said Zimmer, a specialist on turtles who wrote the park handbook on the subject. "It was wonderful to have women in the Park Service. They look so nice in their uniforms, but . . . don't let them get dirty. Don't let them really rough it."[13]

Younger single women guides were often treated differently from their male counterparts. As the only woman historical aide at Colonial National Historical Park in the 1950s, where she led battlefield tours and served on the information desk, Kathleen Lassiter [Manscill] wore the WAC-inspired uniform. She made her own skirt out of uniform material, bought her gray shirt from a military school because she needed such a small size, and kept her overseas cap in her pocket. She found that the chief ranger had been watching out for her without her knowing it: when she decided to spend the night at the home of the people who had hosted her at a party, he noticed her car was missing from her park quarters and spent much of the night looking for her.[14]

The early women guides often came into their positions in indirect ways. Maude Crawford [Harriott] worked her way out of a traditional clerical role into interpretation by learning everything she could about the Everglades. A clerk in Washington, D.C., she took a downgrade in rank to be transferred to the small park office in Homestead in 1954. Because visitors asked so many questions and she herself was eager to learn, she became knowledgeable about the park's natural history. When the new visitor center opened in the early 1960s, she began to lead walks. The park sent her for formal ranger training when she was in her mid-fifties, the retirement age for many Park Service personnel. Fascinated by the breeding behavior of the anhingas, large fish-spearing birds, she published an article about it in the *Florida Naturalist*. By then she knew so much about the Everglades that she was known to the park staff as Mother Nature.[15]

Beginning as a guide with nursing skills in 1943, Olive Johnson continued a Carlsbad Caverns' tradition of hiring nurse-guides that had begun in the early 1930s. During the next twenty-seven years, Johnson trained hundreds of male rangers. Her position titles listed in chronological order reflect the progress of uniformed field women in the 1950s and 1960s: guide, tour leader, first aid attendant, park guide, supervisory park guide, supervisory park technician. The changes in her uniform also reveal the new attitudes about field women. In 1947 she wore the adapted WAC uniform; by the early 1960s she had changed to a white blouse with an open collar and a pillbox hat. Unlike the women guides at Independence, Johnson kept her official badge.[16]

Among the earliest parks to hire women seasonals in the 1960s was Fort Laramie, Wyoming. Local women college students gave tours, staffed the visitor center, and dressed in costume for living history programs. Barbara Erickson Bonds remembers arguing that as the only employee on duty in the early morning, other than the night guard, she should be trained to operate the site's fire-fighting equipment. Her reasoning did not convince the superintendent.[17]

Although Attorney General Kennedy's ruling prevented "male only" from being specified for park ranger positions, the Park Service held on to that restriction, one way or another, for nearly ten more years. Even after women received formal training as rangers at the Albright Training Center at the Grand Canyon, beginning in 1964, literature sent out to applicants for Park Service positions continued to differentiate between park rangers, on the one hand, and park guides, naturalists, archeologists, and historians, on the other. The 1965 statement: "Park ranger positions are restricted to men, due to the rugged, and sometimes hazardous, nature of the duties," was presented in even stronger language in 1967, a sure sign that the policy was being questioned.[18]

Women applicants did, in fact, question the distinction. Secretary of the Interior Stewart Udall responded to one young woman who accused his department of being "'prejudiced against female rangers'" by explaining that it was "our concern and affection for girls that prevents our saddling them with the full load of ranger duties," which he defined as "law enforcement activities, use of firearms, night patrols . . . and occasional need for sheer muscle power in possibly ugly situations." He welcomed her to park naturalist and historian positions, noting that while those jobs were also performed by male park rangers, they could be "done just as well, and indeed, often better, by women."[19]

Role Models for Change: Sportswomen

In contrast with the Park Service's slow acceptance of women in nontraditional roles, a generation of young women was inspired by the new environmental movement. Writers Rachel Carson, whose *Silent Spring* sparked the movement in 1962; Sally Carrigher, whose *One Day on Beetle Rock* dramatized animal life in a corner of Sequoia National Park; and nature essayist Annie Dillard attracted women to the outdoors. Their presence added numbers to the sportswomen who had long demonstrated the potential for women to succeed in outdoor careers by running rivers, rock climbing, caving, and ascending the nation's highest peaks.[20]

Perhaps the most visible sportswoman to make a career in a national park was Georgie White Clark—the "Woman of the River." After ten years of swimming and rafting down the Colorado River through the Grand Canyon, Georgie Clark became the first woman river runner in the park in 1955. She guided hundreds of people on her River Rat trips through the Grand Canyon for more than thirty-five years. She lashed three twenty-seven-foot neoprene boats together and ran the rapids broadside, propelled by oars and a 10-h.p. outboard motor.[21]

Another sportswoman with continuous dedication to national parks since the 1950s is Jan Conn, who, with her husband, Herb, explored and mapped seventy miles of passages in Jewel Cave National Monument in the Black Hills of South Dakota. In 1984, the Interior Department awarded Jan and Herb a citation for conservation for the 13,000 hours they spent inside Jewell Cave. By surveying and mapping routes, they made it the second longest cave in the United States and the fourth longest in the world. Jan Conn was also an accomplished rock climber. With Jane Showacre, she completed the first "manless ascent" of Devil's Tower. Because women rock climbers in the 1950s did not usually lead, Conn had decided that the way to prove women could lead was to climb the tower with someone "who couldn't possibly 'haul me up,' someone who wouldn't get all the credit for my straining muscles." That someone was another woman. They shared in leading the pitches and achieved the summit in six hours, attracting a large crowd.[22]

Women also demonstrated their abilities on park trails. In Olympic National Park, Minnie Peterson, a pack-train operator, began guiding groups of riders throughout the Olympics in the late 1920s and continued for nearly fifty years. She packed lumber for Park Service shelters and trout fingerlings for park streams and lakes. In the mid-1950s, Emma Gatewood, known as Grandma Gatewood, became the first woman "through hiker" of the two thousand miles of the Appalachian Trail—twice, once at the age of sixty-eight and the second time at seventy. A legend of the trail, she carried virtually no camping gear and slept on top of picnic tables or in farmhouses along the way. Only five men had accomplished the feat before her. By 1989, 20 percent of through hikers were women, numbering 175 in that year alone.[23]

As members of teams of men, women continued to make first ascents of mountains in national parks throughout the 1940s and 1950s, but by the 1960s and 1970s all-women teams accomplished difficult ascents. Accompanied by men, the first women to climb the Grand Teton had been Eleanor Davis, a physical education teacher, in 1923, and, in 1924, Gertrude Lucas, a fifty-nine-year-old woman whose homestead looked up at the Tetons. Pat Petzoldt climbed the north face of the Grand Teton in 1939 with her husband Paul, an experienced climber. The first all-woman climb of the north face was accomplished in 1965 by Sue Swedlund and Irene Ortenberger.[24]

In 1947, Barbara Washburn was the first woman to reach the top of Mt. McKinley, located in what is now called Denali National Park and, at 20,320 feet, the highest mountain in North America. Washburn was a member of a three-month expedition, led by her husband, Bradford, to map and film the mountain. She admitted that the climbing "took a lot of will power." What she enjoyed most was "the comradeship" but "actually being on that rope, putting one foot in front of another was hard work for me."[25] The year before, Betty Kauffman, as a member of a team from the Harvard Mountaineering Club that included her husband, Andy, was the first woman to climb the 18,008-foot Mt. St. Elias in what is now Wrangell–St. Elias National Park and Preserve. She carried a fifty-pound pack and helped relay supplies to eleven separate camps before the final ascent.[26]

After Arlene Blum read a notice that women would be accepted for McKinley expeditions "to assist in cooking chores . . . [but] will not be admitted on the climbs," she decided to help organize the first all-woman climb of McKinley in 1970. Led by Grace Hoeman, a physician in Alaska who was making her third attempt, the team consisted of four American women, one woman from Australia, and one from New Zealand. Hoeman suffered severe altitude sickness, but the women helped her struggle to the summit. During the descent, they improvised a stretcher from a pack frame to carry her down to near their third camp, where she recovered.[27]

First climbed in 1953, the three-thousand-foot sheer wall of El Capitan in Yosemite National Park has long been a challenge to rock climbers. In 1973, Sybille Hechtel and Beverly Johnson became the first women's team to climb it. Five years later, Johnson was the first woman to solo the wall in a climb that took ten days, with nine nights spent in a hammock, swinging from bolts in the rock. Johnson also served on the park's search and rescue team.[28]

Sportswomen within the Park Service were beginning to be noticed. In 1956, the Interior Department commended Ruth Heard and Sylvia Reeves, off-duty life guards at the Lake Mead National Recreation Area, with a valor award for saving two women from drowning during a hailstorm after a small boat capsized. Heard swam to the women through heavy waves as Reeves launched a paddle-board through the surf. They pulled one woman onto the board, told the other to hang on, and took them to safe ground.[29]

Role Models for Change: The Student Conservation Association

A direct influence on the Park Service's changing perception of the role of women in the field came from the Student Conservation Program (later Association) (SCA), founded by Elizabeth Cushman [Titus] and Martha Hayne [Talbot] in 1957. Inspired by Bernard DeVoto's suggestion in *Harper's Magazine* in 1953 that Yellowstone and Yosemite should be closed until Congress adequately funded the national parks, Titus's senior thesis at Vassar was a plan to upgrade park facilities by bringing in college and high school women and men as volunteer workers receiving only living quarters and board. From forty-eight students in two parks, the SCA has grown to provide national parks and other land management agencies with 25,000 volunteers over the years, divided evenly between women and men, many of whom later took positions with the agencies.[30] The SCA showed that women who were not exceptional athletes could happily perform such nontraditional tasks as building trails.

After gaining the support of the National Parks Association and extensive net-working with Park Service advocates, Titus and Talbot convinced the superintendents at Olympic and Grand Teton national parks to pilot their project. From the beginning, the women raised money for the program and they were unpaid for their first years of organizing. During the first summer, they supported themselves by camping and working on a ranch near the Tetons.[31]

Although Titus and Talbot assumed that young women would be included from the start, the first parks expected the program to be for young men, somewhat on the model of the Civilian Conservation Corps of the 1930s. Even though they themselves were examples of women with camping, outdoor, and organizational skills, when the first high-school student group was selected for the Olympics, the park superintendent specified that they should all be boys. Titus remembered that the park's assumption was that "girls couldn't cope with this sort of thing." The two women decided to accept the decision at first, rather than jeopardize the trial program, but Titus wondered later, "What did they think *we* were? You know, sitting in front of them, obviously enjoying the out-of-doors and obviously not exactly the clinging vine [types]." Three college women were accepted for the first year, however, and lived and worked in the Grand Teton Museum; one who studied marmots that first summer was Mary Meagher, soon to begin her long Yellowstone career. By 1975, half of the SCA volunteers were women.[32]

Although park staff members were enthusiastic about the program and wanted it to continue, it took them a while to accept mixed groups of men and women. When the one woman of five students was assigned to the protective division at Grand Teton, she was given clerical work, while the men moved hay, put up signs, dug post holes, and removed barbed wire. The chief ranger requested all males from the SCA for the next year "because we are limited in the amount of assignments for a girl."[33] One early success for SCA women was at Cedar Breaks National Monument in Utah in 1960. The services of Peggy Thompson and Margot Schmidt [Haertel] were considered by the staff to be "equal to those performed by the average seasonal park naturalist." Among their duties were raising the flag, staffing the visitor center, giving a campfire program, collecting plants for the herbarium, measuring all the monument trails and laying out a new trail, rebuilding exhibits, counting visitors, mounting slides, typing and filing, answering letters of inquiry, preparing reports, taking photographs, and cleaning up the roadside. At Acadia National Park in Maine, SCA women narrated on boat cruises, led nature walks, worked in the wildflower garden, filed maps, and cataloged items throughout the park.[34]

After Talbot left for other pursuits, Titus continued to operate the SCA, sometimes out of her bedroom, sometimes during nights in the office of the National Parks Association, from which she received a small salary. After a break with the association, the SCA incorporated in 1964, and set up an independent organization. Titus found a new source of financial support from the all-woman Garden Club of America. By 1969, when Titus resigned as SCA director because of illness, the SCA had expanded to fourteen parks. When Senator Henry Jackson of Washington State prepared the legislation for the Youth Conservation Corps (YCC), he used the SCA as a model. The YCC national park programs began in 1971 for young women and men between the ages of fifteen and eighteen and still continue.[35]

Although other persons filled the position of SCA president, Titus continued her role on the board as founding president, raising money, and giving lectures on the program. The Department of the Interior awarded its Conservation Award to Titus in 1974 and to Talbot in 1986. Among Park Service positions held by former SCA women are park superintendent, site manager, acting chief naturalist, resource management specialist, supervisory park ranger, river ranger, facility management specialist, trail crew, park biologist, and backcountry ranger, all jobs not available to women when the SCA began its program in 1957.[36]

Programs like the SCA and the YCC, and the increasing numbers of sportswomen in parks, of women guides, historians, and naturalists combined with new federal legislation to bring change to the Park Service. In 1964, Title VII of the Civil Rights Act prohibited discrimination "on account of sex." Three years later President Lyndon B. Johnson's executive order singled out federal employment and federal contractors as places that must eliminate sex discrimination and established the Federal Women's Program. In 1969 and 1972, President Richard M. Nixon spelled out steps that the government should take to end discrimination in its own employment and put responsibility for ending it under the Civil Service Commission. Although the guidelines for Title IX of the 1972 Education Act providing for equal treatment of women in collegiate athletics would not be made final until 1979, it soon began to enlarge the pool of women athletes.[37] Each of these federal actions had a direct impact on the Park Service.

Ranger and Law Enforcement Training for Women

In 1964, the Park Service took a major step toward ending sex discrimination in employment by assigning two women to the twelve-week ranger training session, "Introduction to Park Operations," at the Albright Training Center at the Grand Canyon. The forty men in the class were surprised at the presence of the women; their reactions ranged from shock and intolerance to deciding to make the best of it. Many of the men had been in the military service and most were married. They saw the position of park ranger as a traditional job that projected a masculine image and allowed them to continue the security of uniformed government service and the camaraderie of men. In contrast, the ranger position was a nontraditional job for women—and it attracted younger, independent women, usually unmarried, who hoped to be treated as full colleagues.

The supervisor of the training center, Frank Kowski, was conflicted himself. To a fellow superintendent, he wrote that he wanted "no part of the job of assigning women to conventional ranger positions;" yet he also believed, he said, that "there may be ranger jobs in the Service where a woman would work out very well." Because he doubted that there was a future for women as park rangers, he did not argue with the Washington office's decision to have the women keep their titles as naturalist and historian, allowing only the men to be designated as rangers.[38]

The first two women at Albright were subject to a great deal of hazing. In addition, they confused the men by having distinct personalities and surviving what must have been a difficult experience by using different strategies. Barbara Lund, who held a bachelor of science degree from Cornell University and was a naturalist at Saguaro National Monument in Tucson, was tall and responded to the hazing by speaking out. The men called her "tall by tough." Barbara Sorrill, who had been a clerk-typist in various government agencies for nearly ten years and had recently been appointed to the post of historian at Colonial, was short and quiet and kept her feelings to herself. The men's name for her was "short by sweet." One of the hazing traditions at Albright was to mix up a trainee's required slide program. To her surprise, when Lund began to show her slides, she projected a nude woman on the screen. The program came to an immediate halt and Kowski called the men together to reprimand them. The women completed the training, but Sorrill left the service within the year. Lund stayed on for ten more years, serving as a naturalist at Saguaro and Zion and as an urban program specialist in Washington, D.C.[39]

During the next two years, the training center began to be more accepting of women trainees. Two—again, the only women in their classes—were particularly successful; both were older women and both were single parents. Betty Gentry, a former Marine and then a junior historian at Vicksburg National Military Park, was called a "backlog" trainee because she had been in the Park Service for nearly five years. Glennie Murray [Wall] was called an "intake" trainee, because she came from outside the service. When she was a graduate student researching petroglyphs at Lava Beds National Monument in northern California, the chief naturalist asked her if she had ever considered a career with the National Park Service. Her immediate response was: "But they don't hire women." He replied, "Oh, but we *do!*" and suggested that she take the Federal Service Entrance Examination (FSEE).[40]

Among the field activities at Albright were hiking and camping, fire control instruction, target practice, and rappelling on ropes over the canyon rim. Since the women were either intake trainees taken right off the FSEE registers or were working as historians or naturalists in parks, these activities were generally new to them. Historians Cindy Kryston and Paige Lawrence, early Albright trainees, attached 12-inch wide pink bows to their hard hats to make the statement that they realized their limits but wanted to participate as much as possible.[41] Pressure continued on the Park Service to increase its affirmative action programs. In August 1969, by the time fifty-six women, representing 9 percent of the total, had taken the training at Albright, the Office of Personnel Management (OPM) issued new, less restrictive standards for park ranger positions. The former standards had required specific outdoor and maintenance-type skills; the new standards were broadened so more people could qualify. From then on, women were no longer restricted to the title of ranger–historian or ranger–naturalist but could call themselves park ranger without a hyphen for the first time.[42]

As the permissive life styles of the 1960s grew, fueled by anti–Vietnam War protests, the Park Service faced other changes in addition to affirmative action. Supervisors became more sophisticated about law enforcement activities and expanded law enforcement operations. In 1970, after mounted park rangers tried to quell a riot lasting most of the night at Yosemite Valley's Stoneman Meadow, the Park Service accepted the reality of urban problems in national parks. Concurrently, the service was developing large urban parks out of decommissioned military sites in prime coastal locations. Both Gateway in New York City and Golden Gate in San Francisco were authorized in 1972. In the same year, the new affirmative action push led Director Hartzog to order the Washington personnel office to set aside 150 ranger intake positions for women and minorities and to recruit them from persons certified by OPM as having high scores on the FSEE and who had indicated they would go anywhere in the federal service. They had not necessarily mentioned the Park Service. The makeup of the classes that resulted was controversial because although there were some places for backlog trainees, outsiders filled slots coveted by seasonal men anxious to go to Albright as a way of achieving permanent status. One-quarter of the slots in the three intake classes went to women; only a few went to African Americans. The trainees left Albright for internships in urban parks.[43]

Only two of the women in the first intake class and two in the second were African Americans. Among them were Martha Aikens and Celia Jackson [Suggs], both of whom had grown up in African-American communities in Mississippi and graduated from historically black colleges. Albright was their first experience in an all-white environment. During Aikens's first assignment as a ranger, at the Everglades, some visitors refused to take her guided walks. When she conducted community planning meetings, she would sometimes have to call a meeting two or three times before enough white participants would come and settle down to discuss objectives. She persisted, however. Rising through the ranks of the service, in 1988 Aiken was appointed superintendent of the Park Service's Mather Employee Development Center. In 1991, Aikens became the first woman superintendent of Independence National Historical Park. Celia Suggs, who began at Independence after her Albright training, was the only African-American ranger out of a staff of fifty, although two other black women started at Independence during the Bicentennial. Later, as site manager of Maggie L. Walker National Historic Site in Richmond, Celia Suggs helped develop a new park.[44]

By 1972, the women's movement had progressed further than the ranger training program. Women trainees reluctantly attended a separate session on grooming conducted by a stewardess from Bonanza Airlines—while the men viewed a movie on Yosemite. When the stewardess told the women that they could remove hair from their legs and faces by using hot wax, one of them broke up the session by asking the stewardess if you could do that over a campfire. They found the Washington personnel officer who was observing the training, backed him into the ladies' room, and demanded that grooming training be discontinued forever.[45]

The first Park Service women to take law enforcement training attended the U.S. Park Police Academy in Washington, D.C., or state training facilities. The first woman to take the training was Helen Lindsley [McMullin] in 1971, the year women were first authorized to wear firearms. While in college, majoring in law enforcement, McMullin responded to an advertisement placed by Yellowstone asking for law enforcement majors to apply as seasonal rangers. Surprised to have a woman respond, the Yellowstone personnel officer wrote, "The possibility of employment of a female for one of our Law Enforcement positions appears rather remote." The park did accept her as a seasonal clerk-typist, calling it a "rather unusual appointment." Although the men in her college class were seasonal rangers, the experience gave her enough law enforcement work, mainly dispatch duties, to meet her college requirement for field work. When she later attended Albright, an instructor recommended that she be sent to the Park Police Academy "to break the ice" for women rangers. She was the only woman in a class of seventy rangers and park police.[46]

The talent many Park Service women have for dispatch duties was demonstrated earlier at Mount Rainier in the 1930s and 1940s, when women telephone operators made the essential connections between victims and helpers during climbing accidents, forest fires, blizzards, and a tragic airplane crash. Beatrice Hall was one of those operators who, after 11 P.M., kept the switches in her bedroom so she could answer nighttime emergencies.[47]

Beginning in 1977, Park Service women and men were trained at the Federal Law Enforcement Training Center (FLETC) in Glynco, Georgia. Through 1994, FLETC had awarded law enforcement commissions to 386 Park Service women rangers who completed the basic law enforcement course, comprising 22 percent of Park Service trainees.[48]

Building Self-Confidence and Protecting Visitors

Several of the women intake rangers met with resistance from staff when they got their first assignments in the parks. What park women call the Old Boy Network stood firm and, as Mary Bradley, one of the personnel supervisors responsible for the intake recruitment, later said, "It took a while for the Park Service to realize it was not a man's world anymore."[49]

Unlike male trainees with military backgrounds accustomed to reporting through the chain of command, most women trainees had little experience with hierarchies. When they left Albright for the real world of the Park Service, they often found that the reality fell short of the vision. One new woman trainee became frustrated because the superintendent spent his time away from the park or meeting the public, leaving administrative duties unhandled. Imbued with a strong sense of mission, she complained to her regional director. When nothing happened, she went directly to an assistant director in Washington. Within a few weeks, Director Hartzog visited the park, interviewed the staff, including her, and transferred the superintendent.[50]

When Mary Jane McDowell from the second intake class was assigned to the protection division at Mesa Verde, the chief ranger did not assign her any work because he did not believe a woman should or could perform law enforcement duties. McDowell taught herself how to operate the fire equipment, joined rangers who were handling traffic accidents, learned how to fire a .38 caliber handgun, and took Emergency Medical Technician (EMT) training on her own. When the Interior Department began to require ten weeks of training for park rangers involved in law enforcement, the park sent her to Washington for training. After transferring to Yellowstone in 1976, she served on winter patrols with male rangers and led a search-and-rescue team that saved the life of a young woman who had been mauled by a grizzly bear.[51]

Most women protection rangers can chronicle the building of their confidence from the first night patrols and traffic accidents to life-saving and life-threatening experiences. One woman ranger using cardiopulmonary resuscitation (CPR) on a man who ate water hemlock brought him back three times before he died. While one woman ranger described delivering a visitor's baby boy in an ambulance, a Park Service couple, both rangers with EMT training, told how they delivered their own baby in the seat of their car during a spring snowstorm, halfway down a mountain.[52]

Women rangers sometimes put themselves in danger while protecting visitors. Before help arrived, a woman ranger struggled with a woman visitor who was threatening suicide on an icy ledge above the Grand Canyon until the ranger was able to handcuff the victim and pull her to safety. The same woman ranger's most difficult moment was the first time she had to draw her gun on a visitor. At Yosemite, a woman ranger spent four months in plain clothes with a partner apprehending visitors for using drugs and disorderly drinking. A Yellowstone ranger saved her own life by playing dead when a grizzly bear attacked her after she came upon the bear's prey.[53]

Visitor and staff protection is also the role of the women who provide medical services in the larger national parks. They practice a combination of family and wilderness medicine. The biggest fear faced by Dr. Cheryl Pagel and nurse Lucy Eagen during their time at the Grand Canyon clinic was that there would be yet another plane crash. Their largest one involved forty-four victims. With help from the rangers, Pagel and Eagen stabilized the survivors before having them transported to a hospital, fifty miles away. In the clinic, no two days were alike. Some days they were chiefly concerned with the year-round community, Eagen doing eye tests and Pagel teaching sex-education in the Grand Canyon School. On other days, emergencies included automobile or bus accidents, broken bones, and mental breakdowns.[54]

The Park Service has publicly recognized the heroism of women rangers. In 1988, Gail Minami, a ranger in Hawaii Volcanoes National Park was honored as the outstanding female law enforcement officer in the federal government; she was particularly cited for her resiliency. Minami's experiences included such varied actions as closing off a highway in the middle of the night because of a lava flow from an erupting volcano and convincing the community that the park would not tolerate the growing of marijuana. The Interior Department awarded Yosemite ranger Kristin Bardsley a citation for valor in 1991. Bardsley, gun in hand, talked with an armed woman who was threatening suicide for three-and-a-half hours before convincing the woman to lay down her weapon.[55]

A Crack in the Old Boy Network

A concern that training women as rangers at Albright and FLETC would be wasted because women would marry and leave the service did not materialize. A study of the retention record of women and men trained at Albright during the first two decades of the program (1964 to 1984) revealed that the women continued in the service at the same rate as the men. Of the 220 women (14 percent of class totals) attending "Introduction to Park Operations" between 1964 and 1979, 65 percent of the women and 66 percent of the men were still employed by the Park Service in 1984. The figures for the shortened "Ranger Skills" courses between 1980 and 1984 showed that, of both the group of 140 women (30 percent of class totals) and the men attending, 80 percent were still working for the service at the end of 1984. Starting with 1985, 40 percent of the approximately one hundred trainees each year have been women.

Attending Albright has had a positive effect on the careers of women rangers. During the twenty-year period studied, the grades of the whole group of women rangers peaked sharply at GS-5 and fell off rapidly. The median grade for women trained at Albright over the twenty-year period, however, was a GS-9, two grades higher. While a comparison of the grades of men and women can be influenced by the length of service, a comparison of the grades of men and women trained over the same period of time is not. In the study, both women and men Albright graduates peaked at GS-9, with the men's grades rising higher than the women's after GS-9. Women Albright graduates exceeded or equaled the whole group of male rangers up through grade GS-11, after which the women's grades declined more rapidly.

A high percentage of Albright women appeared among women rangers in the higher grades in the 1988 roster. When compared with all women rangers, women trained at Albright through April 1989 represented 50 percent or more in the grades of GS-9 and above. Two special occupations also reflect the importance of the Albright experience: of the approximately sixty women who had served as park superintendents by 1994, nearly half attended Albright; of the seventeen women chief rangers serving in 1989, eleven were Albright graduates.

A study of FLETC women graduates was less conclusive, because FLETC lists go back only to 1978. The retention rate for women was 82 percent, a little higher than the rate for the second Albright group. A perception among Park Service women exists that FLETC represents a fast track to promotion. Whether or not that training will translate into superintendencies is unclear, but seven (25 percent) of the women superintendents named in the late 1980s and early 1990s were FLETC graduates. All but one also attended Albright, which made them doubly qualified.[56]

Both the success of the Albright and FLETC-trained women rangers and their retention in the Park Service is the most positive example in the service of training programs designed to increase the representation of women in a nontraditional field. Part of the success can be attributed to the high standards of the initial selection process; more important may be the sense of loyalty and pride engendered by the training; but probably most significant is women's new ability to use new servicewide contacts to crack open the door into the Old Boy Network.

In 1986, the Park Service narrowly avoided a sex-bias class action suit based on the failure to offer women the same opportunities to become law-enforcement rangers as men. Marybeth McFarland, an experienced seasonal law enforcement ranger with a degree in the field, achieved status as a permanent employee by taking a clerk-typist position at Golden Gate with an understanding that she would move to a law enforcement position. When men with less experience than she had were appointed before her, McFarland sued the Park Service. Threatening a class action suit, she settled out of court. She was awarded a park ranger position and training opportunities, including ranger training at Albright and a firearms instructor course. The park was required to train its staff in avoiding "discriminatory selection factors" and to reaffirm to its employees its policy of "non-discrimination against women" and its "commitment to ensuring their training for, entry into, and promotion in law enforcement positions."[57]

Park Police: The Ultimate Challenge

Operating only in Washington, D.C., New York, and San Francisco, the U.S. Park Police is separate from the ranger force. While women rangers may combine law enforcement duties with other activities, women in the Park Police do only police work. In 1942, Beatrice Ball and Lydia H. Barton were the first women to join the Park Police. By 1954, five women served, including Grace Judy [Rowe] who started in 1945 and stayed for thirty-one years. She performed plainclothes assignments before moving into administration. Height and weight restrictions for Park Police limited the number of women who could qualify for positions. After these restrictions were removed in the mid-1970s through a series of court decisions outside the Park Service, seven women entered rookie training in February 1974, more than doubling the number of women on the force.[58]

Jane Marshall joined the Park Police in 1973 before the size restrictions were lifted. Marshall's case is particularly well known because she was the first woman to be shot. She was a veteran of the Peace Corps, serving as a midwife in Senegal, and of the Park Service, where she spent two summers as one of twenty-five college women staffing the information kiosk on the Washington Mall, under the supervision of Betty Gentry. In the Park Police Marshall was assigned to foot patrol. While she was assisting a colleague who was writing a routine citation near the Jefferson Memorial, the driver who had been stopped reached into his glove compartment for what was supposed to be his driver's license, pulled out a gun, and shot them both. Marshall's police radio acted as a shield and saved her, but she was incapacitated, losing the full use of both arms for six months. After she recovered, she became an instructor at FLETC, training recruits whom she later supervised as a sergeant and lieutenant at all three Park Police locations. One of the problems women in law enforcement deal with is the belief by wives of their colleagues that male officers will not be adequately protected if they share patrol duties with a woman. After some of the wives helped give Marshall the around-the-clock care she needed when she was first recuperating, the wives accepted her.[59]

The first woman to become a lieutenant was Valerie Fernandes, who is 5 foot 1 inch tall. In 1980, Fernandes and Pepper Karansky were the first two women in the Park Police to be trained for horse patrol. The third was Gretchen Merkle, who was so determined to become a mounted officer that she persisted even after being thrown eight times. In 1992, Fernandes became the first woman to be named a captain. At that time, 9 percent of the total force of about 740 were women.

Among assignments for Park Police women is undercover work. One of Fernandes's more unusual assignments was at Gateway where, wearing a bathing suit, she did undercover work on a nude beach. Merkle posed as a prostitute in order to get information on narcotics agents, and Jacqueline Anderson was awarded a citation for valor for her actions while serving as a decoy. A felon grabbed her and placed a ten-inch knife blade against her side. She broke his hold and with the help of her backup was able to arrest him.[60]

Probably the ultimate action for any police officer is the taking of another person's life. In 1990, in Lafayette Park, across from the White House, Katherine Heller saved the life of a colleague by shooting and killing the man who grabbed her colleague's gun and was preparing to fire. Group therapy sessions with the Washington police department pulled her through the experience. Heller, a geologist, started as a seasonal naturalist at Glacier, North Cascades, and Grand Teton national parks. She was the first woman chosen as Police Officer of the Year by the International Association of Chiefs of Police.[61]

Maintenance: Jills of All Trades

Since the mid-1970s, the field of maintenance has offered women in the Park Service a direct role in the preservation of park resources. Of the nontraditional fields for uniformed women in the service, however, it is in maintenance that women have had the most difficulty convincing their male peers, their supervisors, and sometimes even themselves that they could perform maintenance tasks, other than cleaning, or that it was even appropriate for women to do so. By the mid-1990s, after more than two decades of recruiting women for maintenance jobs, not quite 6 percent of the wage grade or maintenance workers in the service were women, and only two women held the position of chief of maintenance in a major park. The only woman ever to serve as chief of maintenance for a region (midwest) was Patricia Pusey, a landscape architect, beginning in 1984.[62]

The problem has partly been one of expectations. When one maintenance worker, a widow whose only job in the park was cleaning, was asked what kinds of maintenance tasks she did at home, she said she mowed her lawn, painted her house, and did minor repairs. It did not occur to her to ask to exchange some of the many toilets she cleaned for grounds-keeping tasks. When a male operator of a snow plow at Mount Rainier told Superintendent Jim Tobin that women should not be allowed to plow because they were not physically strong enough, Tobin pointed to the controls to demonstrate that plowing did not take an unusual amount of strength.

On the other hand, women in maintenance have had to show they could meet the physical demands of the tasks. They learned to handle heavy loads without using brute strength and make the point that it is better for men to do the same. When one of her male peers came to help Mary Ellen Snyder pull a 250-pound mixer-shaft out of a waste water tank, she had already attached a hoist to it; she completed the job by herself. Snyder found it difficult to be accepted as an equal. She said that men in maintenance view women workers in one of four roles: a kid sister, a mother, a complaining matron, or a woman with questionable morals. Mary Cannarozzi, on the other hand, believes she taught her peers "that being a journeyman painter has no gender."[63]

Solving unexpected problems is a way of life in maintenance. At Sequoia, Julie Doctor, a chemist, got the highest score on the test for operator of a water treatment plant. But actually keeping the water systems going meant solving one crisis after another. She coped with floods, silted-up dams, redwood roots in pipes, falling branches, and snowstorms. Women in maintenance constantly learn new skills: in just two years Susan Bernotas removed fallen trees after an ice storm, worked in historic preservation stripping paint with dental tools, gardened, laid brick, picked up trash, rebuilt truck starters, lubricated bus motors, mowed grass, took a course in electricity, and drove a truck.[64]

Women have particularly enjoyed mule packing and animal training positions. Mules they packed at the Grand Canyon and Yosemite carried the equipment that Tina Marie Levar and Patricia Haddad took to backcountry trail crews. Edith Roudebush trained personnel to handle the mules who pull the boats on the Chesapeake and Ohio Canal. During the ten years Sandy Kogl managed the kennel for sled dogs at Denali, she developed a smaller, less temperamental breed of dog by not using purebreds. She not only trained dogs to provide park rangers an efficient means of winter travel, but she also developed sled dog demonstrations, attracting thirty thousand summer visitors annually. As ranch manager at Point Reyes National Seashore in California, Gina Muzinich breeds and trains horses for horse patrol, and teaches rangers how to handle them.[65]

Although women worked on trail crews for the SCA and the YCC earlier, most parks resisted adding women to trail crews until the mid-1970s. Lisa Lee Smith, who brought her experience of twelve years of ranching to the Park Service, pioneered trail crew work for women at Pinnacles National Monument in California's coastal range. She demonstrated that women could build dry rock walls and wire fences, split rock, and operate a jackhammer. Dolly Chapman and Annie Barrett Boucher trained on SCA trail crews at Yosemite. Their abilities to construct walls, riprap, fords, and waterbreaks as well as to build the morale of the crews proved to the park that women should be hired on trail crews. After a rockslide wiped out forty-eight switchbacks, Boucher and Sue Brown helped reconstruct the Yosemite Falls trail, all the while looking up to watch for falling boulders.[66]

Adding education, organizational abilities, and budgeting experience to maintenance skills has helped women move into maintenance supervision. Sue McGill's supervisory skills, plus her experience and general knowledge of the trades, helped her become the first woman chief of maintenance at three parks with very different resources. Yet, the question she asks is always the same: "How does what we do as a maintenance staff affect the resource?" Working closely with resource management staff, McGill has faced such problems as containing fuel oil leaking from a sunken ship (U.S.S. *Arizona* Memorial in Honolulu), protecting endangered plants from park development (Bryce Canyon in Utah), and reducing the impact of feral pigs (Great Smoky Mountains).[67]

Women maintenance supervisors have found ways to work effectively with the men who report to them. At Valley Forge, Betty Diamond gave workers more control over their tasks by having groups be responsible for maintaining their own zones, rather than having individuals report to her for different assignments each day. Before the crew began a new project, she met with them to brainstorm the materials and methods to be used. As maintenance foreman for National Capital Parks-East, Martha Ellis has supervised about forty permanent workers, all but two of them men. A trained horticulturalist, Ellis and her crews have handled landscaping around America's most well-known monuments: the Lincoln, Jefferson, and Vietnam memorials. She has often chosen the maternal role and has done a lot of listening. She also acts decisively when necessary: when she wanted to motivate a tree crew, she grabbed a chain saw and cut down a 30-foot tree without help.[68]

Women's Uniform Issues

The struggle to get a uniform equal to men's paralleled women's efforts to gain equity in jobs in the Park Service. It took nearly two decades before the service's definition of women's public roles would become congruent with the demands of women for the authority in the field that the traditional gray and green uniform would give them.

Women throughout the service complained that the "airline stewardess" uniform, adopted in 1961, gave them lower status. When a man in the standard uniform was on duty with them, the visitor invariably went to him first for information, even when the woman was his supervisor. Visitors sometimes thought women rangers were Girl Scout leaders or nurses. Moreover, the uniforms were impractical: the pressure at places with high visitor use meant that a white blouse would stay clean for only a few hours. Regulation skirts caused particular problems. Some superintendents allowed women to wear green jeans on guided walks, but others insisted on skirts. Visitors at Balcony House at Mesa Verde leave by climbing up a tall ladder: women interpreters on that walk quickly learned to have visitors precede them. In the 1960s, the white-bloused, short-skirted women who staffed the eight information kiosks in the District of Columbia were patronized by being called kiosk kuties, and the first women in the Park Police wore short skirts while on foot patrol.[69]

Most controversial was the Park Service's refusal to allow women to wear a Stetson and a full-sized badge. Although the women rangers at Yellowstone in the

1920s and early 1930s had worn Stetsons and badges, when women were designated
rangers in 1969, the Park Service reduced their legitimacy and authority by continuing to oppose their wearing a Stetson and a full-sized badge. The Stetson was
a powerful symbol of masculinity, not easily shared with women. Women began to
ridicule the pillbox hat by calling it a buffalo chip; others went hatless.[70]

Complaints from women and men in the field about the women's uniform were
so common that the Park Service decided to take action: a task force was appointed
and in June 1970 new women's uniforms were displayed in a highly-publicized
fashion show at Independence. At first, the uniforms unveiled in front of the reflecting pool at the park's magnolia garden seemed to answer some of the complaints:
it was the era of the pant suit, the miniskirt, and the identity crisis and all three were
reflected in the new uniforms. Women were given several choices, all in beige
polyester knit with a white ring around the neck. They included a pant suit with a
collarless jacket, culottes with what the women soon called "go-go boots," a one-
piece dress with a short skirt, a "popover apron" for wives, a work dress, a secretary's zip-front dress, and a beige coat with an orange zip-out lining. A Stetson
with the same shape as the traditional Stetson but made of flimsier material was the
new official women's hat, and an embroidered Park Service arrowhead served as a
badge, but to be worn on the right side, not in the traditional place over the heart.[71]

Because they still viewed women as filling a niche much like that filled by their
wives, Park Service officials were pleased with the results. Director Hartzog praised
women as interpreters and said the uniforms were in tune with contemporary fashion and in keeping with Park Service traditions. The superintendent of National
Capital Region said: "In the past, the difficulty with ladies in uniform was that they
tried to adapt from men's materials and styles." When women later asked why the
new uniform standards did not mention the badge, the chairman of the servicewide
uniform committee replied that the badge was not listed because women were not
to wear it; the badge was to be worn "only by men authorized to wear the Class A
(Basic) dress uniform."[72]

Within the year, complaints came pouring in: the uniforms snagged easily, the
collar showed the dirt, the uniform was limp and pulled apart at the seams, and women
were still not recognized as being in charge. The women's version of the Stetson
was "like cardboard" and was rarely worn. In 1974, another task force changed the
uniform to green polyester with a white turtleneck dickie or a scarf printed with
Park Service arrowheads, to be worn at the neck or knotted in front. Worn
throughout the Bicentennial, some women felt this uniform made them look like
workers in a fast-food chain and they soon dubbed it the "McDonald's uniform."
A small-sized badge or embroidered arrowhead was worn in its proper place.[73]

In the late 1970s, the identity crisis for women in the service ended. Although
equity in jobs was still not achieved, both the service and the women themselves
realized that women could and wanted to perform nontraditional tasks and needed
the authority represented by the standard uniform. A Grand Canyon supervisor
said that the uniform affected women's morale: it prevented them from doing their

work, and it fell apart. Women under him wore green jeans, a regulation gray shirt, and a Stetson.[74]

A spontaneous revolution occurring in parks all over the country resulted in women being authorized to wear the traditional gray and green uniform, Stetson, and badge, but an incident in the Southeast Region may have been the catalyst. Two women seasonal rangers had worn the standard men's uniforms and badges at Yosemite, encouraged by their supervisors. When they were not allowed to wear them at the Everglades, they resigned. Their action was enough to convince Southeast acting regional director William Hendrickson. In 1974, he suggested to the Washington office that the uniform standards be reviewed on the basis of equality. He gave the example of women and men performing the same work at entrance stations but wearing different uniforms, with only men wearing badges. His compromise was that standards should be amended to allow women to wear the traditional uniform "when identification with the male counterpart is necessary" and "when women are performing work equivalent to men who are wearing the traditional uniforms."[75]

Although John Cook, who was in charge of park operations in Washington, feared an antidiscrimination lawsuit, he also remembered pictures of the first women rangers in traditional U.S. Cavalry uniforms. He knew how professional those early women looked, and even though the complaint that reached him emphasized the lack of a badge, he took it one step further. He directed the service to issue "ONE NPS Ranger Uniform for men and women." He recommended the addition of a skirt for women who preferred it. Because of necessary approvals and design problems, the gray and green was not made official until the spring of 1978.[76]

Uniform issues did not end there. When the Park Service appointed Linda Balatti to examine uniform standards and procurement, she faced a basket of correspondence "three-feet high." Throughout the 1970s, women had been through four uniform changes and all parts of the traditional uniform were not immediately available. Frustration reached a peak among the large staff of women rangers at Independence. Eighteen women joined to file a class action complaint against the Park Service demanding the missing pieces, especially a winter parka, the lack of which prevented them from taking overtime assignments at night. They also asked for a regulation maternity uniform. When Joyce Grow ordered one, she was sent a medium man's shirt, she said, with "pockets large enough to cover my whole chest." A Kelly green stretch panel replaced the zipper on the pants. Her associate, Jennifer Gamble, who was also pregnant, embroidered a baby buffalo on her stretch panel.[77]

When women finally did achieve the badge, the Stetson, and the full standard uniform, Carol Kruse, a park superintendent, believed their "whole mental image" changed. The full meaning of their positions as park rangers whose job it was to protect the visitors and the resources of the park came home to them. It not only became easier for a woman to be recognized by the public as the person with authority, but it also helped the uniformed women to accept and use that authority.

It took even longer, however, for visitors to expect to see women rangers on duty than it did the service. When Lana Creer Harris, wearing her new gray and green, was putting out an unattended camp fire at the Grand Canyon, a small voice piped up: "Mamma, look, Smokey the Bear is a girl!"[78]

Women Park Service Rangers: An Assessment

Entering the ranger force gave women their greatest opportunity to pursue nontraditional careers in the Park Service. In just twenty-five years from the time the first women became fully fledged park rangers, the proportion of women rangers rose to nearly 30 percent. The change in women's occupations in the service is striking: in 1970, nearly 70 percent of Park Service women held clerical positions and only 3 percent were park rangers; in the mid-1990s, 28 percent of Park Service women held clerical positions and 19 percent were park rangers. Progress for minority women park rangers, however, was slow. They represented only 13 percent of women rangers and 4 percent of all park rangers.[79]

A breakthrough improving the status and grade level of all park rangers implemented in 1994 positively affected the future of women rangers. In the past, one of the reasons women were able to enter the ranger ranks was that, despite the high quality of people attracted to the job, it was a low-pay position, for both men and women. The Ranger Futures initiative, crafted by members of the Association of National Park Rangers (ANPR) working with OPM, succeeded in raising the status of park rangers. Reflecting the Park Service's core mission—protection *and* use of national parks, it redefined the job as a generalist field position responsible for both protecting a park's natural and cultural resources and educating the public about the value of a park's land, wildlife, vegetation, and cultural groups. The service upgraded the knowledge, skills, and abilities required, including new educational requirements in the natural sciences or cultural history, and removed positions formerly included in the park ranger series that properly belonged in such other areas as biologist, historian, or dispatcher. A special appropriation funded immediate increases in the grades of the more than three thousand individuals who qualified to continue as rangers. Park rangers, who can choose to specialize in resource protection or resource education, can now progress up a career ladder to a GS-9 from a trainee grade of a GS-5 in two years, if they meet the new standards. Rangers selecting protection must earn the basic law enforcement commission.[80]

Women profited from the new definition of park ranger in both a specific and a general way. Women and men will continue to receive exactly the same increases in grade from a GS-5 level up through at least the GS-9 journeyman level. Perhaps most significant are possible long-term effects of the change. By placing an equal value on education and protection, the Park Service took a major step toward reducing the influence of the Park Service's male-dominated military culture. Although women now earn nearly one-quarter of Park Service law enforcement commissions, it is still in the field of interpretation that women have shown their greatest strength. By increasing the value of educating the public, the worth of women's particular skills and experiences has been increased.

There are, however, still several areas that could hinder women's progress toward reaching equity as park rangers. Only 35 percent of newly hired rangers have been women, and the Park Service has been slow to appoint women as park superintendents, one of a ranger's traditional means of advancement. Veterans' preference in hiring and sexual harassment, two issues from the past, could still have an effect. A gifted naturalist who proved herself as a summer seasonal at Isle Royale came in second for a permanent position because a less experienced veteran had to be selected. Single women faced the expectation that they were available for affairs with both unmarried and married men. On the other hand, within ANPR itself, women are fully accepted: many members are Park Service dual career couples and, in 1995, ANPR elected Deanne Adams president, supported by officers and a board of four other women and three men.[81]

Park Service field women worked so hard to gain equity in jobs and uniforms that many of the pioneers accepted what amounted to a male-defined model, adopting the male conception of a park ranger instead of finding their own voices. Over and over again in interviews, field women declared that there was no difference between successful female and male rangers. Some were reluctant to marry, but even more were afraid that having a child would make them be seen as different and hurt their careers. An exception was at Independence in Philadelphia, where a large female ranger force offers an informal support group. An analysis of questionnaires from 536 Park Service women in 1985–86 revealed that, although half of women rangers were married, only one quarter had children. Women in the more traditional administrative and clerical jobs cited having to move from park to park as their most difficult problem, but women rangers most often cited the balance between marriage and career. Individual comments pointed up the conflict. One woman ranger simply said that if "you start a family . . . you have to leave the Park Service." Another said, "I need to establish my own independent career before marriage," and another commented, "I fear I'll stay single because of my career."[82]

Expressing Difference

Even though many pioneer uniformed women believed a male-defined model would bring them the most success, it is when they expressed their difference that they made their greatest contributions. It is important to have women in the field because it enlarges the talent pool from which to draw workers, is more representative of the public, and presents role models to the next generation. Equally important are the differences women bring to the role. Women's socialization as nurturers and carriers of culture, their smaller size, and their experience as outsiders with new perspectives on traditional institutions also contribute to the changes they bring to the Park Service. Women working in protection make it clear that if a woman holds that position, she should perform all the attendant duties, including night road patrol, backcountry patrol, search-and-rescue, and making arrests. But several supervisors believe that women also bring special strengths to law enforcement. As superintendent of Denali, Robert Cunningham found women in protection to have "different sensitivities" from men, making them especially valuable in certain situations. Noting that rangers usually check concession bars late in the evening, he said: "It is not uncommon to send a male through there and wind up with a problem, whereas you can send a female through there and not have a problem [because] the female doesn't provide the same threat."[83]

Supervisors mentioned women's judiciousness and expert use of "voice judo." One male chief ranger said of one of the women on his staff that he "was always amazed at how she could talk people into jail." Jane Marshall's major tool in police work has been her sense of humor. As field commander in the patrol branch of the Park Police in the District of Columbia, one of her main goals was to help the officers she supervised protect themselves from escalating situations by being too macho. Partly a holdover from the time she was a training officer at FLETC, Marshall thinks of her officers as sons and, more recently, daughters, to be developed and protected. Valerie Fernandes's style is similar to Marshall's: "Women don't feel they have to prove themselves in . . . fights," she said. "I don't feel I have to fight with the people who are already engaged in assaulting one another."[84]

Women have also changed the field of interpretation. Few women engage in the old-style interpretation, used by some male rangers in the past, that bordered on entertainment and often began with finding out where people came from. Women interpreters assume visitors are interested in the park's resources and tend to act as educators, usually including a preservation or environmentalist message.[85]

Four women interpreters have received Freeman Tilden Awards for excellence in interpretation; each developed environmental education programs. Sandy Dayhoff shared traditions of the Miccosukee tribe at the Everglades; Carol Spears encouraged visitors to assist in resource management activities at Cuyahoga Valley National Recreation Area in Ohio; Sylvia Flowers developed a discovery lab at the Ocmulgee National Monument's visitor center in Georgia; and Kimberly Valentio brought interpretive programs to an Arctic community in northwest Alaska.[86]

In urban areas, women rangers have reached out to children. At Lowell National Historical Park, Marjorie Hicks developed a Junior Ranger program that involved 450 young people over a five-year period. Not only did students assist with park projects, but their positive attitudes about the park reduced vandalism. The staff at Edgar Allan Poe National Historic Site invited neighborhood children to write and publish poetry in a park magazine and to be trained as Junior Rangers.[87]

Women bring a different point of view to interpretation in battlefield parks. Betty Gentry, retired superintendent at Pea Ridge, an Arkansas Civil War park, explained that most male rangers concentrate on military strategy, but "a woman looks at it in terms of the suffering and the impact upon the community around where the battle took place that men don't always look at." Gentry told visitors to the park's Elkhorn Tavern about the family who lived there and retreated to the basement during the battle. "The troops and the fighting were all around with bullets going through the house," she said. "They brought the wounded in and the blood dripped through into the basement where the family was." Becky Lyons developed a Women in War program at Gettysburg and plays the role of a soldier's wife who served as a nurse. She emphasized the cost of war by describing conditions in a town with 24,000 wounded men and quotes Kate Cumming, a young confederate nurse: "The War is certainly ours as well as that of the men. We cannot fight, so we must take care of those who do." At Appomattox Court House, Cynda Carpenter portrays Mary Hicks, a resident there during the Civil War, to show the profound changes the war brought to the lives of Confederate women both during and after the war.[88]

When Pat Lammers was not allowed to portray a soldier or participate in cannon demonstrations using explosive black powder at Antietam, she researched Civil War history and found that four hundred women had been documented as serving as soldiers in disguise. She sued the Park Service and accepted a compromise that uniformed women could fire a cannon but could not dress as soldiers.[89]

Women interpreters have been instrumental in bringing interpretation of their racial and ethnic cultures to parks. At Yosemite, Julia Parker, a Pomo Indian, continued the basket-weaving tradition begun by Tabuce and Lucy Telles decades before; and at Bighorn Canyon, besides presenting Crow Indian culture in her programs, Theo Dean Hugs, a member of the Crow nation, conducts seminars on Native American issues and serves as a liaison between the Crow people and the park, which borders the Crow reservation.[90]

When Althea Roberson, the first African-American woman ranger at Yosemite, presented the history of African-American park employees, she shared the information that an all-black cavalry unit protected the park at the turn of the century. At Martin Luther King National Historic Site, Barbara Tagger described the strong community of African-American business and professional women on Auburn Avenue near King's birthplace. Rose Fujimori, retired site manager of Puukohola Heiau National Historic Site on the island of Hawaii, developed the park's story by introducing native Hawaiian culture. Fujimori believes visitors would like to hear the park story from a native who "will speak from his/her heart and . . . give a little more cultural experience to a visitor."[91]

Two Park Service interpreters who are disabled have introduced their perspectives to visitors. When she was an interpreter at the White House, Erin Broadbent displayed a sign on the back of her wheelchair that said: "I may not be totally perfect, but parts of me are excellent." Catherine Ingram, who is hearing impaired, demonstrated crafts at the Old Stone House in Georgetown, D.C. At Yosemite, Jennifer Jacobs, a hearing person, developed the deaf services program and interpreted in sign language.[92]

Although there are several parks devoted to a famous woman or to women's history, women interpreters in other historical parks have made special efforts to bring women's history to students. At the Arch, in St. Louis, Barbara Consolo switched tours with a male interpreter when Girl Scouts arrived expecting a tour about women in the West: "It was a great feeling to know they learned something about women's roles." At Boston National Historical Park, Lynne Dubiel developed a Rosie the Riveter talk for the Charlestown Navy Yard. Schoolchildren board a destroyer and learn about the eight thousand women who did "men's work" during World War II. Vivien Rose, historian at Women's Rights National Historical Park, believes that when you add women's history "you completely change the perspective on the past." A recent survey found that at least one hundred national parks include women's history in their programs.[93]

In natural parks, women interpreters found historic women to portray in living history presentations. Lucia Perillo was one of the women to play the role of Fay Fuller, the first woman to climb Mount Rainier, using Fuller's own words. At Denali, Jane Anderson chose the role of crusty pioneer and miner Fanny Quigley, and at Sequoia, rangers presented Elizabeth Grant White, who explored the Sierras with her husband in the early 1900s.[94]

Women often present a fresh point of view in solving park problems. Robert Kerr, a former regional director, thinks women are more impatient with decisions based on the past than men. Sandra Key explained that women do not value tradition because they were not part of it. When Key was superintendent at Bryce Canyon, she wanted to reroute a trail that disrupted a rare plant colony and the men on her staff opposed her. Robert Kerr also believes that women are more apt to work with the landscape, rather than to dominate it. A woman seasonal convinced him not to hire his usual contractor with big equipment to remove trees from a campground; instead, he allowed a park crew, more sensitive to the environment, to do the work and preserve the trees. Lisa Lee Smith made a similar point: a wall on a trail is not completed until "mother nature . . . put[s] her finishing touch" on it with "grass and wild flowers growing in between the rocks or lizards living among our work."[95]

Some women have been more willing to speak out to preserve the environment than the traditional male ranger. While serving as a seasonal ranger in the North Cascades, Edie Dillon received a letter of commendation and a letter of reprimand in the same mail. She was reprimanded after the press reported that she dressed as an outhouse at a staff costume party to protest recent Interior Department decisions she believed would endanger the natural resources in parks; she was commended for saving the life of a neighbor who slipped on the ice and broke her hip on a very cold night. Dillon heard her cry out, dragged her inside on a blanket, radioed for help, and kept the woman warm with her own body heat until help came.[96]

The culture of the Park Service was constructed by white men who were anxious to preserve their hegemony and their masculinity. Although the service as a whole was not aggressive in seeking diversity, training opportunities and a new emphasis on education in parks helped women achieve opportunities for field positions.[97] The strength of the male-oriented culture, however, influenced the first Park Service field women to seek a male-defined model and not value their own different voices. As women moved up in the hierarchy, becoming park superintendents and administrators and branching out into such new professional positions as historic preservation and resource managers, they began to search for their own voices, often unconsciously, and to find their own places.

Annie Barrett Boucher found her place on the Yosemite trail crew: "I stop work sometimes and look down at the valley, and across at Sentinel Dome and Glacier Point, and think how insignificant I am in this wilderness. But then I realize that I do have a place and a significance in it. If people were not here would these mountains and waterfalls be really here? It is the experiencing of our world that truly makes reality. . . . So I'm helping to make the experience both possible and real. After me others can come, to love it as John Muir did. . . . And as I do."[98]

Equity Issues for Managers and Support Staff

Early in the spring of 1971, Carol Martin, a young administrative officer at Custer Battlefield, received an unexpected call from Frank Kowski, director of the Park Service's Southwest Region. "I've been keeping an eye on you over the years," he said. "You've been doing a good job. I have a vacancy at Tuzigoot for a superintendent. How would you like to be superintendent of a park?" Martin remembered being "flabbergasted."[1]

That she might become a park superintendent had never occurred to Martin; nor had it occurred to virtually any woman then in the Park Service: a woman superintendent was outside nearly everyone's expectations. Superintendencies are the service's most coveted positions; one woman superintendent compared the holders of these posts to the Knights of the Round Table.[2] Before the thrust for equal opportunity, the Park Service promoted few women to line positions with direct authority over personnel. Male administrators were more comfortable with women as secretaries than as colleagues. Although men depended on women to keep their offices running and to accomplish a myriad of bureaucratic tasks, they did not easily share their authority.

The new women superintendents were joined by the first women in Park Service professional positions, including newly created ones in the preservation of cultural and natural resources in national parks. Women began to enter such fields as landscape architecture and engineering, virtually closed to them before. In the 1990s, three decades of filling the Park Service job pipeline with qualified women for high-level posts began to have an effect. Most important, for the women who found their voices and urged the service fully to honor its mission, there was also the hope that they would be heard.

Three women did achieve high level positions early in the Park Service's history, including the woman who created the agency's first public affairs department and two park superintendents, but their work did not set a precedent for women who followed. Even though Isabelle Story became a legend for her creative and dedicated efforts in promoting the service's mission to the public, by the time she retired, her department was largely taken over by men. Nor was a precedent set by the first two women superintendents because they were selected outside traditional channels. President Franklin D. Roosevelt appointed Gertrude Cooper to Vanderbilt Mansion National Historic Site by executive order, and the Adams family recommended Wilhelmina Harris to oversee Adams National Historic Site. The move in 1971 to promote women park superintendents from the ranks of Park Service personnel was indeed a break with tradition.

Women Superintendents from the Ranks

Carol Martin's appointment represented the cautious beginnings of the new policy to name women as park managers. In many ways, she was a logical choice. Six years before, her husband, Phillip, drowned in a canoeing accident at the Glen Canyon National Recreation Area, where he was a ranger, leaving her with two preschool boys. Because she enjoyed the lifestyle of the service, she decided to bring up her boys in the parks. She began as a clerk-typist at the Tuzigoot Pueblo ruins in the Verde Valley of central Arizona before transferring to Custer Battlefield, where she was promoted to administrative officer. As the widow of a ranger, Martin qualified as Park Service family; her honors in Spanish in college followed by a Fulbright scholarship in Austria proved her ability; and her five years in Park Service administration provided her with the necessary experience.[3]

Like the other regional directors, Frank Kowski was under pressure from Park Service Director George Hartzog; he, in turn, was urged by the secretaries of the interior under President Nixon to promote women and minorities to management positions. Hartzog announced his goal of appointing five women to field management positions at a special Equal Employment Opportunity (later EO) workshop in Washington early in 1971. Kowski, director of the Albright Training Center when the first women rangers entered in 1964, was quick to respond to the challenge.[4]

Other regions also followed Hartzog's directive. The Southeast Region chose historian Kathleen Dilonardo to take charge of Fort Caroline, a reconstructed fort near Jacksonville, Florida. An Albright graduate who developed a successful interpretive program at Fort Pulaski in Georgia, Dilonardo, at twenty-six, became the youngest superintendent. After four years, Independence chose her as its chief of interpretation. The Midwest Region advanced administrative clerk Elizabeth Disrude to superintendent at Perry's Victory, a memorial on an island in Lake Erie, after she trained three park managers who stayed only briefly. Lorraine Mintzmyer, who had risen from secretary to chief of programming and budgeting in the Midwest Region, became manager of Herbert Hoover National Historic Site. Outside Washington, D.C., at Wolf Trap Farm Park, a center for the performing arts, manager Claire St. Jacques brought experience in managing the arts to the job.[5]

The Western Region director, Howard Chapman, developed a plan to train and promote women to superintendencies with Margaret Wilson, regional chief of employee relations and Federal Woman's Program coordinator. The plan was to use the John Muir home in Martinez, California, to train women superintendents. He selected Doris Omundson, chief naturalist at Muir Woods, a coastal redwoods park, as manager of the Muir home. After she acquired experience, Chapman transferred her to Cabrillo National Monument on San Diego's Point Loma. Phyllis Shaw succeeded Omundson at the Muir home. Chapman also selected Mike Hackett, management assistant at Yosemite Valley, for a training position at Fort Point in San Francisco's Presidio. Three years later she was ready for a superintendency in Arizona, combining the Wupatki pueblo with Sunset Crater, a volcanic cinder cone from the same era.[6]

Women Administrators: Public Affairs

The proportion of women administrators to men in the Park Service before Carol Martin's appointment is graphically illustrated in a series of photographs taken at superintendents' conferences. In 1965, Superintendent Wilhelmina Harris is a lone woman, marked by her white blouse, standing with 221 men. The 1941 photograph includes two women, standing with sixty-six men: Superintendent Gertrude Cooper and Isabelle Story, director of public affairs. Before that time, Story was the only woman in any group photograph of administrators; in 1934, for example, she stood in the center of the first row, between the director and the associate director, surrounded by seventy-eight men.[7]

More than any other woman, Isabelle Story personified the Park Service. She dedicated all but six of her forty-four years of government service to building positive attitudes toward national parks. She came into the service at its beginning, in 1916, as secretary to Robert Marshall of the U.S. Geological Survey, who was on loan to Stephen T. Mather during the period when the Park Service was waiting for Congress to make the agency official. When Marshall returned to the survey, Story stayed with the service as secretary to Horace Albright, who was then acting director. Albright, well known for utilizing talent, was so busy and so anxious to publicize the parks that he turned over some of his correspondence to Story and depended on her to help him compile the first annual reports. When he was still expected to produce them after he became superintendent of Yellowstone in 1919, he arranged for Story to work at the park for six weeks to finish the task.

Possessing a talent for writing and an enthusiasm for the parks, Story, who began in her late twenties, soon produced numerous press releases and articles promoting the parks; she took on such special assignments as serving as secretary at park superintendents' conferences and writing speeches for Interior Department officials. She revised Robert Sterling Yard's *National Parks Portfolio* and edited park information publications. In 1934, Story attained the prestigious title of editor-in-chief and expanded her staff, aided by emergency employment funds available during the Depression. She instituted a series of thirty-nine radio programs on the historic parks acquired in the 1933 reorganization and hired Dorothea Lewis to write the scripts. Mary Ryan took over as editor of the employees' *Newsletter*.[8]

Story also developed a network of professional women outside the Park Service.

An active member of the Women's National Press Club, she attended Eleanor Roosevelt's press conferences and was elected to the Society of Women Geographers. Her correspondence shows her, for example, encouraging Mary Rolfe to write her books about national parks; one way she promoted the parks was through talks and communications to women's groups.[9]

Although she dedicated her work to the preservation of the parks, Story once said: "I've tried to follow a middle-of-the-road conservation policy, that is bridging the gap between the so-called long haired conservationists and those who would destroy our scenic beauty solely for financial gain." Much of Story's information was learned first hand: she traveled extensively in the parks. In 1933, she covered 3,716 miles of "roads and non-roads" to see the Southwest monuments with Boss Pinkley and to meet the custodians and their wives.[10]

Isabelle Story's career was radically changed by World War II. During the war, the service transferred its central office to Chicago and reduced Story's staff. Although she went as chief of information, she continued to use the title of editor-in-chief. After the war, when the central office returned to Washington, Director Newton Drury brought in a male chief of information over Story. She kept her grade but was given the title of assistant chief of information. Although there is no record of her response, her correspondence left a clue. She did not use her new title, but continued to sign her letters as editor-in-chief. For the next fifty years, only Priscilla Baker, in the late 1970s, and Joan Anzelmo, in the mid-1990s, broke the tradition of a male chief of public affairs.

When Isabelle Story retired in 1955, the Department of the Interior chose her to be the first Park Service woman to receive the Distinguished Service Award, the department's highest award, citing her for "initiative and ingenuity in acquainting the people" with national parks. The Albright Training Center named a class after her, the first woman they chose; the date was 1969, the year before she died at the age of eighty-one.[11]

Story did demonstrate, however, the skills women could contribute in her field. A decade later, Laurabel Story convinced network producers to use national park topics and developed a "Discovery 67" television series on the parks with the American Broadcasting Company. When the *Newsletter* and the monthly *Courier* needed an editor in 1969, the public affairs office selected Loretta DeLozier [Neumann], who combined the journals into one publication, the *Courier*. Each successive editor, all women, upgraded the magazine until it was discontinued in 1994. Naomi Hunt followed DeLozier in 1975; Mary Maruca took over a decade later.[12]

When Joan Anzelmo became chief of public affairs in 1994, seven of the then ten regional public affairs officers were women. But the nature of the job had changed. Public affairs officers had to be ready to respond to media in times of crisis. Anzelmo trained by serving as chief information officer for Yellowstone. During the 1988 fires, she coordinated a staff of thirty-four to answer the media and the public and serve as fire information officers in fire camps. During the crisis, Anzelmo's office was open eighteen hours a day, seven days a week, and responded to more than three thousand media requests by phone or in person. Another woman who rose to the occasion in an emergency was Sandra Alley, who, in 1981, had to face five hundred reporters during a takeover of the Washington Monument by a man threatening to blow it up. The public affairs officer of the National Capital Region, Alley faced the press again the next year when the Park Service led rescue efforts after a plane crash.[13]

The First Two Women Superintendents

Because of the unusual nature of the appointments of the first two women superintendents, Gertrude Cooper and Wilhelmina Harris, they were not only seen as different but also treated differently from their male peers. In turn, each woman either ignored or successfully opposed Park Service directives they disagreed with. President Roosevelt had several reasons for choosing Gertrude Cooper to be superintendent of Vanderbilt Mansion in 1940. As neighbors of the Roosevelts in a summer colony at Canada's Campobello Island, the Coopers were involved with one of Roosevelt's favorite projects: harnessing the power of the extreme tides of Passamaquoddy Bay. When the Canadian government withdrew its support, the Coopers lost their investment, and when Gertrude Cooper was widowed in 1938, she needed a job. Roosevelt was anxious to preserve the mansion because the property was close to his Hyde Park estate, where both sit high above the Hudson River. The niece of Frederick Vanderbilt, the last owner, offered the property to the government after Vanderbilt's death and Roosevelt pressured the Interior Department to accept it.

Gertrude Cooper believed that a woman should be in charge of the mansion, because, as she said, "the government wants it to appear as a house, not as a museum . . . to show how people of that time and wealth lived." Cooper developed guided tours of the first two floors and refused to put up barriers in the rooms, because she wanted visitors to feel like guests in a home. She worked with CCC men to repair the house, its facilities, and grounds. Her problems ranged from the lack of potable water and replacing a system that discharged raw sewage into the river, to preparing housing on the third floor for forty-five men hired to protect Roosevelt during the war. Roosevelt took a great interest in the mansion; whenever Cooper had a problem, she communicated directly with the president himself. She resigned soon after his death in 1945.[14]

Wilhelmina Harris, the only woman superintendent for the twenty-one years between 1950 and 1971, was the superintendent with the longest period of service in one park when, in 1987, she retired after thirty-seven years. When the Adams Memorial Society decided to give the building in Quincy, Massachusetts, that was home to four generations of the Adams family, including two presidents, to the care of the Park Service, Harris was the logical person to take charge. For seven summers before her marriage, she lived in the house as secretary to Brooks Adams and his wife, the last Adamses to summer there. The family suggested that Harris be hired to arrange the furnishings and objects and interpret the house. Recently widowed, with three sons in college, Harris became a historical aide in 1948; she was made superintendent two years later.

Like Cooper, Harris believed that a woman should be in charge of a historic house, so visitors would feel as if they were entering a family home. Her major goal, she said, was "to fight the trends" in historical interpretation. Backed by members of the Adams family, she opposed a plan to turn the house into a period house and allowed it to reflect all four generations. She removed recorded talks designed to take the place of an interpreter and insisted that visitors be accompanied by a guide as they moved through the house. She resisted efforts to put a superintendent over her and decided not to wear a uniform. Harris instituted a lecture series, published a guide to the house, and documented its furnishings in nine volumes. The Park Service came to respect her as a woman with an independent mind and allowed her to continue as superintendent until she was ninety-one, although the day-to-day work was carried on by Marianne Peak, who succeeded her. The Interior Department recognized Harris with the Distinguished Service Award in 1970. Her "standard of excellence," the citation said, was "unsurpassed by that of any historic house on exhibition in the National Park Service."[15]

Women Managers of Park Concessions

The tradition of women managing hotels, restaurants, and other concessions in parks, pioneered by such families as the Currys in Yosemite, continued into modern times. It was suitable that Evelyn Hill was the force behind the Statue of Liberty concession for fifty years because her life reflected the promise of the symbol she worked to promote. She immigrated to New York from Poland at the age of twenty in 1921 and spoke five languages. She met her future husband, Aaron, when he was in the army, stationed at Fort Wood on Bedloe's Island, now Liberty Island. After his discharge in 1930, they lived on the island while he operated the fort's post exchange and a stand for selling souvenirs. After Aaron died, in 1942, Evelyn ran the greatly expanded concession, which by then included a restaurant, snack bar, and shop, where the Hills sold gifts and souvenirs they designed. Later run by their son Jim, who was born on the island, the operation grew to a staff of forty permanent employees and one hundred and twenty seasonals.[16]

In New Mexico, another long-time woman concessioner was Evelyn Frey, who ran Frijoles Lodge and a gift shop at Bandelier National Monument for a half a century. When Evelyn and her husband, George, arrived at the canyon in 1925, they traveled by pack mule down a steep Indian trail. They kept cows and chickens, raised vegetables, planted fruit trees, and harvested ice for refrigeration. The pioneering days ended after the canyon became part of the National Park System in 1932: CCC men built a road, lodge, dining room, twenty cabins, and a gift shop. After a divorce, Evelyn continued as manager. During World War II, soldiers from the Manhattan Project at nearby Los Alamos were quartered in the lodge and prominent scientists were guests. Evelyn closed the lodge in 1976 but ran the gift shop

until she became a volunteer, still sharing her appreciation of the canyon with visitors.[17]

At Mount Rushmore National Memorial in the Black Hills of South Dakota,
Kay Riordan Steuerwald operated Mountain Company, Inc., for more than forty
years. It grew from a small concession in Gutzon Borglum's old studio to new buildings handling two million visitors a year. Employees are trained to answer visitors'
questions about the giant presidential heads that Borglum sculpted, and college students can earn course credits by working in administration and attending seminars.
A gallery of American Indian crafts provides a sales outlet for the indigenous people. In 1983, the Rocky Mountain Region recognized Steuerwald's service, naming her an Honorary Park Ranger.[18]

Contemporary Women Park Superintendents

Although the women park managers the Park Service selected from the 1970s
to the mid-1990s were, on the whole, just as qualified as the men they chose, it appears that women were often selected because they were in the right place at the
right time. The ups and downs of the number of women appointed to superintendencies has depended greatly on the amount of support from the top administration in the Park Service and Interior Department.

Between 1971 and 1980, the number of women superintendents gradually rose
to twenty-three, about 9 percent of all superintendents, with a jump from about 6
percent soon after the first Park Service Women's Conference in 1979. In that year,
Director William Whalen named women to half of the new superintendencies. He
also selected Lorraine Mintzmyer, by then superintendent of Buffalo National River,
to be the first woman director of one of the service's ten administrative regions.
Beginning in the Southwest Region, Mintzmyer transferred to the Rocky Mountain Region in 1980, where for more than ten years she served as regional director—the only woman at that level. Mintzmyer's appointment was particularly significant, because Rocky Mountain oversees many of the service's premier parks,
including Yellowstone, Glacier, Zion, and Bryce.

Beginning with the administration of Interior Secretary James Watt in 1981, the
situation changed radically. Of thirty new appointments to superintendencies in
1981, only two went to women. This pattern continued for eight years. By then,
retirements had reduced the number of women superintendents to 7 percent.[19]

The downward trend ended with a new administration in 1989. At a public
meeting, where he cut the ribbon opening an exhibit about women's history in the
parks, Interior Secretary Manuel Lujan was asked about the low number of women
park superintendents. He replied: "Come back a year from now and see the
changes that have been made." Within a year, the number of women superintendents nearly doubled, to 12 percent, but it leveled off until 1995 when a new administration pushed it to 16 percent or forty-three women; three were African
Americans and one was the first Hispanic-American women park manager.[20]

One difference between women and men superintendents is the route they take to the superintendency. A study of women superintendents concluded in 1994 showed that of all women who had been superintendents, nearly half came from administrative or professional ranks, and only half from the park ranger job series, the traditional route for male superintendents. Part of the reason for the different pattern is that more women in administration have attained the higher grades necessary for promotion to park manager. Of the women who had been park rangers first, all but a few had attended the Albright ranger training course. Without these alternative routes, the Park Service would have been even slower to promote women and minorities to park superintendencies.[21]

Georgia Ellard, the first African-American woman superintendent, came from administration. When she began as a GS-3 clerk-typist, she was the only person of color in the office of National Capital Parks. After she gained experience at the Design Center and in personnel, the National Capital Region chose her to be administrative officer at the new National Visitor Center in Union Station, prior to the Bicentennial. Promoted to manager, she trained many women who later became managers themselves. After the roof of Union Station literally began to fall down, she had to close the visitor center. When the region selected her as superintendent of Rock Creek Park in the District of Columbia, she had then served more than twenty-five years in the Park Service. A pioneer for both women and African Americans, Ellard noted that many women, including her three daughters, told her that she was a role model for them.[22]

As regions began to select more women park managers, another pattern became clear. They selected women for small or medium-sized historical parks. Of all women who had been superintendents in the 1994 study, three-quarters served in historical parks, and one-third of those were military parks. In 1995, when Barbara J. Griffin took on the challenge of becoming Yosemite's first women superintendent, only five women managed large natural parks: also Karen Wade, Great Smoky Mountains National Park; Maria Burks, Cape Cod National Seashore; Anne Castellina, Kenai Fjords, Alaska; and Judy Cordova, Colorado National Monument.

Another area of difference between women and men superintendents is in the ability to move from park to park as a way of earning higher grades. Once a woman becomes a park manager, she often finds it difficult to be selected for another park. Of the nearly seventy-five women who had been superintendents at the time of the 1994 study, only six moved three times and sixteen moved twice. Although more than half of the women superintendents in 1994 had served less than four years, most of the early superintendents retired in their first positions, even though they applied for transfers to higher-graded parks. The proportion of women park managers to men varied by region. Because of the number of historic parks and the commitment of its directors, the former North Atlantic Region was a leader in appointing women park managers, reaching one-third by 1995. The Park Service recently designated four parks as slots for managers who qualify for the Senior Executive Service. Two were filled by women—Griffin at Yosemite and Martha Aikens at Independence.[23]

Women superintendents, as well as introducing new points of view, have also brought enormous amounts of energy to their positions. They bring an immediacy to local environmental issues on both a large and small scale. During the cleanup of the 1989 Exxon oil spill in Alaska, Ann Castellina, at Kenai Fjords, chaired a multiagency coordinating group, including ten local, state, and federal agencies, that met daily to discuss the cleanup and, speaking with one voice, advise Exxon. The group became permanent, ready to handle other emergencies. Park staff and residents felt such a sense of loss, Castellina said, that managing "the people resources" was as important as managing "the physical resources."[24]

Chewing gum was a serious environmental problem at the Statue of Liberty. Nobody paid attention to the cost of cleaning it up until Ann Belkov became superintendent in 1991. She found that three maintenance employees did nothing else but remove gum, amounting to six hundred pounds a year. Visitors responded to the explanation of the problem and since that time leave their gum in specially marked trash cans as they step off the boat.[25]

Women superintendents have been responsible for coordinating the production of park brochures, exhibits, and new walks and talks. One women superintendent was on hand to implement a radical change in the interpretation of Native Americans. Barbara Booher, of Cherokee and Ute descent, enlarged the American Indian story at Custer Battlefield to support the change of the park name to Little Bighorn Battlefield. The new park brochure emphasized the "clash of cultures," with the pictures of Sioux leader Sitting Bull and Lt. Col. George Custer equal in size.[26]

Before such organizations as the Kiwanis and Rotary Clubs allowed women to join their groups, women park managers found equally effective ways to develop community networks. Jo Ann Kyral was the first woman superintendent at Fort Smith in Arkansas, famous as a frontier federal court and fort. Since community support was essential before she could implement the park's general management plan, Kyral made her contacts through the Chamber of Commerce, United Way, the public schools, and with regular appearances on live talk shows and local television. Using her facility at cutting through paperwork, learned as an administrative officer, she won a park improvement grant to restore the fort's parade ground. The project involved removing an old Coca Cola bottling plant, closing two city streets, and installing a one-hundred-foot Douglas fir as the flagstaff. When she supervised the repointing of the brick and repair of the roofs, she rigged up and wore a hard hat in order to check on the contractors' work. She also found funding for a curator and published a new park brochure. In addition to handling the crew and actors filming part of the TV miniseries, "The Blue and the Grey," Kyral was the first woman on the annual rodeo committee and joined members to lead the grand entry into the arena after only one riding lesson.[27]

The price of becoming a pioneer woman superintendent in the Park Service was the acceptance of a male-defined model on an even greater scale than the pioneer women park rangers. From the beginning, women superintendents were different from men superintendents: men were not only expected to be married but to bring the unpaid services of their wives to the post. The pattern set by women superintendents in the early 1970s was continued by many of the women who followed. The majority were either single, or the person on whom the family depended for its financial support. In the 1994 study, of all the women who had been park superintendents, two-thirds were single, including women who were divorced or widowed. Nearly one-third of those were also single parents. Changes were on the horizon. As wives of park superintendents undertook their own careers, either inside or outside the Park Service, the traditional services performed by wives were assumed by park personnel—and there was a twist on the perception that if a woman wanted to be a park ranger she had to marry one. Three women who received their first training in the role of volunteer wives eventually became superintendents themselves: they developed independent careers after being divorced from park managers.[28]

Modern Women Administrators

Having women park superintendents in the field is relatively new to the Park Service, although women administrators have always worked behind the scenes. In 1970, just as the push for equal opportunity for women was taking hold, less than 20 percent of Park Service women held administrative positions; 70 percent held clerical positions. The clerical and secretarial workers in the service were virtually all women. Womens' grades in 1970 reflected their positions. Including women in public affairs as well as administrators, women held less than 5 percent of all GS-11 positions; only 2 percent of women held a GS-11, compared with 10 percent of men. Women were even more absent from the highest ranks: women held 2 percent of all positions of GS-12 and over; only 1.5 percent of women held a grade of GS-12 and over, compared with 18.5 percent of men. Women's overall median grade was a GS-5.[29]

Besides public affairs, the areas with high-graded women were personnel, concessions management, and the park position of administrative officer, the person responsible for implementing park activities according to federal guidelines. The first woman administrator to reach the position of an assistant director of the Park Service was Imogene LaCovey, in 1974. LaCovey, a specialist in concessions management, entered the Park Service as a clerk-typist in the mid-1930s and took time out to raise her family before returning in 1953. She played a large role in getting relations with concessioners "back on track," as she described it, after World War II. She recognized the complexity of a field that reflects the issue at the core of the Park Service: the tension between use and preservation of the parks, as she worked to keep a balance between service to the public and protection of a park's resources. When she retired, in 1974, she became the second woman in the Park Service to receive the Distinguished Service Award.[30]

The first women to achieve the highest level positions in the Washington directorate came from outside the Park Service. The only woman to be deputy director was Mary Lou Grier, appointed by James Watt in 1982 and serving for three years. She supported the administration's policy of using available funding to improve facilities in existing parks rather than adding new areas to the National Park System, carrying out the policy by administering the Park Restoration and Improvement Program, through which parks applied for funding. The first woman associate director for administration was Nancy Garrett, selected by Director William Whalen in 1978 from another agency. Although she was committed to women's advancement in the service, she was not seen as holding her position legitimately by the rank and file of the Park Service, partly because she did not have "green blood"—Park Service lingo for persons who worked their way up through the ranks, and she left after two years.[31]

During the two decades of the 1970s and the 1980s, Park Service women began to achieve a more equitable share of administrative positions and gain a larger proportion of higher grades. An extensive work-force profile prepared for the Women's Conference in 1991 revealed that women held 45 percent of all administrative positions at that time. Overall, 8 percent of women held a grade of GS-11, compared with 9 percent of men; 9.5 percent of women held grades of a GS-12 or over, compared with 19 percent of men. Women held 30 percent of all GS-11 positions and 20 percent of all positions of GS-12 and over. In 1995, six women reached the Senior Executive Service, the service's highest level.[32]

Three women have held the post of director of one of the Park Service's regions, which were reorganized in the mid-1990s, reducing the total from ten to seven. Each director is a member of the Senior Executive Service. The Rocky Mountain regional director, Lorraine Mintzmyer, retired in 1992, six months after Director James Ridenour transferred her to the Mid-Atlantic Region. He then chose Marie Rust as director of the North Atlantic Region. The following year, Roger Kennedy, new Park Service director, chose Barbara J. Griffin as head of the Mid-Atlantic Region. Transferring from another federal agency, in 1974, Rust set up the first personnel office in the new North Atlantic Region. As an associate and then deputy regional director, Rust was an advocate for equal opportunity and employee development. Her youth in Brooklyn, a few blocks from what became Gateway National Recreation Area, made her particularly sensitive to a region with urban parks. Griffin began as a program and budget analyst in the Southeast regional office and gained significant field experience as manager of Castillo de San Marcos National Monument in Florida, assistant superintendent at Yosemite, and associate regional director of the Western Region. In 1995, after Griffin became superintendent of Yosemite, Rust was the only woman to head a regional office, and only one woman was chosen to head one of the ten new support offices.[33]

In 1994, Director Roger Kennedy appointed women to three of five associate director positions in the Park Service Washington directorate. Each rose through the ranks, demonstrating that nearly twenty-five years of filling the pipeline with qualified women was having an effect. Mary Bradford, a former Interior Department attorney who began her career as a seasonal ranger/historian in 1967, became associate director for administration, after serving as deputy of the Southwest Region. Maureen Finnerty, first woman president of the Association of National Park Rangers, became associate director for park operations and education after being superintendent of Olympic National Park, and Katherine Stevenson was promoted to associate director for cultural resources from a position as associate regional director for planning and resource preservation in the Mid-Atlantic Region. Stevenson had previously been chief of cultural resources for the Rocky Mountain Region.[34]

Minority women, in the mid-1990s, were still underrepresented in administrative positions. Although 18 percent of all women administrators were minorities (half of those African Americans), the total represented only 6 percent of all administrators. The first African-American woman in the Park Service to receive the Interior Department's Distinguished Service Award, in 1994, was Mary E. Jackson, a special assistant to the Chief of Personnel, for her skill in planning the automation of personnel systems.[35]

The Woman Administrator/Secretary Nexus

Although individual women in the Park Service had achieved notable advances after 1970, the majority of women in the 1991 profile still held a grade of GS-5. The traditional explanation for women's low overall average grade, that women have not been employed in the Park Service as long as men, offers only a partial explanation. In the 1991 profile, nearly 35 percent of women had worked for the Park Service between ten and nineteen years, compared with 50 percent of men; those in the service for more than twenty years broke down to 15 percent of women and 25 percent of men. Moreover, when a comparison was made between men and women in all administrative positions, including personnel, a traditional field for women, men held an average of nearly two grades higher than women with the same length of service. On the other hand, in a field being taken over by women, that of administrative officer, men held less than one grade higher than women with the same length of service.[36]

A more likely explanation for women's low overall grade is the issue of pay equity in the clerical/secretarial field. A study in 1995 illustrates the problem. The study found that while 87 percent of Park Service clerical and secretarial staff were women, 94 percent of the maintenance staff were men; 28 percent of Park Service women were in clerical occupations, compared with 26 percent of men in maintenance under a wage grade scale. Although the skills, training, education, and value to the Park Service of a superintendent's secretary, who takes a great deal of responsibility for the park and its clerical staff, is at least as much as, if not more than, the work of a mason or painter, she was paid less than he was. When figured by actual salary, the average for wage grade men was 17 percent higher than the average salary of women clerical and technical (administrative and budgetary assistants) workers.[37]

The disparity between women clerical workers and male maintenance workers could be addressed by using pay equity standards to determine a person's grade by reclassifying clerical work. The issue is one economists call "comparable worth," a plan that supports equal pay for work of comparable value. It rejects the premise of lower wages for jobs primarily held by women based on the assumption that women can be paid less because their salaries supplement a husband's or father's income.[38] Comments from clerical women revealed they were aware of the issue. One woman said: "A WG-3 laborer can make almost twice as much as I and I am doing important clerical and budget functions"; others stated: "If men were secretaries, the jobs would be higher paying" and "We need pay equity so much!"[39]

Many women who were classified as secretaries actually performed administrative work. Irma Buchholz, a widow, retired in 1991 as secretary to the superintendent of Sequoia–Kings Canyon National Park after working for fifteen different superintendents over a period of forty-eight years. When new managers arrived, she quietly introduced them to the special needs of the park and its personnel. She also kept the superintendent's office running between superintendencies, sometimes for a period of several months. Yet because she was classified as a secretary, the highest level she could achieve was a GS-7. Although she enjoyed her job so much that she said she sat in a "magic chair," she also believed she was underpaid. She said she was "in a channel, not a rut," and advised young women not to stay in the channel.

If Buchholz had moved into administration by becoming an administrative or personnel officer, she could have achieved a higher grade. Yet, as Barbara Teaster, former secretary to the superintendent of Great Smoky Mountains National Park, said, in the past, women felt that becoming the superintendent's secretary was the most desirable job for a woman in a park. The service appreciated Buchholz's work to such a degree that in 1983 she became the first Park Service secretary to receive the Distinguished Service Award, but nothing could be done to raise her grade.[40]

Irma Buchholz is an example of the loyalty shown to the Park Service, its values and its people, by both long-term secretaries and women who moved into administration from the clerical ranks. Terry Wood devoted more than a decade of her retirement to building up the membership and programs of the Park Service Employees and Alumni Association, serving as its executive secretary and president, because she wanted to preserve the sense of family among Park Service people. Her entire career, from her first job, just out of high school, as a clerk at Castillo de San Marcos National Monument in Florida to being a legislative affairs specialist in the Washington office, was dedicated to the Park Service.[41]

Before opportunities outside the clerical field opened up for women, several women worked as park secretaries because, like many men, their wanderlust attracted them to national parks; but unlike men, they knew that working as a secretary was their only route. Alvina Zimmerman, secretary to a succession of regional directors in the Southwest before the late 1960s, traveled in parks all over the country before choosing to work in San Francisco and Santa Fe. Her rule, she said, was "to take any transfer you can get."[42]

Using pay equity systems does not eliminate the necessity for training and upward mobility programs that help women move up into management. Beginning in the early 1970s, the Departmental Management Program trained fourteen Park Service women, including two of the three women who have been regional directors and five park managers. By the mid-1990s, twenty-four Park Service women, including five park managers, had participated in the Women's Executive Leadership Program, originating in OPM in 1987.[43]

Upward mobility plans help women reach middle management. They are designed to solve a two-part problem women face in the federal system: a person cannot skip a GS grade in a promotion, yet many women clustered in the lower grades cannot apply for middle management positions. Using an upward mobility plan, the selecting official lists a vacancy at a grade below its rated level, but states that in a specific length of time, and often with training, the position will be raised to a higher grade or, even two. Cecila Matic, a Hispanic American, for example, began as a clerk-typist in the Southwest Region. After she became a secretary in the Public Affairs Office, they recognized her talents and offered her an upward mobility position, progressing from a GS-7 to a GS-9 to a GS-11 public affairs officer. The new ranger career ladder also expedited the movement of those women rangers who previously were stalled at a GS-5 level.[44]

The life patterns of women in administrative and secretarial positions reflect the more traditional nature of their jobs and personal choices. In the 1985 survey of 536 Park Service women, 78 percent of clerical workers and 63 percent of administrators were married, with virtually the same numbers reporting children. Many women in administrative or clerical positions were wives of rangers or maintenance men who chose to follow their husband's moves and find clerical work in a park when they could, often starting at the bottom with each move. The problem they found most frustrating was the practice of being able to advance only by rating for a position in a different park. While virtually all the women surveyed cited the mission of the Park Service as a job satisfaction, women in clerical and administrative positions also mentioned security, a reason rarely mentioned by women rangers and superintendents. It appears that the price for conforming to the expectation of the male-defined culture of the Park Service—that women on the job serve as assistants to men—was low pay and slow advancement.[45]

Toward Equity I: Positions in History and Historic Preservation

Perhaps the area where Park Service women made the most progress between the early 1970s and the 1991 work-force study was in professional positions in the social sciences—fields with strong educational requirements, including public history, historic preservation, archeology, and curatorship. Because these pioneering professional women brought their expertise to the Park Service from the outside, they also contributed an independent point of view and added a pool of talent to Park Service operations. Highly motivated to preserve cultural resources in national parks, they reflected a sensitivity to social history and the details that bring life to parks. Although, in the 1985 survey of Park Service women's attitudes, nearly half of them cited the mission of the Park Service as a key motivating factor, almost as many mentioned the challenge of working in their own disciplines.[46]

The inclusion of women in professional positions in the Park Service was influenced by external as well as internal factors. The increased interest in historic preservation generated by the negative effect of urban renewal in the 1950s and the positive response to the nation's bicentennial in 1976 expanded the Park Service's need for historians and architectural historians. The National Historic Preservation Act of 1966 gave the Park Service the task of determining which state and local properties, in addition to sites of national significance, were worth listing in the National Register of Historic Places. The supply of trained women historians also increased, both because of new opportunities in public history and because of efforts by women themselves to increase the status and numbers of women historians. In 1970, only 13 percent of Park Service historians were women, clustered at a GS-7, indicating a probable role as interpreters. The 1991 study revealed that 38 percent were women and the average grades for women and men historians were the same when the factor of length-of-service was included.[47]

On the surface, the experiences of Nan Rickey and Penny Batchelder, who pioneered in public history and historic preservation in the Park Service, appear to be quite different, but because they were tuned in to the details of daily life in historic buildings, they shared some basic insights about public history. The work of Nan Rickey, former chief of cultural resources for a regional team at the service's design center in Denver, was broad-based; she served as an interpretive planner for more than eighty parks during her twenty-five years with the service. She worked with imagination, always with the goal of bringing park buildings to life. When she designed the furnishings plan for the officers' quarters at Fort Laramie, she pored over officers' wives' diaries until she felt a personal identification with life in an isolated fort on the Wyoming frontier. Her plans revealed how army families kept up personal standards and combatted feelings of isolation by furnishing their quarters in up-to-date Victorian fashion and trying—unsuccessfully—to grow roses.[48]

During her thirty-eight years at Independence, Penny Batchelder tried to keep her colleagues focused on how people actually lived in a building so they would avoid presenting the historic scene as sterile and rigid. She still saw a need to bring the Assembly Room at Independence Hall "down to the level where it really was" from the present "high level of attractiveness." She would add stoves to the Assembly Room during the winter months and remove and clean them in the summer, the way they did in 1776, and would not have installed air conditioning. Like Rickey, Batchelder enjoyed uncovering mysteries from the past. After apprenticing with a paintings conservator, she pioneered in analyzing building paint. She cut through layers with a surgeon's scalpel to find evidence for dating parts of a building, a method now standard in such preservation work. Although Independence Hall was her major focus, Batchelder prepared historic structure reports for more than a dozen other buildings.[49]

Many women historians have been involved with saving buildings by preparing or evaluating nominations to the National Register. Carolyn Pitts looked for buildings so prominent they were missed by others. She nominated the Empire State Building and the Metropolitan Museum of Art. As Rocky Mountain regional historian, Mary Culpin devoted much of her time to "putting out fires." When a historic building was in danger of development or removal, the staff moved quickly to document it for evaluation. Culpin also used her research skills to protect natural resources. When she documented the history of efforts to maintain a minimum flow of the Yampa River through Dinosaur National Monument for a case before the Colorado Water Court, she demonstrated that historical research was a tool that could be used to preserve park lands.[50]

Melody Webb, who was the first woman regional historian in the Southwest, broadened her definition of historic preservation to include living cultures. During five previous years in Alaska, she directed the Alaskan Native Historic Sites program and conducted cultural resource studies for several of Alaska's proposed parks, often traveling by foot and canoe. Drawing on her Alaskan experience, she championed a controversial Park Service philosophy that allowed living cultures to exist and even evolve in park landscapes. She supported the managers at Buffalo National River, who developed a plan to sell back the land originally acquired for the park in order to bring back people to the river valley and thereby "maintain the historic scene." She brought her organizational skills to park administration, first as superintendent of Lyndon B. Johnson National Historical Park, a place showing, she said, "how a man was shaped by his environment," and next as assistant superintendent of Grand Teton National Park.[51]

Mary Culpin was one of several Park Service historians who found stories of women's lives in natural parks. At Florissant Fossil Beds she researched the 1878 homestead of a single woman, Adeline Hornbeck, and in Bighorn Canyon she documented writer Carolyn Lockhart's ranch. The first Park Service historian publicly to voice the necessity for including women's history in park programs was Heather Huyck, an interpretive specialist in Washington in the early 1980s. She advocated using Park Service sites to interpret women's history in the broader historical community by presenting papers at national meetings.[52]

Toward Equity II: Archeologists

The Park Service's tradition of hiring women archeologists began with Mesa Verde in the 1930s, when women served as archeological interpreters during the summer season. Although the Park Service discouraged women from serving in field positions after the mid-1930s until the early 1970s, two women archeologists bridged the old and new eras: Sallie Harris, whose first assignment was at Montezuma Castle in 1934, and Jean Pinkley, who was associated with Mesa Verde for twenty-five years.

Throughout the 1930s, Sallie Harris worked as a volunteer partner of her husband, Jim Brewer, in the Southwest monuments. During the war, and after her divorce from Brewer, she began her formal Park Service career as a ranger at Casa Grande. Despite the many ups and downs of her career, during which she held various titles at fluctuating grade levels, Harris contributed her archeological skills to seven Southwestern monuments. Before she retired in 1967 as a museum specialist in the Southwest Archeological Center, she published results of a site survey of the ruins in the north rim of Walnut Canyon, test trenching at the Tumacacori mission, and salvage excavations at Wupatki.[53]

Jean Pinkley survived the era when Park Service archeology was virtually all male by remaining at Mesa Verde for the majority of her career. The war widow of Boss Pinkley's son, Jean Pinkley was accepted as Park Service family and allowed to demonstrate her competence. In turn, she looked upon Mesa Verde as a substitute for a family, and she at times almost seemed to take on the role of her lost husband. At Mesa Verde, by 1960 Jean Pinkley had risen from museum assistant to supervisory archeologist and chief of interpretation. She trained large numbers of male interpreters, particularly in the summer, but did not reopen the field to women. Tall and slender, she assumed what could be called a paternal role, calling the seasonals who reported to her "boys," wearing slacks, and pitching in to help whenever needed.

In 1966, Jean Pinkley took on a new challenge, the excavation and stabilization of the ruins of an eighteenth-century Spanish mission at Pecos National Monument, near Santa Fe. Beneath the ruins, she discovered the foundations of a seventeenth-century church, probably burned during the 1680 Pueblo rebellion. She developed such a sense of place at the site that one day she reported seeing a friar looking at her. The vision frightened the local Native American workers, who had to be persuaded to return: they believed it proved that the monument was cursed. Pinkley continued her work at Pecos until her death in 1969.[54]

Between 1958 and 1964, the remarkable Wetherill Mesa Project at Mesa Verde provided opportunities for several women archeologists and museum aides. Partially funded by the National Geographic Society, the project was the largest in the country. In addition to its research goals, the project hoped to relieve the pressure of visitor use by opening up more cliff dwellings. It benefited from talented husband-and-wife teams. Carolyn Osborne, wife of Douglas Osborne, the director of the archeological work, was a specialist in preindustrial textiles and analyzed twines and yarns discovered on the project and in the Mesa Verde Museum. She replicated twines made of yucca, using methods that would have been available to the Anasazis. Park wives, hired and trained by the project, cleaned and organized artifacts.[55]

By 1970, there were only two women in archeology in the Park Service, and each was at an entry level. Although women had a long tradition in Southwest archeology, men dominated professional organizations. By the early 1980s, one-third of doctorates in the field were awarded to women, but because university teaching was difficult to find, women archeologists looked for careers or contract work in federal and state agencies. Legislation helped increase the demand for archeological surveys. The 1960 Reservoir Salvage Act that gave the Interior Department the responsibility for collecting archeological data endangered by dam construction was amended in 1974 to include all federally funded projects.[56]

Women who contracted with the Park Service to undertake surveys engaged in original archeological research. When the Western Archeological and Conservation Center (WACC) was excavating for its new building in Tucson, for example, the staff discovered evidence of an 1882 ranch house. Carol Martin, WACC chief, hired Nancy Curriden, who literally worked with her crew in front of bulldozers in over 100-degree heat to save artifacts and document the homestead. She used a combination of approaches to reconstruct daily life in the ranch: oral history from a descendent, contextual history about Tucson's growth, and artifacts, mostly glass and ceramic, showing an expanding economic network.[57]

The first two women designated as archeologists in the new era of the late 1960s were Marion Riggs [Durham] and Karen Lindquist. Lindquist was an interpreter at Mesa Verde and Tonto; Riggs, an interpreter at Walnut Canyon, was also an active field archeologist. She helped George Fischer start the service's underwater archeological program. After earning their scuba diving certificates, Riggs and Fischer did a test dive to a Spanish galleon off the Florida keys before trying to find artifacts in the murky waters of Montezuma Well. Riggs eventually moved to administration after finding it difficult to be accepted as a professional by her park manager.[58]

The second woman in underwater archeology was Toni Carrell, who entered the Park Service in 1976 as part of the inundation study research team while still a graduate student. Combining her love of scuba diving with her interest in archeology and anthropology, Carrell joined the Submerged Cultural Resources Unit. Although she began her career on teams studying prehistoric sites submerged by reservoirs and as the Southwest Region's dive officer, she developed a specialty in documenting shipwrecks. She combined her skills in diving, underwater photography, video, and mapping to help make an inventory of resources the Park Service did not know were there. In her first ten years with the service, she logged over six hundred dives on archeological projects. She was a supervisory archeologist on teams that documented more than a dozen Lake Superior shipwrecks off the Apostle Islands and Isle Royale, and as a team member surveyed three wrecks near California's Point Reyes. Carrell's model for evaluating shipwrecks became the standard for National Register nominations. After fifteen years, Carrell left to work on a Ph.D., leaving the service with no women in her field.[59]

Among the Park Service's first women with a Ph.D. in archeology was Michele Aubry, the first woman supervisory archeologist in Washington's interagency program, and Adrienne Anderson, who became the first regional archeologist when the Rocky Mountain Region selected her. In addition to advising federal agencies on archeological issues, Michele Aubry prepared testimony for Congress, preventing the army, for example, from issuing a dredging permit that would have destroyed two Civil War shipwrecks. During Adrienne Anderson's five years in the Midwest Archeological Center, she pioneered in archeology of the historic period, where she felt she had the most freedom, because her male supervisor respected historic less than prehistoric archeology. Anderson's style is to consult parks about what they need and let them frame the questions, rather than telling them what to do. When she worked on Golden Spike's cultural resources plan, she was interested in learning the culture of railroad building. She and the park historian wanted to answer questions about life in end-of-track towns. They located sites of blacksmith shops, boarding houses, whorehouses, and tents. By lining up the hills in a period photograph with the actual hills, many sites were immediately apparent.[60]

Both prehistoric and contemporary Native American culture are valued by Park Service women in archeology. As part of an interdisciplinary team, Ann Johnson helped determine the chemical "fingerprint" of Yellowstone's Obsidian Cliff and prepare a National Historic Landmark nomination for the cliff. Native Americans used the obsidian for tools eleven thousand years ago; its fingerprint helps document prehistoric trade networks.[61] Because Grand Canyon archeologist Janet Balsom recognizes the "living cultures" of the Native American people of the region who "call the Grand Canyon sacred," she believes in setting up dialogues with American Indian communities. Communications with tribes revealed that the canyon and the Colorado River are central to each tribes' creation story and rituals. Identifying places and resources sacred to the tribes calls for "care to make sure these things are not disturbed," she explains. For Balsom, the "living nature of the culture keeps it vibrant and exciting."[62]

Archeology in the Park Service has only recently opened up to women. Because the service did not hire an equitable number of women archeologists until the 1980s, men dominated the higher grades in the 1991 study of the work force: only a little more than one-quarter of archeologists were women. Women archeologists found various ways of coping with the male domination of the field. Some, like Jean Pinkley, chose the androgynous route; others pioneered in new fields, notably historic archeology; and others left the service or the field. The scope of published reports of archeological projects by women hired only on contract suggests the amount of talent lost to the service in the past.[63]

Toward Equity III: Curators and Exhibit Specialists

Once historians and archeologists uncover documents and artifacts, parks need to preserve and display them. Women have a long tradition in the Park Service as museum curators, nearly equal with men in numbers by 1991. Although women pioneered in the related area of exhibit specialist, men still dominated the field, many employed at the Harpers Ferry Center, where exhibits are produced for parks throughout the country. In 1993, however, Mary Herber was named chief of a new Division of Exhibits, combining planning, design, and production.[64]

Despite technical assistance from the Museum Division, until the last decade, preserved and cataloged museum collections in individual parks depended largely on a park's priorities. Responsibility for the collection was often a collateral duty of naturalists or rangers. With the appointment in 1980 of Chief Curator Ann Hitchcock, the first woman in that position, efforts to attack the problem of uncataloged and unpreserved objects were stepped up. Hitchcock worked with regional and park curators to revise the service's Museum Handbook and to assist parks in defining and managing their collections. Her staff offered technical assistance, training, and supplies. By 1993, 16 million out of an estimated 25 million objects were included in the National Catalog's database.[65]

The first full-time women curator, Vera Craig, who began as a museum assistant at Morristown National Historical Park in 1947, was largely self taught. During her ten years at Morristown, she became a specialist in cataloging and preserving the park's Revolutionary War collection. An initiative to professionalize records in park museums, begun during Mission 66, brought Craig to Washington in 1957 at the time the service appointed the first regional curators. Working with them, Craig standardized a classification system for museum records. Earlier, she prepared a housekeeping manual for historic houses. Her attitude, that she "never said 'no' to any Park Service project," led her to learn to clean rifles, muskets, and cannons as well as to become a furnishing and fabric specialist. Among her projects were cataloging the furnishings in the White House and creating the service's first furnishing plan—at Andrew Johnson National Historic Site.[66]

The first woman to become a regional curator, Elizabeth Albro, was one of the initial group of five regional curators hired in 1958. Albro was encouraged by Ralph Lewis, chief of the Museum Branch, to bring her experience to the Park Service. She spent 85 percent of her time on the road, training the all-male cadre of historians and naturalists who had curatorial work as a collateral duty. Although the men were not used to having a woman offer technical assistance, they accepted it, she said, because she "worked alongside of them" rather than "tell[ing] them how to do it." Before Albro retired, she took on the massive project of curating the collection at Thomas Edison's home and laboratory in New Jersey, cataloging and selecting for salvage nearly 30,000 items, still only one-third of the collection.[67]

Before Mission 66 began, in 1956, the majority of park exhibits were produced on site. One of Mission 66's goals was to offer parks exhibits that had been produced centrally. Hired as an exhibit artist in 1956, Marilyn Wandrus was one of two women (in a group of thirty people) who produced exhibits in the Washington Museum Laboratory. She painted exhibits until exhibit styles changed to using photographs, when she became a specialist in graphics research. One of her most meaningful projects was finding still photographs of Eleanor Roosevelt for the film produced by Corinne Erlebach for the Eleanor Roosevelt National Historic Site.[68]

As a jill of all trades, Jean Rodeck Swearingen combined creating exhibits with curatorial work. Because her father was director of the University of Colorado Museum, she grew up in the museum world, making exhibits while still in high school. After working as an exhibit artist in the Western Museum Laboratory, she left to become a park wife and volunteer. When she became a single parent, she returned to museum work at Yellowstone as a GS-3 clerk-typist with museum duties. She worked up to Southwest regional curator, becoming the second woman to achieve that rank, and rehabilitated exhibits in fifty-six of the region's fifty-seven areas. As Alaska's first regional curator, she was challenged to "keep fragile things intact" and preserve "bits and pieces of the nation." She likes "coming into a mess and leaving it in order" and thinks women are better equipped than men for that task.[69]

Part of the work of a curator is conservation of objects. As a pioneer conservator for the Park Service, Janet Stone broke new ground in solving problems of how to preserve some of the service's most valued possessions. During her later career, she specialized in paper conservation, attacking the problem of conserving the large collection of blueprints of landscape architect Frederick Law Olmsted at the Olmsted Historic Site near Boston. Among earlier artifacts she conserved were beaded American Indian bags and baskets, early profiles of the Yellowstone mountains, paintings of birds by Louis Agassiz Fuertes, a charcoal of Frederick Douglass on newsprint, and Theodore Roosevelt's mounted birds.[70]

Curators face complex contemporary issues. An area of particular controversy is that of the storage and return of human remains. As a member of the Santa Clara Pueblo, Virginia Salazar, regional curator for the Southwest and former curator at Bandelier National Monument, brings a special sensitivity to her post. Her perspective was broadened even more when she received a research grant from the International Partnership Among Museums program. Paired with a Canadian research partner, Salazar investigated relationships between museums and native peoples on the Canadian Northwest Coast and introduced her partner to similar issues in the Southwest. Both concluded that it was essential for museums to establish meaningful connections with the community of native people.[71]

In the few national parks devoted to the fine arts, curatorial work is the central issue. For this reason, Sarah Olson left her post as chief of historic furnishings for the superintendency of Weir Farm, a new site in Connecticut that incorporated the home and studio of impressionist artist J. Alden Weir. Olson, who apprenticed at Boston's Museum of Fine Arts, was especially qualified for her new responsibilities of directing the rehabilitation of the buildings and grounds, curating paintings and furnishings, and the development of an interpretive program.[72]

Curatorial work continues to be a challenge in the Park Service. Although the function has been shuffled around on the organizational chart, the enormity of the task is ongoing. Curators see their field as central to the Park Service's mission: they rate the preservation of the park's objects on the same continuum as that of the protection of its major resources. Chief Curator Ann Hitchcock believes that park collections, particularly in natural history, can provide baseline data that will reveal to future researchers the impact of the industrial society on the country's resources. By bringing in women historians, archeologists, and curators, the Park Service not only expanded its talent pool but brought in a new group ready to give voice to the diversity of lifestyles and cultures represented in national parks by paying close attention to the details that reveal the differences.[73]

Moving into Science and Resource Management

Women's entrance into positions requiring a scientific background is dependent partly on the pool of women available for those jobs, partly on opportunities offered by the service itself. In 1970, there were virtually no women in scientific fields in the Park Service. In the 1991 study, only 20 percent of the service's biologists were women, an underrepresentation of women graduating from college in biology, and only a handful of women worked in the physical sciences. On the other hand, when the Park Service revitalized the field of natural resource management, it encouraged women to enter the new training programs.[74]

A strong devotion to the stewardship of park landscapes has been the common bond among women in science. This tradition goes back to Herma Albertson Baggley and Pauline Patraw, pioneer park naturalists with graduate training. The service's first woman Ph.D. in wildlife biology was Mary Meagher, who, because there were no jobs for women scientists, began her extensive career at Yellowstone in 1959 as a museum curator. Known particularly for her research on the park's bison, she also kept records over time of the habitat and status of elk, bear, and bighorn sheep. Combined with her photographs of park landscapes, taken periodically from the same viewpoint, her work provides essential baseline data for input into decisions about managing the park's wildlife and landscapes. Because of her knowledge, commitment, and outspoken manner, Meagher comes as close to serving as the conscience of the park as anyone could. She served as an expert witness in controversies ranging from brucellosis and bison management to poaching and was an early spokesperson for closing campgrounds located in prime bear habitat, including Fishing Bridge.[75]

In addition to her field research, conducted at first alone and without a two-way radio, Meagher has also served on the front line. A part of bear management teams, she helped move problem bears and analyze the events and causes of bear attacks on humans. Among her activities during the fires of 1988 were monitoring bison and convincing fire crews not to destroy park resources by using heavy-handed fire-fighting methods. One night during the fire she returned to her cabin and witnessed her "very own fire storm." She said, "I stayed 'til the fire was between the barn and the cabin and running to cut the road, then it was time to go. . . . Barn and cabin survived, root cellar and outhouse burned out."[76]

In a variety of research projects, women scientists express their commitment to enlarging the knowledge of park resources that is essential before action can be taken or testimony given. They hope the accumulation of their findings will have an impact beyond park boundaries. After years of fighting for protection of air quality in parks in the Pacific Northwest, Shirley Clark's efforts culminated in an agreement by a large power plant west of Mt. Rainier to meet EPA emissions standards. At the Grand Canyon, Christine Shaver's study of air quality helped limit emissions from a nearby power plant. When Susan Bratton set up the Uplands Field Research Laboratory in Great Smoky Mountains National Park, it was the first step in viewing the park as a biosphere reserve. The lab monitored acid rain, compiled a computerized botanical database, surveyed backcountry water quality, analyzed trail and campsite damage, and studied fire ecology. She disseminated the findings through training programs and publications. At Mt. Rainier, botanist Regina Rochefort not only monitors threatened plant species but also directs a long-term revegetation project.[77]

Several women park scientists are particularly committed to the preservation of specific species of wildlife, past and present. The service's only woman paleontologist, Ann Schaffer Elder, adds to knowledge about how dinosaurs lived. In the summer she excavates dinosaur bones in the quarry at Colorado's Dinosaur National Monument and follows this with laboratory analysis and preservation of the fossils in the winter. Kate Kendall conducted grizzly bear habitat research for an interagency team out of Glacier National Park. For a study of bear food, she looked for a link between fluctuations in the availability of such food as whitebark pine nuts and berries and annual bear activity. Based at Padre Island National Seashore, near the Texas/Mexican border, Donna Shaver managed the project to restore Kemp's ridley sea turtle, an endangered species, to the Gulf of New Mexico. Participants collected eggs, incubated them, and released hatchlings, experimentally imprinted, to Padre Island.[78]

Donna Shaver is one of forty-five women who completed the Natural Resource Management Trainee Program between 1982 and 1993. The multidisciplinary program trains women and men with scientific backgrounds in the application of scientific methods and data to the management of natural resources in parks. Trainees study such topics as the management of wildlife, vegetation, fisheries, fire, pests, air and water resources, environmental policy and law, budget, and interpersonal relations. About one-third of the trainees in the first six classes were women. Before the program, fewer than 1 percent of Park Service employees worked full time on resource management. The graduates' new network has begun to have a positive impact on both the parks and opportunities for women.[79]

Katherine Jope, who was in the first resource management class, went to her successive posts as resource management specialist for the Pacific Northwest and Mid-Atlantic regions from Katmai National Park and Preserve in Alaska. As the Alaskan park's first full-time resource manager, she developed both a natural and cultural management program. She not only defined projects but also found funding and personnel for them. They gathered baseline data on the parks' natural resources, restored its historic trails and cabins, and developed a plan to allow visitors to observe grizzly bears fishing in a stream. Guiding her is the belief that "resources can't be sacrificed for today's uses." Echoing the views of early women park visitors, she said: "Parks are places where you experience wonder, and preserving that opportunity is our job."[80]

The network includes Judith Hazen Connery and Sue Consolo. At Maine's Acadia National Park, Connery developed a plan to reduce loose strife, an exotic plant that displaces native species. Consolo helped reintroduce the swift fox, a threatened species and a nocturnal hunter, to Badlands National Park in South Dakota. After long, nighttime hours of searching, she and a ranger spotted the foxes, but that was only the beginning of their work. It took four months to trap a whole family. After they moved them eighty miles to a designated park wilderness area with acres of prairie-dog towns, they penned them in yards with artificial dens for a month before releasing them in the park.[81]

That the overlapping of natural and cultural resources management can make preservation issues complex is demonstrated in the work of Nora Mitchell, manager of the Olmstead Center for Landscape Preservation, a partnership between the Park Service and the Arnold Arboretum of Harvard, located in Boston. After studying the conservation of "heritage landscapes" in England while on a sabbatical funded through the Horace M. Albright Employee Development Fund, Mitchell recommended that the Park Service develop policies for conserving historic landscapes, including associated historic plant material. Mitchell believes that certain plants, slated for removal because they were introduced and are not native, should be preserved because they reflect the cultural history of a landscape. Preserving varieties of plants and trees no longer widely cultivated, such as a nineteenth-century apple, she explains, also contributes to the conservation of biological diversity.[82]

The woman who has made the greatest contribution to networking scientific practices in the service is Jean Matthews, editor of *Park Science* from 1980 to 1994. A former speechwriter for the Interior Department, Matthews wrote the first five conservation yearbooks and prepared environmental education materials for schools. After a year of editing *Pacific Park Science* for the Pacific Northwest, Matthews responded to requests to publish it nationally. Each issue contains articles by park personnel on science and resource management studies and practices. The journal's goal is to help preserve park resources by encouraging the incorporation of scientific information into park management.[83]

Women in science and resource management play the role of double pioneers, as scientists and as women. Some of the newer principles in resource management are controversial; for example, the fire policies that received national coverage during the 1988 Yellowstone fires. Because resource management was the province of park rangers in the past, resource managers who are women do not always find it easy to convince traditional park rangers that certain resource management practices are necessary. Charisse Sydoriak, a fire management officer, is an example of a woman who deals with controversy. She has succeeded in convincing several park managers of the need to reduce hazardous underbrush with a prescribed burn or to let natural fires burn out.[84]

The women resource managers represent a new wave of women in the field. Well qualified academically, they bring a high level of enthusiasm and energy to their positions and support the Park Service initiative to increase scientific research in the parks. On the personal side, however, a difference between the men and women resource manager trainees noted from the beginning is that most of the women have been single and most of the men married. Some of the single women meet their generative needs by rehabilitating wildlife and plants. Others among them say they do not want to settle for a single life. As some of them married, dual-career issues, unresolved by the service, resulted in the loss, at least temporarily, of a few of these valuable trainees.[85]

Project Managers in Landscape Design and Engineering

Fields with a strong male tradition, like civil engineering, were still resistant to change in the 1991 work-force study. Less than 10 percent of Park Service engineers were women, reflecting the slow growth of the numbers of women in the field nationally. In contrast is women's rise to 30 percent of Park Service landscape architects in the past ten years, reflecting a national shift. Often engaged in projects to develop national parks for public use, women landscape architects and engineers share a goal of mitigating intrusions into the parks. Like women scientists and resource managers, they see as their primary goal the protection of park landscapes.[86]

When Laura Wilson became the first woman landscape architect in the Park Service, in 1957, she entered a man's world: contractors would not allow a woman to supervise their work. Some of the male students in her classes had chosen the field because they had failed in architecture or engineering, whereas for the women, landscape architecture was first choice. Women brought a sense of design and a sensitivity to the integrity of a site. Wilson's goal was to work "a transition between the man-made and the natural." Her challenge was to "provide for visitor access without destroying the area." In her own mind, her most memorable project was at Cabrillo National Monument, where visitors look out at San Diego Harbor. There, Wilson's attention to details made a difference. She noticed that the architect's design of the visitor center made it difficult for a visitor to view the sea through the windows. By having the floor lowered, excavating 30 inches more, she solved the problem.[87]

The service's second woman landscape architect had an unusual assignment. To all intents and purposes, Kathryn Simons [Cochrane] became Lady Bird Johnson's personal landscape architect in her beautification program for the District of Columbia in the mid-1960s. Johnson raised $2.5 million from private sources and kept Simons so busy that the design office detailed a team and a secretary to work with her. The only woman in her classes at Pennsylvania State University, Simons was the first woman landscape architect in the Eastern Office of Design and Construction, beginning in 1960. Her first job was to landscape the grounds around a new visitor center in the Great Smokies. Her superiors were reluctant to have her supervise the project's installation, but she prevailed and her supervisory style was so accepted by the team of sixteen local men that they gave her a handcrafted stool when they finished. Simons also respected the historic integrity of a site; she convinced planners to reroute a highway crossing Burnside's Bridge at Antietam battlefield.

Soon after she transferred to the National Capital Region in 1964, Simons began to specialize in designing plantings for small parks. For nearly three years she was deeply involved in carrying out Lady Bird Johnson's projects. When Mary Lasker, chair of the Committee for a More Beautiful Capital, donated ten thousand azaleas and other plants for Pennsylvania Avenue, Simons had to meet a deadline. In the month of April 1965 alone, Simons and her team designed sixteen spaces that also included play areas and benches, as well as flowers, shrubs, and trees. When Johnson moved her projects into low-income neighborhoods, where she hoped to develop community pride, Simons followed and developed beautification plans for housing projects and schools. One of Simons's largest neighborhood projects was Watts Branch Linear Park, thirty-five acres in Northeast D.C. In all, more than one hundred city sites received some attention.[88]

One of the landscape architects in the Beautification Task Force was Darwina Neal, who entered the Park Service in 1965 and became Chief of Design Services for the National Capital Region in 1989. Neal influenced not only practices in the Park Service but also in the American Society of Landscape Architects (ASLA). The ASLA elected her to be president in 1983–84, the first woman, following thirty-five men. Earlier she served as chair of the ASLA Task Force on Women in Landscape Architecture, established to learn whether or not women in the profession were being treated on an equal footing with men. Published in 1973 in the *ASLA Bulletin,* the survey paved the way for the women who followed. By then, nearly half the students in some landscape architecture classes were women. The report called for a major change in the acceptance of women. The survey, answered by 50 percent of ASLA women members, documented discrimination ranging from lower salaries and unfair advancement policies to the assumption that women would also do clerical work and were unsuited for field work or supervision. It would still be ten years before the Park Service would begin to hire equitable numbers of women landscape architects, and in 1991 women's promotion rates still lagged behind men's.[89]

Darwina Neal's long service in the National Capital Region brought a pragmatic attitude to her work. "What *appears* to be the 'best,' 'flashiest' design . . . is *no good,*" she emphasized, "unless it can be *constructed, used,* and *maintained* at a realistic level of maintenance." She is committed to the integration of natural and cultural elements in a design. In Meridian Hill Park, a formal, designed historic landscape in the city, she recommended that original plant materials be used unless they proved to be susceptible to pollution and disease. But in Rock Creek Park she advised planting native or local species. At the presidents' retreat at Camp David, she planted native trees and shrubs, eliminating exotics like spruce, to enhance the natural qualities of Camp David as a true retreat. Her favorite project is the Lyndon Baines Johnson Memorial Grove, for which she coordinated the design and construction. The seventeen-acre grove is within Lady Bird Johnson Park, across the Potomac River from the Tidal Basin. Dedicated in 1974 and still in good condition, the grove meets Neal's criteria of the practicality of postconstruction evaluation, design, and maintenance.[90]

To Eleanore Williams, landscape design in large Western parks is as essential as it is in a city. Williams, supervisory landscape architect at Yellowstone, had a prime opportunity to put her ideas into practice during the 1988 fires. She worked with the fire lines, taking only two half-days off in four months, to protect the future regeneration of the landscape. She showed firefighters how to remove top soil when digging trenches in order to preserve roots and seeds. During the year before the fire, Williams had developed a bank of seeds, hand collected from indigenous plants. After the fire, the seeds were essential in the rehabilitation of thirty miles of bulldozer-line and five hundred miles of hand-line. When the Fishing Bridge campground was removed, her crews restored the natural scene by seeding and planting whitebark pines. Her long-term project is to restore dignity to the park's roads and public areas by making signs, guard rails, fencing, tables, and benches meet standards of uniformity in construction and appearance.[91]

The crews that women landscape architects and civil engineers supervise are primarily men, and most of the women met resistance to their authority from the crews and contractors because they were women. Describing her method of working with male crews, Nancy Ward, roads and trails engineer at Yellowstone, said, "I don't play Mr. Know-it-all." When Kim Titus was the engineer in charge of buildings and utilities at Yellowstone, she supervised men in carpentry, plumbing, and electricity. She learned to ask questions, admire skills, and find out why a worker used a certain method to accomplish a task before she suggested changes. Williams, Ward, and Titus all reported to Yellowstone's chief of maintenance, Tim Hudson, a man whom they all found supportive.[92]

One of the first women civil engineers working out of the Denver Service Center, Titus moved to Yosemite where she supervised the building of a treatment plant for waste water, a visitor overlook at Glacier Point, and phase one of the project to move employees out of the park to El Portal. When the projects ran into trouble, and they always did, she tried to resolve the problem on the spot, sometimes reworking the plans or specifications. Titus found she was more successful when she identified herself as a woman. When she married, she felt a new respect from the men, probably, she thought, because there was no longer any question among them about whether or not she would make a good date, and they began to see her more in the role of coworker.[93]

Titus's career issues point up actions the Park Service could take if it expects to retain women in technical fields where experienced women are scarce. After nearly ten years with the Park Service, in 1990 Titus moved on to the Forest Service, finding greater opportunities there. Two issues made her leave: one was that she remained a GS-11 for eight years, despite her growing proficiency and the increasing complexity of her projects; the other, following the birth of her son, was the denial of her request for leave (without pay) until he was four months old, the age at which the Yosemite Day Care Center would accept him. The service also lost Tammy Gorden Scholten, after ten years the longest serving woman civil engineer at the Denver Service Center, to the Bureau of Reclamation over a dual-career issue: the Park Service failed to offer her a different position when she moved to a new area because her husband was transferred. Scholten spent six years as a project supervisor at Sequoia/Kings Canyon, where she supervised construction projects connected with moving the buildings and utilities out of the sequoia groves at Giant Forest to Wuksachi, one mile south of Lodgepole in the high country. Among her projects were a sewage treatment plant and a fire station.[94]

Women civil engineers are examples of the new wave of Park Service women in technology ready to tackle unexpected events. As a coop student, Scholten supervised the installation of nineteen concrete-vault toilets at Yellowstone and learned to run a BobCat back hoe. When she backed up in soft fill, she dumped the Bob-Cat and herself into one of the vaults and came up smiling. When a snowmobile she was driving packed with 400 pounds of supplies went over a 150-foot bank at Yellowstone, she called for a gas winch; it took more than three hours for her and her companions to inch it up to the trail, supplies and people still intact.[95]

Although Kathleen Gavan trained as a landscape architect, her experience as a planner out of the Denver Service Center and background in engineering made her eligible to be project supervisor of the $3,000,000 rehabilitation of the Boott Mill in Lowell National Historical Park, an old five-story brick mill with 100,000 square feet of space. While she supervised the first phase, which included roughing in utilities and elevators and rehabilitating the structure, the architectural and engineering firm was designing the second phase and making constant changes. The old building also produced surprises. Despite the daily pressures of the assignment and her reputation as a stickler for quality, Gavan lasted three years on the assignment. She found construction particularly satisfying: she liked to see things being built, whereas in planning she rarely saw results. Like other women entering male-dominated fields, Gavan believes that a woman has to be better than men in comparable positions before she will be respected.[96]

Park Service women are relative newcomers in most scientific and technical fields. They bring a willingness to listen but are also ready to buck the status quo and look for new solutions to old problems. They contributed a sense of scale and a pragmatism lacking in grandiose projects sometimes planned to enhance the reputation of the designer, not the resource. When park resources were at stake, women were also willing to speak out.

Finding A Voice

In April 1992, Lorraine Mintzmyer, the highest ranking woman in the Park Service and former director of the Rocky Mountain Region, a position she held for more than ten years, retired from the service after thirty-two years. Less than four years before, the Interior Department had rewarded her with its highest honor, the Distinguished Service Award, making her only the fifth woman in the Park Service ever to receive the award.[97] Her decision to retire followed several months of protest against what she believed was the subversion of the Yellowstone "vision plan" by mining and timber interests who had lobbied Interior Department officials.

The previous September, she joined John Mumma, Forest Service regional forester for the northern Rockies, to tell her story before the House Subcommittee on Civil Service. Mintzmyer and Mumma were members of a committee that released a draft of a plan spelling out ways to conserve the Yellowstone ecosystem by involving lands surrounding the park. Called *Vision for the Future: A Framework for Coordination in the Yellowstone Area,* the report was originally sixty pages long. Mintzmyer stated that in October 1990, Scott Sewell, then the Interior Department's deputy assistant secretary for fish and wildlife and parks, told her the document would have to be completely rewritten. She testified that her meeting with Sewell followed a secret meeting between Sewell, Senator Alan Simpson of Wyoming, and others who opposed the report. When it was published in June 1991, she said, the report was watered down to ten pages, the word *vision* removed, and the "position on almost all major issues reversed." At the same time, both Mintzmyer and Mumma were transferred out of the Rocky Mountain region. Mumma retired and Mintzmyer accepted her transfer to the Mid-Atlantic Region, but she stayed only six months.[98]

After years of speaking for the Park Service, Mintzmyer had found her own voice. The month after she resigned, she addressed the annual meeting of the Greater Yellowstone Coalition, organized to protect the ecosystems of Yellowstone and its surrounding territory. "I have made many speeches in my career," she said, "but to the best of my recollection, this is *my* first speech. It is certainly the first time in over a third of a century that someone has asked me for my *personal* thoughts." She went on to spell out the dangers to Yellowstone from mining, energy, timber, and grazing interests. "There is simply too much taking. The takers have obtained help to take just a little more than the system can absorb." She received a standing ovation at the end of her talk. Some critics believed she should have spoken earlier, but it was the political interference with the Yellowstone "vision plan," combined with her removal from the arena, that radicalized her. A few months later, Mintzmyer went on national television with her message, appearing on NBC's *Dateline.* She reaffirmed her concerns, saying, "Someone, somewhere, sometime had to stand up. . . . You can't do these sorts of things in isolation, in closed meetings." She concluded: "Wouldn't it be a tragedy if because we didn't pay attention and raise the specter . . . that tomorrow or fifty years from now it [Yellowstone] is no longer here?"[99]

Mintzmyer joined a long line of women whose passion was protecting the living land in national parks, like the Sierra Club women who fought alongside John

Muir to save Yosemite's Hetch Hetchy Valley, Minerva Hamilton Hoyt, who preserved the desert at Joshua Tree, and Rosalie Edge, who battled timber interests in the Olympics. The difference was that Mintzmyer was a product of the Park Service itself. When she believed its mission was at stake, she stepped away from the Park Service's male-defined culture that labeled her actions as insubordinate, and spoke out.

While the new generation of Park Service women continued to support the service's mission by working inside the service, a second wave of women on the outside, also inspired by a revived environmental movement, pressed for the preservation of new kinds of landscapes and historic spaces. Their successes changed the very nature of national parks themselves.

Left: The first women interpreters in the new era, hired in 1961 at Independence National Historical Park, wore an adaptation of an airline stewardess uniform. *From left:* Judith Rhodes, Margaret Ciborowski, and Ruth Friday. (*Courtesy of National Park Service.*)

Right: According to Charlie, the new woman ranger reinterpreted history. (*Reprinted by permission: Tribune Media Services.*)

Left: New uniforms for women unveiled at Independence in 1970 set women apart from men. Park Service women modeling the uniforms are, *from left:* Marion Riggs, Carole Scanlon, Louise Boggs, Inger Garrison, Ellen Lang, Elaine Hounsell, and Helen Hartzog. (*Courtesy of National Park Service.*)

Women at the 1941 superintendent's conference were Gertrude Cooper, the first woman park superintendent, who served at Vanderbilt Mansion National Historic Site, New York, from 1940 to 1945 and Isabelle Story, Park Service editor-in-chief for nearly forty years beginning in 1916. (*Courtesy of National Park Service.*)

Isabelle Story directed the National Park Service's twenty-fifth anniversary radio broadcast in 1941. *From left:* Story; Carl P. Russell; Paul Woodbridge; Dorothea Lewis; Newton B. Drury, Park Service director; and Horace M. Albright, former director. (*Courtesy of National Park Service.*)

Georgia Ellard, the first African-American woman park superintendent, began as a clerk-typist and rose through the ranks to manager of Rock Creek Park in Washington, D.C. in 1977. (*Photo by Bill Clark, National Park Service.*)

Lorraine Mintzmyer, the first woman regional director in the Park Service, served as head of the Rocky Mountain Region for more than ten years, beginning in 1979. Here she receives the Distinguished Service Award from Interior Secretary Donald Hodel in 1988. (*Courtesy of National Park Service, Rocky Mountain Region.*)

Irma Buchholz with Superintendent
Jack Davis at Sequoia/Kings
Canyon National Park where she
was superintendent's secretary
under fifteen different superinten-
dents, including Davis's father,
John, *above center*. Buchholz was the
first Park Service secretary to be
awarded the Interior Department's
Distinguished Service Award.
(*Courtesy of National Park Service,
Sequoia/Kings Canyon National Park.*)

Virginia Salazar, a member of the Santa
Clara Pueblo, served as Southwest Re-
gional Curator. (*Courtesy of National
Park Service.*)

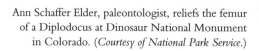

Ann Schaffer Elder, paleontologist, reliefs the femur
of a Diplodocus at Dinosaur National Monument
in Colorado. (*Courtesy of National Park Service.*)

Above: Operating a backhoe at Timpanogas Cave is Sue McGill, who has served as chief of maintenance in three national parks. (*Courtesy of Dutch Scholten, National Park Service, Timpanogos Cave National Monument.*)

Erin Broadbent, a disabled park ranger, shown on duty at the White House in Washington, D.C. (*Photo by Bill Clark, National Park Service.*)

Left: Marjorie Stoneman Douglas, crusader for Florida's Everglades, autographs copies of her book on the park. (*Courtesy of Florida State Archives.*)

Right: Celia Hunter, the first woman president of the Wilderness Society, serving from 1976 to 1979, was a leader in the campaign for the Alaska lands. (*Courtesy of Celia Hunter.*)

Margaret E. Murie, long-time advocate for national parks in Alaska and the Grand Tetons, with Park Service Director William Whalen after speaking at the superintendent's conference in 1977. (*Courtesy of National Park Service.*)

At the signing of the act establishing the Frederick Douglass Home in 1962, President John F. Kennedy hands a pen to Rosa Gragg, president of the National Association of Colored Women, while Mary Gregory, president of the Frederick Douglass Memorial and Historical Association, looks on. (*Courtesy of Library of Congress.*)

Sue Kunitomi Embrey speaks to participants at the 1992 pilgrimage to Manzanar, a World War II Japanese internment camp in California, at its designation as a national historic site on the camp's fiftieth anniversary. (*Courtesy of Sue Kunitomi Embrey.*)

Kathy Phibbs portrays Fay Fuller while leading thirty-three women on the 1990 Fay Fuller Centennial Climb of Mount Rainier. (*Photo by Rachel da Silva.*)

Sculptor Glenna Goodacre, *at left,* and Diane Carlson Evans, leader of the Vietnam Women's Memorial project, dedicate the statue to women nurses on Veterans Day 1993. (*Photo by Terry Adams, National Park Service.*)

Modern young women meet sculptured likenesses of the historic participants in the 1848 Women's Rights Convention at Women's Rights National Historical Park, Seneca Falls, New York. (*Photo by Michael Okoniewski, New York Times Pictures.*)

Recent Park Founders
and Advocates

*W*ith the new environmental movement and the second wave of feminism stirred into the already burgeoning civil rights movement, the preservation of landscapes and historic sites as national parks took on a new urgency for women activists. In the early 1960s, Rachel Carson's appeal for people to stop poisoning the earth, Betty Friedan's call for women to lead more meaningful lives, and Rosa Parks's demand that African Americans be integrated into American life, all called for new actions. Development and pollution threatened natural life on the last great landscapes, and urban unrest endangered the quality of human life in cities.[1]

As a new generation of women activists defined history in terms of their own experiences and recognized that landscapes were theirs to preserve, they joined other groups in pushing the National Park Service to redefine itself. A new method for acquiring land to be used as national parks opened up the process of creating new parks. With Cape Cod National Seashore as a precedent in 1961, Congress authorized direct purchase of lands for natural or recreation areas and, soon, for historic sites. Traditionally, parks had been carved out of existing federal or state lands or created from philanthropic gifts.[2] No longer would it be a presidential site that automatically became the new national historical park, new areas would honor the home of a playwright and the desegregation of the nation's public schools. No longer would national parks be created mainly from open space in the West, with sparse populations, but they would be carved out of shorelines and disconnected urban spaces near large concentrations of people. Like the women preservationists before them, women in the 1960s through the 1990s used the political process to rescue natural and historic spaces. For many, it was their life's work.

Backyard Environmentalists: Atlantic Shorelines

When the Park Service published *Our Vanishing Shoreline* in the mid-1950s, documenting the rapid loss of seashore to private development, the service challenged "public-minded citizens" and local, state, and federal governments to act "before it is too late—to preserve this priceless heritage."[3] Several women up and down

the East Coast were ready to act on this new imperative. As each woman faced situations that varied with the shorelines and local politics, the commonality of the
goal of saving land and the life it supports for future generations was clear. When
testifying before Congress for Cape Cod National Seashore, Miriam Hapgood De-
Witt explained that she believed "that this wild and lovely bit of country should
become a part of a national park, to be preserved for the enjoyment of future generations."[4] Each woman activist was first inspired to preserve natural landscapes by
an environmental issue in her own "back yard."

Local public opinion often opposed a national park, especially in prime real estate near well-populated areas. People slated to become inholders (owners of land
inside a park boundary) were often suspicious of federal control, even though national seashores allowed owners who met new zoning regulations to retain their
property. DeWitt joined other Provincetown residents to gather the names of 325
supporters of a national seashore that would include not only Cape Cod's great outer
beach but also the state-owned Province Lands surrounding Provincetown that form
Massachusetts's hook. DeWitt's goal was to keep real estate interests and land owners from whittling away the boundaries until there was nothing left for the seashore.[5]

The state-owned Province Lands were crucial to the success of the seashore, but
some local politicians proposed that the town take them over for potential development. When DeWitt learned by accident that these men had quietly presented
a development plan to the town selectmen, she organized the Emergency Committee for the Preservation of the Province Lands and published their plan. She
found and publicized a state report revealing that the developers, who included members of the Provincetown planning board and the board of selectmen, would be in
charge of the proceeds from the sale of the Province Lands if the state ceded the
lands to the town. Her committee fought the developers with a simple flyer: "If
Provincetown takes the Province Lands, who takes the money?" When the town
realized that individuals were going to profit if the town took over the lands, public opinion turned around and the town meeting voted to include the Province
Lands in the national park. Cape Cod National Seashore, with the contested lands
intact, came into being in 1961.[6]

In New York, at about the same time, Grace Barstow Murphy founded Conservationists United for Long Island to create public opinion to protect undeveloped parts of Long Island. The group was especially concerned about Fire Island,
a barrier island close enough to Manhattan to make it valuable real estate. Totally
deaf, Murphy met with her group monthly and had them submit issues and news
to her on slips of paper. For more than ten years, until she was past eighty, she organized the slips into monthly newsletters to convince the public to preserve threatened Long Island landscapes. They supported land use planning, parks, preservation of wetlands, and pesticide control. Their opposition to Robert Moses's plan to
build roads on Fire Island helped save the thirty-two mile barrier island from development and paved the way for the national seashore authorized in 1964.[7]

Once Congress established a national park, however, it did not mean that the landscape was free from future threats. In 1965 Congress authorized a national seashore for Assateague Island, a wild barrier island off Maryland's Eastern shore. The Park Service's first management plan called for building a road the length of the narrow thirty-seven mile island and setting aside six hundred acres of land for commercial concessions.[8] Judy Johnson, a Garden Club activist, and her twelve-year old son, Reid, often visited the island, which was about 150 miles from the Johnsons' home in the Baltimore suburbs. They particularly valued its bird life. It was Reid who inspired Johnson to take action: when they realized that the unspoiled area where they stood was slated for development by the Park Service, Reid turned to her and said, "Mom, I think the most important thing you can do is save Assateague."[9]

Judy Johnson agreed to join the National Parks Association in opposing the Assateague management plan by testifying before the House Environmental Committee in 1970. There she learned the importance of organizing support in numbers. When asked how many people she represented, she said "five." The chairman suggested she return when she could speak for more people. With great energy and conviction, Johnson was spurred to organize the Committee to Preserve Assateague Island and enlisted 1,400 dues-paying members in five years. As she led the group in preservation efforts, Johnson learned the importance of group action and "eternal vigilance." She built the committee into a textbook preservationist organization and circulated her report, "A Primer for Citizen Action" to other groups. "Never be discouraged!" she wrote. "If your cause is right, if it is economically and environmentally sound and for the public benefit, you can win!" Essential were extensive publicity, lobbying, and the readiness to "drop everything else when crises appear." She added, "Your opponents will hope you will get tired and give up."[10]

Johnson's tenacity paid off. Besides being a major force in the revision of the Park Service's master plan, Johnson's group played key roles in stopping the state of Maryland from building a sewage treatment plant that would impact the island; in preventing the Army Corps of Engineers from building a road, research pier, and laboratory in the middle of the island; in forestalling a projected museum in the adjoining Fish and Wildlife Refuge devoted to hunting water birds; and in opposing an intercoastal waterway between the island and the mainland. The committee defeated demands for increased use of off-road vehicles on the beach and dune areas and convinced the refuge to close off three-and-a-half miles during the nesting season of the Piping Plovers, a threatened species. In the early 1990s, they helped the park acquire land for a buffer zone next to a planned visitor center.[11]

In Florida, another woman environmentalist saw another barrier island off the Atlantic coast as endangered. Inholder Doris Leeper devoted more than twenty-five years to preserving Canaveral National Seashore, literally her back yard. The seashore protects the twenty-five miles of the barrier island adjoining the Kennedy Space Center. Before the seashore was established in 1975, Leeper rallied support to protect the island so there would be something left to preserve, including preventing the building of a 350-unit trailer court on the beach. When the national seashore became a reality, the governor appointed her to the park advisory committee to help develop a management plan. She asked for basic protection: no cars driving on the beach, no man-made cut-throughs destroying the dunes, and an end to trash dumps.

Establishing the national seashore did not put an end to Leeper's concerns. She unsuccessfully led a campaign to have part of the seashore designated as a wilderness area. After the advisory committee expired, she soon felt the need to organize the Friends of Canaveral. The impetus was the Park Service's bulldozing of a hammock of oak trees and palmetto scrub for a small parking lot. Her concern led to the reestablishment of an advisory commission. Believing that there will always be pressure for development, she explained her philosophy for preserving a fragile barrier island: "I don't think you should bring anything here that you can't take out, and just as important, you should take nothing out that you didn't bring in." Leeper, who is an artist, did take herself out of the park in the late 1980s. She moved to nearby New Smyrna, where she developed the Atlantic Center for the Arts and became active in the state's environmental issues.[12]

Backyard Environmentalists: Nationwide

The woman environmentalist who outlasted the most opponents was writer Marjory Stoneman Douglas, who lived past one hundred years, and has been associated with the Everglades since the publication of her book, *The Everglades: River of Grass,* in 1947, the year Congress established Everglades National Park. A native New Englander, Douglas moved to South Florida in 1915 and became a reporter on the *Miami News Record,* owned by her father, Frank B. Stoneman, who opposed plans to drain the Everglades for development. When Douglas first knew the Everglades, she watched "great flocks of birds, amazing flights of 30,000 to 40,000 in one swoop." She remembered the thrill of watching the nuptial flight of the white ibis. Although the Everglades were in her back yard, Douglas said she hardly ever went into them. "I know it's out there and I know its importance," she explained. "I suppose you could say the Everglades and I have the kind of friendship that doesn't depend on constant physical contact."[13]

Over the years, Douglas wrote about threats to the region and its wildlife, particularly the endangered Florida panther and egrets, ibises, and roseate spoonbills who were killed "for every reason" from food to plumes. But it was not until she was in her eighties that preserving the Everglades became, as she put it, "a central force in my existence." Of the estimated 200,000 wading birds in the 1930s, only 2,000 to 4,000 remained by the 1990s.[14]

In 1970, the Miami National Audubon Society had used up all its energy winning a fight against a proposed oil refinery on the shores of lower Biscayne Bay. When Douglas congratulated an Audubon member on the victory, the reply was, "What are *you* doing?" To Douglas's answer, "I wrote the book," the member countered, "That's not enough. We need people to help us." A drive to oppose a jetport and industrial park in Big Cypress Swamp, north of the national park, now faced them. The Audubon member asked the group's leader, Joe Browder, to call Douglas. When he asked her to make a public statement opposing the jetport, Douglas protested, saying nobody would "care about my ringing denunciation of anything," and that "such things are more effective if they come from organizations." If she felt that way, he said, she should start one—and Douglas did, launching the Friends of the Everglades. She became convinced that the Central and South Florida Flood Control Project had done irreparable damage to natural life in the Everglades by draining and channeling the waters that fed it. She began "making speeches," she said, "to every organization that would listen to me." The group soon had three thousand members from thirty-eight states.[15]

After the jetport was defeated and Big Cypress National Preserve authorized, the Friends of the Everglades turned to the "general predicament of the water." Douglas campaigned to increase the water flow into the Everglades by plugging or breaking down canals to allow the Kissimmee River to flow in as near its original channel as possible into Lake Okeechobee from the north. Her organization also aimed to restore acres of marshland south of Lake Okeechobee to purify water flowing into the Everglades of agricultural pollutants. A restored flow in the Everglades, she argued, would also increase levels in the Biscayne Aquifer, the source of water for South Florida. With others, Douglas started the Coalition to Repair the Everglades.[16]

Douglas received many honors, including the Presidential Medal of Freedom in 1993. To celebrate her one hundredth birthday, the Park Service unveiled a statue of a Florida panther as a memorial to Ernest F. Coe, whom Douglas long championed as the founder of Everglades National Park. The National Parks and Conservation Association and Bon Ami Company instituted an annual Marjory Stoneman Douglas Award to recognize "an individual for an outstanding effort that results in protection of a unit . . . of the National Park System."[17] In 1993, the Interior Department announced a $465 million plan to increase the flow of water through the Everglades by 25 percent and to plant 40,000 acres of marshes below Lake Okeechobee to filter pollution. Although environmentalists believed the new plan was too limited, it was Douglas's concept of a flowing "river of grass" that made the public able to grasp the essence of the Everglades as a fragile ecosystem of rare tropical plant, bird, animal, and fish life that plays a crucial role in protecting Florida's water supply.[18]

In southeast Texas, across the Gulf of Mexico from the Everglades and about twenty miles inland, lies the beginning of Big Thicket National Preserve. Because it is a "biological crossroads," supporting life normally seen in four other climactic zones as well as its own, the preserve is a treasury of biodiversity. In 1964, when Maxine Johnston accepted the role of chair of the Big Thicket Association's committee to build a Big Thicket museum, she did not expect her involvement to include extensive lobbying for a national preserve that would take ten years and, after a hiatus, another seven to extend its boundaries. Divided into units representing different natural zones and habitats and based on a green corridor concept, the units of the preserve are connected by land alongside rivers that drain the area into the Neches River, which flows into the Gulf of Mexico at Port Arthur.

Johnston was reference librarian at the Lamar University library in Beaumont, on the edge of Big Thicket, and knew how to find information quickly. When the association received a grant from the American Heritage Society, they converted the cafeteria of an old school into the museum, began a herbarium, and organized historical artifacts. Although the association's goal was to create a national park, they did not know how to go about it. They contacted other environmental groups, including the Lone Star chapter of the Sierra Club and National Audubon Society branches, and elected Pete Gunter, a philosophy professor at North Texas State University, as president. He stumped the state to find supporters. Meanwhile, Johnston, drawing on her experience in the League of Women Voters, worked behind the scenes. She ran the museum, developed a slide talk, edited a newsletter mailed to 1,400 people, wrote letters, and took groups on tours.[19]

Maxine Johnston followed Gunter as president of the Big Thicket Association. Sent by the group to Washington, she testified at every congressional hearing on the project, making the trip several times a year. In all, between 1966 and 1974, the year Congress approved the preserve, twenty-eight Big Thicket bills were introduced. Women from the Texas League of Women Voters and Federation of Women's Clubs, the Garden Club, and the American Association of University Women joined other groups in giving testimony for the park or sending letters of support. In 1972, when park opponents said the removal of 100,000 acres from the tax rolls and the forest industry "would result in economic blight," she argued that a national park would contribute to economic growth, as parks had in other regions, and that the forest industry's pine farms would not be affected. In order to counter the impression of a lot of local opposition, she emphasized that it was Big Thicket residents who "initiated this movement" and explained who opposed the park and why. In the final year of testimony, she added a note of urgency as she showed photographs of trees recently cut in areas proposed for the park.[20]

When Congress established Big Thicket National Preserve in 1974, no appropriations were included, but the association produced explicit maps and worked with the Park Service on boundaries. With the help of Congressman Charles Wilson, annual appropriations slowly came through and land was acquired. In 1987, the Texas Committee on Natural Resources asked Johnson to chair a Big Thicket Committee Task Force to work on adding land to the preserve. She testified before Congress five more times. By 1993, 90 percent of the preserve was complete and the association voted to give the museum to the Park Service for an environmental education center. When asked what she was going to do next, Johnston immediately outlined current threats to the preserve: Houston's demands for water and a problem with barriers built to prevent saltwater intrusions on the lower Neches River. "Once you get a preserve established," she said, "you can't quit; there's always some issue that impacts the preserve in a certain way."[21]

Having Glacier National Park in her back yard kept Sharlon Willows alert. When the state and federal highway agencies planned to build a super-highway at the eleven-mile west entrance to the park, Willows created a nonprofit educational research organization called the Coalition for Canyon Preservation. The group found a sympathetic attorney, sued the agencies, and stopped the project on the basis of an inadequate Environmental Impact Statement (EIS). Willows said that their strongest opponents were local promoters of large-scale development and "entrenched bureaucrats" who did not understand environmental law. The lawsuit lasted for eight years and ended in the Ninth Circuit Court in San Francisco in 1980; there, the coalition prevailed and set a national precedent for EIS requirements.

For her leadership, Willows received the Montana Wilderness Association's 1984 Conservationist of the Year award. A paralegal, Willows did the legal and technical research herself and raised $20,000 for the lawsuit. As do many of the other women activists, Sharlon Willows noted that environmental battles come "at great personal sacrifice," but her satisfaction came from saving the park from the incursions that a super-highway would have brought. Instead, a specially designed two-lane road was built at the six-mile west entrance to the park. The coalition expanded its work to monitor park development in the entire state, sending out a "news alert" when protests were needed. At Yellowstone, they supported the removal of the campgrounds at Fishing Bridge, a grizzly bear habitat, and demanded reduced park use by snowmobilers in the winter.[22]

Professional Environmentalists: Fossils, Lakeshores, and Rivers

Some women who worked with environmental issues in their professions contributed their specialized knowledge to identifying potential sites. But for these women, too, the political struggle was the same and only persistence brought success in projects to save an ancient fossil bed, Great Lakes shorelines, and wild and scenic rivers.

The Florissant Fossil Beds lie thirty-five miles west of Colorado Springs and are the site of a collection of fossilized trees, leaves, insects, birds, and fish living in or near ancient Lake Florissant and frozen in time by volcanic action 38 to 34 million years ago. The beds have been well known to scientists for nearly one hundred years and more than 80,000 specimens have been removed to museums, but many remain, and the landscape itself holds significant clues to the earth's story. Past attempts to protect the site languished in Congress because there was not enough political pressure to push them through, until two women took on the cause.[23]

Beatrice (Bettie) Willard and Estella Leopold brought unusual credentials to the campaign: Willard, in 1948 a student at the Yosemite Field School, became an early woman seasonal naturalist for the Park Service; Leopold was the last of five children born to Estella and Aldo Leopold, whose *Sand County Almanac* was a key text for the new environmental movement. When Willard, by then a scientist with the Thorne Ecological Institute in Boulder, looked for an issue to unify the groups in the Colorado Open Space Council, she learned that Leopold represented the Colorado Mountain Club on the council. Leopold was a professor at the University of Colorado and a paleobotanist with the U.S. Geological Survey. They agreed that a prime project was protection of the fossil beds.[24]

At first there appeared to be no opposition from the people who owned the land, and the two women scientists took small groups to view the site. U.S. Senator Gordon Allott agreed to introduce the measure, but instead of including the essential 6,000 acres, he cut the proposal to 1,000 acres. The women used contacts in the business field to pressure Allott to revise the figure and within two weeks he agreed to meet them on the site. Arriving by helicopter, he gave them thirty minutes to tell him only what he "needed to know." As a result, Allott restored the acreage to the bill. After he introduced the bill early in 1969, field hearings on Memorial Day weekend proceeded, apparently without opposition. But ten days before the Washington hearings, everything changed. Leopold learned that developers had bought 1,800 of the 6,000 acres and planned to build an A-frame community of second homes. The women contacted a lawyer who joined them in creating the Defenders of Florissant and suggested they meet with the developers. When that plan fell through, they found an environmental lawyer in New York with a national reputation. Together they prepared a legal brief documenting the value of the site and asked the federal court for an injunction. By then the Senate had passed the bill, but while the Defenders waited for the court and the House to act, there was nothing to prevent the bulldozers from stripping off the irreplaceable volcanic earth covering the fossil beds.[25]

At this point, dramatic citizen action came into play. Leopold had aroused the interest of a bird-watcher, Vim Crane Wright, at an Audubon meeting when she mentioned there were bird fossils at Florissant. In July, Leopold took Wright up on her offer of help. Although the court was considering a stay order, during the interim, said Leopold, using language that showed the depth of her feelings, nothing could prevent the developers from "having their way with Florissant." Wright asked what would happen if they lost the case; Leopold answered, "The bulldozers would roll." And without, as she later put it, "intellectualizing" her words, Wright said: "I'll go sit in front of the bulldozers to buy some time."[26]

Wright led a cavalcade with her red jeep covered with signs saying, Save the Florissant Fossil Beds. She took along children and a pregnant mother. Because activism was new to her, she was, she said later, "scared"; but she believed, or at least hoped, that no bulldozer operator would harm them. Wright left messages in local truck stops to let operators know she would be ready to meet them at six the next morning. At the site, where a local supporter gave them lemonade and coffee, Wright instructed her group in tactics. Then came the reprieve: Leopold sent a message that the federal circuit court had issued a temporary injunction even though a federal district judge ruled only hours before that the developers had a right to proceed. By the time the injunction expired, the monument bill was on its way to be signed.[27]

Vim Crane Wright was changed by her involvement with Florissant Fossil Beds and became an environmental educator. To her, the fossils were once living birds. When asked why she was willing to take such extreme action as lying down in front of a bulldozer, she knew she should say she did it "for my children and grand-children and posterity" or that she had "such a feeling for the scientific verity of this wonderful piece of land that I wanted to preserve it." But, in truth, what "I really thought about was the birds . . . in some way this is my offering to the birds. It was to me inconceivable that anyone would desecrate the burial grounds of these creatures." She continued, "You never know why any of the citizen types ever do anything. It's very personal to them and this land is really personal to me."[28]

Meanwhile, in Michigan, another woman with special expertise in environ-mental issues, landscape architect Genevieve Gillette, was already deeply involved in developing state parks. When she learned that private funding was available for a shoreline survey of the Great Lakes, but that the National Park Service believed it could act only if citizens requested it to do so, she called a meeting in her house. The five people who came, all active in state parks, formed the nucleus of the Michi-gan Parks Association. They expanded their goals to supporting Michigan parks "on every level of administration from the local to the federal." Their first order of business was to submit a request that the survey be carried out; it was published by the Park Service in 1959 as *Our Fourth Shore: Great Lakes Shoreline Recreation Area Survey*.[29]

Gillette became involved in creating parks when, as the first woman to gradu-ate with a degree in landscape architecture from Michigan State University, in 1920, her only job offer was answering the telephone in the office of Friends of the Na-tive Landscape, a philanthropic group surveying Illinois for sites suitable for parks. When she returned to Michigan, she organized a Michigan branch of the Friends. She worked as an unpaid expert to make detailed studies of proposed parks and, a master at networking, developed financial and political support.[30]

Gillette was in her sixties when she began to agitate for national parks on Michi-gan's shorelines. Of the sites listed in the Park Service survey, Gillette and the Michigan Parks Association pursued Sleeping Bear Dunes, on the lower peninsula, where rugged dunes reach nearly five hundred feet above Lake Michigan, and Pic-tured Rocks, on the upper peninsula, noted for multicolored sandstone cliffs rising out of Lake Superior. Each site includes about forty miles of shoreline and is backed by forests and inland lakes. In 1966, Pictured Rocks became the nation's first na-tional lakeshore; Sleeping Bear Dunes followed in 1970.[31]

Gillette's efforts to create the national lakeshores encompassed a variety of ac-tions. Her firsthand knowledge of the state made her help invaluable in selecting the specific areas to be included. She led the lobbying effort in the state legislature to transfer D. H. Day State Park, a key parcel in Sleeping Bear Dunes, from state to federal ownership. Through extensive research she learned that the Valley of the Giants on South Manitou Island, part of Sleeping Bear Dunes, with old-growth white cedars and sugar maples, could be acquired from a concerned owner. As president of the Michigan Parks Association, she convened a conference designed to develop supporters for the national lakeshores, testified before many hearings in Washington, and lobbied for federal funds. She defused opposition from influential summer residents by visiting Cape Cod National Seashore and finding that many inholders had become park supporters when they saw their property values increase after the park opened.[32]

Gillette believed that the state had fewer resources than the federal government to develop and maintain parks. She wanted parks to allow the land to "tell its story" to a "considerable number of Americans." The National Park Service, she said, could provide "a quality of recreation" that neither private, local, nor state funds could give. Her primary goal was educational, but her definition of education was broad. "Wherever a National Park is we find the most delightful sort of education . . . a wholly painless experience of such inspiration and spiritual renewal."[33]

The method chosen by biologist Liane Russell to protect two wild rivers that cut deep channels in the Cumberland Plateau of Tennessee and Kentucky was to marshal evidence, provided by volunteer experts, for submission as testimony before Congress or as inputs into park planning. Russell convinced colleagues at Oak Ridge National Laboratory in Tennessee and experts from the University of Tennessee in ecology, geology, and archeology to help her do the studies that became essential in protecting the Big South Fork of the Cumberland River and the Obed River and its tributaries, Clear Creek and Daddy's Creek. What motivated her, she said, was not only the beauty of the areas but the quality of wilderness there. "The scientific worth of an unspoiled natural area," she said, "is beyond description."[34]

Russell's environmental activism began in 1965, after she and her husband joined a canoe trip on the Obed River. Totally wild, with no sign of human habitation until the take-up place, the clearwater river runs through a deep gorge of huge sandstone bluffs and supports mixed vegetation and diverse wildlife. A tiny item in the local paper alerted Russell that the Tennessee Valley Authority (TVA) was studying the Obed as a possible site for the Nemo Dam. A local Wilderness Society leader suggested that the Russells form an organization to do some fact-finding. A year later, Tennessee Citizens for Wilderness Planning (TCWP) took shape, after the Russells had attended Great Smoky Mountains wilderness hearings. Several participants who disagreed with the Park Service's plans for the Smokies joined the Russells for supper and, stimulated by their concern for the Smokies as well as the threatened Obed river, the group became the nucleus for TCWP. After a brief period during which members believed a man should be president (because, they thought, he would have more clout), Liane Russell took over the position. In the mid-1990s, more than twenty-five years later, she was still the sparkplug of TCWP and had personally edited two hundred editions of its newsletter and mailed out hundreds of action calls.[35]

Although TCWP worked on such projects as mitigating strip mining in Tennessee,[36] they soon confronted another proposed dam, this time the Devil's Jump Dam planned by the U.S. Army Corps of Engineers as a power supply on the Big

South Fork River in Kentucky, near the Tennessee border. TCWP's expert witnesses demonstrated that the dam would provide only 11 percent of the power projected by the corps and did not include navigation locks or flood-control systems. At first, Kentucky Senator John S. Cooper, the ranking Republican on the Senate Public Works Committee, supported the dam because he believed it would help the region. When he saw that the bill was stalled, he called for new surveys of Big South Fork. Using TCWP as the core, Liane Russell convinced thirty environmental and recreational groups to form a Big South Fork Preservation Coalition. She found experts to study all aspects of the river, including its prehistoric rock shelters. Members also provided many hours of free guide service on the river. Cooper agreed to support the coalition and gained backing from Senator Howard Baker of Tennessee. President Nixon pocket-vetoed the public works omnibus bill that included naming Big South Fork as a national river and recreation area under the Corps of Engineers, but it passed in 1974, after the House Interior Committee chair, Wayne Aspinall, asked for dual jurisdiction over the bill and separated out the Big South Fork proposal. With great efficiency, the Corps of Engineers acquired 80 percent of the acreage before turning it over to the Park Service.[37]

Meanwhile, the Obed River was still in danger from TVA's proposed Nemo Dam. When TCWP showed how low the cost-benefit ratio would be, TVA restudied the plan and eventually dropped it. A Bureau of Recreation study led to designating the Obed and two of its tributaries as a wild and scenic river in 1976, but because of pressure from a local landholder, TCWP's proposal to preserve one hundred miles was cut in half. The general management plan, with TCWP still actively involved, was delayed until 1992.[38]

Threats to the Obed continued. Despite the opposition of TCWP, the Farmers Home Administration built Otter Dam on a tributary to the Obed, flooding one hundred acres, and planned a similar one on the Clear Creek tributary. Liane Russell organized the Friends of the Obed to meet the threats to the river in the mid-1990s, believing that another dam would have a cumulative effect on the Obed and "starve the system" of water, much like the Colorado River in the West. Once again, the volunteer experts calculated water flow and counted wildlife to accumulate evidence to block a dam. They demanded a thorough EIS. Russell recognizes that threats to the rivers will always be there and wonders how to develop a "follow-up generation." A plan to tap in to branches of national environmental organizations, however, was already in place. When the National Parks and Conservation Association published news of the possibility of a Clear Creek Dam, Russell received support from all over the country.[39]

Moving National Organizations to Action

Some women dedicated to preserving resources in national parks became professional, full-time volunteers who, early in the new environmental era, helped move branches of national organizations to action. Women assumed leadership in regional branches of environmental groups, including the Sierra Club, still male-directed on the national level, and activated county branches of the League of Women Voters to provide essential support for preservation efforts.

When Polly Dyer moved to Seattle in the 1950s, she helped start a Pacific Northwest chapter of the Sierra Club and joined the Mountaineers, with whom she climbed Mount Rainier. Her concurrent positions on regional boards of environmental groups made her able to network and quickly produce constituencies for action, particularly in saving old-growth forests in the Olympic mountains. After years of controversy, she concluded: "You always have opposition if there are any trees involved anywhere."[40]

Her first political struggle was during one of the timber industry's efforts to decrease the size of the Olympic National Park boundaries. In May 1953, Governor Arthur Langlie, who was sympathetic to the timber industry, appointed a commission to review the boundaries and management of the park. In order to be fair, he invited Emily Haig, of the Seattle Audubon Club, Rosamond Engle, of the Seattle Garden Club, and Polly Dyer, of the Mountaineers, to join the fourteen-member commission. The three women joined two trade union men in a minority report advising that the park's boundaries should remain as announced by President Harry S. Truman the previous January. When the majority report insisted that the boundaries be reduced to a 1934 proposal, the commission deadlocked. The women rallied their organizations to lobby the governor, who, inundated by mail, dropped the proposal.[41]

Threats to the Olympic forests continued. In 1954, the Rayonier Corporation launched a campaign to resume logging with a full-page advertisement in national magazines portraying the opposition as finger-shaking women who wasted forests by allowing "trees to reach maturity, die, topple over and rot."[42] No doubt the company was reacting to the years of battling Rosalie Edge and her Emergency Conservation Committee; now, a new generation of women preservationists opposed them. The next year, Dyer, representing the Mountaineers, revealed her goals when she testified against logging in parks before a Senate committee. Park values, she said, give "aid to the physical well-being of the millions seeking relief from deskside or factory jobs" and "support the spiritual well-being of those seeking respite from crowded urban areas." At a follow-up meeting between environmentalists and Park Service Director Conrad Wirth, Dyer's shorthand notes put Wirth on record as opposing salvage logging in the park.[43]

Dyer also worked to protect the Olympic coastline. In 1959, she organized a three-day hike along the coast, led by Supreme Court Justice William O. Douglas, in a successful protest of a plan to build a road along the Olympic coastal strip. In the early 1970s, Dyer, who was then president of the Olympic Park Associates, and her committee convinced Governor Dan Evans to advocate extending the park's coast to Shi-Shi beach, a wilderness beach in the northwest corner of the park. She identified the inholders and testified before Congress in time for the area to be included in the 1976 Omnibus Park Bill.[44]

Dyer joined the push to create North Cascades National Park, an alpine wilderness in Central Washington. She backpacked with Jane and Grant McConnell, longtime summer residents in Stehekin Valley, a base for alpine trails, and leaders in the drive for a national park. When the U.S. Forest Service began to log Agnes Creek, the McConnells became alarmed. They believed a national park would protect the area. With others from the Mountaineers, the Sierra Club, and the Federation of Western Outdoor Clubs, Dyer formed the North Cascades Conservation Council and with Emily Haig, wrote its bylaws. The council became the principal lobbying group for the park. At House hearings, Haig asked for a wilderness park of adequate size—protected for "all of America."[45] The park was created in 1968, but it took supporters another twenty years to win wilderness designation for the majority of its land.

Between 1960 and 1976, the environmental consciousness of the League of Women Voters grew from listing only water quality issues on its national agenda to including all natural resources.[46] When the Cuyahoga River burned for three days at its entrance to Lake Erie in 1969, local league members were already sensitized to pollution issues but the event startled other Ohio citizens into facing the depth of the pollution of their landscape. Within five years, their concerns were transformed into widespread support for a new national recreation area in the valley where the Cuyahoga River flows between Akron and Cleveland. The efforts of the League of Women Voters members in Cuyahoga and Summit Counties were major forces that developed the grassroots support essential for passing the park bill.

Janet Hutchison, who held the water quality portfolio for the interleague organization, an umbrella group coordinating issues in the twelve leagues in Cuyahoga County, had joined an ad hoc group to explore creating a national park in the valley. The group merged with the Cuyahoga Valley Association, newly revitalized by journalist James Jackson and his wife, Margot. As soon as Congressman John Seiberling, newly elected from Akron, introduced the first version of the park bill during Earth Week, April 1971, Hutchison wasted no time in starting the process to win support for the park among the 2,500 league members in both counties.[47]

Because the League of Women Voters cannot support an issue until its members study it and agree by coming to a consensus, Hutchison gathered information about the natural and cultural resources in Cuyahoga Valley that qualified it for a national recreation area. She narrated hundreds of bus tours through the valley to inform league members and other community groups about the plan. After the leagues' county conventions accepted the proposed recreation area as a study item, they divided subjects for research among women from the Cuyahoga County leagues and the five leagues in Summit County. Hutchison pulled the information together in a brief that was mailed to all members with a ballot for a write-in consensus. In order to answer questions before the vote, in February 1974 the leagues produced a television call-in show with Seiberling, Hutchison for the Cuyahoga County leagues, and Delores Warren for the Summit County leagues answering the calls. Of those who completed ballots, 100 percent were in favor of the park proposal. Once the league had consensus, Hutchison explained, they "could dive in and get busy." Members, along with women from the Junior League and the Garden Club, collected thousands of signatures on hundreds of petitions supporting the park. Congress passed the bill in the closing moments of its session in December 1974. Realizing the strength of the grassroots support, President Gerald Ford signed it. Funds were forthcoming and, within a decade, the park was 80 percent complete.[48]

League members continued to define the park. As chair of the first park advisory commission, Delores Warren asked Janet Hutchison to head a group to consider future directions. After consulting with park historians and archeologists, Hutchison's group proposed that the park be extended so it would follow topographical features and include omitted historic and prehistoric sites. These were added in 1976. As a member of the second commission, Hutchison led a committee that developed hiking, biking, horse, and cross-country ski trails that she called "a magnificent gift to the future." Perhaps the league's most dramatic action was to join the Sierra Club in producing, and distributing by hand, a flyer, written by Hutchison, disputing a documentary film, fueled by the conservative National Inholders Association, that claimed the park was destroying communities and property rights.[49]

Meanwhile, the Cuyahoga Valley Association hired a staff and opened an environmental education center. Hutchison added Cuyahoga Valley National Recreation Area (NRA) to her league portfolios. She kept up the complicated map of land ownership—a map that constantly changed as Congress allocated funds for acquisitions, compiled the park's legislative history, and chaired the citizens' committee for its tenth birthday. When asked why she undertook what in essence was a full-time unpaid position, Hutchison responded: "We are part of the universe, not lords of it. If it perishes, we do too."[50]

The Struggle for Urban Parks: Golden Gate

One of the ways President Lyndon B. Johnson proposed to alleviate urban unrest in the mid-1960s was to improve the quality of life in cities by expanding parks and recreational facilities, projects that strained municipal budgets could not afford. Lady Bird Johnson's beautification program for the District of Columbia included projects in low-income areas, including a thirty-five acre park at Watts Linear Branch Park.[51] The two Gateway parks, one on each coast, arose from Director Hartzog's study of surplus federal property in New York City and San Francisco. Signed by President Nixon in 1972, the acts creating Gateway and Golden Gate national recreation areas activated the new concept of bringing "parks to the people." Congressman Seiberling promoted Cuyahoga Valley NRA as Gateway Midwest.

Although William Whalen, first manager of Golden Gate NRA, said some form of a national park would have happened without the work of Amy Meyer, he believes she made the essential difference in "pulling" the spaces "together into a cohesive national park." When some citizens, many active in the Sierra Club, found that a study was underway to use surplus forts and federal land on both sides of the

Golden Gate for a park, they formed People for a Golden Gate NRA. Edgar Wayburn, former Sierra Club president, and Amy Meyer were co-chairs. Her role, Meyer said, was to provide "the nuts-and-bolts and the spider web" for the group.[52]

To develop support for the park, Meyer organized a coalition of 4,500 individuals and seventy organizations, ranging from the Contra Costa Hills Club to the Committee for Better Parks and Recreation for Chinatown. She became an expert on the land and topography of the area. Although the strategy was to keep newspaper publicity at a minimum to avoid stirring up opposition, members presented slide talks to hundreds of groups, made thousands of phone calls, and, using the Sierra Club outings program, led innumerable trips to proposed sites. They enlisted Congressman Philip Burton, who shepherded the bill through the House.[53]

At the House hearings, Meyer and her associates turned out more than ninety speakers. Meyer expressed her philosophy of urban parks: "People living under increasing urban and suburban tensions must have peaceful places for recreation." Warning that society "cannot afford to be divided between those who live in green enclaves of privilege and the deprived residents of decaying cities," she concluded, "we must face the problems of our environment together." At Senate hearings a year later, Meyer introduced the concept of "conservation of people."[54]

Once the park was established, Meyer continued to direct People for a Golden Gate NRA with new goals of acquiring park lands and developing the park. She has served as vice chair of the Citizens' Advisory Commission for the park for more than twenty years. By incorporating state, city, and other national park sites, Golden Gate "strings together what others had set in motion," she explained. The park took a giant step forward in 1994 when the U.S. Army transferred the Presidio, a former army base on 14,000 acres of prime land on the San Francisco side of the Golden Gate, to the NRA, presenting a new challenge for park planners.[55]

The Struggle for Urban Parks: Indiana Dunes and Santa Monica Mountains

Not all new urban park projects were able to start with a core of federal land, however; without such a start, creating parks near America's largest cities, out of land poised for development, was even more costly in citizen energy. Both the campaigns to save what is now Indiana Dunes National Lakeshore, lying along Lake Michigan, directly across from Chicago, and the Santa Monica Mountains National Recreation Area, contiguous with Los Angeles, attracted women to the cause and converted them into militant activists.

The fifty-year struggle to save the Indiana dunes from development by the steel industry that circumscribes and intrudes on a landscape considered "sacred" by many preservationists was one of the hardest-fought preservation battles in U.S. history. Bills supporting the park numbered nearly one hundred. Begun just a few weeks after the Park Service's own birth in 1916, the push for a dunes national park was first led by the service's first director, Stephen Mather, a Chicagoan and member of the city's conservation-minded Prairie Club. Although a great outdoor pageant in 1917, connecting the dunes with the history and soul of the nation, drew 25,000 people, the movement died with World War I. This first effort was replaced by a local movement for a state park, led by Richard Lieber and Bess Sheehan, head of the Dunes Park Committee for the Indiana Federation of Women's Clubs. The state park was established in 1923 after Sheehan, convinced legislators by rallying members of six hundred women's clubs.[56]

Nearly thirty years later, steel industry plans to carve a deep-water port out of the Central Dunes, west of the state park, revived the movement. Dorothy Buell, who lived in Ogden Dunes and as a girl performed in dunes pageants, inadvertently became a leader in the new phase of the movement: a trip to White Sands National Monument in New Mexico made her appreciate the Indiana Dunes even more. On their way home, she and her husband stopped for dinner at a hotel in Gary, where a sign announcing a meeting to save the dunes propelled her life in a new direction. By 1952, at an age when many think of retiring, Buell organized the Save the Dunes Council; she served as its president for sixteen years. Twenty-one women attended the first meeting, in her home, where Bess Sheehan described the earlier campaign. After the council decided its goal was adding five miles of unspoiled lakeshore in the Central Dunes to the state park, Buell announced to the press: "We are prepared to spend the rest of our lives if necessary, to save the Dunes!"[57] The opposition was formidable: a group of business and political leaders were united in the opposite goal of developing the Central Dunes.

The Save the Dunes Council launched a national membership drive, acquired Cowles Tamarack Bog, networked with many groups, organized a Children's Crusade to Save the Dunes, and sponsored a Day in the Dunes, at which Park Service Regional Director Howard Baker spoke in favor of a national park. Not long after the council established an advisory board of scientists, environmentalists, and philanthropists, the governor announced plans to develop a port in the Central Dunes. Convinced by the board that the council would have to enter hardball politics, Buell decided to invite men to be members, although women continued to serve as president. When the Indiana congressional delegation refused to introduce legislation for a dunes park, Buell turned to Illinois Senator Paul H. Douglas after learning from the Prairie Club that he used to live in the dunes. Reluctant to enter a controversy in another state, Douglas did not respond until naturalist Donald Culross Peattie, a Dunes Council board member, interceded.[58]

In Buell's home, on Easter Sunday 1958, Douglas announced his plans to introduce a bill making Indiana Dunes a national monument, saying that the large national constituency built by the Save the Dunes Council gave him the backing he needed to oppose Indiana's political and business leaders. Within a year, Buell and her council gathered a quarter of a million signatures on petitions from all over the country, including many from organized labor. They lobbied Congress and produced a film depicting industry as poised to destroy the dunes.[59]

The struggle between the factions supporting a port, led by Indiana Congressman Charles Halleck, and those supporting a park, led by Douglas, was protracted and bitter. When a power company, without a public hearing, began to bulldoze parts of the Central Dunes for a new facility, the Save the Dunes Council protested "legislation by bulldozer." In 1961, Douglas led a pilgrimage to the dunes that convinced Interior Secretary Stewart Udall and Senator Alan Bible, chair of the Senate subcommittee on parks, to back a bill to save the dunes. But in 1962, Bethlehem Steel removed 2.5 million cubic yards of sand from the Central Dunes, which became fill for Northwestern University's expansion. All Dorothy Buell and Senator Douglas could do was watch; within a year the Central Dune was gone. Reluctantly, in 1963 Douglas agreed to accept a compromise proposed by President John F. Kennedy: the port would be built on the site of the Central Dune and the park would be established on both sides of the port, with the eastern portion contiguous to the state park. Armed with petitions at each hearing, Buell and the Save the Dunes Council had to wait for three more years of jockeying between park and port supporters for Indiana Dunes National Lakeshore to become a reality.[60]

The bill was only an entering wedge. About 8,000 acres were protected, including the nearly 2,000-acre state park, and Congress was slow in appropriating funds. Sylvia Troy, president of the Save the Dunes Council from 1966 to 1976, and Charlotte Read, who became executive secretary in 1974, led successful lobbying efforts for park expansion in 1976, 1980, and 1986, when the park reached nearly 14,000 acres. They also led the council in facing unusual threats to the park. They defeated proposals for a jet airport and a railroad marshalling yard and worked to stop sand mining within the park and to mitigate air and water pollution. The most dramatic threat was the plan to build the Bailley Generating Station, a nuclear power plant. The site bordered Cowles Bog, valued for its diverse plant life. The Dunes Council spearheaded a coalition of civil rights, peace, environmental, and labor activists to protest against the plant, culminating in a major protest in 1981. Although excavation had already begun, protests, site problems, and legal delays caused the company to cancel the project.[61]

Led by women for more than forty years, the work of the Save the Dunes Council is a remarkable testament to the tenacity and persistence of women citizens. They assumed women's traditional moral role and believed they were crusading against the forces of materialism by protecting sacred land essential for renewal of the human spirit. Senator Douglas called them "one of the most unselfish groups . . . who it has ever been my pleasure to know." At the same time, he gave them a warning that they continue to heed. "The enemies of the Dunes have not given up the battle," he said, as he urged them "to keep together and push on."[62]

Another intense effort to preserve open space contiguous to an urban area was in Los Angeles and Ventura counties, where several women became allies in the all-consuming task of saving the Santa Monica Mountains from what has been called the "Octopus" of development.[63] With its butt end at Griffith Park, a 4,000-acre city park east of the Hollywood Hills, the Santa Monica Mountain range stretches fifty miles west to Point Mugu and the Channel Islands. A series of steep canyons, supporting a variety of wildlife and plants, run from Pacific beaches and bluffs for five to ten miles up to a 3,000-foot crest, traversed from the city by Mulholland Drive and falling off on the north to the Ventura Freeway and the San Fernando Valley. The Los Angeles basin is plagued by smog, caused by polluted air trapped by a ring of 10,000-foot mountains.

Part of the insurgent homeowners movement of the 1960s and 1970s, hundreds of people engaged in the move to preserve the Santa Monica Mountains. They ranged from property owners, anxious about their home values and who wanted to maintain class and ethnically homogeneous neighborhoods, to citizens who believed that saving open space was one way to mitigate urban problems.[64] Even though the initial movement to save the Santa Monicas succeeded in preserving a few large landscapes as state parks, the areas were scattered, and the parks were not immediately accessible to the public: the largest, Point Mugu, sat on the eastern end, as far from development pressure as it was possible to be.

For three of the women involved in the national park movement, the twin goals were: first, to integrate the public land by adding federal land to create canyon wildlife corridors from the mountains to the sea and link the mountain parks with a protected Backbone Trail from east to west; and, second, to open up public space utilizing the National Park Service's interpretive skills. Sue Nelson's political action, Jill Swift's educational campaigns, and Margot Feuer's legal and governmental approaches all helped establish Santa Monica Mountains NRA in 1978. Although the original impetus for each woman was opposition to development in her own neighborhood, qualifying her as a member of the Not in My Back Yard (NIMBY) movement, each progressed beyond to work on broad environmental issues. Sierra Club lobbyist Margot Feuer said before the Senate national parks subcommittee, the Santa Monicas were an "air shed for an already critically polluted air basin" and "a recreational resource for the millions of urban dwellers in the country's second largest metropolitan area."[65]

For Sue Nelson, joining in a housewives' petition in 1963 to defeat a freeway proposed to enter undeveloped areas of the Santa Monicas—a signal that developers were looking for access points—led to a thirty-year volunteer career in environmental activism. She also joined the signature effort to introduce an initiative for what became a successful bond issue for state parks. A year later, the new Friends of Santa Monica Mountains Park chose her to be president, succeeding her mentor, Ralph Stone, who started the group. By working with petition lists and neighborhood associations, organizing groups where none already existed, and connecting them with a newsletter and an annual conference, Nelson and Stone developed a constituency of two thousand paid members. Although paying for state parks instead of for the infrastructure for developers was their initial goal, in 1970, at their first annual conference, Stone suggested that the Friends support a national park for the Santa Monicas.[66]

Meanwhile, Jill Swift, who was leading young people on Sierra Club walks, decided that one way to build a constituency for the Santa Monicas was through education and by using the land already owned by the state. Her goal was to get people "off the concrete, into the natural areas, and into the voting booth." In 1971, she organized a March on Mullholland, publicized by a popular columnist, that drew five thousand adults and children. She participated in a weekly television program on hiking in the mountains and led weekly hikes. She was not always welcome. When she tried to check out the route for a Sunday hike in new Topanga State Park, a man who had leased a ranch on the property stopped her. Only her complaint to the state attorney general opened the park. Swift founded the Sierra Club's Santa Monica Mountains Task Force and worked to limit concession development in state parks. In 1973, Mayor Tom Bradley appointed her to a five-year term on Los Angeles's first Commission on Recreation and Parks.[67]

Margot Feuer's first activism as an environmentalist was to help found Stamp Out Smog in the late 1950s. When she moved to Malibu in 1965, she was "catapulted into community action" by the threats of a nuclear plant, sewer projects, and a freeway through Malibu Canyon. Noting her work as a watcher at the Los Angeles County Board of Supervisors' meetings, the Sierra Club chose her as co-chair of the task force founded by Jill Swift. Feuer became the club's principal lobbyist for the national park. She was a founding board member of the Center for Law in the Public Interest. When the center sued a developer for wrongdoing, the monetary award brought endowment for mountain restoration projects.[68]

By June 1971, after nearly ten years of preparatory work, the stage was set for the introduction of legislation to create a national park. The two Gateways were well on their way to fruition and California's congressional delegation believed Los Angeles, too, deserved an urban park. The first hearing was delayed until 1974. Held in Los Angeles, the hearing gave many women a public voice. Jill Swift documented the numbers of people using the new state parks; Margot Feuer explained how a park would improve the region's air quality; Sue Nelson described the size of the constituency supporting a national park. Nelson and Feuer also testified at hearings in Washington in 1976 and in 1978.[69]

The final drive for the bill came in 1977. While working on strategy, Sue Nelson was guided by Loretta Neumann, legislative aide for the House subcommittee on parks member John Seiberling, who had sponsored Cuyahoga Valley NRA. Nelson networked with Sylvia Troy, of Indiana Dunes, and Amy Meyer, of Golden Gate, before helping newly elected Representative Tony Beilenson draw up a new bill. She created a huge map that indicated land ownership and desired parcels. Philip Burton, chair of the House subcommittee on parks, agreed to hold final hearings in Los Angeles. The large turnout brought even Horace Albright, then in his late eighties, to speak for the park. Included in Burton's 1978 Omnibus Bill, the park passed with a spending ceiling of $155.5 million.[70]

Santa Monica Mountains NRA is still a park in process: pressure from developers continued to influence park acquisitions, Congress held back allocations, land purchases were complex and slow, and disagreements occurred over priorities for purchase. Sue Nelson persisted in lobbying for the park, making annual visits to Washington.[71] After ten years, with only half of the park's ceiling allocated, Margot Feuer helped form the Save the Mountains Coalition to demand completion of the national park. By the mid-1990s, however, the patchwork of federal, state, county, city, and conservancy lands began to make sense. Thirty years of activism by citizens, sustained by women who made saving the Santa Monicas their lifetime careers, had withstood the pressure of the Los Angeles Octopus and created more than 150,000 acres of public land. Canyon corridors began to be filled in with protected space and the Backbone Trail was nearly complete. Starting with Jill Swift's filebox of hiking trails, the National Park Service was coordinating programs for all the public lands, including environmental education for inner-city young people.[72]

The Drive to Save Wild Alaska

Everything about the drive to preserve wild Alaska was on a larger scale than any other national park preservation effort. With a territory one-fifth the size of the continental United States, Alaska is made up of a series of spectacular glaciered mountain ranges, divided by the Yukon River basin, which runs east to west from Yukon Territory to the Bering Sea. The mountains and islands of southeast Alaska extend six hundred miles south along the coast of British Columbia. At odds over land use are the environmentalists who see Alaska's value as the nation's greatest and last unspoiled wilderness and the developers who measure Alaska's wealth by its oil, minerals, coal, and timber. With the passage of the Alaska National Interest Lands Conservation Act (ANILCA) in December 1980, the size of the entire National Park System was doubled from 39 to 79 million acres. The bill's proponents had to build a national constituency because of opposition from the Alaskan congressional delegation. Alaskan women were thrust into national leadership positions as they spoke out to the entire country. They added credibility to the cause, because unlike many concerned men, the women were outside the state and federal power structure and believed they had nothing to lose.

A series of events and congressional acts led up to ANILCA. Allowed to select 103 of Alaska's 375 million acres by the 1959 Alaska Statehood Act, the state chose its land using criteria of economic value. In 1968, two oil companies struck oil in Prudhoe Bay, below the North Slope of the Brooks Range; five years later President Nixon signed an executive order allowing a pipeline to be built through federal lands to carry the oil 850 miles south, to Valdez, on Prince William Sound. In 1971, Congress enacted the Alaska Native Claims Settlement Act (ANCSA), allowing Alaskan Natives the right to select 44 million acres. The act included Section 17-d-2, which temporarily set aside 80 million acres of public lands to be studied for possible national parks, forests, wildlife refuges, or wild and scenic rivers. The struggle to make the withdrawal permanent by passing ANILCA took nearly a decade.[73]

Among the women who spoke out on the national level was longtime activist Margaret (Mardy) Murie. As pioneer environmentalists, Olaus and Mardy Murie were instrumental in protecting the first piece of Alaskan wilderness, the Arctic

National Wildlife Range of 19 million acres in northeast Alaska. Olaus, a wildlife biologist, in 1945 left the U.S. Biological Survey to become director of the Wilderness Society. Great champions of Alaskan wilderness (where they spent their honeymoon on a field expedition for Olaus's caribou survey), the Muries as a team publicized wilderness values for nearly twenty years. In 1950, their first major environmental victory convinced local and national activists to support the addition of Jackson Hole National Monument to Grand Teton National Park, where they had settled during Olaus's elk survey. In 1960, the Arctic Wildlife Range resulted from their all-out effort to publicize the need to preserve Alaskan habitats. After Olaus died in 1963, Mardy had to represent their team alone, first at the signing of the Wilderness Act in 1964.[74]

For the next thirty years, Mardy Murie continued to speak out in print and in person for wilderness preservation, particularly in Alaska. A native of Alaska and the first woman graduate of its university, she brought enormous authority and credibility to the drive to save Alaska's wild lands. In 1975, the Park Service hired her to study the lands being considered for national parks. She flew and camped all over Alaska, talking with Alaskans about the future of their lands. "This is Alaska's time," she told a meeting of national park superintendents. "Alaska needs all your help." Stating that "the main thing about Alaska is that it is different," she urged them to "adopt the ecosystem approach" and consider the right of Native Alaskans to continue subsistence living. She testified before Congress at every phase of the struggle, and when the lobbyists assembled in the East Room of the White House to begin the final drive for Senate support for ANILCA, it was she they called upon for inspiration.[75]

Although passing ANILCA was a national effort involving hundreds of women and men, the participation of Alaskan women was especially important, because Congress needed to know that many Alaskans supported ANILCA. Among women leaders were Celia Hunter and Ginny Wood, who moved to Fairbanks following World War II after careers in the Women's Airforce Service Pilots. They set up Camp Denali for visitors at the end of McKinley (now Denali) National Park road and worked as bush pilots. While flying to the far corners of Alaska, they became aware of both the magnificence of Alaska's wilderness and the threats to its integrity. Inspired by the Muries's goal of an Arctic wildlife range, in 1960 they helped found the Alaska Conservation Society, with Hunter as president. The Wilderness Society appointed Hunter to its national governing council. With the discovery of oil, a new urgency prompted the Conservation Society to hold a wilderness conference in 1969. Participants formed the Alaska Wilderness Council and enlisted support from national environmental groups.[76]

Meanwhile, Mark Ganopole [Hickock] helped start a Sierra Club chapter in Anchorage and led the effort to establish Alaska's first state park, located at Kachemak Bay on the Gulf of Alaska. She became the secretary-director of the new Alaska Wilderness Council and asked two hundred Alaskans concerned about wild Alaska to prioritize the lands they believed essential to preserve. With the help of

Sierra Club members and others, she drew up the wish list of selected landscapes and plotted them on maps that grew so large the group called themselves the Maps on the Floor Society. When Interior Secretary Rogers C. B. Morton withdrew the lands specified in 17-d-2 of ANCSA, he followed their suggestions.[77]

With the support of national groups, the fight for the Alaska lands attracted countrywide support and much of the action shifted to Washington. Alaskan women took on central leadership positions in national organizations. In 1976, the Wilderness Society named Celia Hunter its first woman president. She moved to Washington and later served as interim director. The Sierra Club elected Mark Ganopole to its national board, but she broke with them when they opposed the plan to allow Native Alaskans to continue subsistence living on national park lands. Pam Rich [Minier], of Friends of the Earth, and Dee Frankfourth and Peg Tileston, of the Alaska Center for the Environment, joined Chuck Clusen to build the Alaska Coalition—an effort, aimed at convincing Congress that ANILCA was an issue of national importance. Fifty-two national and Alaska-based organizations eventually joined the coalition.[78]

Although President Jimmy Carter's election in 1976 and Morris Udall's position as chair of the House Interior Committee brought new support, Alaskan senators Ted Stevens and Mike Gravel blocked the bill in the Senate. When John Seiberling, by then chair of the House subcommittee on parks, assisted by Loretta Neumann, took the Alaska lands hearings on the road continuously from April to September 1977, hundreds of people testified, including Carolyn Carr, of the Alabama Sierra Club, who organized grassroots support in the southeast, women from the Appalachian Mountain Club in the northeast, and Audubon Societies in Columbus and Denver. Despite success in the House, the Senate had not passed a bill by December 1978, the deadline for protecting land set aside by 17-d-2 of ANCSA, forcing President Carter to take the emergency action of invoking the 1906 Antiquities Act. Naming seventeen new national monuments in Alaska and preserving 56 million acres, he supported his action with a mailgram put together by the Alaska Coalition and signed by one thousand groups, totaling 10 million members.[79]

Two more years of building grassroots support both within Alaska and in the nation against unflinching opposition from the Alaskan senators, backed by powerful industrial lobbies, resulted in a Senate bill that was at first unacceptable to the Alaska Coalition. It allowed oil and gas exploration on the coastal plain of the Arctic National Wildlife Refuge and mining and timber harvesting in old-growth forests in southeast Alaska. It reserved, however, 104.3 million acres, including 56 million acres of wilderness and 44 million acres for the National Park System. When Carter lost his bid for reelection in 1980, the Alaska Coalition accepted the Senate bill as the only possible measure. Because the coalition had finally agreed to accept hunting, trapping, and fishing in parks for subsistence living among the Native Alaskan and rural populations, lands were designated as national parks and preserves.[80]

Mardy Murie, Celia Hunter, and Mark Ganopole Hickock know the drive to save wild Alaska is not over. The 1989 oil spill and the Republican party's support of oil drilling on the North Slope of the Brooks Range were immediate threats. Subsistence use was interpreted to allow hunting in all-terrain vehicles that plow up the tundra; timber was harvested at a loss in national forests; staffing in national parks was low; and potential wilderness areas awaited designation.[81]

Preserving the National Memory

Women in every region hoped to preserve the national memory by adding historic sites in their own localities to the National Park System. Sites that women believed had national significance commemorated the Hispanic and Native American heritage of the Southwest, the fur traders of the Pacific Northwest, the first transcontinental railroad, and a Civil War battlefield.[82]

The San Antonio Conservation Society, organized by women in 1924 to protect the cultural heritage of San Antonio, Texas, acquired properties and sponsored events that contributed to the development of San Antonio Missions National Historical Park. The park was authorized in 1978 and established five years later. An early goal of the Conservation society was to celebrate the Spanish, Mexican, and Native American ancestry of their city by preserving the remains of its eighteenth-century Franciscan missions. Their efforts over fifty years to preserve Mission San José, the queen of the four missions now included in the national park, was the catalyst that led to the park and the restoration of the church itself.

When the missions were secularized, the Roman Catholic Church gave land in the mission compounds to the Native people. In 1929, the threat that a gasoline station would be built in the remains of the Mission San José compound led the society to buy the land as its first purchase. Although the walls of the abandoned mission church were still standing, its roof had fallen in. The mission's granary was the society's next purchase. The society furnished the materials WPA workers used to restore the building and commissioned their architect to draw up plans to restore the mission church. They generated enough interest from public agencies that the church was eventually restored and reopened for services.

In 1941, after the Conservation Society rehabilitated the Mission San José compound, a project that included convincing the county to close a road running through it, they deeded the compound and the granary to the State of Texas for a state park, paving the way for the future national historical park. Their work was not over, however. When the Army Corps of Engineers planned, as part of a flood-control project, to destroy the eighteenth-century aqueduct the Franciscans had built to carry water from Mission Espada to surrounding farms, the society saved the structure by suing the corps and the San Antonio River Authority. They acquired the Espada Aqueduct and, in 1983, transferred it to the new national park.

The Conservation Society's many restoration projects and its extensive historic buildings survey have contributed to preserving the multicultural character of the old city of San Antonio. The three-thousand-member society also sponsors cultural events: at Christmastime they present the miracle play, *Los Pastores,* at Mission San José—a play first performed there in 1776.[83]

Across the state line, to the west, twenty-five miles from Santa Fe, New Mexico, Pecos National Historical Park also reveals the story of contact between Spanish colonizers and Native Americans. Intertwined ruins of two Spanish missions, a century apart, lie next to the remains of a large, fifteenth-century pueblo. Pecos became a focus for the philanthropy of actress Greer Garson [Fogelson] and her husband. Residents of nearby Forked Lightning Ranch for more than thirty years, the Fogelsons donated land for a buffer zone around the monument, increasing the site from 70 to 300 acres, and funded a visitor center and its expansion. They took a personal interest in the programs, and Garson sometimes led tours for senior citizens.

At the groundbreaking for the visitor center in 1983, Garson stated that the park showed "that when citizens and their government work together good things can happen and will happen." When she first saw the ruins, thirty years before, she said, they were "of rather dubious outlines and thistles and weeds everywhere." Garson sometimes visited the ruin in the evening "when nobody was about, with a pair of muleskin gloves on, to clear the trails." Pecos made her "think with reverence and appreciation of the people who lived here" and gave her "serenity and strength of spirit from the beauty of the surroundings" and "inspiration for the future." After the death of her husband in 1990, Garson donated the entire ranch of 5,500 acres to the monument, a gift that resulted in its change of status from a national monument to a national historical park.[84]

The period of contact between Europeans and American Indian nations is also the theme of Fort Vancouver in the Pacific Northwest, a park that focuses on the era of the fur trade between the Hudson's Bay Company and the indigenous people. Because the fort's remains could be identified only by archeological excavation, and it had more than one location, its reconstruction was controversial. By the time Julia Butler Hansen was elected to Congress in 1960 (after serving twenty years in the Washington state legislature), Congress had designated the fort's 1825–1849 location as a national monument. Made up of land transferred from the U.S. Army after long negotiations, the monument had no appropriations for development. In the first month of her term, Hansen introduced a Fort Vancouver bill, the first bill of her Congressional career, with a goal of rebuilding the fort so that young people could learn that it was "the outpost and bastion of trade and civilization."[85]

Within six months, Hansen's bill establishing Fort Vancouver as a national historic site had sailed through Congress, expanding the acreage to nearly twice the original size, and within a year a new museum and visitor center were completed. Hansen's power increased in 1963 when she was appointed to the House Appropriations Committee and to its subcommittee for the Interior Department. Although she supported many national park projects, Fort Vancouver was always at the top of her list. She insisted on the early development of the master plan for the park and pushed through appropriations for a five-year archeological study, for buying private land adjoining the site, and for reconstructing the stockade wall and bastion.[86]

Hansen's interest in national parks grew throughout her career. She supported many of Director Hartzog's requests, among them increases in the overall Park Service budget, authorization to purchase private land within national parks, and planning for the nation's bicentennial. Two years after her retirement in 1974, the Department of Interior awarded her a citation for conservation service.[87]

A one-woman campaign waged by Bernice Gibbs Anderson produced Golden Spike National Historic Site at Promontory Summit, Utah, in 1965. Robert Utley, former chief historian of the Park Service, called her struggle a "splendid elementary lesson in civics." Anderson—mother of six children and a large woman with a presence—wanted the nation to commemorate the joining with a golden spike, on May 10, 1869, of the Central Pacific and the Union Pacific railroads. Inspired by her childhood memory of the sounds of the transcontinental railroad speeding along tracks half a mile from her home in Corinne, Utah, she wrote nearly three thousand articles, press releases, and letters to congressmen, railroad officials, and presidents, campaigning from the mid-1920s to the mid-1960s.[88]

In an exchange of letters with President Dwight D. Eisenhower in 1954, she invited him to the third annual reenactment of the driving of the golden spike. If it had not been completed in 1869, she explained, California would have "seceded from the Union, taking the other western states and territories with her and we would have had to fight another Civil War." Not only should the national government "preserve this spot," but it should "build a museum, landscape the area, provide trackage . . . and provide a permanent caretaker-historian." She reminded him that President Lincoln signed the act that built the railroad and "you, as president could render this beloved country of ours another service by preserving this sacred spot for future generations." After he thanked her for a piece of the original rail, she said she would treasure his letter of thanks, but "as a fighting General" he could "understand the struggle that has been made and will still go on, to secure National recognition for this National event to which we owe so much."[89]

When Utah congressmen approached the Park Service in 1949, Director Newton Drury told them the site did not have national significance, but in 1957 the Park Service designated Golden Spike as a national historic site in non-Federal ownership with no commitment other than a plaque. By then, Anderson, as chair of the Golden Spike Committee, had been organizing annual reenactment ceremonies for five years and attendance had increased to more than one thousand people. At this point, Park Service Director Conrad Wirth asked Robert Utley to evaluate Promontory Summit as a national historic site. Anderson was heard at last; in 1960, Utley recommended that the Park Service support the project. Utah senators introduced legislation the following year and the bill passed in 1964, just five years before the centennial celebration. Anderson's decades-long crusade was won.[90]

The proponents of the most heated historic preservation battle of the last few decades, known as the Third Battle of Manassas, were victorious over odds that seemed insurmountable to all but its leader, Annie Snyder, and her army of supporters. A former lieutenant in the Marine Corps, Snyder and her family had lived on a farm overlooking Manassas National Battlefield Park in Virginia for nearly forty years. They saw the park as ground made sacred by the nearly 25,000 soldiers who died or were wounded in the two battles fought there early in the Civil War. Called the First and Second Battles of Manassas by the Confederate Army and the First and Second Battles of Bull Run by the Union Army, the conflicts demonstrated to an overconfident Union that the war would not be won by a few skirmishes. Stuart's Hill, site of General Robert E. Lee's headquarters, lay just outside the park.

For Annie Snyder, who in 1988 led an army of preservationists in the Save the Battlefield Coalition to defeat a plan to build a shopping mall on Stuart's Hill, it was the sixth, shortest, and most intense Third Battle of Manassas. She was "hooked on Manassas" in the 1950s, when Superintendent Francis Wilshin guided her over the battlefield and brought it to life for her. Wilshin was enlisting supporters to defeat an interstate highway planned to bisect the park and invited Snyder to join them. The campaign was successful and the highway was redirected to south of the park.

After participating in a few skirmishes to protect the battlefield, Snyder joined the Save the Battlefield Committee to defeat an annex to Arlington National Cemetery planned for the park. In their next encounter, the committee defeated a Marriott Corporation plan to build a theme park on Stuart's Hill. Realizing that the Prince William County Board of Supervisors, who supported the Marriott plan, was looking for tax revenues from development, the committee joined other Manassas supporters to ask Congress to extend the park boundaries. When Congress expanded the park in 1980, however, the preserved area still did not include Stuart's Hill.[91]

The 1988 preservation battle was joined after the Hazel/Peterson Company bought Stuart's Hill. The Board of Supervisors supported the company's plan for a corporate park with residences. Believing the plan was the best they could hope for, the Battlefield Committee joined others to negotiate with the company to reduce the number of residences, fund archeological research, and build buffers to protect the park. Unexpectedly, Hazel/Peterson switched plans and announced its intention to build a shopping mall on the site and level Stuart's Hill. The only permission they needed was the county permit they already possessed.[92]

Snyder moved into action. She pulled together Manassas supporters to create a new group, the Save the Battlefield Coalition, and, as chair, devoted full time to the fight. When the Hazel/Peterson Company began to bulldoze the site, they raised the stakes: the coalition, having at first expected only to stop the mall, now, with the support of several congressmen, decided that nothing short of acquiring Stuart's Hill would satisfy them. By the June congressional hearing, they had collected 36,000 signatures on petitions, a number that more than doubled over the next few months, and garnered the support of more than a hundred organizations, representing 1.5 million members. In July, Snyder organized a reenactment weekend and rally that was attended by four thousand people, including Virginia Senator John Warner, who announced his support. Each weekend, coalition members staffed a table at the park to collect signatures and sell T shirts, visors, and bumper stickers that read: Don't Mall the Battlefield.[93]

As the campaign gained momentum, help came from many quarters. Jody Powell, former press secretary to President Carter, helped turn the cause into a national issue, gaining publicity in national publications. In all, more than six hundred articles and newspaper stories were printed. The National Parks and Conservation Association, the National Trust for Historic Preservation, veterans' associations, and Civil War roundtables all put pressure on their delegates to Congress.[94]

On Armistice Day 1988, ten months after the Third Battle of Manassas began, President Ronald Reagan signed the bill adding 558 acres, including Stuart's Hill, to the park. The cost was approximately $118 million. Betty Rankin, president of the Save the Battlefield Coalition, said the message was clear: "The American people will not sit down and let people destroy historic resources." Linda McCarthy, who staffed the Coalition's Manassas booth every weekend, agreed: "People could not comprehend video vendors, fast food factories, and Reebok retailers holding court where brave men died to preserve a country." There was a major difference between the Third Battle of Manassas and the first two, she noted. In 1988, it was "women who made up the bulk of the foot soldiers" and "toiled the longest and the most."[95] It seemed as though it was a reverence for life that led women to honor the dead with such passion. The women who led the Third Battle of Manassas, combined with a wave of public interest in the Civil War expressed by thousands of participants at weekend reenactments, had helped the Park Service gain support to preserve a landscape commemorating the sacrifices of war.

Bringing the Arts to the Park Service

A national heritage that the Park Service did not recognize as significant until recently was the arts. Even in the 1990s, only a handful of its sites represent the creation of America's literature, fine arts, and the performing arts.[96] Women who spoke out for the arts helped propel the Park Service in a new direction. Wolf Trap Farm Park, a center for the performing arts located on rolling Virginia countryside outside Washington, D.C., was the brainchild of Catherine Filene Shouse; rehabilitating playwright Eugene O'Neill's Tao house on the eastern slope of the California Coast Range in the San Francisco Bay Area owed its success to the woman-run Eugene O'Neill Foundation; and the drive to establish Weir Farm National Historic Site, home and landscape of painter J. Alden Weir in southwestern Connecticut involved many women activists.

Catherine Shouse, the daughter of Lincoln Filene, founder of Filene's department store in Boston, and wife of Jouett Shouse, a former congressman and chair of the Democratic National Committee, knew how to marshall the financial and political resources needed to carry out her goals. A patron of the performing arts, Shouse became concerned about preserving open space after a highway bisected her extensive Virginia farm. She connected the two ideas in the mid-1960s by offering to donate half of her farm to the National Park Service for a performing arts center. Her pattern of working was clear from the beginning. When she met a luke-warm reception from a regional director, she went directly to Interior Secretary Stewart Udall. He immediately authorized Park Service Director Hartzog to ex-plore the possibilities. In keeping with the service's mission, planners included the interpretation of the performing arts in American culture along with building an open-sided theater.[97]

From the time that Shouse first approached Udall until Congressional approval of the project, less than two years elapsed. Shouse sweetened her donation of land with funds for the amphitheater, and Hartzog drew up a bill for Congress. Park Service responsibility included operating the facility and the surrounding park, and, as the plan developed, the Wolf Trap Foundation became a cooperating asso-ciation to raise money, determine the theatrical program, hire the artists, and sell tickets.[98]

Shouse remained in charge. She chose the architect and the site, disregarding Park Service recommendations. She kept the project politically secure by asking First Lady Lady Bird Johnson to break the ground for the building and First Lady Patricia Nixon to signal the raising of a Virginia pine to top off the structure. She kept up the pressure for a 1971 opening season, despite cost overruns, strikes by workers, a fire, and a crack in the theater's supporting trusses. At the opening on July 1, a major social event, she named the theater the Filene Center to honor her parents. The Park Service accepted the building but was left to solve problems of public access, parking, design flaws, leaks, roosting birds, and traffic noise. Over and over again the service had to return to Congress for additional appropria-tions. Each time Shouse used carefully cultivated political relationships to gain the funding.[99]

Another woman helped Wolf Trap to succeed, but from within the Park Ser-vice: Claire St. Jacques, formerly production manager at the Kennedy Center, served as Wolf Trap's administrator for nearly twenty years. She was committed to its mis-sion. "The performing arts is our heritage;" she said, "we had performers before we could write." St. Jacques developed programs to interpret the arts for adults and children, preserved the facility, including the grounds, and kept the operation steady. Although she had been Shouse's choice, after St. Jacques opposed some of Shouse's ideas on the basis of cost and feasibility, Shouse tried to have her removed. Con-gress's watchful eye brought St. Jacques unsolicited support and she continued in her position.[100]

Wolf Trap's Filene Center burned to the ground in 1982. Both public and po-litical support convinced Congress, which in 1966 had expected to allocate only $500,000 a year to support the park, to appropriate 9 million dollars and loan 8 mil-lion to the Wolf Trap Foundation to reconstruct the building. Characteristically, Shouse pressured contractors to rush the construction and problems developed. The center reopened in 1984 for a short season and a full season the next year. Wolf Trap now hosts more than half a million visits a year.[101] With its opening, the Park Service redefined its mission to include the nation's heritage in the performing arts. A well-connected woman whose great persistence kept her in the center of controversy made it happen.

Meanwhile, in California, a group of women organized to establish a national historic site for Eugene O'Neill, the only American playwright to be awarded the Nobel Prize for Literature and the winner of four Pulitzer prizes. Their goal was to save Tao House, the home O'Neill designed and built with his money from the Nobel prize in the Las Trampas Hills, east of the Oakland Hills. In 1974, with Darlene Blair as president and Lois Sizoo as executive vice president, the group formed the Eugene O'Neill Foundation: their goal to raise money to buy Tao House. When the house had come on the market, nearly ten years earlier, concerned citizens blocked the sale and formed an association for the purpose of establishing a national monument. Although bills were introduced into Congress, no action was taken; but Tao House did receive National Landmark status in 1971.

The impetus for the new foundation was a plan by the East Bay Regional Park District to buy land surrounding Tao House and include an option on the Tao House property to allow the foundation time to raise the funds. Fifteen benefit performances of O'Neill's play *Hughie,* acted by Jason Robards and Jack Dodson, raised funds for a down payment that secured a mortgage and access to the property. A high point of the fundraising program was an outdoor presentation at Tao House of *A Moon for the Misbegotten,* performed by Oregon Shakespeare Festival actors. Plans were made to open a major theater library, remodel a building on the property for artists-in-residence, and hold readings and seminars.[102]

California Senator Alan Cranston and Congressman George Miller persuaded the Park Service to accept Tao House as a national historic site, with the understanding that the building would be donated. The foundation and its supporters convinced the California legislature to appropriate the remaining funds from a special park preservation fund in time for the ensuing Congressional hearing. Stating that it was time for the government to "preserve our cultural heritage," Darlene Blair noted that only two national parks represented literary achievement. Congress passed the Tao House bill in 1976.[103]

The foundation worked on returning furniture, or duplicates, to the house, and even found the same model of O'Neill's beloved Rosie, a player piano. Foundation members believe the Park Service did a "beautiful job of restoration," but many of their plans were put on hold. The Park Service opened Tao House to the public in 1985, but, because of legal problems with access roads, visits are limited to two small groups transported by a van five days a week. But by 1996, the O'Neill Foundation was able to offer performances of early modern plays at Tao House and the research library was up and running.[104]

Women were among the key players in the chain of concerned people responsible for preserving the landscape and home of J. Alden Weir, an American Impressionist painter. Weir Farm National Historic Site protects the landscape painted at the turn of the century by Weir and his associates, as well as his house and studios. Visitors who follow a painting trail recognize sites depicted by these artists and see them being painted again by a new generation, this time including children.

The first person in the preservation chain was Weir's daughter, Dorothy, who married sculptor Mahonri Young, and kept the property unchanged during her lifetime. In 1957 it was sold to artists Doris and Sperry Andrews, who were also determined to protect it. When some of the land that had been previously sold was threatened by development, Doris Andrews rallied support. In the adjoining towns of Ridgefield and Wilton, she contacted Lillian Willis and Nancy Fasey, chairs of each town's Conservation Commission, who lobbied the state to protect the site's open space and wetlands as a state park.

When Andrews involved the Trust for Public Land (TPL), she found the link that led to the Park Service. TPL assigned planner Katherine Barnar to the project and took options on the land. When Barnar told Sarah Peskin, a Park Service planner, about Weir Farm, Peskin suggested she contact the service.

By the time of the congressional hearings in 1990, supporters had created the Weir Farm Heritage Trust, chaired by Terry I. Tondro, a law professor; convinced the state of the Connecticut to buy a ring of lands around the house and studios; and developed countrywide support. When the director of the Park Service, James M. Ridenour, opposed the project, suggesting that Weir might not be the best artist to interpret, Barnar faxed twenty art museums and received immediate support. Senator Joseph Lieberman led the Connecticut congressional delegation in favor of the bill, noting that Connecticut had no other national park. Barbara Cairnes on Lieberman's staff drummed up support on Capitol Hill and President George Bush signed it into law in 1990.

Still a partnership between the Weir Farm Heritage Trust and the National Park Service, Weir Farm is the only Park Service site recognizing a painter. Katherine Barnar became the volunteer chair of the Trust's Council of Overseers charged with working cooperatively with the Park Service to raise funds and develop programs. Barnar believes having national park status "nails down its national importance." She said, "Art is important," adding, "and the rural lifestyle is there forever."[105]

Promoting Racial Pride and Healing

Giving voice to racial pride and healing, African-American and Asian-American women headed drives to add sites to the National Park System that represent times of racial division and reconciliation.

Two women's organizations worked for half a century to protect the home of former slave and civil rights leader Frederick Douglass, on Cedar Hill, in the Anacostia section of Washington, D.C. The National Association of Colored Women's Clubs (later NACW) and the Frederick Douglass Memorial and Historical Association applied scarce resources to protect the house. NACW President Mary Talbert expressed their reasons in 1916 when the group announced a campaign to save the home. She compared the modern struggle with that of their enslaved ancestors:

"We realize today is the psychological moment for us women to show our true worth and prove that Negro women of today measure up to those sainted women of our race, who passed through the fire of slavery and its galling remembrances."[106]

Although Douglass's second wife, Helen Pitts Douglass, left the house with its contents as they were when Douglass died in 1895 to the all-male Memorial Association, the house was tied to a small mortgage. After unsuccessfully trying to raise funds, the association asked the NACW to take over. The women created a committee from the NACW membership that became the nucleus for a new all-woman Memorial Association. After 1916, when the NACW accepted the charge at its national convention, saving the Frederick Douglass Home was the responsibility of African-American women.[107]

By 1921, the women had raised enough money to burn the mortgage and improve the structural condition of the house and its grounds. The following summer, the NACW and the association, justly proud of their achievement and anxious to generate continued support, dedicated the Douglass Memorial Home and hired a caretaker to live in a cottage they built on the property. But the onset of the Depression and the efforts of the NACW to fund a national headquarters drained the organization of resources, and only a minimum was available to maintain the home. Small donations—some of them pennies from children in segregated schools—barely paid utility bills and taxes. Workers assigned by Mary McLeod Bethune, director of the Division of Negro Affairs of the National Youth Administration, landscaped the grounds. When Nannie Helen Burroughs, a prominent Memorial Association trustee who lived in the area, chastised both the NACW and the association for allowing the home and grounds to deteriorate, the NACW voted funds at its 1941 biennial meeting, but, in 1950, after a controversy over which group should possess the title to the home, the NACW voted to provide no more funds to the project.[108]

Meanwhile, in 1949, the Memorial Association had the good fortune to find an effective caretaker. Gladys Parham, who worked at Walter Reed Medical Center, was not paid for her work at the home until the Park Service hired her as an interpreter in 1965, but she showed great resourcefulness in maintaining the property. Her reaction to the withdrawal of NACW support was, aided by her Cub Scout troop, to clear the weeds and plant a garden.[109]

The rift was healed in 1961. After a joint fund-raising effort had met with little success, the women decided that only the federal government could save the Frederick Douglass Home. The civil rights movement was in full swing and set the tone. The NACW president, Rosa Gragg, and the Memorial Association president, Mary Gregory, joined forces. Gragg's godson, Charles Diggs Jr., a congressman from Detroit, and Phillip Hart, a Michigan senator and old friend of Gragg's, agreed to introduce the bill. Gragg stayed in Washington to lobby for the bill; hearings were held in May 1962 and President John F. Kennedy signed it into law that September, transferring care of the home to the Park Service, and presenting pens to Gragg and Gregory at the ceremony. The Memorial Association had to return to Congress for increased appropriations in 1969, before the Park Service could complete its re-habilitation of the site, including curating the historic contents, so carefully pro-tected over the years by the women.[110]

The Frederick Douglass Home reopened in 1972, in wintery weather to a thou-sand people on Douglass's birthday, February 14. In keeping with the kind of effort it had been, Gladys Parham, Dorothy Benton, Park Service community relations coordinator, and Benton's aunt worked on shortening curtains, found at the last minute to be a foot too long, until 2 A.M. the night before. Both Gragg and Greg-ory spoke, each representing their organizations, after some discussion about who should be first. In 1985, a new visitor center and a major film followed; the park became a national historic site three years later. Always on the women's consciences but needing more funds than were ever available, the Frederick Douglass Home was finally redeemed, in the words of Mary Talbert, "so that our children and chil-dren's children will know who sacrificed and left this heritage to them."[111]

Linda Brown Buckner and her sisters Cheryl Brown Henderson and Terry Brown Tyler are the figurative granddaughters of the African-American women who wanted history to mentor the future by preserving Frederick Douglass' legacy. Their father's name was first on the pivotal civil rights case, *Brown vs. Board of Education of Topeka* that led the U.S. Supreme Court to declare that racially segre-gated schools violated the equal protection clause of the U.S. Constitution. In 1951, Lucinda Todd, secretary of the Topeka National Association for the Advancement of Colored People (NAACP), wrote the national office that their branch and a local law firm were ready to challenge school segregation in Topeka. Encouraged by the national office, the Topeka NAACP looked for parents who were willing, as Henderson later expressed it, to "walk their kids to that [white] school to docu-ment denial."[112]

Oliver Brown, the Brown sisters' father, was the only male to volunteer. An as-sistant pastor at the St. John A.M.E. Church, he was also a welder whose job was protected by union membership. Although the Browns lived only four blocks from the white Sumner School, Linda, the eldest daughter, had to walk six blocks along railroad tracks to catch a bus to the black Monroe School. Oliver Brown joined Lucinda Todd and eleven other African-American mothers as plaintiffs after each of their children in turn was refused admittance to a Topeka white school.[113]

In 1990, Cheryl Brown Henderson, by then an educator herself, learned that the Monroe School was up for sale. Two years before, she and Linda had set up the Brown Foundation for Educational Equity, Excellence and Research to honor their father's memory. Henderson realized that the Monroe School was a site of national significance and went on a "one-woman letter writing campaign" to find a black leader to buy it. She got no response until she wrote the Kansas congressional del-egation. After Senator Nancy Kassebaum suggested that Henderson contact the In-terior Department, she learned that in 1987, after completing a theme study com-memorating the bicentennial of the Constitution, Park Service historian Harry Butowsky had nominated the Sumner Elementary School as a National Historic

Landmark. Henderson told Butowsky that the job was only "half done" because it did not include the Monroe School.[114]

Only two years elapsed from the time Henderson first talked to the Park Service until Brown v. Board of Education National Historic Site was established in 1992. Butowsky helped her apply for landmark status for the Monroe School, an essential step, and she hand-carried it to a National Park Advisory Board meeting at Estes Park for immediate approval. The Kansas congressional delegation requested a feasibility study for a national historic site and Henderson faxed their request to Michael Hayden, assistant secretary of interior, a former Kansas governor, and prompted local groups to support a park. Henderson's input added important sites to the park: the post office, where, on the second floor, the federal district court first heard the Brown case; Lucinda Todd's home, where strategy was planned around the dining room table; the law office for the NAACP; and her family's former home.[115]

Henderson worked with Kansas congressional staffers to draft the bill. By then she had the support of Senator Robert Dole who scheduled a Senate hearing. When she found it was too late in the session for a House hearing, she located women to pressure Bruce Vento, chair of the House subcommittee on parks, to hold a special hearing. When Vento added other park needs to the bill, Dole hesitated, but Henderson asked him to pass it anyway, saying that she was not "going away," she was not "giving up."[116]

In her testimony, Henderson noted that only 5 percent of national historic landmarks and sites "relate directly to the role of African Americans" and the new site helps "ensure a more representative National Parks system." In 1996, inspired by the success of the Brown site, Angela Bates concluded a five-year campaign to establish Nicodemus National Historic Site, also in Kansas, the location of a black pioneer community founded by freed slaves in 1877.[117]

Errors in America's past are also acknowledged at Manzanar National Historic Site. Established in 1992, Manzanar is another site that honors the persons who were wronged in an effort to ensure that the action is part of the national memory so it will not be repeated. For more than twenty-five years, Sue Kunitomi Embrey, chair of the Manzanar Committee, has been giving voice to the story of the Japanese Americans interned by the United States government in ten relocation camps during World War II.[118]

Embrey was one of ten thousand Japanese Americans sent to the Manzanar War Relocation Center, a mile-square camp, surrounded by barbed wire and topped by eight guard towers, in the Owens Valley below the Sierra Nevada Mountains. Taken from their homes and livelihoods, they were gathered in assembly centers before being sent to camps to live in barracks. Tiny units housed four families with common lavatories and mess halls. Part of the Japanese-American story is the community they created with gardens, schools, an orphanage, a cemetery, newspapers, and poetry, all essential for their spiritual and emotional survival. When they were released, most remained silent and tried to put the experience behind them.[119]

In 1969, during the Free Speech Movement in California sparked by Vietnam War protests, a Buddhist priest and a Christian minister organized the first pilgrimage to Manzanar for students at the University of California at Los Angeles. Embrey and her husband joined the participants; afterwards, Embrey gave interviews to students about her experience. Anxious to have the U.S. government admit the wrong, Embrey organized the Manzanar Committee. Joining with the Japanese-American Citizens League, the committee convinced the state to designate Manzanar a California State Historic Landmark in 1972. The Park Service followed in 1985, designating it a National Historic Landmark. Annual pilgrimages continued each April, with growing participation. Embrey also developed a lending library with materials about the internment camps.[120]

The effort to bring Manzanar into the National Park System had to wait until the campaign for redress was over. Although Congress established a commission to review the internment in 1980, it was not until 1988 that President Ronald Reagan signed a bill expressing an official apology. It took two more years before the federal government produced reparations payments. In 1990, Embrey and the Manzanar Committee asked California Representative Mel Levine to introduce the bill making Manzanar a National Historic Site. Rose Ochi, who often had business in Washington, helped with the lobbying. After a year in committee, the bill passed, but there was opposition from the Los Angeles Department of Water and Power, owners of the property. Before the Senate would release the bill, the Los Angeles City Council had to pass a resolution supporting it and requesting the department to cooperate.[121]

On the fiftieth anniversary of Manzanar, in 1992, the pilgrimage attracted more than two thousand people. Park rangers from Death Valley donated their time. Although only a few buildings remain on the site, eight Japanese-American landscape architects who were themselves interned have volunteered to help the Park Service with its plans. Sue Embrey wants visitors to enter through the guard posts and walk to the cemetery at the rear so they will experience the impact of being confined in one square mile. The site is also about reconciliation. The American Legion, who at first opposed the site, in 1994, at the twenty-fifth annual pilgrimage, carried their colors at the request of the Manzanar Committee. The occasion was the Oasis Garden Club's designation of the highway outside Manzanar as a Blue Star Memorial Highway to honor the Japanese Americans who served in a regimental combat team and in military intelligence during World War II.[122]

A remarkable group of women, whose causes were pursued independently of one another, unknowingly spoke with one voice. They were determined to expand the country's definition of national significance to include urban landscapes; contested shorelines, wetlands, and tundra; artistic endeavors; and racial pride and conflict.

Meanwhile a new generation of women continued to support the service's mission by working as employees inside the Park Service. At the same time, women on the outside, anxious to bring issues of equity for women to a national forum, found women allies within the Park Service to help them redeem historic sites representing the struggles and achievements of women themselves.

Claiming Women's
Legitimate Place

*A*t Seneca Falls, New York—in 1848, the place of the nation's first women's rights convention—Women's Rights National Historical Park today makes a bold statement in support of equal rights for women. The restoration of this historic space and the opening of its first permanent exhibit brings both women and national parks to the threshold of the twenty-first century.

Preserved to the east of the visitor center are the remains of the Wesleyan Chapel, the site of the 1848 convention, and Declaration Park, where a 140-foot, bluestone water wall is inscribed with the *Declaration of Sentiments,* the resolutions passed at the convention that became the cornerstone of the first women's rights movement, proclaiming: "All men and women are created equal." The opening of the Wesleyan Chapel Block in July 1993 was the culmination of an effort that had roots in a hundred years of commemorative celebrations. Authorized in 1980, the park opened, in 1985, the house where Elizabeth Cady Stanton, the major author of the *Declaration of Sentiments,* lived at the time of the convention. The park is particularly significant because women inside the park service joined women outside to create it.

Parallel to the creation of a women's rights national park were movements of other women to claim women's legitimate place in the nation's history. Inspired by the second wave of feminism, they defined and preserved the roles of historic women in new national sites and landmarks. Within the Park Service itself, women came together in two major conferences to define their own roles, to assume legitimacy within the agency, and to seek advancement.

A Park for Women's Rights

The movement that created a women's rights national park in Seneca Falls can be dated back nearly a century. Successive groups of women used the anniversaries of the 1848 convention to press for women's rights. In 1908, on the sixtieth anniversary of the convention, Harriot Stanton Blatch, Elizabeth Cady Stanton's daughter, organized the celebration to spur the still-unrealized drive for women's suffrage. Ella Hawley Crossett, president of the New York State Suffrage Association, unveiled a commemorative sculptured bronze tablet on the Wesleyan Chapel site, followed by an address, given by Mary Church Terrell, the first president of the National Association of Colored Women. Terrell reminded the audience that in 1848 Frederick Douglass seconded the suffrage resolution, at the time considered to be the most radical in the *Declaration of Sentiments.* Blatch then embarked on a campaign for the vote in New York, traveling with visibility on canal-boats and trolley-cars.[1]

The National Woman's Party launched its campaign for the Equal Rights Amendment (ERA) at Seneca Falls in 1923, on the convention's seventy-fifth anniversary, but they had to choose an alternate location because the chapel had become a garage and the owner had removed the tablet. Summoned by bugles, the audience watched one hundred young women in Grecian robes portray the progress of women through the ages. The next day, five hundred young women, dressed in white and carrying purple and gold banners, heralded an illuminated banner printed with the text of the ERA. This event introduced speeches by the National Woman's Party leaders, Alice Paul and Alva Belmont.[2]

Members of the League of Women Voters from three counties organized a celebration in 1928. They met to restore the commemorative tablet at the chapel site, because the building had become a car dealership, with a sympathetic owner. A centennial celebration in 1948 produced a new pageant and an assembly at which prominent women urged the two thousand women participants to become more involved in government. Beginning in 1970, the fiftieth anniversary of the passage of the women's suffrage amendment, celebrations were also held on August 26, named Women's Equality Day.[3]

Although there was talk, especially during anniversaries, of buying the chapel site or a house connected with the women of 1848, the only purchase was of a building, a few blocks from the Wesleyan Chapel site, by the National Women's Hall of Fame in 1979. Organized by local women in 1969 but directed by a national board, the Hall of Fame selects notable women for induction and displays. By the end of 1994, they had chosen 107 women.[4]

Meanwhile, women in the Park Service, too, were responding to the second wave of feminism. When Judy Hart, legislative affairs specialist for the North Atlantic Region, was scouting for new projects in 1978, she looked for sites portraying women. She conferred with Peggy Lipson, her counterpart in Washington, and when they searched in the eight-state region for women's sites that were already National Historic Landmarks they found only two, both in upstate New York and both commemorating women's rights leaders: the Susan B. Anthony house in Rochester, New York, and the Elizabeth Cady Stanton house in Seneca Falls. Hart and landscape architect Shary Berg decided to visit the area. Because Berg had recently worked on a project with Nancy Dubner, staff assistant to Maryanne Krupsak, New York lieutenant governor, she called Dubner, who seized the opportunity to recommend Seneca Falls. Rochester women had preserved the Anthony house, she explained, but the Stanton house was for sale and local women had already asked for help. The national significance of the Wesleyan Chapel had been newly demonstrated to Dubner when, present at both the start, at Seneca Falls, and the finish, at Houston, she had watched women runners relay a lighted torch to open the 1977 National Women's Conference, linking the two conventions. As she stood by the Wesleyan Chapel remains, Dubner remembered thinking, "This was the critical place."[5]

Local events made the visit of the Park Service women to Seneca Falls particularly propitious: the business community was upgrading the central business district and open to fresh ideas. By then the Wesleyan Chapel had become a laundromat, but Hart discovered that the original roof line and some of the supporting walls still existed. An unexpected offer from Ralph Peters, a member of the National Organization for Women (NOW) in Seattle, to buy the Stanton House had impelled the local women to organize. On a pilgrimage to Seneca Falls, Peters and his wife, Marjorie Smith, had been shocked to find the house for sale. The realtor introduced Peters to Lucille Povero who pulled women together from an inactive chapter of NOW to form the Elizabeth Cady Stanton Foundation. Peters purchased the house and was willing to hold it until the foundation could raise the funds to take it over.[6]

Community enthusiasm and resources convinced the Park Service to move ahead with the necessary studies. Encouraged by Dubner, New York's Representative Jonathan Bingham and Senator Daniel P. Moynihan introduced bills for the park into Congress. Senate hearings reflected a wide-ranging community interest in a park. Testimony was offered by Stanton's great-granddaughter, Rhoda Jenkins; a women's historian; the deputy mayor; the director of the Women's Hall of Fame; the president of the Stanton Foundation; and Peters, owner of the house. President Carter signed the bill in 1980 at the end of his term.[7]

But the difficult work of creating a park out of disparate elements lay ahead. Before Judy Hart was named the first superintendent, early in 1982, she acted as park coordinator, spending a week of each month in the area. After the Stanton Foundation finished raising the funds to buy the house, with help from Stanton's great-grandchildren, a New York State matching grant, and actor Alan Alda, Ralph Peters was no longer sure he wanted to sell. He disapproved of new Interior Secretary James Watt and did not trust the department to take proper care of the Stanton house. A meeting arranged by Judy Hart between Peters and Park Service Director Russell Dickenson convinced him that the house would be in safe hands.[8]

Although the park had received only limited appropriations, Hart and her advisory committee opened it in July 1982 on a shoestring budget. They invited women's historians to a concurrent conference and the Stanton great-grandchildren hosted breakfast at the Stanton house. At the dedication, Alan Alda drew a large crowd, surprising his followers with his feminism. "These modest buildings of Seneca Falls," he said, "are as much a part of the soul of our democracy as those revered halls in which white, propertied men granted themselves freedom, liberty, and democracy." Corinne Guntzel, a founder of the Stanton Foundation, said that although for many businessmen the goal of the park was "to encourage tourism, a lot of consciousness raising went on at the same time."[9]

As the vision of the women in the Park Service and in Seneca Falls began to expand, local and national interest developed. Appropriations were forthcoming. In 1985, the Park Service completed its rehabilitation of the Stanton house and purchased the Wesleyan Chapel building. Acquisition of the Wesleyan Chapel Block was completed when the village of Seneca Falls donated its former office building to the park for a visitor center. The challenge of how to treat the area when so little remained of the chapel, the primary site, was resolved by a national design competition, held in cooperation with the National Endowment for the Arts. Park Service Director William Penn Mott announced the competition in 1987 in the rotunda of the U.S. Capitol as he stood in front of a statue of his ancestor, Lucretia Mott, a principal organizer of the 1848 convention. Senator Moynihan and Representative Frank Horton's presence signified their crucial support. From the 212 entries, a national jury of architects and landscape architects selected the design of Ray Knoshita and Ann Wills Marshall.[10]

By the groundbreaking for the Wesleyan Chapel Block in the fall of 1991, a $12 million federal appropriation for park development expressed the commitment of Congress, the Park Service, and the local community to the significance of the issues raised at the 1848 Women's Rights Convention. The park also expected to rehabilitate the M'Clintock House in nearby Waterloo, where the convention was planned. The park joined the National Women's Hall of Fame to set up a Women's Educational and Cultural Center, offering off-campus courses and women's history workshops in conjunction with local colleges.[11]

When visitors walk into the Women's Rights visitor center, they mingle with nineteen life-sized bronze statues of women and men who attended the 1848 convention. A multicultural display on two floors includes interactive video exhibits, speaking to the issue of equal rights by posing open-ended questions such as "Is there a sexual double standard?" Visitors are invited to leave behind responses to the question, "What will it be like when men and women are truly equal?"[12]

Defining History Through Women's Lives

As the women's movement gained momentum in the 1970s, independent groups of women sought to change the Park Service's view of history by lobbying for historic sites and national landmarks about women whose primary achievements were in the twentieth century. They began with women who had personally inspired them: Eleanor Roosevelt, Mary McLeod Bethune, and Maggie Walker. Although the Park Service accepted as the first historic site devoted to a woman's life the home and work place of Clara Barton because she was the founder of the American Red Cross, women interpreters soon set Barton's life in the context of women's history.

The addition of these new sites represented a major change in the Park Service's definition of what is significant in history. In 1975, when Nancy Dubner first proposed Val-Kill, Eleanor Roosevelt's home in Hyde Park, New York, as a national historic site, the Park Service historian assigned to review the proposal dismissed it, saying: "Mrs. Roosevelt's position in history is not clear." Dubner's interpretation of the reply was that, to the reviewer, "the position of *women* in history was not clear."[13]

Nowhere in the rationale for the addition of the Clara Barton historic site into the National Park System in 1974 is the significance that it represented a woman's life mentioned. A Park Service official testified that the "principal purpose . . . is, of course, to tell the early story of the American Red Cross through the interpretation of the life and times of its founder, Clara Barton." Many of the members of the Friends of Clara Barton who preserved the house and offered it to the Park Service were volunteers for the Red Cross. Both men and women, they worked for more than a decade to buy and maintain the house, by holding benefits, by soliciting for funds, and by renting apartments within the house. They conducted tours of the remarkable building, designed as a warehouse for disaster and war relief supplies, that was used by Barton as both Red Cross headquarters and her home. For the Friends, she represented a model of "patriotism and heroism"; that she was also a woman was not mentioned.[14]

In addition to telling the Red Cross story after the park opened in April 1975, however, women interpreters tied Barton's life story to the lives of Victorian women. Supervisor Heather Huyck introduced Barton to public school classrooms during women's history month and started Sunday afternoon events. At a "Suffragist Lawn Party," where speakers in period clothing presented the words of suffragists, the woman playing Clara Barton told the audience that women were entitled to the vote because of the strength they exhibited during the Civil War. The Park Service began to list the site as one "commemorating American women." [15]

Nancy Dubner's quest to preserve Val-Kill—the cottages that had been Eleanor Roosevelt's place of renewal as well as her primary residence from 1945 until her death in 1962—was both personal and feminist. In the mid-1950s, as student vice chair of the Collegiate Councils for the United Nations, she worked with Eleanor Roosevelt and was inspired by her. Twenty years later, after representing Lieutenant Governor Maryanne Krupsak at a meeting, Dubner visited Eleanor Roosevelt's grave at the Roosevelt home in Hyde Park. There Dubner had what she described as "close to a religious experience": she felt a strong desire to talk with her. After Dubner toured the house, guided by Eleanor Roosevelt's voice on tape, she asked to visit nearby Val-Kill. Not only did she learn that it was not part of the historic site, but she also found that Val-Kill was in jeopardy. John Roosevelt inherited Val-Kill when Eleanor Roosevelt died in 1962 and sold it in 1970, auctioning off its contents. The two new owners were trying to get a zoning variance to build a senior citizen complex on the 180-acre site.

Dubner contacted county and state planning and preservation officers to set up a meeting and visit to Val-Kill with park superintendent Warren Hill and William Emerson, director of the Roosevelt Library. The cottages, rented to six families, were falling into disrepair. Because the state had a budget crisis, Dubner decided that only the Park Service could protect Val-Kill. When, with the blessing of Krupsak, she wrote on official stationery to her congressmen, the proposal was turned down.[16]

Meanwhile, a local effort to protect the landscape at Val-Kill was underway, particularly because the area represented the last open space in Hyde Park and included important wetlands. Joyce Ghee and Joan Spence, of the Hyde Park Visual Environment Committee, were working to develop trails to connect the Val-Kill space, the three-hundred acres of the Roosevelt home, and the two-hundred acres of the Vanderbilt Mansion, also a national historic site. They knew that the Hyde Park community would be reluctant to have any more land withdrawn from the tax rolls and hoped to work with the potential developers to allow access to the area and to mitigate the effects on the environment of any project. Superintendent Hill put Dubner in touch with Ghee and Spence; together they formed the Eleanor Roosevelt Cottage Committee with Ghee and Dubner as co-chairs. Because both state and federal governments had turned them down, they thought they would have to raise the money privately.

A serendipitous catalyst, as unexpected as Ralph Peters's purchase of the Stanton home at Seneca Falls, propelled Val-Kill into being authorized as a national historic site in only one year. It was actress Jean Stapleton's visit to the Roosevelt Library to study the words and voice of Eleanor Roosevelt. She hoped to change her image from the role of scatterbrained Edith Bunker on the television series "All in the Family," by playing the role of Eleanor Roosevelt, whom she greatly admired. She had also asked to see Val-Kill and was shocked at its condition. When library director Emerson told the cottage committee about Stapleton's interest, they asked her to perform a benefit to convince the town to support the preservation of Val-Kill.[17]

In June 1976, only six weeks after Stapleton's acceptance, the benefit played at a local high school to a standing-room-only audience. Curtis Roosevelt, a grandson, explained that Val-Kill was Eleanor Roosevelt's *place:* "She had no other place," he said, "it was her only place." He called her a "model of constructive rebellion" who fought for "the individual against dehumanizing bureaucracies." Maryanne Krupsak asked them to give "that outstanding human being the proper recognition and place she deserves in history." Stapleton's performance of a fifteen-minute fictional monologue, "Soul of Iron," written by Rhoda Lerman, was warmly received.[18]

Newly convinced of community support for the project, Nancy Dubner went back to Congress. Representative Jonathan Bingham agreed to introduce the bill and the New York congressional delegation fell into line. The cottage committee, now called Eleanor Roosevelt's Val-Kill (ERVK), made a film of "Soul of Iron," and Dubner aired it at the 1977 Women's Conference in Houston. The House hearings in Hyde Park revealed strong community support. At the Senate hearings in

Washington, Dubner reminded the national parks subcommittee how few national historic sites related to "the accomplishments of women," and Esther Peterson, who was a member of the President's Commission on the Status of Women chaired by Eleanor Roosevelt in 1961, testified on short notice. Identifying herself as an ERVK board member, Jean Stapleton introduced her film.[19]

Although Eleanor Roosevelt National Historic Site was authorized in May 1977, it did not officially open until her one hundredth birthday, October 11, 1984. Delays were caused by litigation with the owners over the price, extensive rehabilitation, and the search for the original furnishings. Several unique features were contained in the legislation. Upon the recommendation of the first site manager, Margaret Partridge, money designated for a memorial was used for a cutting garden instead of a statue, because Eleanor Roosevelt always prepared bouquets for guests. The act also created "a living memorial" to Eleanor Roosevelt, a role taken on by ERVK, with headquarters in the Val-Kill stone cottage. Among their programs is Youth Against Racism, which runs workshops and retreats where high school students explore racism, sexism, and homophobia. ERVK also awards medals to citizens whose lives exemplify Eleanor Roosevelt's principles.[20]

Two Park Service locations in Washington, D.C., commemorate Mary McLeod Bethune, one of the most prominent of all African-American women leaders in the first half of the twentieth century. The Bethune locations bring out the two major facets of her career. A statue in Lincoln Park showing her handing a copy of her legacy to two African-American children, signifies her role as an educator and founder of Bethune-Cookman College. Near Logan Circle, the Mary McLeod Bethune Council House National Historic Site represents her role as founder and president of the National Council of Negro Women (NCNW) and as an active participant in national politics. As director of the Division of Negro Affairs of the National Youth Administration, Bethune became the informal leader of President Roosevelt's Black Cabinet, as it was called. Connecting the themes of the two sites is the cane he willed to her that she carries in the statue.[21]

Dorothy Height, who became the fourth president of the NCNW, in 1957, saw Bethune as her mentor and led the drives for both sites. Congress authorized the statue in 1960 and the U.S. Fine Arts Commission approved the design, but the exigencies of the civil rights movement put the project on hold. When Height took it over in 1973, she raised more than $500,000 in less than a year. The crowd of 250,000 people attending the unveiling on July 10, 1974, the ninety-ninth anniversary of Bethune's birth, was welcomed by Shirley Chisholm, the first African-American congresswoman.[22]

The second Bethune site, the Bethune Council House, fulfilled one of Bethune's goals: it houses a facility to encourage the study and public awareness of African-American women's lives. When the NCNW left the building where she directed the organization and lived until her death in 1955, Bethune's plans could be carried out. In 1979, the Bethune Museum and Archives opened, with Dorothy Height as chair of the board. It soon became apparent that the project needed assistance and in 1982 the board asked Congress to designate the elegant Victorian residence as a national historic site, affiliated with the Park Service but still owned by the NCNW. Under Bettye Collier-Thomas, executive director, documents essential for researching the history of African-American women were protected and the museum flourished, presenting forums on contemporary issues, art exhibits, and programs featuring black women poets, dramatists, and musicians.[23]

Within a decade, the cost of maintaining the museum and archives at the level it deserved was cutting too deeply into the NCNW's ongoing programs. Dorothy Height and the museum board decided to return to Congress to ask the Park Service to take over the building and its interpretation. Georgia Congressman John Lewis introduced the bill and it passed in 1991. Lewis testified that Bethune's work "laid the foundation for the success of the civil rights movement." Within the Park Service, Dorothy Benton began the task of directing the planning. Cooperative agreements with groups connected with Bethune, assisted by an advisory commission, were invited to provide programs. Benton saw the site as an opportunity for the Park Service to put African-American women's history on center stage.[24]

The home in Richmond, Virginia, of community builder Maggie L. Walker was the first Park Service site devoted to interpreting the life of an African-American woman. Authorized in 1978, the park opened in 1985. When the Park Service was looking for sites expressing the black experience, the groundwork laid by the women of the Maggie L. Walker Historical Foundation paved the way.

Maggie Walker's goal was to uplift the status of African Americans by establishing black-run community institutions. Women were well represented on the governing boards of her enterprises. Among them was the St. Luke Penny Savings Bank. When Mozelle Sallee [Baxter] learned that the Consolidated Bank and Trust Company, successor to the St. Luke bank, was planning to raze Walker's original bank building because the company was moving into a new location, she called together a group of women to help save the old bank. Although the women lost their bid to save the bank building, they were already organized when the Walker house came on the market in 1974. They quickly changed their objective and incorporated as the Maggie L. Walker Historical Foundation.

Located in Jackson Ward, considered to be one of the most enterprising African-American neighborhoods in the nation, the Walker house expresses an important era in black life and was an excellent candidate for preservation. After Walker's death in 1934, her daughter-in-law lived in the house and kept its original contents intact for forty years. Maggie Walker's granddaughter, Dr. Maggie L. Lewis, inherited the house in 1994 and decided to sell it. The Walker Foundation moved in two directions at once: while raising funds to purchase the property, they began the process of convincing city officials of the significance of the house. With the help of a specialist in historic preservation, they succeeded in placing the house on the Virginia Landmarks Register and the National Register of Historic Places. They also applied to the city for funding to restore the house as a community development project.

In 1978 everything came together. The Richmond City Council decided to provide a grant that would not only purchase the house but also provide money for its restoration. When Park Service officials in the Mid-Atlantic Region expressed interest in the project, the women of the Maggie L. Walker Foundation proudly escorted them through the house. When the Park Service decided to purchase, restore, and interpret the home, the foundation returned the city's check. On Maggie Walker's 112th birthday, July 15, 1979, at a well-attended ceremony, Dr. Lewis presented the deed to the Park Service. Exactly six years later, at the ceremony to open the house, Director William Penn Mott presented the foundation with a citation for service.[25]

The significance of the Walker site continued to grow. The Jackson Ward neighborhood became a National Historic Landmark district. At a Park Service symposium on Maggie Walker in 1992, prominent historians presented papers. Founder of a fraternal insurance company, a black-run department store, a newspaper, and a bank, Walker served on the national boards of the National Council of Colored Women, the National Training School for Women and Girls, and the NAACP. Scholar Elsa Barkley Brown pointed out that "sisterhood . . . was Walker's base, her support, her strength, and her source of wisdom and direction."[26]

"Who Decides Who America Will Remember?"

The question of who determines what will be remembered or preserved from the past was raised by two quite different groups of women in the 1980s and 1990s. The ten-year endeavor to share sacred ground for a memorial to women Vietnam War nurses caused their leader, former combat nurse Diane Evans, to raise the fundamental question. "Who decides who America will remember?" she asked. "If it is the American people who decide, then we are truly a democratic nation."[27] Page Putnam Miller, who directed a project to add sites significant in the history of women to the list of National Historic Landmarks, took the issue one step further. "If Americans had to rely on existing historic sites for their understanding of women's history," Miller said, "a very limited and distorted picture would emerge."[28] Even women mountain climbers claimed historical space. In 1990, on the one-hundredth anniversary of Fay Fuller's ascent of Mt. Rainier, Kathy Phibbs, dressed in a skirt and a ribboned straw hat, reenacted Fuller's climb.[29]

In 1974, when Diane Evans conceived of the idea of placing a Vietnam Women's Memorial near the Vietnam Veterans Memorial (the Wall), she thought the primary task would be raising funds for a sculpture and gaining support from veterans' groups. Her goal was to aid the healing process for the 11,500 American military women who served in the Vietnam War, of whom 90 percent were nurses, and to honor the 265,000 military women who served during that era. As the committee grew and collected stories of individuals in their Sister Search, she became even more convinced of the rightness of the project. They incorporated as the Vietnam Women's Memorial Project, with Donna-Marie Boulay as chair.

At a press conference in St. Paul, Minnesota, in 1984, the women revealed their proposed statue, designed by Roger Brodin: a single nurse in uniform cradling a combat helmet, with medical instruments tucked in her pockets and hanging around her neck. By 1987, they had raised nearly $300,000 and started a newsletter. Early approvals came from the Vietnam Veterans Memorial Fund and Interior Secretary Donald P. Hodel, but in October 1987, the project suffered a major setback. The U.S. Fine Arts Commission rejected the proposal. The memorial to the Vietnam War was complete, they said, and if they included the women's sculpture, they would be open to projects from many other minority groups.

The rejection acted as a spur to the women. They protested by generating hundreds of letters to the commission and Congress. "Women make up half the population of the world," they said. "They are neither a minority nor a special interest group."[30] They convinced Senator Dave Durenberger of Minnesota to introduce a bill authorizing the completion of the Vietnam Veterans Memorial with a Vietnam Women's Memorial. At the Senate hearings, Evans asked that a statue for women stand "beside our soul mates, our brothers who served." Boulay listed twenty-seven groups who supported the project, and Park Service Director Mott added his approval. President Ronald Reagan signed the bill a few days after Veterans Day, 1988. Although the women's committee was now assured of a site, they still had to select a sculpture acceptable to the Fine Arts Commission and to two other commissions.[31] By then located in Washington, the project directors realized they had to leave Brodin's statue behind. In 1990, they held a design competition. A panel of architects and military people examined three hundred entries. Approvals and feasibility studies led to the selection of a sculpture by Glenna Goodacre, of Santa Fe.

The groundbreaking in July 1993, followed by the dedication the following Veterans Day, were emotional events, the latter attended by an estimated 25,000 people, thousands of whom were Vietnam War veterans. By then the project had raised $3.2 million of the $4 million needed. The statue depicts a nurse cradling a soldier's head, both figures supported by sandbags. A second nurse scans the sky and a third kneels. Diane Evans opened the ceremonies with "Welcome home, daughters of America." Now, certain that this piece of women's history was secure, she said, "Thank you for what you did. Let no one ever forget."[32]

When women's historians proposed the Women's History Landmark Project, only about 2.5 percent of the nation's two thousand National Historic Landmarks focused on women. Running from 1989 to 1994, the project nearly doubled the number of such landmarks. The goal of the project was to identify sites as signifiers of the work, art, lives, and causes of women throughout American history, and list them as National Historic Landmarks. Directed by Page Putnam Miller, the project was a cooperative agreement between the National Park Service and the Organization of American Historians and the National Coordinating Committee for the Promotion of History.

The effort raised many issues, however. Miller believes regulations for nominations lead to "an elitist approach to history." Some proposed sites, though local, were representative examples of women's work or lives. Because they did not appear to have the national significance needed for nomination as a landmark, the Park Service did not nominate them. Other women's sites were rejected because they did not meet standards of physical integrity. Miller believes such standards are more applicable to buildings nominated for architectural, not historical, significance.[33]

The addition of nearly fifty new National Historic Landmarks restored important examples of women's lives and work to public awareness. These included the Triangle Shirtwaist Factory Building in New York where 146 young women workers died in a fire in 1911; the New England Hospital for Women and Children, built and staffed by women, that opened in Boston in 1862; and Nannie Helen Burroughs's National Training School for Women and Girls, founded in 1901 in Washington to educate African-American women so they could move beyond domestic service. Miller also explained that many previous landmarks, like the Lowell mills, have women's stories to tell.[34]

When Senator Paul Tsongas opened the hearing for Women's Rights National Historical Park in 1980, he wryly stated that it would be the "complement to the Men's Rights National Historical Park." When asked where the location for that park was, Tsongas answered, "Probably right here in Washington."[35] The reality of Tsongas's remark has been slow to change, but within the National Park Service there has been change. As the service enters the twenty-first century, the nature of the historic space it manages is fundamentally different. Women outside the National Park Service, often allied with women inside, have organized to weave threads into the historic fabric of national parks. A concurrent step was for women inside the service to organize to achieve power within so that their voices could be heard.

Conferences for Park Service Women

The contrast between the two National Park Service Women's Conferences, one in 1979 and the other in 1991, is striking. The call for the first was feminist and arose out of the Federal Women's Program (FWP) and the push for equal opportunity that climaxed at the end of the 1970s. It was a cry for legitimacy from women who asked for full acceptance as colleagues within the Park Service. Women from a diversity of occupations and grade levels made up its planning committee, and it revealed to participants the complexity of issues that faced women within the agency. The 1991 conference, on the other hand, reflected a decade of incremental change. Run by the service's Stephen T. Mather Employee Development Center, it was feminist only in its basic assumption of equal opportunity for women. Although the women planners hoped to inspire women and teach them how to be successful, the overall result was simply an exuberant celebration of Park Service women. Underlying both conferences was a sense that women needed to continue to work to change the male-oriented Park Service culture.

In November 1979, the message women sent to the Park Service leadership was that it was time to take women seriously. More than eighty women, including a significant group of African-American women, representing the ten regions and a variety of occupations and grade levels, worked together for four days to identify issues that held women back and to propose solutions. Each regional director and Washington associate director attended the final dinner, where committees presented reports. "They saw women who were GS-4s, -5s, -7s getting up, making the most articulate well-written reports," Priscilla Baker, then chief of public affairs remembered, "and I saw jaws drop all over that room."[36]

More than a decade of Federal Women's Program and Equal Opportunity Program (EO) affirmative action plans, workshops, newsletters, and formal complaints of discrimination had created a consciousness of the need for change. FWP Manager Jeanetta Foreman, an African American, called the planning group together when she found that Director William Whalen would fund a women's conference. Because Peggy Lipson, a legislative affairs specialist, was in the midlevel management training program and able to take on special duties, she agreed to serve as chair. Priscilla Baker invited Lipson to work out of the public affairs office. Baker had been inspired by the 1977 National Women's Conference in Houston—opened by the relay torch, lighted at Seneca Falls.[37]

Lipson, Foreman, and Baker formed a sixteen-member planning committee to identify key issues and assign each one to a group of women. The committees researched their subjects and prepared position papers, including information on pertinent federal regulations, and these were sent to conference participants ahead of time to prepare them for their workshops. Many issues represented problems for everyone in the Park Service, but with a women's twist. Women found that poor communications resulted in a highly developed "old-boy network" that kept women from receiving information that would both help their advancement and improve their job performance. A major issue affecting women and family life was the problem of geographic mobility, a perception that the only way Park Service personnel could advance to positions of greater responsibility was to move to different locations. A corollary was the dual career issue for employees with spouses or partners, a particular problem in the Park Service because couples who meet in the parks are often separated when they accept opportunities for advancement. Minority women said they experienced a double discrimination that led to dead-ended jobs. Limits on maternity leave were frustrating to many. Knowledge of personnel practices that could help women were explained and documented, as were EO regulations, career development plans, training programs, and EO complaint and personnel grievance procedures.[38]

The conference was dedicated to Dorothy Boyle Huyck, a freelance journalist whose study of the history of women in the National Park Service was halted by her death the summer before the conference. Peggy Lipson noted that during Huyck's interviews with nearly two hundred Park Service women, she served as a "confidant and inspirational mentor." Shortly before Huyck's death, Director Whalen named her an Honorary Park Ranger, only the third woman to receive that award. She used the opportunity to suggest that the service address problems of isolation, sexual harassment, and dual careers. Her daughter, Heather Huyck, then program supervisor at Clara Barton, revealed some of her mother's findings at the opening session of the conference.[39]

Several recommendations from the conference represented new thinking. One in particular was creating "geographic complexes" to address the issue of dual-career couples. Career ladders, it was suggested, should be designed within groups of parks and regional offices so that commuting between them would be possible. Bridge positions and premanagement training were proposed to allow clerical workers to move into management positions. Upward mobility plans, temporary details into vacant positions for training purposes, and mandatory workshops in EO regulations for supervisors were recommended. The women agreed that long-term support for their advancement needed to come from two directions: from the Park Service leadership and from women working together.[40]

The radical shift in the leadership of the Park Service and particularly in the Interior Department that soon followed the first women's conference made some women believe the conference had little lasting effect on the service as a whole. Recommended follow-up conferences never materialized and the women themselves did not organize an active women's network. But it was evident in April 1991, when four hundred women gathered in New Orleans for the second National Park Service Women's Conference, that the Park Service was indeed taking women seriously.

Billing the 1991 conference as an "extraordinary employee development opportunity" for Park Service women, Martha Aikens, who chaired the conference, an African-American woman and superintendent of the Mather Employee Development Center, wanted to prepare women and minorities to step into leadership positions expected to open up when male top and middle managers retired during the next decade. The theme of the conference, "Learn the past, seize the present, lead the future," meshed with the Park Service's seventy-fifth anniversary.[41]

Despite a myriad of informational sessions, ranging from changing career fields to breaking the glass ceiling, and speakers including the highest ranking women in the Canadian Parks Service and the Department of the Interior, networking with other women was by far the most frequently chosen highlight in conference evaluations—just as it had been in 1979. Many old issues still persisted. When asked what problems should be passed on to the Washington office, participants replied: opportunities for dual-career couples, flexibility in maternity and family leave, better communication between employees and managers, the chance to evaluate supervisors, active recruitment of women for senior management positions, upward mobility plans, and mentoring programs. On the other hand, the conference demonstrated that Park Service women were resources for its future, representing talent, experience, commitment, and energy.[42]

At a Career Fair on the third afternoon, women, along with several supportive men, were available for answering questions from individuals. Marie Rust, soon to become a regional director, offered counseling on administration in a regional office; Anne Castellina, superintendent at Kenai Fjords, helped with questions about park management; Sandy Dayhoff, a Freeman Tilden award winner in interpretation, suggested ways of helping visitors appreciate the value of park resources; and Bill Walker, head of the Resource Management Training Program, encouraged women to apply for training. A team discussed women's future in maintenance jobs: Sue McGill, who had just been promoted from chief of maintenance at Bryce Canyon to superintendent at Timpanogos Cave, and Lisa Lee Smith, trails supervisor at Pinnacles.

Two women who had each worked closely with the Park Service for twenty years offered special perspectives: Mary R. Bradford, an attorney in the Interior Department, a 1971 graduate of the Albright ranger training program, told about her training program for the Senior Executive Service. Heather Huyck, who began her career as a park technician, answered questions about national park legislation and working on Capitol Hill, based on her eight years of experience as a professional staff member for Representative Bruce Vento, chair of the House Subcommittee on Parks and Public Lands. Huyck began the position after winning the American Historical Association's Congressional Fellowship. She worked on legislation resulting in nearly eighty laws and amendments to such acts basic to the Park Service's operations as the National Historic Preservation Act and the Archeological Resources Protection Act. Building on her earlier efforts to promote women's history in parks, she helped convince the Park Service to undertake the women's history landmark study. In 1994, Huyck returned to the service as chief of the Office of Strategic Planning.[43]

Women in the Park Service have also reached out to professional women outside the service. For nearly ten years, Lowell National Historical Park has sponsored an annual women's history conference for public school teachers who share curriculum projects with each other.

Solving Women's Career Issues

Throughout the 1990s, as before, women continued to experiment with creative solutions to career issues in the Park Service. Most of the problems they tackled arose out of women's difference; most of the remedies contributed to enhancing the quality of life for both women and men. Many women and men were no longer willing to allow work to push family aside.

One of the most longstanding issues was the problem of dual careers for couples. Everglades rangers Lorrie Sprague and Duncan Hollar were first faced with the dual-career issue when Hollar accepted a ranger position at Yosemite. Everglades put Sprague on leave without pay so she could keep her permanent federal status while looking for a position. As a result of her experience, in 1986 she worked with a committee of the Association of National Park Rangers (ANPR) to create the first Dual Career Directory. Primarily a method of networking, it listed the qualifications and goals of each partner. ANPR listed arguments that showed how hiring a couple helped the Park Service: it utilized talent and experience that might otherwise be lost, it helped parks in remote areas or with housing shortages to find qualified personnel, and addressing the low-pay problem faced by rangers, ANPR said dual hiring offered some couples their "only chance for financial survival." Such parks as Everglades, Big Bend, and Carlsbad Caverns pioneered dual-career placement by including the possibility for such assignments in vacancy announcements. In 1994, the issue was addressed servicewide. The Interior Department instituted a computerized listing of all department vacancies, offering couples a wider range of job options, and each park appointed a Quality of Worklife Coordinator to help employees handle dual career issues.[44]

Women took the lead in solving another family issue in parks—child care. The day care center with the longest record of continuous operation in the parks is Yosemite's, which opened in 1984 after two years of planning. A year later, the Park Service issued a policy allowing parks to provide space, utilities, access to restroom facilities, emergency telephone service, and surplus furniture for child care facilities. In the Midwest Region, archeologist Ann Dial-Jones worked with other federally employed women to start a day care facility. Alternate work schedules and flex-time allows couples to share child care. Carlsbad Caverns was among the parks that encouraged job sharing: four women shared two interpretive positions and helped each other with child care.[45]

By clarifying situations specific to women, women sometimes helped with broader issues; for example, by looking at pregnancy and childbirth as a temporary disability, women helped solve problems for anyone with a short-term disability. When Ivette Ruan, a law enforcement ranger in a large Rocky Mountain park, told her supervisor she was pregnant, he demanded that she give up her commission on the spot. After eighteen months of presenting her case to meetings of chief rangers and regional law enforcement personnel, she was able to develop the support she needed to influence the Park Service to revise the regulations. Now all law enforcement rangers with temporary disabilities can keep their commissions while they take on less physically demanding law enforcement duties.[46]

Career development activities outside formal training programs offered extra support to women. With backing from Regional Director Marie Rust, Beryl Stella-Meszaros, as North Atlantic Federal Women's Program manager, organized a mentoring program, pairing fifteen women with more highly graded employees, ten women and five men. Within the year, all fifteen were either promoted, received awards, or had decided to take college classes. In the Southwest Region, Michelle Pelletier designed a mentoring program specifically planned to raise the skills and aspirations of women administrative technicians, pairing them with women administrative officers.[47]

Equal opportunity officers serve as the consciences of employee relations. When policy decisions are made or promotions are recommended, their voices speak for equity for women, racial/ethnic minorities, the disabled, and older employees. When all else fails, women can file complaints of discrimination with EO officers. Not being selected for a position for which they are qualified or not being assigned duties that will help them build the knowledge, skills, and abilities that will qualify them for promotion are among the complaints most often filed. Sexual harassment complaints, made most often by young, single women stationed in parks, are defined as discrimination; remedies are backed by Park Service policies. Most EO officers provide training for managers. EO officers believe that the expensive load of complaints stemming from perceived discrimination against women and other specified groups, as well as the service's failure to meet affirmative action goals, would be reduced if there were an increase in training and recruitment.[48]

The Park Service was slow to accept lifestyles that arise from differences in sexual orientation. Until 1992, homosexuality was underground in the Park Service. Being branded as womanly guides posed such a threat to some male ranger-naturalists and historians that homosexuality remained hidden. The fear of being seen as different stopped lesbian women from identifying themselves. In 1992, Don Henry, an EO specialist in the Western Region, led the region in including sexual orientation in its EO policy statements. Gay and straight men, lesbian and straight women responded positively in print. Four regions and the Denver service center followed. One of the first to respond was the only region with a woman director at the time—North Atlantic, headed by Marie Rust. Early in 1994, Interior Secretary Bruce Babbitt expanded the department's EO goals to include sexual orientation, thus opening up grievance procedures for Park Service personnel. Rust allowed employees to use work time and travel allocations to attend meetings of a regional sexual orientation issues group. In announcing the policy, Rust repeated the goal that the region would "strive to build a work force that reflects the nation's diversity [because] we cannot afford to waste the valuable talent, creativity, and different perspectives which people from all backgrounds can bring to it."[49] In adding her voice to the issue, Rust reflected a sensitivity to discrimination arising from every woman's struggle to move beyond the restrictions imposed by the concept of woman's place.

Greeting the Twenty-First Century

Career women inside the National Park Service and women park advocates outside shared the goal of preserving each special space that is a national park. In more than three hundred interviews, not one Park Service career woman faltered when asked to state the mission of the agency. "We are the caretakers of our nation's treasures," Peggy Lipson, chair of the first women's conference, explained, "that the American people through their members of Congress deem . . . as being nationally significant. We are a gatekeeper and a defender."[50]

From the time in May 1857 that high-spirited San Francisco teachers Harriet Kirtland and Anna Park rode sidesaddle into Yosemite Valley, when the spring water was high, to Mardy Murie's eloquent appeals to save Wild Alaska more than one hundred years later, women have played major roles in the national park story.

Whether cast as travelers or wives, rangers or scientists, mountain climbers or environmentalists, their role has been a legitimate one. Some national parks owed their very existence to women; others were protected by women's commitment to the future. As women in national parks greet the twenty-first century, they also know that the caretakers of national parks have been transformed by their presence.

Notes

Introduction

1. Horace M. Albright to Stephen T. Mather, 14 October 1926, Education Division Correspondence, 1926–34, Yellowstone National Park Archives. For Albright's efforts to remove the military presence and influence from Yellowstone, see Horace M. Albright, *The Birth of the National Park Service, The Founding Years, 1913–33* (Salt Lake City: Howe Brothers, 1985): 56–57, 97. The 340 Park Service women, from all ten regions, interviewed by the author from 1985 to 1986, who were asked, "Do you think the Park Service is male-dominated?" answered unanimously, "Yes."

2. Granville and Mary Liles interview with author, 10 August 1986; see also Richard West Sellars, "Manipulating Nature's Paradise: National Park Management under Stephen T. Mather, 1916–1929," *Montana* 43 (spring 1993): 2–13 The National Park Service mandate is quoted on page 4.

3. To the Division of Interpretation Chief (Daniel B. Beard), from Staff Historian (Roy) Appleman, 26 September 1968, National Park Service Library, Harpers Ferry, WV; hereafter cited as NPS Library.

4. Herma Albertson Baggley, "Report of the National Park Housing Survey," 1953: 12, National Park Women file, NPS Library.

5. Christine A. Littleton, "Equality and Feminist Legal Theory," in Kathryn Kish Sklar and Thomas Dublin, *Women and Power in American History* (Englewood Cliffs, NJ: Prentice Hall, 1991), v. 2: 282–86.

6. Marcia Myers Bonta found that only two of the twenty-five women naturalists she studied had children, although fifteen were married. Her interpretation is that the women were "freed . . . to do as they wished with their lives." Another conclusion could be that these women met their generative needs by preserving birds and wild flowers. Bonta, *Women in the Field: America's Pioneering Women Naturalists* (College Station: Texas A. & M. University Press, 1991): xiii.

7. White males, at 53.5 percent, still dominate the Park Service. The total of all minorities is 20 percent, of which 38 percent is female: "Total Employees in National Park Service," 31 March 1995, courtesy Eleanor Pratt.

Chapter One

1. In 1856 Madame Gautier and Jean Frances Neal, of Mariposa, and Mrs. Thompson, of Sherlocks, may have been the first white women to visit Yosemite Valley. Lafayette Bunnell, *Discovery of the Yosemite* (Chicago: Fleming H. Revell, 1880): 308–09.

2. Harriet J. Kirtland, "Journal of a Trip through the Southern Mines," 13 May to 3 June 1857, California State Library; James Denman, "First Two Days in the Yosemite Valley," *San Francisco Evening Bulletin*, 8 July 1957, and "Vernal Falls and Yosemite Valley," *San Francisco Evening Bulletin*, 9 July 1957, courtesy of the California State Library. See Shirley Sargent, *Pioneers in Petticoats: Yosemite's Early Women, 1856–1900* (Yosemite: Flying Spur Press, 1966): 15–16.

3. The story of the Mariposa Battalion and their leader James Savage is told by Carl Russell in *One*

Hundred Years in Yosemite (Berkeley: University of California Press, 1947): 15–49. Russell interviewed Maria Lebrado in 1928. She later demonstrated Native American customs and food preparation at the recreated American Indian Village behind the park's museum. She died in 1931, aged about one hundred years. For her story, see the following articles in *Yosemite Nature Notes:* C. P. Russell, "A Last Link with the Past" 7 (June 1928): 41–46; C. P. Russell, "Last of Yosemite Indians Visits Valley" 8 (July 1929): 69–70; and George C. Crowe, "The Last Member of Chief Tenaya's Band" 10 (July 1931): 57–60. See also Harold E. Perry, "Native Daughter," *Sierra Club Bulletin* 37 (December 1952): 17–20. Ta-bu-ce's Americanized name was Maggie Howard. She worked as a maid in the Sentinel Hotel before becoming a cultural demonstrator for the park in 1930. See Sargent, *Pioneers in Petticoats:* 12–13.

4. The Phillips diary is reprinted in M. E. Phillips, "Side-Saddle Days in Yosemite," *Touring Topics* 23 (July 1931): 18–20, 39–40.

5. For other early Yosemite hotelkeepers' wives who kept family businesses going, see Sargent, *Pioneers in Petticoats:* 19–26.

6. Phillips, "Side-Saddle Days": 19–20, 39.

7. Grace Greenwood (Sara Jane Lippincott), *New Life in New Lands: Notes of Travel* (New York: J. B. Ford & Co., 1873): 303–370. John Muir guided Lippincott and her friends on a "tramp" to Tenaya Falls and the cascades of Porcupine Creek.

8. H. H. (Helen Hunt Jackson), *Bits of Travel at Home* (Boston: Roberts Brothers, 1878): 87–133; Susan Coolidge, "A Few Hints on the California Journey" *Scribner's Magazine* (May 1873): 29–31. Helen Hunt journeyed to Yosemite three years before her marriage to William Jackson of Colorado Springs. She first published her account of the trip in the *Independent* in 1872, nearly ten years before *A Century of Dishonor*. See Valerie Sherer Mathes, *Helen Hunt Jackson and Her Indian Reform Legacy* (Austin: University of Texas Press, 1990): 21–94; Ruth Odell, *Helen Hunt Jackson* (New York: D. Appleton-Century Co., 1939): 120–55.

9. Mary Cone, *Two Years in California,* (Chicago: S. C. Griggs & Co., 1876): 198, 231–33; Constance Gordon-Cumming, *Granite Crags* (Edinburgh: Wm. Blackwood & Sons, 1884); Therese Yelverton, *Teresina in America* (London: Richard Bentley & Son, 1875), v.1: 58–90; Therese Yelverton, *Zanita: A Tale of the YoSemite* (New York: Hurd & Houghton, 1872). See also: Sargent, *Pioneers in Petticoats:* 27–32 and David Robertson, *West of Eden: A History of the Art and Literature of Yosemite* (Yosemite Natural History Association, 1984): 34, 48–49.

10. E. C. Stanton, *Eighty Years and More* (New York, 1898): 289–94. Alice Van Schaack, who stayed at Hutchings at the same time as did Stanton and Anthony, said, "Mrs. H.B. Stanton . . . described her journey down the mountain in such a sprightly way we were all greatly entertained." Alice Van Schaack, *A Familiar Letter from a Daughter to Her Mother . . . at Yo-Semite* (Chicago: 1871): 10–11, Yosemite National Park Research Library.

11. Olive Logan, "Does It Pay to Visit Yo Semite?" *Galaxy* 10 (October 1970): 498–509. The Yosemite Library has a collection of unpublished writings by women travelers to Yosemite.

12. Jane Apostol, "Jeanne Carr: One Woman and Sunshine," *American West,* 25 (July–August 1978): 31–32. See also James Mitchell Clarke, *The Life and Adventures of John Muir* (San Francisco: Sierra Club Books, 1980): 124–25. Jeanne Carr was also a close friend of Helen Hunt Jackson, who wrote "One Woman and Sunshine" about Carr's horticultural genius for the *Christian Union* in 1885. Odell, *Helen Hunt Jackson:* 176–78, 209–10, 279.

13. Elizabeth H. Godfrey, "Chronicles of Cosie Hutchings Mills," Yosemite Library; Sargent, *Pioneers in Petticoats:* 36–40, 45–48; Russell, *One Hundred Years in Yosemite:* 58–60, 96–97, 149–52. Hutchings was evicted from his Yosemite land-claims in 1875 but the family camped in Yosemite in the summer. Floy and Cosie's mother Elvira left the family in 1875, but their grandmother Florantha Sproat stayed. In 1876, Florantha, at the age of sixty-five, and Augusta Sweetland, who later married Hutchings, may have been the first white women to climb Yosemite's Mount Lyell.

14. Shirley Sargent, *Pioneers in Petticoats:* 71–73. Degnan's Restaurant is still in operation. For the story of the Yosemite Valley School, see Laurence Degnan's reminiscences in *Yosemite Nature Notes* 35 (February 1956): 15–21; (March 1956): 27–30; (April 1956): 41–47; (May 1956): 54–61. For the affect

of Yosemite's early tourism on the natural environment, see Peter J. Blodgett, "Visiting 'The Realm of Wonder': Yosemite and the Business of Tourism, 1855–1916," *California History* 69 (summer 1990): 118–33, 222–23.

15. Herbert Evison interview with Mary Tresidder, 15 October 1963, NPS Library; Mary Curry Tresidder file, Mather Collection, National Archives; "Mary Curry Tresidder," National Park Service *Courier,* 18 (January 1971): 8 (hereafter, NPS *Courier*); Shirley Sargent, "Westways Women," *Westways* 69 (May 1977): 37–38, 80. The Curry Company merged with the Yosemite National Park Company in 1925, with Dr. Tresidder as president. They built the Ahwahnee Hotel two years later. In 1932, Stanford University Press published Mary Tresidder's *Trees of Yosemite,* with block prints by Della Taylor Hoss. Jennie Curry died in 1948; Mary Tressider died in 1971.

16. Adolph D. Sweet, "Down a Glacier a Mile a Minute," *San Francisco Chronicle,* 25 August 1896, copied for Sweet file, Yosemite Library; "A Daring Woman's Exploit," *Leslie's Illustrated Weekly,* 20 October 1900: 290; letter to the *Sierra Star* from Hattie Harris, 23 August 1962: 8, in Tatch file, Yosemite Library. Tatch's photographers were George Fiske and Julius Boysen. Harris reports that Kitty Tatch drowned in a whitewater canoeing accident. See also Sargent, *Pioneers in Petticoats:* 25–26, 49–50.

17. Louise S. Shunk, "Recollections of Hiram and Emma Stone," including a copy from *Historical Records,* 1931–33, History Collection, Yellowstone National Park Library.

18. Mabel Cross Osmond, "Memories of a Trip through Yellowstone Park in 1874," History Collection, Yellowstone.

19. "Mrs. George Cowan" in Paul Schullery, ed., *Old Yellowstone Days* (Boulder: Associated University Press, 1979): 1–25. Apparently two "lawless" American Indians fired the shots. A Nez Perce Indian, Poker Joe, who spoke English, was sent back to prevent further trouble and to retrieve Emma, her sister, and her brother. When Emma was taken to meet Chief Joseph, she said, "The 'noble red man' we read of was more nearly impersonated in this Indian than in any I have met." Poker Joe guided them to a trail, telling them to ride "all night, all day, no sleep." The original manuscript is in the Montana Historical Society.

20. Lee H. Whittlesey, "Marshall's Hotel in the National Park," *Montana, the Magazine of Western History* 30 (autumn 1980): 42–51; Carrie Adell Strahorn, *Fifteen Thousand Miles by Stage* (New York: G. P. Putnam's Sons, 1911): 254–286. An English traveler, Margaret Andrews Cruikshank, complained that the Marshalls were "over-worked and all cross." Margaret Andrews Cruikshank, "A Lady's Trip to Yellowstone, 1883," *Montana, the Magazine of Western History* 39 (winter 1989): 8–9. Surveyors for the Northern Pacific named Rosa Lake for the child. Robert Strahorn was an advertising agent for the Union Pacific.

21. O. S. T. Drake, "A Lady's Trip to the Yellowstone Park," in *Every Girl's Annual* (London: Hatehard's, 1887): 346–49; Georgina M. Synge, *A Ride Through Wonderland* (London: Sampson Low, Marston, 1892), History Collection, Yellowstone.

22. Louise S. Shunk, "Recollections of Hiram and Emma Stone," Flora Chase Pierce letters, 26 July 1897 and 8 August 1897, History Collection, Yellowstone.

23. Alice Wellington Rollins, "The Three Tetons," *Harpers New Monthly* 74 (May 1887): 869–90; Caroline L. Paul, "Notes on Yellowstone National Park," 28 June to 4 August 1897, History Collection, Yellowstone; David A. Clary, *"The Place Where Hell Bubbled Up"* (Washington, D.C.: USDI, 1972): 56. Calamity Jane or Martha Cannery Burk symbolized the new freedom travelers to the Old West believed frontier women possessed.

24. Jean Crawford Sharpe, "This is Me . . . and This is What I Remember," History Collection, Yellowstone.

25. Memoirs of Letitia Follett Bradley, 1933–34, Grosse Pointe Farm, MI, History Collection, Yellowstone. A bibliography of officers' wives' accounts, many in forts that are now national military parks, is in Sandra L. Myres, "Army Wives in the Trans-Mississippi West; a Bibliography" in Teresa Griffin Viele, *Following the Drum* (Lincoln, University of Nebraska Press, 1984): 257–73.

26. Marguerite Lindsley Arnold, "Early Impressions," *Yellowstone Nature Notes,* 11 (March/April 1934): 15–17. See chapter 3 for Marguerite Lindsley Arnold's career. Her father first went to Yellowstone in 1894 to visit his brother, a cavalry lieutenant.

27. Bessie Haynes Arnold, diary, letters, and photographs, History Collection, Yellowstone.

28. Harriet Monroe, "The Grand Cañon of the Colorado," *Atlantic Monthly,* 84 (November 1899): 816–21; Mary Wager Fisher, "A Day in the Grand Cañon," *Outing* 22 (July 1893): 261–64.

29. "Two Women at the Grand Canyon: Ada and Edith Bass," from Lisa D. Madsen, "The Grand Canyon Tourist Business of the W. W. Bass Family," M.A. thesis, University of New Mexico, December 1980: 73–93; Sharon Spangler, *On Foot in the Grand Canyon* (Boulder, CO: Pruett, 1989): 107–09, 121. For the Harvey Girls, Eastern women who served as waitresses at the Fred Harvey restaurants along the Santa Fe Railroad, including the Grand Canyon, see Lesley Poling Kempes, *The Harvey Girls: Women Who Opened the West* (New York: Paragon House, 1989).

30. Isabella L. Bird, *A Lady's Life in the Rocky Mountains* (Norman, OK: University of Oklahoma Press, 1960): 83–101.

31. Anna E. Dickinson, *A Ragged Register of People, Places and Opinions* (New York: Harper & Brothers, 1979): 265–71; Louisa Ward Arps and Elinor Eppich Kingery, *High Country Names: Rocky Mountain National Park* (Denver, Colorado Mountain Club, 1966): 51–53; Enos A. Mills, *Early Estes Park* (Estes Park, CO, 1959): 15–16. Following a proposal by Enos Mills, Mount Dickinson, in the Mummy Range, was named for Anna Dickinson. Mills supposed her to have been the first white woman to climb Longs Peak. Addie Alexander, of St. Louis, who climbed Longs in 1871, may have been the first white woman to make the climb. See Janet Robertson, *The Magnificent Mountain Women: Adventures in the Colorado Rockies* (Lincoln, NE: University of Nebraska Press, 1990): 7–8. Rocky Mountain National Park was established in 1915.

32. Ibid.: 20–22; Mills, *Early Estes Park*: 23–26.

33. Laura and Guy Waterman, *Forest and Crag: A History of Hiking, Trail Blazing, and Adventure in the Northeast Mountains* (Boston: Appalachian Mountain Club, 1989): 122–24, 262. Women formed the majority on the first Appalachian Mountain Club excursion to Mount Katahdin, in 1887. The Appalachian National Scenic Trail has been managed by the Appalachian Trail Conference in cooperation with the Park Service since 1984.

34. Lynn Sherr and Jurate Kazickas, *Susan B. Anthony Slept Here,* (New York: Random House, 1994): 41.

35. Anna Mills Johnston, "A trip to Mt. Whitney in 1878," *Mt. Whitney Club Journal* 1 (May 1902): 18–28, courtesy of the Annie Mitchell Local History Room, Tulare County Free Library, Visalia, CA, reprinted in Leonard Daughenbaugh, "On Top of Her World: Anna Mills' Ascent of Mt. Whitney," *California History* 64 (winter 1985): 42–51. Daughenbaugh reports a recent effort to rename the peak Mount Anna Mills. The other three women climbers in 1878 were Hope Broughton, Mary Martin, and Ella Baker Redd.

36. Beatrice Scheer Smith, "The 1872 Diary and Plant Collections of Ellen Powell Thompson," *Utah Historical Quarterly,* 62 (spring 1994): 104–31. Thanks to Miriam B. Murphy.

37. Maurine S. Fletcher, *The Wetherills of Mesa Verde* (Lincoln: University of Nebraska Press, 1987): 195–213; Alice Eastwood, "Notes on the Cliff Dwellers," *Zoe* 3 (January 1893): 375–76; Carol Green Wilson, *Alice Eastwood's Wonderland* (San Francisco: California Academy of Sciences, 1955): 35–48.

38. Eliza R. Scidmore, *Alaska, Its Southern Coast and the Sitkan Archipelago* (Boston: D. Lathrop, 1885): 135, 139–140, 145–150; Isabel C. McLean, "Eliza Ruhamah Scidmore," *Alaska Journal* 7 (autumn 1977): 238–43. See also Eliza Ruhamah Scidmore, "The Muir Glacier in Alaska," *Harper's Weekly* 36 (23 July 1892): 711–12; *Appleton's Guide-Book to Alaska and the Northwest Coast* (New York: D. Appleton, 1893); and "Recent Explorations in Alaska," *National Geographic Magazine* 5 (3 January 1894): 173–79. Glacier Bay became a national monument in 1925 and a national park and preserve in 1980. Its Scidmore Bay, created from the melting Scidmore Glacier on the side of Mount Fairweather, is named for Eliza Scidmore. She joined the new National Geographic Society in 1890 and served as corresponding secretary, associate editor, and foreign secretary, and was the only woman to serve on the board of managers. When she lived in Japan, she was responsible for transporting Japanese cherry trees to Washington, D.C.

39. Mary Chipman Lawrence explored the Alaskan coast in 1857 and 1859, with her husband, Cap-

tain Samuel Lawrence, on the whaler *Addison*. She wrote of Mount St. Elias as "lofty and grand" and of Mount Fairweather, "its hoary summit clothed in snow," from Stanton Garner, ed., *The Captain's Best Mate: The Journal of Mary Chipman Lawrence on the Whaler Addison, 1856–1860* (Hanover, NH: University Press of New England, 1986): 39, 42, 163, 168.

40. Septima M. Collis, *A Woman's Trip to Alaska* (New York: Cassell, 1890): 3, 144–50; Abby Johnson Woodman, *Picturesque Alaska: A Journal of a Tour Among the Mountains, Seas and Islands of the Northwest, from San Francisco to Sitka* (Boston: Houghton Mifflin, 1889): 158, 161–68. Sitka became a national monument in 1910 and a national historical park in 1972.

41. The buttercup was *Ranunculus Cooleyae*. Grace E. Cooley, "Impressions of Alaska," *Bulletin of the Torrey Botanical Club* 19 (6 June 1892): 178–89; Grace E. Cooley, "Plants Collected in Alaska . . . July and August, 1891," *Bulletin of the Torrey Botanical Club* 19 (10 August 1892): 239–49; Maxine Williams, "Dr. Cooley and Her Buttercup," *Alaska Magazine* 47 (June 1981): 49.

42. Frances Knapp and Rheta Louise Childe, *The Thlinkets of Southeastern Alaska* (Chicago: Stone and Kimball, 1896): 7–15, 165, 194–97, passim.

43. Laurie Alberts, "Petticoats and Pickaxes," *Alaska Journal* 7 (summer 1977): 144–59. By July 1898, English journalist Flora Shaw said she was one of 27,000 persons to climb over the passes. Melanie J. Myer, *Klondike Women: True Tales of the Gold Rush* (Athens: Ohio University Press, 1989): 140.

44. Grant Pearson, "Fannie Quigley, Frontierswoman," *Alaska Sportsman* (August 1947): 6–7, 31–32; Thomas K. Bundtzen, "A History of Mining in the Kantishna Hills," *Alaska Journal* 8 (spring 1978): 151–60. Thanks to Jane Anderson for Quigley's story. Klondike Gold Rush National Historical Park was established in Skagway, Alaska, and Seattle, Washington, in 1976. Mt. McKinley National Park, first established in 1917, became Denali National Park and Wilderness Preserve in 1980.

45. An 1896 graduate of Bryn Mawr College, Dora Keen was one of four daughters of a prominent Philadelphia physician. She later became the first woman to cross Skolai Pass to the Yukon River, traveling three hundred miles by foot and open boat. In 1914 she was made a fellow of the Royal Geographical Society, London. In 1911, she described seven of her Alpine ascents before the Appalachian Mountain Club (AMC). Joseph Adelman, *Famous Women* (New York: Ellis M. Lonow, 1926): 312; *Appalachia* 12 (July 1911): 324; Dora Keen, "Mountain Climbing in Alaska: The First Expedition to Mount Blackburn," *Appalachia* 12 (April 1912): 327–39; Dora Keen, "First Up Mt. Blackburn," *The World's Work* 27 (November 1913): 80–101. Wrangell–St. Elias National Park and Preserve (including Mt. Blackburn) was established in 1980.

46. Cicely Palser Havely, ed., *This Grand Beyond: The Travels of Isabella Bird Bishop* (London: Century Publishing, 1984): 40–59. Kilauea's lake of molten lava sank in 1924 and was replaced by steam explosions and eruptions. In 1995 Kilauea had been erupting for twelve years, sending lava into the ocean and destroying buildings, including a Park Service visitor center.

47. Emma Shaw Colcleugh, Scrapbook #2: 4–18; Red Scrapbook 17–29, Haffenreffer Museum of Anthropology, Brown University. My thanks to Barbara Hail for showing me the scrapbooks. Shaw also rode down into the inactive crater of Haleakala on the island of Maui. She published a curriculum on Yellowstone included in the Red Scrapbook, page 40. For the catalog of an exhibit including items from Colcleugh's subarctic collections, see Barbara A. Hail, *Out of the North: the Subarctic Collection of the Haffenreffer Museum of Anthropology* (Providence, RI: Brown University, 1989). Hawaii National Park, including Haleakala (island of Maui) and Mauna Loa and Kilauea (island of Hawaii) was established in 1916. They were separated into Haleakala National Park and Hawaii Volcanoes National Park in 1960 and 1961.

48. Margaret Howard, "A Woman's Ascent of Mauna Loa," *Mid-Pacific* 3 (March 1912): 311–17.

49. "Sierra Club Women, 1972–1977," Sierra Club Oral History Collection, Bancroft Library, University of California; *Mazama* 2 (October 1900): 57–58; the *Mountaineer* 1 (March 1907): 1, 26–28; Robertson, *Magnificent Mountain Women*: 24–25. The Mountaineers were formed from the Seattle members of the Mazamas.

50. Fuller's account is reprinted in Paul Schullery, *Island in the Sky: Pioneering Accounts of Mt. Rainier, 1833–1894* (Seattle: The Mountaineers, 1987): 125–40. Fay Fuller Von Briesen, New York City, to C. A. Tomlinson, superintendent, Mount Rainier National Park, 4 May 1933, courtesy William F. Dengler

and Lucia Perillo, park ranger, who presented a program on Fuller at the park; *Mazama* 2 (October 1900). It was Len Longmire's first ascent of Rainier and began his twenty years of guiding climbers. Fay Peak is named for Fay Fuller. In 1927, at the age of twelve, Dixy Lee Ray (who later was elected state governor) became the youngest girl to climb Rainier. Associated Press obituary, 3 January 1994.

51. Dee Molenaar, *The Challenge of Rainier* (Seattle: The Mountaineers, 1979): 41–43; Gertrude Metcalfe, "The Rainier Climb," *Mazama* 2 (December 1905): 224–34; Anne Shannon Monroe, "Climbing Mount Tacoma," *World Today* 9 (October 1905): 1047–53. For early women climbers in the Pacific Northwest, see Rachel da Silva, ed., *Leading Out: Women Climbers Reaching for the Top* (Seattle, Seal Press, 1992): 68–84.

52. Helen M. Gompertz, "A Tramp to Mt. Lyell," *Sierra Club Bulletin* 1 (May 1894): 136–43; E. T. Parsons, "The Sierra Club Outing to Tuolumne Meadows," *Sierra Club Bulletin* 5 (January 1902): 22–23; Josephine Colby, "Kern River Canyon," *Overland Monthly* 43 (January 1904): 16; Helen Gompertz LeConte, "The Sierra Club in the Kings River Canyon," *Sunset Magazine* 11 (July 1903): 250–266.

53. Roger W. Toll, *Rocky Mountain National Park* (Washington, D.C.: USDI, 1919): 33–34; Arps and Kingery, *High Country Names:* 2–10; Robertson, *Magnificent Mountain Women:* 44–56. Harriet Vaille's sister Agnes, an experienced climber, died in an attempt to make a winter ascent of the east face of Longs Peak in 1925.

54. Cora Smith Eaton, "First Aid in the Mountains," *Mountaineer* 3 (September 1907): 100–03; "Record of Ascents to the Summits of Peaks of the Olympic Range," *Mountaineer* 1 (September 1907): 80–86; Mary Banks, "Mountaineers in the Olympics," *Mountaineer* 1 (September 1907): 75–79.

55. Harvey Monroe Hall and Carlotta Case Hall, *A Yosemite Flora* (San Francisco: Paul Elder, 1912); Winona Bailey, "A Few Flowers of the Higher Olympics," *Mountaineer* 6 (1913): 59–64; Elizabeth Van E. Ferguson, "Field Notes of the 1920 Outing," *Sierra Club Bulletin* 11 (January 1921): 147–150. For Sara Plummer Lemmon, see Frank S. Crosswhite, "'J. G. Lemmon & Wife,' Plant Explorers in Arizona, California, and Nevada," *Desert Plants* 1 (August 1979): 12–22 and J. G. Lemmon, "A Botanical Wedding-Trip," the *Californian* 4 (December 1881): 517–25.

56. Naming geographical features for their wives were Joseph Le Conte (Lake Marion and Marion Peak in Kings' Canyon) and Stewart Edward White (Elizabeth Pass in Sequoia). J. S. Hutchinson, "Helen Marion Gompertz Le Conte," *Sierra Club Bulletin* 12, no. 2, 1926: 154; Stewart Edward White, *The Pass* (New York: Outing Publishing, 1906): 157. High Sierra lakes named for women include: Florence (for Floy Hutchings), Elizabeth, Marie, Evelyn, Helen, May, Mildred, Rose, Eleanor, Elizabeth, Rae, and Dorothy. The only peaks named for women using last names are Mount Mills (see note in this chapter, above) and Amelia Earhart Peak, named in 1967. Peter Browning, *Place Names of the Sierra Nevada* (Berkeley, CA: Wilderness Press, 1986).

57. Marion Randall Parsons, "The Ascent of Mount Olympus," *Mountaineer* 6 (November 1913): 33–41; Marion Randall Parsons, "Through the Olympics with the Mountaineers," *Sierra Club Bulletin* 9 (January 1914): 149–58. In 1907, Marion Randall married Edward T. Parsons, a founder of the Sierra Club. When he died in 1914, she succeeded him as a director, serving until 1936. She helped John Muir edit his *Travels in Alaska,* bringing it to publication after his death. Marion Randall Parsons, "John Muir and the Alaska Book," *Sierra Club Bulletin* 10 (January 1916): 33–36; "Marion Randall Parsons," *Sierra Club Bulletin* 38 (October 1953): 35–39.

58. Alfred Runte called tourists' railroad destinations "the romantic terminus." For women in railroad advertisements, see his *Trains of Discovery: Western Railroads and the National Parks* (Flagstaff, AZ: Northland Press, 1984): 48, 54, 57, 70, 78. See also Kerwin L. Klein, "Frontier Products: Tourism, Consumerism, and the Southwestern Public Lands, 1890–1990," *Pacific Historical Review* 62 (February 1993): 39–71.

59. For other women painters who sold canvases to railroads to promote tourism, see Phil Kovinick, *The Woman Artist in the American West, 1860–1960* (Flagstaff, AZ: Northland Press, 1976).

60. Thanks to Ronald Fields for sharing his research on Hill. See his *Abby Williams Hill and the Lure of the West* (Olympia: Washington State Historical Society, 1989); "Abby Williams Hill," *Columbia* 2 (winter 1989): 21–29; and "Abby Williams Hill: Northwest Frontier Artist," *Landmarks* 2 (spring 1984): 2–7.

61. Abby Williams Hill diary, 24 and 26 Aug.; 24 and 5 Sept. 1905, courtesy of Ronald Fields; Fields, *Abby Williams Hill:* 65–69. Thanks to Karen Blair for alerting me to Fields's research.

62. Ibid.: 70–75, 88–91. Hill also did portraits of Nez Perce and Yakima Indian people.

63. See Mary Roberts Rinehart, *Call of the Mountains: Vacations in Glacier National Park* (St. Paul, MN: Great Northern Railroad Co., n.d.); "Through Glacier National Park with Howard Eaton," *Colliers* 57 (22 April 1916): 11–13, 34–36, (29 April 1916): 20- 21, 16–28; *Through Glacier Park: Seeing America First with Howard Eaton* (Boston: Houghton Mifflin, 1916); and *Tenting Tonight: A Chronicle of Sport and Adventure in Glacier Park and the Cascade Mountains* (Boston: Houghton Mifflin, 1918).

64. Rinehart, *Through Glacier Park:* 66–69; Mary Roberts Rinehart, *My Story: A New Edition and Seventeen New Years* (New York: Rinehart, 1948): 202–05.

65. Rinehart, *Through Glacier Park:* 51; Rinehart, *My Story:* 200; Mary Roberts Rinehart, "My Country Tish of Thee," in *Tish* (Boston: Houghton Mifflin, 1916): 257–372.

66. Virginia L. Grattan, *Mary Colter: Builder Upon the Red Earth* (Flagstaff, AZ: Northland Press, 1980): 2–6, 14–19. For the arts and crafts movement, see Eileen Boris, *Art and Labor: Ruskin, Morris, and the Craftsman Ideal in America* (Philadelphia: Temple University Press, 1986).

67. Grattan, *Mary Colter,* 25–39, 67–80, 110–11; "The Watchtower Guide," (Grand Canyon National Park, AZ: Fred Harvey, n.d.). For Colter's role in the making of Native American culture into a commodity, see Marta Weigle, "Exposition and Mediation: Mary Colter, Erna Fergusson, and the Santa Fe/Harvey Popularization of the Native Southwest, 1902–1940," *Frontiers* 12 (3) (1992): 117–130.

68. Kitson's other Vicksburg sculptures are busts and relief portraits of individual men. Her papers are included in the Henry Hudson and Theo Alice Ruggles Kitson papers, Archives of American Art, Smithsonian Institution. Theo Ruggles Kitson, List of Works, Reel 3929: 101-02; "Cordial Welcome . . . ," *Vicksburg American,* 14 November 1903; "How Kitson Stormed the Heights of Vicksburg," *Boston Sunday Herald,* 7 February 1904, and newspaper articles, Reel 3929: 1091–1103. See also Charlotte Streifer Rubenstein, *American Women Artists* (Boston: G. K. Hall, 1982): 106. Vicksburg National Military Park, established in 1899, was transferred from the War Department to the National Park Service in 1933. Thanks to Michael W. Panhorst for guiding me to Kitson's work.

69. "Cordial Welcome . . . ," Reel 3929: 1091–1103; McClellan model, Reel 3930: 814; Bickerdyke Memorial, Reel 3930: 1119.

Chapter Two

1. American Association for the Advancement of Science *Proceedings,* 36th meeting, August 1887: 317; *Proceedings,* 37th meeting: 35–37.

2. Mrs. Gilbert M. McClurg, "The Colorado Cliff Dwellings Association," ms., n.d.; Virginia McDonaghe M'Clurg, "The Mesa Verde Cliff Dwellings and the Women's Park," *Colorado Springs Weekly Gazette,* 14 April 1900, in Geographical File, Stephen H. Hart Library, Colorado Historical Society; Maurine S. Fletcher, ed., *The Wetherills of the Mesa Verde* (Lincoln: University of Nebraska Press, 1977): 192–94. Thanks to Linda Martin and Duane Smith for helping me find information on the founding of Mesa Verde. See his *Mesa Verde National Park: Shadows of the Centuries* (Lawrence: University Press of Kansas, 1988): 40–66. For McClurg, see also Robertson, *Magnificent Mountain Women:* 61–72.

3. "The Colorado Cliff Dwellings Association;" "Enthusiastic Women Hew a Pathway to the Lofty Ruins of the Mesa Verde Cliff Dwellers," *New York Herald,* 29 September 1901; Bertha Damaris Nobe, "Colorado Women," *Women's Home Companion,* July 1901, clippings in Mesa Verde National Park Museum.

4. M'Clurg, "Mesa Verde Cliff Dwellings and the Woman's Park."

5. Ibid.; Patricia A. Hoben, "The Establishment of Mesa Verde as a National Park," M.A. thesis, University of Oklahoma, 1966: 42–45.

6. "Scientists Visit Cliff Palace," *The Daily News* (Denver), 20 September 1901 and "Denver Women as Cliff Climbers," *Denver Republican,* 10 September 1901, clippings, Mesa Verde Museum.

7. "Resents Slurs on Hard Work," *Rocky Mountain News,* 11 March 1906, clipping, Mesa Verde Mu-

seum; Hoben, "Establishment of Mesa Verde": 58. Artifacts excavated by Gustaf Nordenskiold in 1891 are in the National Museum of Helsinki, Finland.

8. "Society Women of Colorado are Rent in Twain . . . " *Rocky Mountain News,* 25 October 1906, clipping, Mesa Verde Museum; Lida Gertrude Frowe, "The Mesa Verde National Park," *The Modern World* (Denver, CO.) 7 (November 1906): 9–11; General Federation of Women's Clubs (GFWC), *Proceedings, Seventh Biennial Convention,* May 1904: 184.

9. When the women of the Cliff Dwellings Association found the boundaries in the bill did not include the major cliff dwellings, they pushed through an amendment to include them. "Make it a National Park," *Denver Post,* 23 February 1906 and "Resents Slurs of Hard Work," *Rocky Mountain News,* 11 March 1906, clippings, Mesa Verde Museum; Virginia McClurg, "The Making of Mesa Verde Into a National Park," *Colorado Magazine* 7 (November 1930): 218; Margaret Keating, "Knowledge of Ages is Buried in Mesa Verde," *The Modern World* (Denver, CO) 8 (October 1907): 149, 155.

10. *Denver Post,* 24 February 1906: 1, clipping, Mesa Verde Museum; McClurg, "The Making of Mesa Verde": 218. Lucy Peabody (1863–1934) died in Denver and Virginia McClurg (1857–1931) in Stonington, Connecticut, clippings, Mesa Verde Museum.

11. *Denver Post,* 24 February 1906: 1, Mesa Verde Museum.

12. Mary S. Gibson, ed., *A Record of Twenty-Five Years of the California Federation of Women's Clubs, 1900–1915,* v. 1: 220–221, The Bancroft Library, University of California. For other accounts of the Hetch-Hetchy controversy, see Stephen Fox, *John Muir and His Legacy: The American Conservation Movement* (Boston: Little Brown, 1981): 139–47 and Roderick Nash, *Wilderness and the American Mind* (New Haven: Yale University Press, 3rd. ed., 1983): 161–81.

13. Lydia Phillips Williams, "Address," *Proceedings of the American Forest Congress,* 2 to 6 January, 1905 (Washington, D.C.: American Forestry Association, 1905): 428–35; *Forestry and Irrigation* 13 (February 1907): 62–63; Lydia Adams-Williams, "Forestry at the Biennial," *Forestry and Irrigation* 14 (August 1908): 435–37. The women's Forestry Committee also supported the Weeks bill setting aside forest reserves in the White Mountains of New Hampshire and the Southern Appalachian mountains. Thanks to Carolyn Merchant for sending me her crucial article, "Women of the Progressive Conservation Movement: 1900–1916," *Environmental Review* 8 (spring 1984): 57–85.

14. Gifford Pinchot, *The Fight for Conservation* (New York: Doubleday, Page, 1910): 101–08; *Forestry and Irrigation* 13 (July 1907): 302. The Daughters of the American Revolution continued to support Pinchot, awarding him a special certificate at the 1910 National Conservation Congress. That Pinchot's mother was a former chairman of the DAR's Committee on Conservation is included in Samuel P. Hays, *Conservation and the Gospel of Efficiency: The Progressive Conservation Movement 1890–1920* (Cambridge: Harvard University Press, 1959): 142. *Proceedings of the Second National Conservation Congress at St. Paul,* 5–8 September 1910 (Washington, D.C.: National Conservation Congress, 1911): 276–77.

15. Harriet Monroe, "Camping Above the Yosemite—A Summer Outing with the Sierra Club," *Putnam's Magazine* (May 1909): 221–26; Harriet Monroe, "The Hetch-Hetchy," *Century Magazine* 89 (June 1910): 441; Cora Calvert Foy, "Save the Hetch-Hetchy," *Outwest* 1 (December 1910): 1–18.

16. U.S. Congress, House, Committee on the Public Lands, Hearings, *San Francisco and the Hetch Hetchy Reservoir,* 60th Cong., 2nd sess. (9 January 1909): 130–332; Senate, Committee on the Public Lands, Hearings, *Hetch Hetchy Reservoir Site,* 60th Cong., 2nd sess. (11 February 1909): 30–33.

17. *GFWC Bulletin* 7 (January 1910): 107; Kent quoted in Hays, *Conservation:* 194. For the federation's full arguments for the presevation of Hetch Hetchy Valley, see *GFWC Magazine* (December 1913): 11–13. For the efforts of dam proponents to discredit the preservationists by making them appear to be feminine and unscientific, see Michael L. Smith, *Pacific Visions: California Scientists and the Environment, 1850–1915* (New Haven: Yale University Press, 1987): 178–81.

18. Ellen T. Emerson, "Through the Tuolumne Canon," *Sierra Club Bulletin* 9 (January 1915): 258–60; Bertha Pope, "With the Sierra Club in 1914," *Sierra Club Bulletin* 9 (January 1915): 247–57.

19. For the increasing professionalization of the conservation movement, see Hays, *Conservation:* 265–66 and Merchant, "Women of the Progressive Conservation Movement": 79–80.

20. Frances Drewry McMullen, "'The National Park Lady,'" 17 May 1924, Mary Belle King Sherman file, Rocky Mountain National Park.

21. Ibid.; Alcyon Robinson, "Home Glimpses of Mrs. John D. Sherman," *Better Homes and Gardens* (December 1924): 10–11, 46–47, Sherman file. Sherman was born in 1862 and died in 1935.

22. Mrs. John Dickinson Sherman, "Conservation," *GFWC Magazine* (March 1915): 23. For the role of Enos Mills in creating Rocky Mountain National Park, see C. W. Buchholtz, *Rocky Mountain National Park: A History* (Boulder: Colorado Associated University Press, 1983): 104–05.

23. *Proceedings of the National Park Conference Held at Berkeley, California, March 11, 12, and 13, 1915* (Washington: Department of the Interior, 1915): 140–42, hereafter, USDI.

24. Sherman GFWC Magazine, October 1915: 21; Mrs. John Dickinson Sherman, "Report of Conservation Department," GFWC *Proceedings, Thirteenth Biennial Convention*, 27 May 1916: 250.

25. Linda D. Vance, "May Mann Jennings and Royal Palm State Park," *Florida Historical Quarterly* 55 (July 1976): 1–17; Linda D. Vance, *May Mann Jennings; Florida's Genteel Activist* (Gainesville: University of Florida Press, 1985): 81–100, 117–18, 129–33. Jennings was born in 1872 and died in 1963.

26. Mrs. William S. Jennings, "Woman's Work in Florida," *Florida Magazine*, April 1922: 13–14, 18; Mrs. W. S. Jennings, "Royal Palm State Park—God's Own Garden," *Southern Women's Digest* 1 (April 1936): 6; Vance, "Mary Mann Jennings and Royal Palm State Park": 16–17.

27. Sherman, *GFWC Magazine,* April 1916: 19; June 1916: 53–54.

28. GFWC, *Proceedings, Thirteenth Biennial Convention*: 273–76; Sherman, *GFWC Magazine,* August 1916: 10; Albright, *Birth of National Park Service*: 38–39.

29. Mrs. John Dickinson Sherman, "Women's Part in National Park Development," *Proceedings of the National Parks Conference, Washington D.C., January 2–6, 1917* (Washington: USDI, 1917): 45–49. Anne M. Davis is sometimes called the Mother of Great Smoky Mountains National Park. In 1923, while on a tour of Western national parks, she suggested to her husband, Willis P. Davis, that the Great Smokies should be a national park. He agreed and the meeting he called to set up the Great Smoky Mountains Conservation Association is considered the beginning of the park movement. As a member of the Tennessee legislature, Anne Davis introduced the bill providing for state purchase of a tract that later became part of the national park. Carlos C. Campbell, *Birth of a National Park in the Great Smoky Mountains* (Knoxville: University of Tennessee Press, 1960; rev. 1978): 14–23, 31–33.

30. Mrs. John Dickinson Sherman, "Report of the Conservation Department," GFWC *Proceedings, Thirteenth Biennial Convention,* 27 May 1916: 251; Kay Franklin and Norma Schaeffer, *Duel for the Dunes: Land Use Conflict on the Shores of Lake Michigan* (Urbana: University of Illinois Press, 1983): 41, 85–88; Ron Cockrell, *A Signature of Time and Eternity, The Administrative History of Indiana Dunes National Lakeshore, Indiana* (Omaha, NE: NPS, USDI): 28–29. See chapter 7 for women's involvement in establishing Indiana Dunes National Seashore in the 1960s and 1970s.

31. Sherman, *GFWC Magazine* (January 1918): 28–29; *GFWC Bulletin,* August 1920: 7; October 1921: 2; January–February 1923: 4.

32. Elizabeth Spencer, "The Great Sand Dunes . . . " undated speech; "P.E.O. Chapters Deserve Credit for Designation," *Alamosa Courier,* 1 April 1932: 1, Great Sand Dunes National Monument Archives. My thanks to Jean Corlett, the daughter-in-law of Jean and George Corlett, of Chapter V of the PEO Sisterhood in Monte Vista. Letters to author from Jean Corlett, 26 March 1987; 13 April 1987; 15 May 1987; 13 June 1987.

33. "P.E.O. Chapters Deserve Credit"; petitions to Senator Lawrence C. Phipps and Senator A. Elmer Headlee, undated; George M. Corlett to Anna R. Darley, 24 December 1930; Elizabeth Spencer, Jean Corlett, Myrtle C. Woods, and Anna R. Darley to Edward P. Costigan and to Guy U. Hardy, 29 December 1931; Guy U. Hardy to Elizabeth Spencer, 7 January 1932; Horace M. Albright to Elizabeth Spencer, 27 January 1932; Guy U. Hardy to Elizabeth Spencer 14 March 1932; A.E. Demaray to Elizabeth Spencer, 25 March 1932; Great Sand Dunes Archives.

34. See *Fifty Blooming Years* (New York: Garden Club of America, 1963), the club's fiftieth anniversary book. A forerunner of the Garden Club movement was Sarah Louisa Rittenhouse. She led a group of women in a successful campaign to save Montrose Park, in Washington's Rock Creek Park,

from development in 1911. Citizens of Georgetown dedicated an armillary sphere and rose garden to her memory. Montrose Park folder, NPS.

35. "Annual Meeting, 1916," *Garden Club of America Bulletin* 14 (May 1926): 2–12, hereafter, *GCA Bulletin.*

36. Ibid.; Ellen Rooksby, "Hillcrest, the Home of Mrs. Hoyt," *Desert,* 2 (July 1930): 34–35.

37. Mrs. A. Sherman Hoyt, "The International Deserts League," *Americana,* 25 (July 1931): 315–19; "Minerva Lockhart Hamilton Hoyt," *National Cyclopaedia of American Biography* 35 (James T. White, 1936; reprint, Ann Arbor: University Microfilms 1967–71): 374–75. Minerva Hamilton Hoyt was born in 1866 and died in 1945. Thanks to Linda Green for leading me to Hoyt's remarkable story.

38. Hoyt, "The International Deserts League;" Marshall A. Howe, "The Mrs. A. Sherman Hoyt Collection of Living Desert Plants," *Journal of the New York Botanical Garden* 29 (May 1928): 108–11; *GCA Bulletin* 16 (March 1928): 52–55; 17 (January 1929): 84.

39. Hoyt, "The International Deserts League;" *GCA Bulletin* 17 (May 1929): 3–6, 96–97; (July 1929): 78; Ada King Wallis, "Remarkable Achievement of One Representative Western Woman," *Western Woman* 6 (December 1919–January 1930): 11–16, courtesy New York Botanical Garden.

40. Hoyt, "The International Deserts League;" Walter Sylvester Hertzog, "'Apostle of the Cacti'," *Los Angeles Saturday Night* reprint, 16 May 1931, courtesy Twentynine Palms Historical Society.

41. Conner Sorensen, "'Apostle of the Cacti:' The Society Matron as Environmental Activist," *Southern California Quarterly* 58 (fall 1976): 415–17.

42. Ibid.: 419–23; Beatrice Willard interview with author, 29 June 1988. See Linda W. Greene, *A History of Land Use in Joshua Tree National Monument* (Denver: NPS, USDI, 1983): 375–80.

43. Lucille Weight, "Mother of Joshua Tree National Monument," newspaper clipping in biography file, Twentynine Palms Public Library, courtesy Twentynine Palms Historical Society. The Keys View plaque was stolen in the 1960s and in 1980 the Billy Holcomb Chapter of the Order of E. Clampus Vitus installed a new plaque at the entrance to the visitor center, saying, "Minerva Hamilton Hoyt, Apostle of the Cacti. Her tireless efforts to establish Joshua Tree National Monument contributed to a heightened appreciation, not only of the Joshua tree but of the total environment." Letter and dedication program to author from Joshua Tree National Monument, 15 March 1988.

44. The Desert Protection Act also upgraded Death Valley to a national park and created the Mojave National Preserve protecting 4.3 acres of California desert. *National Parks* 69 (January/February 1995): 12; interviews with author: Kathryn Lacey, 30 March, 1995; Judith Anderson, 31 March, 1995; U.S. Congress, Senate, Hearings, Subcommittee on Public Lands, National Parks and Forests, Committee on Energy and Natural Resources, *California Desert,* 102nd Cong., 2nd sess. (4 April, 1992), 309–10.

45. Mrs. William A. Lockwood, "National Parks Committee," *GCA Bulletin* 22 (September 1934): 16–18. The Garden Club of America Redwood Grove now totals 5,130 acres, including the whole watershed of Canoe Creek. Garden Club of America Fact Sheet, 1985.

46. After Aurelia Harwood became the first woman president of the Sierra Club (1927 to 1928), only two women held that position: Michele Perrault (1984–1986; 1993–1994) and Susan D. Merrow (1990–1991). For Harwood see *Sierra Club Bulletin* in 14 (1929): 64–68. For Merrow, see Susan D. Merrow, *One for the Earth, Journal of a Sierra Club President* (Champaign, IL: Sagamore Publishing, 1992). For a discussion of the male dominance of the Sierra Club, see Helen King Burke, "Women in the Environmental Movement," oral history by Waverly Lowell (1979), Sierra Club History Committee, Regional Oral History Office, The Bancroft Library, University of California, 1980: 14.

47. *GCA Bulletin,* 31 (July 1943): 5; 36 (September 1948): 70, 94–95; 37 (July 1949): 72; 38 (September 1950): 74–75; 40 (July 1952): 87; 41 (March 1953): 84–91; 42 (November 1954): 82; Mrs. Robert Wright, "In Defense of National Monuments," *GCA Bulletin* 29 (January 1941): 61–62; Mrs. Le Roy Clark, "History of National Parks Committee, *GCA Bulletin* 49 (July 1961): 92–93; Mrs. Charles Willing, "Dedication of the Magnolia Garden, Independence National Historical Park," *GCA Bulletin,* 47 (September 1959): 3–5. The Bar Harbor (Maine) Garden Club, affiliated with the Federated Garden Clubs, created a wildflower garden of more than three hundred species in thirteen habitats at Acadia National Park in 1961. It was rededicated in 1986. "Wild Gardens 25th Anniversary is Noted," *Bar Harbor Times,* 19 June 1986, courtesy Acadia.

48. Rosalie Edge, "Good Companions in Conservation: Annals of an Implacable Widow," unpublished manuscript, Hawk Mountain Association Archives: 2–9; Rosalie Edge, "Motor Power," *Nature Magazine* 33 (December 1940): 156.

49. Edge, "Good Companions": 2a, 25–27; Irving Brant, *Adventures in Conservation with Franklin D. Roosevelt* (Flagstaff, AZ: Northland Publishing, 1988): 13–18. An extensive collection of Rosalie Edge's papers and ECC publications are included in the Conservation Library of the Denver Public Library. ECC publications are also in the Peabody Museum of Comparative Zoology, Harvard University. My thanks to Stephen Fox and Peter Edge, Rosalie Edge's son, for helping me locate these sources.

50. See ECC's annual reports, from *Conservation To-Day, Report for the Calendar Year, 1932*, to *Conservation-Up and Doing, Annual Report, 1944*. Robert Lewis Taylor, "Profiles: Oh, Hawk of Mercy!" *New Yorker Magazine* 24 (17 April 1948): 31–45; Edge, "Good Companions": 35–38; Brant, *Adventures in Conservation*: 4, 17–22; [Willard G. Van Name], *A Crisis in Conservation*, ECC Pub. #1, June 1929; [Irving Brant], *Compromised Conservation: Can the Audubon Society Explain?* ECC Pub. #6.

51. [Rosalie Edge], *The Slaughter of the Yellowstone Park Pelicans*, ECC Pub. #20, September 1932; Brant, *Compromised Conservation*: 17; Fox, *John Muir*: 181–82; Edge, "Good Companions": 97–100; [Willard G. Van Name], *Hands Off Yellowstone Lake*, ECC Pub. #25, February 1933. In 1934, Edge established a sanctuary for migrating hawks on Hawk Mountain in eastern Pennsylvania. She continued as president until her death.

52. Edge, "Good Companions": 91–96; U.S. Congress, House, Committee on Public Lands, *Acquisition of Lands for Yosemite National Park, HR 5394*, 75th Cong., lst sess. (20 April 1937): 26–31; Brant, *Adventures in Conservation*: 55–68. The national DAR conservation chair and the DAR California regent submitted a letter from the national president putting the entire DAR membership on record as supporting the pines. Ibid: 53–54.

53. Edge, "Good Companions": 102–07; [Rosalie Edge] *Twelve Immediately Important Problems of the National Parks and of Wild Life Conservation*, ECC Pub. #48, May 1935.

54. Ibid.: 107–10; U.S. Congress, House, Committee on Public Lands, *Mount Olympus National Park*, 74th Congress, 2nd sess. (25 April 1936): 76–81. See Brant, *Adventures in Conservation*, chapters 4–8, 13 for the creation of Olympic National Park.

55. Edge, "Good Companions": 111–12, 117–18; [Rosalie Edge] *Double-Crossing the Project for the Proposed Mount Olympus National Park*, ECC Pub. # 63, March 1937; Brant, *Adventures in Conservation*: 110–13.

56. Edge, "Good Companions": 118–20; [Rosalie Edge], *The Raid on the Nation's Olympic Forests*, ECC Pub. #93, May 1947; Brant, *Adventures in Conservation*: 281–86.

57. Ibid.: 148, 165–71, 197–98, 207–08, 216–17; Irving Brant, *The Proposed John Muir–Kings Canyon National Park*, ECC Pub. #74, January 1939.

58. Mrs. C.N. Edge to Harry S. Truman, 29 December 1952; Oscar L. Chapman to Mrs. C. N. Edge, 16 January 1953; Rosalie Edge to the President of the United States, 29 March 1954; Mrs. C. N. Edge to Senator Ives, 6 January 1954; to Herbert H. Lehman, 14 February 1954; to Fred M. Packard, 14 April 1954; to Sherman Adams, 5 May 1954; Conservation Library, Denver Public Library; Edge, "Good Companions": 96, 122, 210–12.

59. Edge, "Good Companions": 96, 122, 210–12; Taylor, "Profiles: Oh, Hawk of Mercy!"; Edwin Becker, "Ladies Afield," *Independent Woman*, 25 (April 1946): 108. Edge (1877–1962) died three weeks after receiving a standing ovation at the annual meeting of the Audubon Society. Fox, *John Muir*: 266.

60. The Native Daughters of the Golden West placed a marker at Lava Beds National Monument in 1926 to honor pioneers and Native Americans killed in the Modoc Indian War. Dorothy V. Gloster, "Monument for Historic Spot," *The Grizzly Bear* 36 (March 1925): 4; *Modoc Country Record*, 12 February 1987, clipping, Lava Beds, NM.

61. Ruth E. Finley, *Lady of Godey's: Sarah Josepha Hale* (Philadelphia: J. P. Lippincott, 1931): 64–73; G. W. Warren, *History of the Bunker Hill Monument Association* (Boston: James R. Osgood, 1877): 285–312.

62. Everett W. Burdett, *History of the Old South Meeting-House* (Boston: B. B. Russell, 1877): 86–103; Edwin D. Mead, "The Old South Work," reprint from *Journal of Education*, 30 August–13 September 1894. Bunker Hill and Old South became part of Boston National Historical Park in 1974.

63. Charles B. Hosmer Jr., *Preservation Comes of Age: From Williamsburg to the National Trust, 1926–1949* (Charlottesville: University Press of Virginia, 1981): 525–26.

64. James M. Lindgren, "'For the Sake of our Future': The Association for the Preservation of Virginia Antiquities and the Regeneration of Traditionalism," *Virginia Magazine of History and Biography* 97 (January 1989): 47–50, 59–61; "Report by Miss Galt to the APVA concerning the excavation of ruins on Jamestown Island, VA," Mary Jeffrey Galt papers, Virginia Historical Society.

65. Lindgren, "'For the Sake of Our Future'": 62–64, 72–73; letter to author from Belle Pendleton, Programs Coordinator, APVA, 7 July 1986; Mary Jeffrey Galt obituary, in the Norfolk *Virginian-Pilot,* 1 July 1922: 3, courtesy Virginia State Library.

66. Hosmer, *Preservation Comes of Age,* v.1: 478–83.

67. Ibid.: 483–90; ibid.: 607–610. Louise du Pont Crowninshield, helped furnish the Richard Derby House at Salem National Historical Park. Hosmer, *Preservation Comes of Age,* v. 2: 924.

68. Founded in 1891, the Society of Colonial Dames preserved Sulgrave Manor in England, home of Lawrence Washington, the president's ancestor. S. Price Gilbert, "The Part Played by the Colonial Dames in Establishing the Fort Frederica National Monument," *Georgia Historical Quarterly* 27 (1943): 175–81.

69. The prison and cemetery became Andersonville National Historic Site, administered by the National Park Service, in 1970. Marion Tinling, *Women Remembered: A Guide to Landmarks of Women's History in the United States* (Westport, CT: Greenwood Press, 1986): 135; G. Michael Strock, *Anderson National Cemetery* (Eastern National Parks and Monument Association, 1983).

70. Mary B. Poppenheim et al., *The History of the United Daughters of the Confederacy* (Richmond: Garrett and Massie, Inc., 1938): 1–2. See also, Drew Gilpin Faust, "Altars of Sacrifice: Confederate Women and the Narratives of War," *Journal of American History* 76 (March 1990): 1200–28; Richard West Sellars, "Vigil of Silence: The Civil War Memorials," NPS *Courier* 32 (March 1987): 12–13, reprinted from *History News,* July 1986.

71. Poppenheim, *History of the UDC:* 52–57, 66–67. The UDC sponsored the first Confederate memorial at Arlington National Cemetery. Created by sculptor Moses Ezekiel, a Confederate veteran, it was unveiled on 4 June 1914. The central figure is a woman as a symbol of peace high on the monument, her head crowned with olive leaves and her hand on the proverbial plow and pruning hook. Poppenheim, *History of the UDC:* 57–62.

72. "Mrs. Andrew Johnson Patterson," typescript in the Mather Collection, National Archives. The Lincoln Club of Southern Indiana, a member of the Indiana Federation of Women's Clubs, sponsored a bill changing Nancy Hanks Lincoln State Memorial to federal status in 1962 to become Lincoln Boyhood National Memorial. The club holds an annual Lincoln Day Program at the grave of Nancy Hanks Lincoln, President Lincoln's mother. Letter to author from Norman D. Hellmers, Lincoln Boyhood National Memorial, 18 April 1986.

73. Hugh A. Lawing, "Administrative History of Andrew Johnson National Historic Site," 21 October 1971, typescript, NPS: 57–67, 98–106; Margaret P. Bartlett interview with Dorothy Huyck, 8 April 1978, NPS Archives.

74. Hosmer, *Presence of the Past:* 146–50.

75. *Woman's Roosevelt Memorial Bulletin* 1 (December 1919): 1-2; 1 (February 1920): 1,4; 1 (April 1920): 1–3; Judith Paine, *Theodate Pope Riddle: Her Life and Work* (New York: NPS, USDI, 1979).

76. Hosmer, *Presence of the Past:* 151–52; *Roosevelt House Bulletin* 1 (February 1921): 4; 2 (fall 1923): 1–6; 2 (summer 1926): 10; letter to author from John A. Gable, Theodore Roosevelt Association, 3 April 1985. Roosevelt's daughter, Ethel Roosevelt Derby, helped preserve Sagamore Hill, Roosevelt's home on Long Island, New York, from 1885 until his death. Bertha Rose supervised the restoration until 1962 when it became Sagamore Hill National Historic Site. Jessica Kraft, former secretary to Edith Kermit Roosevelt, Roosevelt's wife, became curator in 1953 under the Theodore Roosevelt Association, continuing under the Park Service until 1974.

77. Lonnelle Aikman, "The DAR Story," *National Geographic Magazine* 50 (November 1951): 569; letter to author from Elva B. Crawford, National DAR, 2 February 1988. Other catalysts for saving his-

toric sites were women advocates of zoning for historic districts. In the 1930s, when Eva Hinton worked to save historic Georgetown, D.C., from development, the first place she helped protect was the Old Stone House, built in 1765, now administered by the National Park Service. Willard Clopton, "The Busiest Body in Georgetown," *Washington Post,* 16 June 1963; obituaries: *Georgetowner,* 26 April 1985, *Washington Post,* 20 April 1985, courtesy Columbia Historical Society.

78. Hosmer, *Presence of the Past:* 86–87. For a discussion of problems about the accuracy of the restoration see Hosmer: 87–88, and Constance M. Greiff, *Independence: The Creation of a National Park* (Philadelphia: University of Pennsylvania Press, 1987): 36–39. The Colonial Dames restored the Old Senate Chamber in Congress Hall, completing it in 1896. Hosmer, *Presence of the Past:* 86. A national drive by the General Federation of Women's Clubs between 1953 and 1963 raised $215,000 to restore and refurnish the first floor of Independence Hall as a "campaign of Americanism." In addition to restoration work, the Park Service used the funds to purchase three hundred pieces of furniture and a painting and reinforced the yoke of the Liberty Bell. *GFWC Clubwoman* 33 (February 1953): 12–13; *The Role of the General Federation of Women's Clubs in the Restoration and Refurnishing of Independence Hall, 1953–1954* (Washington, D.C.: NPS, USDI, 1963).

79. "National Memorials: The Valley Forge Shaft" in Mrs. Henry T. Kent et al., *History of the Origin and Work of the National Society of the Daughters of the American Revolution* (Rumford Press, 1931): 113–140. The DAR monument to the Washington Light Infantry of Charleston, SC, at Cowpens National Battlefield, preceded that park. Letter to author from William T. Spring, Cowpens NB, 28 May 1986.

80. Kent, *History of the . . . DAR:* 113–16. The all-male Centennial and Memorial Association of Valley Forge placed the task of raising money to purchase Washington's Headquarters "in the hands of the ladies" under a "Lady Regent." Mary Bean Jones, "Origin," *Valley Forge Journal* 1 (June 1982): 9–12.

81. Letter to author from James J. Anderson, Kings Mountain National Military Park, 9 May 1986.

82. Gertrude S. Carraway, "How, Why—Moore's Creek," speech at the Memorial Service, 27 February 1965, Moore's Creek National Military Park Archives; Russell A. Gibbs, "A History of Moores Creek National Military Park," typescript, NPS, 1965: 21–23. For Republican Mothers, see Linda K. Kerber, *Women of the Republic: Intellect and Ideology in Revolutionary America* (Chapel Hill, University of North Carolina Press, 1980): 269–88.

83. Carraway, "How, Why—Moore's Creek"; letter to author from Fred Boyles, Moores Creek NB, 27 March 1986; John Albright, "Historical Base Map . . . Moore's Creek National Historical Park," Denver Service Center, NPS, April 1974: 23–27.

A ladies' auxiliary to the Washington Association of New Jersey raised money and provided curatorial and guide service for George Washington's headquarters (1779–80) at Morristown, bought by the association in the 1880s. Altha Hatch Cutler, curator from 1909, continued to advise Morristown National Historical Park when it was established in 1933. James Elliott Lindsley, *A Certain Splendid House: The Centennial History of the Washington Association of New Jersey* (Morristown, 1974): 72–74; letter to author from Ralph H. Cutler Jr., 30 June 1986. DAR chapters provided funds for furnishings or restoration in the following national parks: Mount Washington Tavern, Fort Necessity National Battlefield; Moore House, Colonial National Historical Park; the Old Commissary, Fort Smith National Historic Site. See Lewis Barrington, *Historic Restorations of the DAR* (New York: Richard Smith, 1941): 107, 126, 150.

84. *Bent's Old Fort* (Denver: State Historical Society of Colorado, 1979): 53–63.

85. Ray H. Mattison, "Homestead National Monument: Its Establishment and Administration," typescript, NPS, 1961: 11–12, 20–26; plaque at Nez Perce National Historical Park; "The Old Trail" and "Mississippi Daughters of the American Revolution Discover the Natchez Trace," typescript, Natchez Trace Parkway Archives. In North Dakota a DAR chapter cared for Theodore Roosevelt's Maltese Cross cabin, the only surviving structure from his ranch, before it was moved from the State Capitol grounds in Bismark to Theodore Roosevelt National Park. Letter to author from Harvey D. Wickware, Theodore Roosevelt National Park, 3 April 1986.

86. William P. Corbett, "Pipestone: The Origin and Development of a National Monument," *Min-*

nesota History 47 (fall 1980): 83–84; Robert A. Murray, "Administrative History of Pipestone National Monument," typescript, NPS, 1961: 81–83; Winifred Bartlett taped interview by William Corbett, 19 April 1976, American Indian Research Project, University of South Dakota. Bartlett (1885–1982) was born on a farm in Pipestone County. Thanks to Betty McSwain for help with this research.

87. Bartlett interview; Corbett, "Pipestone": 87–88.

88. Bartlett interview; Corbett, "Pipestone": 91–92. Bartlett set up a museum after she found the county museum collection dumped on the courthouse lawn. See also: Hal K. Rothman, *Managing the Sacred and the Secular: An Administrative History of Pipestone National Monument* (Omaha: NPS, 1992).

89. *Woman's Journal,* 19 June 1875: 196; 28 February 1885: 68.

90. Elizabeth Cady Stanton, *Eighty Years and More* (New York, 1898): 311–14; Elizabeth Cady Stanton, Susan B. Anthony, Matilda Joslyn Gage, eds., *History of Woman Suffrage* (Rochester, NY, 1887), v. 3: 27–47.

91. Sally Roesch Wagner, *A Time of Protest: Suffragists Challenge the Republic, 1870–1887* (Sacramento: Spectrum Publications, 1987): 11–17.

92. "Notes on the Mount Rushmore Struggle," 13 July 1945, Box 1: 1; Mary R. Beard to Gutzom Borglum, 23 May 1935, Box 2: 27; Gutzon Borglum to Rose Arnold Powell, 27 December 1939; January 1940, 10 April 1940; Box 2:28; "In Sympathy with Mount Rushmore Effort," Box 5: 84, Rose Arnold Powell Collection, A-107, Schlesinger Library, Radcliffe College.

93. "Sequoia Park is Site of Memorial," Box 3: 74, undated clipping, Powell Collection; Alma Whitaker, "Tribute Paid to Feminist," *Los Angeles Times,* 27 June 1938, California State Library. The Utopian Kaweah Colony named a tree in Giant Forest for Clara Barton in the 1880s. Letter from Wm. Tweed, 14 December 1990.

Chapter Three

A version of this chapter was published as "Challenging Tradition: Pioneer Women Naturalists in the National Park Service," *Forest and Conservation History* 34 (January 1990): 4–16.

1. Isabel Bassett, "Archives of 1919," *The Purple Book,* 1920, Wellesley College Archives, Wellesley, Massachusetts.

2. Isabel (Bassett) Wasson, U.S. General Services Administration, Civilian Personnel Records (hereafter cited as USGSA CPR); Isabel B. Wasson, "Summer of 1920, First Naturalist Ranger in Yellowstone National Park," Yellowstone National Park Archives; Albright, *The Birth of the National Park Service*: 120. The Civilian Personnel Records used for this book were collected by Dorothy Boyle Huyck from the Personnel Records Center, St. Louis, MO, and are now filed in the Dorothy Boyle Huyck Collection, National Park Service Library, Harpers Ferry Center; hereafter cited as Huyck Collection.

3. Wasson, *The Purple Book,* 1921: 10; Wasson, "Summer of 1920"; Elizabeth Wasson Bergstrom interview with author, 9 January 1994. Wasson worked as a geologist for Pure Oil Co. for seven years. She developed a program in natural science for the River Forest, Illinois, public schools and published *Birds* in the Follett Beginning Science series in 1963. Wasson died in 1994.

4. "Report of Progress in Educational Activities in National Park Service," 1931, Library, Yosemite National Park. Also listed was Florence Taylor, as a seasonal ranger-naturalist at Yosemite, and Thelma McKinnon, as a seasonal museum caretaker at Sequoia.

5. Horace M. Albright and Frank J. Taylor, *"Oh, Ranger!"* (Stanford, CA: Stanford University Press, 1929): 31.

6. Alice Eastwood, *Key and Flora, Rocky Mountain edition* (Boston: Ginn, 1900); Alice Eastwood, *Key and Flora, Pacific Coast edition* (Boston: Ginn, 1901); "Bibliography of the Writings of Alice Eastwood" in *Proceedings of the Academy of Sciences,* Fourth Series, 25 (1943–49): xv-xxiv; Alice Eastwood, "A Plea for the Protection of the Wild Flowers," *California Out-of-Doors,* April 1921: 190. Alice Eastwood's correspondence with the Gray Herbarium at Harvard University runs from 1891 to 1950. Her role as a botanical explorer is discussed in chapter 1.

7. Florence Merriam Bailey, *Among the Birds in the Grand Canyon Country* (Washington: USDI, 1939); Florence Merriam Bailey, *Wild Animals of Glacier National Park: the Birds* (Washington: USDI, 1918); Florence Merriam Bailey, *Birds of New Mexico* (Santa Fe: New Mexico Department of Game and Fish, 1928); Florence Merriam Bailey, "The Birds" in *Cave Life of Kentucky* (Notre Dame University Press, 1934): 81–192. For the use of *Birds of New Mexico* in the Southwestern Monuments, see *Southwestern Monuments Monthly Reports,* June 1934: 15; August 1935: 107; September 1937: 223.

8. Florence Merriam Bailey, "How to Conduct Field Classes," *Bird-Lore* 2 (June 1900): 83–87. See also: Harriet Kofalk, *No Woman Tenderfoot: Florence Merriam Bailey, Pioneer Naturalist* (College Station, Texas A. & M. Press, 1989); Joseph Kastner, *A World of Watchers* (New York: Alfred A. Knopf), 1986): 110–11.

9. Mrs. William Starr Dana (also Frances Theodora Parsons), *How to Know the Wild Flowers* (New York: Scribner's, 1893); Buckner Hollingsworth, *Her Garden Was Her Delight* (New York: Macmillan, 1962): 155–58; Mary Elizabeth Parsons, *Wild Flowers of California* (San Francisco: California School Book Depository, 1930).

10. Katherine Chandler, *Habits of California Plants* (San Francisco: Education Publishing, 1903). See Peter J. Schmitt, *Back to Nature* (New York: Oxford University Press, 1969).

11. Anna Botsford Comstock, *Handbook of Nature-Study* (Ithaca: Cornell University Press, 1911): 1–24. For the split between amateurs ("lovers of science") in the Nature Study movement and professionalized New Botany, see Elizabeth B. Keeney, *The Botanizers: Amateur Scientists in Nineteenth Century America* (Chapel Hill, University of North Carolina Press, 1992): 123–46.

12. Anna Botsford Comstock, "New Years Greetings," *Nature Magazine* 3 (January 1924): 45; Mrs. John Dickinson Sherman, "The Study of Nature for Children," *Nature Magazine* 1 (January 1923): 45–46. *Nature Magazine* became *Natural History* in 1960.

13. Winona Bailey, "A Few Flowers of the Higher Olympics," *Mountaineer* 6 (1913): 59–64; L.G. Richards, "And We Learned About Fungi From Her," *Mount Rainier Nature Notes* 8 (September 1930): 4; Elizabeth Eaton Morse, "Features of Our Fungi," *Mount Rainier Nature Notes* 9 (September 1931): 4–5; "The Spined Puffball," *Nature Magazine* 17 (June 1931): 382–83.

14. Other women hotel nature guides were Gertrude Norton at the Glacier National Park Hotel in 1919 and Zillah Pocock White for the Yellowstone Park Camps Company at Old Faithful geyser in 1921. C. Frank Brockman, "Park Naturalists and the Evolution of National Park Service Interpretation through World War II," *Journal of Forest History* 22 (January 1978): 24–43; Zillah Pocock White, "Notes on Early Development of Information Services in Yellowstone National Park," History Collection, Yellowstone.

15. Enos A. Mills, "The Development of a Woman Guide" in *Adventures of a Nature Guide* (Boston: Houghton Mifflin, 1932): 259–71.

16. Hildegarde Hawthorne and Esther Burnell Mills, *Enos Mills of the Rockies* (Boston: Houghton Mifflin, 1935).

17. Superintendent's Annual Report, Rocky Mountain National Park, 1917: 8–9.

18. Luther E. Wyman and Elizabeth F. Burnell, *Field Book of Birds of the Southwestern United States* (Boston: Houghton Mifflin, 1925). Elizabeth married Norman Smith, a mining engineer, in 1932.

19. Esther edited editions of Mills's works and wrote his biography. Hawthorne and Mills, *Enos Mills of the Rockies.*

20. Yosemite School of Field Natural History, class rosters and 1985 alumni address list, Yosemite Library; letters to author from Clare McGee Lennox, 3 January 1987 and 1 April 1987; "Training for National Park Service," *Sierra Club Bulletin* 22 (April 1937): iii; Mildred Ericson interview with Herbert Evison, 1962, NPS Library, Harpers Ferry, WV. Unless otherwise noted, all interviews are filed in the NPS Library at Harpers Ferry.

21. Lennox to author, 1 April 1987.

22. Ruth A. Nelson, USGSA CPR; Ruth Ashton Nelson interview with Dorothy Huyck, 28 June 1978; Ruth Ashton Nelson, *Plants of Rocky Mountain National Park* (Washington: NPS, USDI, 1933).

23. Roger W. Toll to Ruth E. Ashton, 9 April 1928, Ruth Ashton Nelson folder, Huyck Collection.

24. Ansel F. Hall to Ruth E. Ashton, 18 January 1929, ibid.; Roger L. Williams, *Aven Nelson of Wyoming* (Boulder: Colorado Associated Universities Press, 1984): 257–59, 302–08. Ashton contributed over ten articles to *Nature Notes* and published a guide to the plants of Zion National Park in 1970. She and her husband collected plants at Mount McKinley National Park in 1939 as collaborators with the National Park Service. "Rocky Mountain National Park" in Hazel Hunt Voth, compiler, *General Index to the "Nature Notes". . . in National Parks, 1920–1936,* (Berkeley: USDI): 6, hereafter, *Index to Nature Notes*. Ruth Ashton Nelson died in 1987.

25. "Reminiscences of Bert Harwell" in a letter to Frank Kittridge, 23 June 1947, Yosemite Library.

26. Mildred J. Ericson, USCSA CPR; Ericson interview with Evison. See Mildred J. Ericson, "Washington Takes to the Woods," *Nature Magazine* 39 (May 1946): 253–55; "Animal Accidents in Geyersland," *Nature Magazine* 41 (June–July 1948): 317-18. Mary Louise Oswald [Griffitts], who held a Ph.D. in geology from the University of Colorado, was also a ranger-naturalist at Yellowstone in the summer of 1946. Mary Griffitts to author, 23 June 1989.

27. Beatrice E. Willard, USGSA CPR; Bette Willard interview with author, 29 June 1988; Ann H. Zwinger and Beatrice E. Willard, *Land Above the Trees: A Guide to the American Alpine Tundra* (New York: Harper & Row, 1972). For Willard's role in saving the Florissant Fossil Beds, see chapter 7.

28. "Women's Number," *Yosemite Field School Alumni Newsletter,* November, 1936, Yosemite Library.

29. Ibid. The only field school graduate listed as working for the Park Service as a naturalist was Mabel Hibbard, a children's guide at Yosemite for one summer. Mabel E. Hibbard, USGSA CPR.

30. Helene Wilson, USGSA CPR; Mount Rainier superintendent's monthly reports for June, July, August, 1918.

31. Clare M. Hodges, USGSA CPR; *Sunset Magazine* 42 (February 1919): 47–48, Yosemite Library; Clare H. Wolfsen, "Once Upon a Time," *Yosemite Nature Notes* 31 (January 1952): 6–10.

32. Ibid. Clare Hodges Wolfsen died in 1958. See also Clare M. Hodges folder, Huyck Collection.

33. Letter to author from Phyllis Freeland Broyles, 6 January 1988; Martha Bingaman, USGSA CPR; John W. Bingaman, *Guardians of Yosemite* (Lodi, CA, 1961): 18. Ernest Reed and his wife also received equal pay at the Arch Rock Entrance Station.

34. Eva McNally, USGSA CPR; letter to author from Charles McNally, 16 January 1988, with clipping; photograph, Yosemite Library; Eva McNally interview with author, 9 June 1988. The Classification Act of 1923 required equal pay for equal work for federal employees. The park no longer used paid couples at entrance stations after 1932, the year the Economy Act, a response to the Great Depression, went into effect. Section 213 required that one member of a married couple working for the federal government be discharged before individuals. Although the act expired in 1935 and only thirty-four women and fifteen men from the entire Department of the Interior were affected, its more far-reaching effect was to discourage the hiring of Park Service wives to work in tandem with their husbands. U.S. Department of Labor, Women's Bureau, "Preliminary Study on the Application of Section 213 of the Economy Act of June 30, 1932." I would like to thank Joy A. Scime for sending me this information.

35. Enid R. Michael, USGSA CPR; quotation in Enid Michael, "Recollections of Thirty-Two Summer Seasons in the Ranger Naturalist Service," Enid Michael File, Yosemite Library; *Index to Nature Notes,* Yosemite: 42–44. See also Enid Michael folder, Huyck Collection.

36. Michael, "Recollections;" Lisa Rhudy, "Enid Michael," *Yosemite Nature Notes* 46, no. 2, 1977: 25–27; Enid Michael, "Wild Animal Friends of Yosemite," *Nature Magazine* 8 (July 1926): 9–12; "Winter Bird Group in the Yosemite," *Nature Magazine* 7 (March 1926): 162–63. A red phalarope raised her bird count to 131. "A Stranger Calls at Yosemite," *Nature Magazine,* 14 (August 1929).

37. C. H. Adams to Mrs. Robert Fisher, 12 September 1923; Bess Hayne Fisher to Stephen T. Mather, 26 October 1923; C. H. Adams to Stephen T. Mather, 5 November 1923; Enid Michael file, Yosemite Library.

38. A. E. Demaray to W. B. Lewis, 5 November 1923; W. B. Lewis to The Director, 24 November 1923, Enid Michael File, Yosemite Library.

39. Her appointment was for "When Actually Employed." Acting superintendent to C. L. Snyder, U.S. Civil Service District, 24 October 1931; Michael, "Recollections," Yosemite Library.

40. Bert Harwell to C. G. Thomson, 20 December 1934; Thomson to Enid Michael, 14 January 1935; Michael to Harwell, 6 February 1935; Harwell to Thomson, 14 February 1935; Harwell to Thomson, 6 March 1935; Thomson to Bryant, 9 March 1935; Bryant to Thomson, 20 March 1935; Thomson and Harwell to Michael, 4 April 1935; Harwell to Thomson, 9 July 1935, Enid Michael File.

41. Charles Michael, who was often called the Yosemite Bird Man, died in December 1941. Enid married Herbert Benson, who outlived her. After she died on 11 February 1966, many tributes were printed in the *Yosemite Sentinel,* 18 May 1966. Mary Curry Tresidder said that the Michaels were the persons who gave people at Yosemite their beginning knowledge of birds and flowers.

42. Margaret F. Boos, USGSA CPR; Toll to Ashton. Boos studied the exposed pre-Cambrian schists and granites. See Margaret Bradley Fuller, "The Physiographic Development of the Big Thompson River Valley in Colorado," *Journal of Geology* 31 (February–March 1923): 126–37; "Contact Metamorphism in the Big Thompson Schist of North Central Colorado," *American Journal of Science* 11 (March 1926): 194–200. She married C. Maynard Boos in September 1927.

43. C. Maynard Boos interview with Dorothy Huyck, 29 June 1978; Lloyd Musselman, *Rocky Mountain National Park Administrative History* (Washington, NPS, USDI, July 1971): 153; Margaret Fuller Boos, "Guide to the Geology of Rocky Mountain National Park, Colorado," 1919, revised 1963, unpublished manuscript, Rocky Mountain National Park; Rocky Mountain, *Index to Nature Notes:* 11. A relative who made a first ascent in Alaska's Talkeetna Range named the mountain Peggy's Peak in her honor. Boos died in 1978. See also Margaret Fuller Boos folder, Huyck Collection.

44. Pauline Mead, USGSA CPR; Pauline Mead Patraw interview with Dorothy Huyck, 29 September 1978; Pauline and Preston Patraw interview with Herbert Evison, 22 January 1964. See also Pauline Mead Patraw folder, Huyck Collection.

45. Pauline Mead Patraw interview with Julie Russell, 3 August 1981, Grand Canyon National Park Library; Grand Canyon, *Index to Nature Notes:* 21–22; Pauline Patraw, *Flowers of the Southwest Mesas* (Globe, AZ: Southwest Parks and Monuments Association, 1977); "Plant Succession in Kaibab Limestone," *Grand Canyon Nature Notes,* November, 1931: 6–9. For a discussion of the role of the women couriers in interpreting Native American culture in the Southwest during this period, see Weigle, "Exposition and Mediation,": 130–45.

46. Mary A. Rolfe, USGSA CPR; Mary A. Rolfe, *Our National Parks* (Chicago: Sanborn, 1937), Books I & II.

47. Marguerite L. Arnold, USGSA CPR; "In Memoriam for Marguerite Lindsley Arnold" *Yellowstone Nature Notes* 27 (May–June 1952), entire issue devoted to her writings; Yellowstone, *Index to Nature Notes:* 18, 47.

48. Marguerite Lindsley Arnold, "Early Impressions," *Yellowstone Nature Notes* 11 (March–April 1934); quotes in Marguerite Lindsley to Miss Stolz, 26 November 1927, Marguerite Lindsley Arnold file, Huyck Collection. Lindsley's father became the postmaster at Yellowstone.

49. "She's a Real Ranger," *Sunset Magazine* 27 (November 1927): 48; quotes in Lindsley to Miss Stolz, 26 November 1927.

50. Marguerite Lindsley, "Yellowstone Wolves," *Nature Magazine* 30 (August 1937): 111–12; Marguerite Lindsley, "Coyote Replies to Imitation Call," *Yellowstone Nature Notes* 4 (September 1927): 7.

51. Irene Wisdom, USCSA CPR; Irene Wisdom interview with Dorothy Huyck, 18 October 1977. Also working at Yellowstone as rangers in the mid-1920s were Margaret Thone and Ruby Anderson. Luis A. Gastellum to Aubrey Haines, "History of Women's Uniform in the National Park Service," 13 October 1961, Yellowstone Archives.

52. Frances Pound, USGSA CPR; Frances Pound Wright interview with Tim Manns, 11 July 1981, Yellowstone Archives.

53. Frieda Nelson, USGSA CPR; Elizabeth Conard, USGSA CPR; photographs of Frieda Nelson, Yellowstone Archives.

54. E. K. Burlew and J. F. Gartland to the Secretary [of the Interior], 4 October 1926 in Education

Division Correspondence, 1926–34, Yellowstone Archives. I am indebted to Denise Vick for bringing this significant correspondence to my attention.

55. George Rhule interview with Dorothy Huyck, May 1977; Brockman, "Park Naturalists": 43.

56. All quotations in the preceding paragraphs are contained in Horace M. Albright to Stephen T. Mather, 14 October 1926, in Education Division Correspondence, 1926–34.

57. Henry S. Conard to Horace M. Albright, 26 December 1926; Horace M. Albright to Henry S. Conard, 11 January 1927, Education Division Correspondence, 1926–1934. It should be noted that the many women who worked for the park concessions found housing, as, of course, did the many women visitors.

58. Geo. D. Fuller to Stephen T. Mather, 24 January 1927; Arno B. Cammerer to Geo. D. Fuller, 9 February 1927; Henry S. Conard to H. C. Work, 24 January, 1927; Hubert Work to Henry S. Conard, 5 February 1927, Education Division Correspondence, 1926–1934.

59. E. Lucy Braun to Stephen T. Mather, 31 January 1927; Arno B. Cammerer to E. Lucy Braun, 9 February 1927, Education Division Correspondence, 1926–1934.

60. "She's a Real Ranger," *Sunset*; Esther W. Clements to Marguerite Lindsley, 16 February 1927; Marguerite Lindsley to Esther W. Clements, 23 February 1927; Frances E. Bradshaw to Marguerite Lindsley, 18 February 1927; Marguerite Lindsley to Frances E. Bradshaw, 23 February 1927, Marguerite Lindsley Arnold file, Huyck Collection. Marietta McDaniels (Sumner) testified that naturalist jobs were closed to women in the mid-1930s. After she passed the Civil Service examination for junior park naturalist in 1932, the telegram offering her a position as a park naturalist failed to reach her. By the time she learned of her eligibility, she said, "they were closing that job to women." Lovell and Marietta Sumner interview with Herbert Evison, 16 February 1973.

61. Geo. C. Ruhle, "Qualifications of a Nature Guide," in "Proceedings of the First Park Naturalists' Training Conference, 1–30 November 1929": 116, Yosemite Library.

62. Herma A. Baggley, USGSA CPR; Baggley interview with Herbert Evison; Herma Albertson Baggley, "I was born in a small town . . . " Baggley file, Yellowstone Archives.

63. Ibid.

64. Horace M. Albright to Roger W. Toll, 29 September 1931, Herma Albertson Baggley file, Huyck Collection.

65. W. B. McDougall and Herma A. Baggley, *Plants of Yellowstone National Park* (Yellowstone Park, Wyoming, 1956). Herma Baggley contributed more than twenty articles to *Nature Notes*. Yellowstone, *Index to Nature Notes*: 1, 19. Baggley died in 1981.

66. Barbara A. Babcock and Nancy J. Parezo, *Daughters of the Desert: Women Anthropologists and the Native American Southwest, 1880–1980* [exhibit catalog] (Albuquerque: University of New Mexico Press, 1988): 39, 47, 73. For the proceedings of the conference connected with the above exhibit, see Nancy J. Parezo, Editor, *Hidden Scholars: Women Anthropologists and the Native American Southwest* (Albuquerque: University of New Mexico Press, 1993). The pioneering work in the Gulf of Alaska of archeologist and ethnologist Frederica de Laguna for more than fifty years paralleled the work of the women in Southwestern anthropology. She was also a student of Franz Boas, at Columbia, and her studies at the Cook Inlet, now bordered by two national parks, was the first periodization of the Pacific Eskimo culture in the area and demonstrated the antiquity of that culture. Her ethnology of the Yakutat Tlingit people who live "under Mount Saint Elias" preserved their history, culture, and names for places and inhabitants of the natural world. Frederica de Laguna, *The Archeology of Cook Inlet, Alaska* (Philadelphia: University of Pennsylvania Museum, 1934; Anchorage: Alaska Historical Society, 1975, 2nd edition); Frederica de Laguna, *Under Mount Saint Elias: The History and Culture of the Yakutat Tlingit* (Washington: Smithsonian Institution Press, 1972).

67. The Chaco Canyon Field School was sponsored by the School of American Research at Santa Fe and the University of New Mexico. Florence Hawley Ellis interview for *Daughters of the Desert*, 4 August 1985, used with permission from Barbara Babcock, with thanks; Florence M. Hawley, *The Significance of the Dated Prehistory of Chetro Ketl*, University of New Mexico Bulletin, Monograph Series, v. 1, 1 July 1934; *Field Manual of Prehistoric Southwestern Pottery Types*, University of New Mexico Bulletin, Anthropological Series, v. 1, 1 August 1936.

68. Bertha P. Dutton, *Leyit Kin; A Small House Ruin, Chaco Canyon, NM Excavation Report,* University of New Mexico Bulletin, Monograph Series, no. 7, 5 October 1938; *NPS Courier* 21 (January 1974): 2.

69. Ann Axtell Morris, *Digging in the Southwest* (Garden City, NY: Doubleday, Doran, 1933); Will Logan interview with the author, 7 May 1985. Will Logan, a Park Service archeologist, remembers being excited about the field after reading Morris's book.

70. Bertha P. Dutton, "Report on Senior Girl Scout Archeological Mobile Camp," *Southwestern Lore* 21 (September 1955): 35–41. By 1955, 207 Girl Scouts from thirty-four states had participated.

71. Interview with Kate Peck Kent for *Daughters of the Desert,* 4 September 1985; Kate Peck Kent, "Textiles," in *Montezuma Castle Archeology,* Southwestern Monuments Association Technical Series, v. 3, 1954; Kate Peck Kent, "An Analysis and Interpretation of the Cotton Textiles from Tonto National Monument," in Louis Caywood, ed., *Archeological Studies at Tonto National Monument,* Southwestern Monuments Association Technical Series, no. 2, 1962.

72. Caroline M. Thompson, USGSA CPR; Caroline Thompson Simmons interview with author, 25 June 1988; Caroline Thompson, "Exterior Ornamentation of Mesa Verde Bowls," *Mesa Verde Nature Notes* 3 (October 1933): 40–43. Thompson married John Farr Simmons, a career foreign service officer, and lived in many parts of the world.

73. Elizabeth Yelm, USGSA CPR; Elizabeth Yelm Kingman interview with Dorothy Huyck, 29 September 1978; Elizabeth Yelm Kingman interview with author, 23 September 1985; Rocky Mountain, *Index to Nature Notes:* 27; Mesa Verde, *Index to Nature Notes:* 10. Elizabeth Yelm Kingman later became the librarian at the School of American Research at Santa Fe. See also Elizabeth Yelm Kingman file, Huyck Collection.

74. Virginia S. Harrington, USGSA CPR; Jean C. Harrington, USGSA CPR; letters to author from Virginia Harrington, 14 March 1986; 22 June 1986; Mr. and Mrs. J. C. Harrington interview with Charles B. Hosmer, Jr., 18 May 1970, NPS Library.

75. For Pierce: Sallie Pierce Harris, USGSA CPR; Sallie Harris interview with Dorothy Huyck, 11 October 1978; Robert H. Rose to Horace M. Albright, 16 February 1934; Horace M. Albright to Robert H. Rose, 20 February 1934, Sallie Harris file, Huyck Collection. For Jean McWhirt Pinkley: Jean Pinkley, USGSA CPR; Ellis interview for *Daughters of the Desert*; Ardy Ptolemy, "Mrs. Mesa Verde? Could be Jean Pinkley," *Durango-Cortez Herald,* 10 April 1966; Chester A. Thomas, "Jean McWhirt Pinkley, 1910–1969," *American Antiquity* 34 (October 1969): 471–73. See also Jean McWhirt Pinkley file, Huyck Collection.

76. Harris interview with Huyck; letter to author from Sallie Harris, 9 August 1989. Women hired as guides at Aztec National Monument in the 1930s were Gay Rogers, Zelda Mae Abrams, Joyce Clubb, and Georgia Akers. Letters to author from Homer Hastings, 22 June 1986, and Zelda Mae Abrams McWilliams, 28 June 1986.

77. Ptolemy, "Mrs. Mesa Verde?"; Thomas, "Jean McWhirt Pinkley."

78. "Proceedings of the Second Naturalists' Conference," Grand Canyon National Park, 13–17 November 1940, NPS Library: 1, 56, 116, 289, 300–01, 325. Conference resolutions on pages 347 to 361. Long-time naturalist George Rhule said that football players were selected for seven of the eleven naturalist positions at one park in the 1930s in order to counter what the park viewed as the "effeminate stigma." Rhule interview with Huyck.

79. Carl Russell to Natt [Dodge], 8 November 1945, Western Archeological Center Files, Tucson, AZ. Jean Pinkley, USGSA CPR.

80. See John E. Cook, "That Cover Girl—A Living Treasure," *Courier* 33 (May 1988): 21; Martelle W. Trager, *National Parks of the Northwest* (New York: Dodd, Mead, 1939): 12.

81. Nelson interview with Huyck.

Chapter Four

1. Margaret Merrill, *Bears in My Kitchen* (New York: McGraw-Hill, 1956); Margaret Merrill interview with author, 7 November 1985. The taped interviews between the author and forty-three NPS wives made between 1985 and 1989 are in the NPS Library.

2. Besides Ann Axtell Morris, *Digging in the Southwest,* (cited in chapter 3), other examples of companion-wives are: Osa Johnson, *I Married Adventure* (New York: J. B. Lippincott, 1940); Anne Morrow Lindbergh, *North to the Orient* (New York: Harcourt, Brace, 1935); Miriam MacMillan, *Green Seas and White Ice* (New York: Dodd, Mead, 1948); Grace Barstow Murphy, *There's Always Adventure* (New York: Harper & Brothers, 1951). For army officer's wives, see Sandra L. Myers, "Army Wives in the Trans-Mississippi West, a Bibliography" in Teresa Griffin Viele, *Following the Drum: a Glimpse of Frontier Life* (Lincoln: University of Nebraska Press): 257–73.

3. Interviews with author: Phelma and Bob Jacobsen, 10 April 1986; Hap Dodge, 25 June 1988.

4. Dama Margaret Smith, *I Married a Ranger* (Stanford, CA: Stanford University Press, 1930). Her articles include: "Going Down 'Bright Angel'," *Good Housekeeping,* 76 (June 1923): 30–31, 181–85; "White Medicine Man of the Navajos," *Desert 1* (March 1938): 16–18, 30. See also articles in *Desert* 1938 through 1942 under Dama Margaret Smith and under Dama Margaret Langley for 1945 and after. She married Henry Langley of the NPS Washington office. For Smith, see Adrian Howard, "White Mountain Smith of the Petrified Forest," *Desert Magazine* 1 (October 1938): 4–7.

5. Elizabeth Compton Hegemann, *Navaho Trading Days* (Albuquerque, University of New Mexico Press, 1962): 1–42.

6. Marta Weigle, "Civilizers, Art Colonists, Couriers, and Civil Servants: The Role of Women in Popularizing the Native American Southwest, 1902–1940," Daughters of the Desert symposium paper, Tucson, AZ, March 1986: 37–39; Elizabeth Shepley Sargent, "Journal of a Mud House," *Harper's Magazine* 144 (June 1922): 416–17.

7. T. Stell Newman and Harold A. La Fleur, "Mesa Verde Historical Administrative District: An Architectural and Historical Study," (Denver: NPS, USDI, November 1974): 20–21; 51–56; 71–81; Herb Evison, "Jesse L. Nusbaum, Defender of American Antiquities," NPS *Courier* 4 (January 1981): 25–26.

8. Aileen O'Bryan, *The Dine: Origin Myths of the Navaho Indians,* Bureau of Ethnology Bulletin 163 (Washington: Smithsonian Institution, 1956); Laura Gilpin, "The Dream Pictures of My People," *Art and Archaeology,* 22 (July–August 1926): 12–19, 46. As Aileen Nusbaum, she also published *Zuni Indian Tales* (G. P. Putnam's Sons, 1926).

9. Weigle, "Civilizers, Art Colonists": 38–39. Jesse Nusbaum married again in 1947 and served as superintendent of Mesa Verde from 1936 to 1939 and 1942 to 1946. Evison, "Jesse L. Nusbaum." Although there appears to be no direct connection between Smith, Hegemann, O'Bryan, and Mabel Dodge Luhan's Taos community, in the same era, they shared an impulse to identify with Native American peoples' sense of community in which art and daily life are integrated into a belief system. Lois Palken Rudnick, *Mabel Dodge Luhan: New Woman, New Worlds* (Albuquerque, University of New Mexico Press, 1984): xi–xiii. For the pull of "restless and rebellious" Eastern women to the Native American Southwest, see also: Babcock and Parezo, *Daughters of the Desert:* 1–5.

10. Letter to author from Irene C. [Evans] Stewart, 10 April 1989; Lois Kowski interview with author, 21 September 1985. Leon Evans died in 1967. Irene Evans married Everett Stewart in 1974.

11. Letter to author from Irene C. Stewart, 23 March 1989.

12. Letters to author from Icel Wright, 30 January, 14 February 1989; Stewart, 23 March 1989.

13. The Kowskis' honeymoon was winter in a Yellowstone back-country ranger station, where they experienced a unique kind of hazing. When they arrived, they found all the labels had been removed from the canned food, making every meal all winter a surprise. Kowski interview with author.

14. Ibid.; Louise Chapman interview with Dorothy Huyck, 28 July 1978; letter to author from Wright, 30 January 1989. The Chapmans met as students at Colorado State College. For wives employed during World War II, see Luis A. Gastellum, to Chief, Division of Interpretation, 13 October 1961, Yellowstone Archives.

15. Letter to author from Stewart, 23 March 1989.

16. Chapman interview with Huyck; Lon and Inger Garrison interview with Julie Russell, 22 July 1981, Grand Canyon library.

17. For Pinkley's odes to the HCWP's see *Southwestern Monuments Monthly Report,* 1939 (July): 80–81; 1940 (February): III–VI, 115 (hereafter, *SWMMR*). See also Hal Rothman, "Forged by One Man's

Will: Frank Pinkley and the Administration of the Southwestern National Monuments, 1923–1932," *Public Historian* 8 (spring 1986): 83–100.

18. *SWMMR*, 1934 (July): 35; Earl Jackson and S. Pierce, "Second Preliminary Archeological Report for Montezuma Castle C.W.A," *SWMMR*, 1934 (February): 21–23. See chapters 3 and 5 for Sallie Pierce [Harris]'s career as a Park Service professional.

19. Sallie Van Valkenburgh [Harris] interview with Herbert Evison, 9 March 1964; *SWMMR*, 1934 (July): 2; (August): 51, 70–71; 1935 (June): 292; (July): 28; (August): 107, 125; (September): 177; 1936 (February): 136–7, (May): 343.

20. They called it a "Kishmus" Party. *SWMMR*, 1935 (December): 417–19; 1936 (December): 436–37.

21. *SWMMR*, 1936 (February): 102–03; (April): 255–56; (June): 423–26, 488–49; (December): 437. The Brewers' efforts to revive Navajo crafts were part of a generally successful effort to revitalize Navajo weaving during the Depression. The exhibit was the forerunner of the Museum's "Navajo Craftsman."

22. *SWMMR*, 1936 (February): 123–5; (June): 422–23; (December): 437.

23. Letter to author from Sallie Harris, 18 April 1989; Sallie Pierce Brewer, "The 'Long Walk' to Bosque Redondo, As told by Pehslakai Etsedi," *Museum Notes, Museum of Northern Arizona* 9 (May 1937): 55–62; *SWMMR*, 1935 (January): 53.

24. *SWMMR*, 1938 (November): 379; 1939 (January): 52; (September): 222. Sallie Brewer contributed her time unpacking and arranging material at the Museum of Northern Arizona from a public works dig at Keet Seel. *SWMMR*, 1939 (April): 255. For pictures of the Brewers' house, see Hal K. Rothman, *Navajo National Monument: A Place and Its People* (Santa Fe: Southwest Cultural Resources Center, Professional Papers no. 40, 1991): 50–51.

25. While being guided by the Wetherills, Theodore Roosevelt noted that Louisa knew "and feelingly understands their [Navajo] traditions and ways of thought." Theodore Roosevelt, "Across the Navajo Desert," *Outlook* 105 (October 1913): 311–17, quoted in Frances Gillmor and Louisa Wade Wetherill, *Traders to the Navajos: The Story of The Wetherills of Kayenta* (Boston: Houghton Mifflin, 1934): 265–67.

26. Courtney Jones taped self-interview in possession of her sister, Edna Emerson, spring 1988; Courtney Jones to James and Lillian Reeder, 18 June 1935, Courtney and David Jones Papers, Museum of Northern Arizona, hereafter, Jones Papers. Selections from the Courtney Jones letters were published in Courtney Reeder Jones, "Memories of Wupatki: Life in an Ancient Ruin," *Journal of the Southwest* 35 (spring 1993): 2–52. Courtney, a student at the University of Nebraska, believed she was accepted at the Kinishba Ruin dig because they interpreted her first name as a man's.

27. Courtney Jones to James G. Reeder, August 1939; "Background information—Davy and Corky Jones," Jones papers; *SWMMR*, 1939 (July): 48; (December): 449. Courtney Jones described Sally Peshlakai's art in "A Navajo Weaver In Her Home," *All Indian Pow-Wow Program*, July, 1940, Flagstaff, Arizona, Museum of Northern Arizona. She described spinning in "Spindle-Spinning: Navajo Style," *Plateau* 18 (October 1945): 43–51.

28. Courtney Jones to James G. Reeder, 26 February 1939; August, 1939; 29 March 1942, Jones papers; *Grapevine*, June 1942: 1, NPS Archives; Katharine Bartlett to author, 27 April 1988; Courtney Jones, "Rock Wrens at Wupatki," *SWMMR*, 1939 (July): 69–72; (August): 143; (September): 225–26.

29. Courtney R. Jones, "This Wife Lives in an Old Ruin," *Christian Science Monitor*, 24 July 1940: 12. Petroglyphs depicting Kokopelli, an Anasazi flute player, were found in pueblos of that period.

30. *SWMMR*, 1938 (June): 489, 535; (September): 233–34; (November): 403, 415–16; 1939 (May): 347; (December): 475–76; 1940: (January): 66–67; (August): 98; (September): 178; Betty Budlong, "One Woman's Unselfish Vision Launches Desert Library," *Christian Science Monitor*, 25 November 1941: 17.

31. Interviews with author: Jennie Heaton Brown, 25 September 1985; Edna Heaton, 25 September 1985; letter to author from Leonard Heaton, 30 March 1986; Robert Shankland, *Steve Mather of the National Parks* (New York, 1951): 140–41; Jeffrey A. Frank, "Legacies," NPS *Courier* 33 (March 1988): 20–22.

32. *SWMMR*, 1934 (November): 232; 1936 (July): 25; 1939 (March): 199; letter to author from Betty Jackson, April 1988.

33. Earl Jackson underwent a thoracoplasty and fully recovered after eight years of reduced activity. Letter to author from Jackson, April 1988; Frank Pinkley to Earl Jackson, 26 August 1935, in possession of the Jacksons; Betty Jackson, "Joys of Park Service Life Outweigh Its Problems," *Christian Science Monitor,* 14 August 1940: 14; *SWMMR,* 1934 (June): 15; 1936 (June): 469, 478; 1937 (February): 84–85; (March): 165–67; (May): 305–08; 1938: (March): 233–34; (December): 518–19; 1939 (January): 59–60; (March): 204–05; 1940 (December): 350.

34. *SWMMR,* 1937 (July): 5; (December): 456; 1938 (April): 346-h; (May): 429.

35. *Round Table,* September 1941: 1–2, NPS Archives; *SWMMR,* 1940 (June): 359; 1941 (April): 183; letter to author from Charles and Frances Sharp, 28 August 1988.

36. Courtney Jones, "Housing Report," *SWMMR,* 1939 (August): 161-69; Courtney Jones to George and Hazel Reeder, February, 1939, Jones Papers; Mary Jane Nichols, "They Live in an Ancient Ruin," *Desert Magazine* 3 (June 1940): 11–14.

37. *SWMMR,* 1940 (February): I–VI, 115–118, 118 I.

38. Marguerite Schmidt, whose husband, Hank, was custodian at Arches National Monument, offered to be the first editor. She was succeeded by Courtney Jones whose coeditor was Winnie Caywood, from Tumacacori. When the newsletter became *Grapevine,* Sallie Brewer became Jones's coeditor. Courtney Jones to Edna Reeder, 14 July 1942; to George and Hazel Reeder, 7 September 1942, Jones Papers; *Roundtable,* 1940: April, November; 1941: June, September; *Grapevine,* 1942: June, August, September, November; 1943: January, NPS Archives.

39. *Grapevine,* January 1943, NPS Archives; Courtney Jones to Hazel and Lillian Reeder, 22 October 1942; to Edna Reeder, 12 January 1943, Jones Papers.

40. Courtney Jones to Edna Reeder 14 March 1943; to Marian Reeder Prentice, 26 May 1944, Jones Papers; Ross A. Maxwell to Sallie Pierce Brewer, 13 February 1943, Sallie Harris file, Huyck Collection, Schlesinger Library; Van Valkenburg [Harris] interview with Evison.

41. Kay Mayer, "Organ Pipe," *Arizona Highways,* April 1987: 40–45; letter to author from Frances and Charles Sharp.

42. Courtney Jones to Margaret Love, 30 January 1950, 28 April 1950, Jones papers; Courtney Jones taped self-interview, spring 1988.

43. Dani and John Cook interview with author, 14 July 1985.

44. Fred and Amy Binnewies interview with Herb Evison, 27 April 1973; Dixon and Annie Freeland interview with author, 9 April 1986; Garrison interview with Julie Russell.

45. Gertrude Hieb interview with author, 27 November 1989.

46. Nattalie Dodge and Zorro Bradley later married. Interviews with author: Nattalie and Zorro Bradley, 30 August 1985; Dodge. Hap Dodge died in 1991.

47. William and Beverly Holloman interview with Herbert Evison, 28 October 1980; Susan Parsons interview with author, 25 June 1985.

48. Interviews with author: Rebecca Kurtz, 14 August 1985; confidential interview, 11 June 1985; Stella Johnson, 10 April 1986; Vera and Ray Schaffner, 10 April 1986.

49. Barbara McKee first went to the Grand Canyon as a field assistant to Vernon Bailey of the U.S. Biological Survey, husband of ornithologist Florence Merriam Bailey. For her contributions to *Nature Notes,* see *Index,* Grand Canyon: 19. Letter to author from Barbara McKee, 14 November 1988; interviews with author: Barbara McKee, 20 November 1988; Margot Haertel, 5 September 1985; Jacobsen; letter to author from Kay Shevlin, 10 February 1988.

50. Interviews with author: Sharon and Bruce Paige, 12 August 1985; Jacobsen; Moore; Karen and Eldon Reyer, 22 September 1985. One of the boarding schools Park Service families sent their teenagers to was Wasatch Academy in Mount Pleasant, Utah.

51. Jacobsen interview with author; letter to author from Doris Howe, 31 May 1989.

52. Interviews with author: George and Helen Fry, 9 April 1986; Mollie O'Kane, 13 April 1985; Dave O'Kane, "Wives keep fingers crossed, bags packed," NPS *Courier* 20 (August 1973): 10; Mollie O'Kane, "Life Experience Petition," prepared for Goddard College, August 1979, NPS Library.

53. Letter to author from Mitzi Chandler, 12 December 1985; interviews with author: Helga Raftery, 2 June 1986; confidential interview, 11 June 1985.

54. Interviews with author: O'Kane; Jane Ring, 29 August 1985; letters to author: Eileen Gallagher, 25 May 1985; Barbara Bohanan, 20 April 1985.

55. Letter to author from Leila Miller, 19 March 1986.

56. Interviews with author: Barbara Evison, 19 May 1985; Freeland.

57. Binnewies interview with Herb Evison, 27 April 1973; Rosemary Ryan, "Hot But Not Bothered," *Woman's Day*, July 1956: 30–31; 83–84; Jean Valens Bullard, "We Live in Death Valley," *Saturday Evening Post*, 235 (5 May 1962): 18–23; "Summer Routine for a Family of Six," *Desert*, July 1960: 14–15.

58. Ruth Kirk, "Emergency," *Westways*, 52 (April 1960): 12–13; letters to author from Roberta Davis, 29 May 1985; Dorothy James, 15 October 1986; O'Kane, "Wives Keep Fingers Crossed."

59. In addition to the following article, Frances Judge published articles on the history of the Yellowstone area and two stories in the *Atlantic*, one as an "Atlantic First." Frances Judge, "The Park and I," *Colliers* 132 (21 August 1953): 66–69; letter to author from Frances Judge, 12 April 1986; *Atlantic Monthly* 190 (November 1952): 58–62 and 194 (July 1954): 47–52; letter to author from Donald A. Dayton, 31 January 1986; Merrill interview with author.

60. Letter to author from Maureen Cutler, 4 May 1988.

61. Freeland interview with author. Perhaps the most isolated station in the NPS is Fort Jefferson, a small island seventy miles from Key West, Florida, part of Dry Tortugas National Park. Nancy Klingener, "Park Ranger's Family Appreciates Solitude of Isolated Fort Jefferson," NPS *Courier* 38 (January 1993): 5.

62. Interviews with author: Merrill; Hieb; O'Kane; letter to author from Ann Parks, 27 October 1986; Judge, "The Park and I"; Marian Andrews, "Bears Flee Noise: New Yorkers Love It—Says Ranger's Wife," *Christian Science Monitor*, 31 July 1940: 12.

63. Letters to author from Esther Macy, 4 August 1985; Carolyn Miller, 10 December 1985; Jacobsen interview with author.

64. "Of webs and word-artists," *Sequoia Bark*, 13 (December 14–March 21, 1985): 4; Fern B. Bernard, "Winter Glory," *Yellowstone Nature Notes*, 9 (December 1932): 54–5.

65. Ione Gunderson self-interview, 10 March 1988; letters to author from Sharp; Dorothy James; Bonnie Campbell, 4 October 1988.

66. Interviews with author: Nancy Doerr, 8 November 1985; Jane and Jim Sullivan, 10 April 1986; Mary Ellen Rutter, 6 November 1985.

67. Ed and Carolyn Gastellum interview with author, 21 September 1985.

68. Bradley interview with author.

69. Interviews with author: Lois and John Dalle-Molle, 2 September 1985; Reyer.

70. Maxine Dickenson, "Indian cultural/spiritual tradition," NPS *Courier*, 31 (October 1986): 6–7; Inger Garrison, "Living Interpretation" in Grant W. Sharpe, *Interpreting the Environment* (New York: John Wiley, 1976): 177–92. Inger Garrison purposely did not use Native American designs in her pottery because she did not want to exploit American Indian people. See also Inger Garrison file, Huyck Collection.

71. DPT shots are a combination of diphtheria, pertussis (whooping cough), and tetanus inoculations. Letters to author from Phyllis Freeland Broyles, 1 June 1988; Marilyne Mabery, 24 October 1984.

72. "Morristown woman elected," NPS *Courier*, 25 (August 1978): 14; "Civil War Haute Couture Susie Overton's Specialty," NPS *Courier*, 20 (January 1973): 5.

73. Laura Joyner interview with Dorothy Huyck, 22 June 1978, Huyck Collection; letter to author from Evelyn Luce, 17 September 1986; Robert Utley interview with author, 22 September 1985.

74. Florence Stupka interview with Dorothy Huyck, April 1977, Huyck Collection; "Birds of the Smokies," NPS *Courier*, 8 (May 1963): 2; *Index*, Acadia: 11.

75. Bradley interview with author.

76. Doerr interview with author.

77. Gene Scovill testimony, U.S. Congress, House, Joint Oversight Hearing, Subcommittee on Na-

tional Parks and Public Lands and Subcomittee on Civil Service, 101st Cong., 2nd sess. (5 April 1990): 156–59.

78. Interviews with author: Raftery; Reyer; letter to author from Elinore Herriman, 4 September 1986.

79. Ruth Kirk's books include: *Exploring Death Valley* (Palo Alto: Stanford University Press, 1956, 1981); *Exploring the Olympic Peninsula* (Seattle, University of Washington Press, 1964, 1986); *Desert Life* (New York: Doubleday, 1970); *Yellowstone* (New York: Atheneum, 1961); *Northwest Coast Indians, Land and Life* (Seattle: Pacific Science Center, 1979). She was awarded the John Burroughs Medal for "outstanding natural history writing" in 1978. Ruth Kirk interview with author, 7 November 1985; *Westways*, 52 (April 1960).

80. Letter to author from Ann Sutton, 24 May 1989; Moore interview with author. The Suttons' *Wildlife of the Forests* (New York: Harry Abrams, 1979) and *Audubon Society Book of Trees* (New York: Harry Abrams, 1979) were published in five languages.

81. Confidential interview with author, 6 December 1985; confidential letter to author, 10 May 1986.

82. Interviews with author: Haertel, Reyer, Cook.

83. Interviews with author: Jacobsen, Hieb.

84. The first area chairmen were: Janet Palmer, Northeast; Ettabelle Northington, Southeast; Muriel Kennedy, Central; Berenice Scoyen, Northwest; and Betty Frank, Southwest. Amy Binnewies, "National Park Service Women's Organization," Box 83–6, National Park Women file, NPS Archives. General chairman for 1955–57 was Amy Binnewies; 1957–59, Rosemary Vintin; 1959–61, Inger Garrison; 1961–63, Helen Abbott; 1963–65, Nancy Doerr; 1965–67, Ruth Linder; 1968–69, Phil Jacobsen. *NPS Newsletter* 3 (31 October 1968): 2–3.

85. Conrad Wirth, *Parks, Politics, and the People* (Norman: University of Oklahoma Press, 1980): 244–67; Herma Albertson Baggley, "Report of the National Park Housing Survey," 1953: 12, National Park Women file.

86. Baggley, "Housing Report": 2, 5, 12, 19, 27.

87. Ibid.: 3, 10, 28, 33, 35.

88. Binnewies, NPS Women's Organization: 4; Phil Jacobsen, "National Park Service Ladies," 1 December 1966 in National Park Women file, Box 83–6. The continuing problems of NPS housing are spelled out in a special issue of the NPS *Courier* 36 (August 1991). In 1995, the NPS rated 56 percent of its housing in poor or fair condition. An initiative planned to triple the employee housing improvement program, including replacing 659 trailers with standard housing. "Parks to benefit," NPS news release, 6 February 1995.

89. A group of wives from the Southwest Region prepared the booklet: Lyn Broadbent, Pat Binnewies, and Susan Wilson. "Dear Friend," booklet in National Park Women file, Box 83–6. National Park Service Wives, "Live with Beauty," attributed to Inger Garrison, emphasized the responsibilities and pleasures of park life.

90. About the same time, the NPS *Courier* published a series of biographical sketches of park wives under the title, Silhouettes. See NPS *Courier*, 16 (May–June 1970): 13. The collection of the newsletters in the National Park Women file include the *Breeze*, Pacific Northwest, fall 1971-continuing, but national since 1981; *Roundup*, Midwest, January 1970 to spring 1979; *New Voice*, Northeast, February–March 1973 to November 1978; *Smoke Signal*, Southwest, November 1967 to summer 1975; *Trailblazer*, Rocky Mountain, November 1974 to November 1976; *Trade Winds*, Southeast, May 1974 to February 1977; *Yankee Doodles*, North Atlantic, April 1975 to 1978; *Lava Flow*, Western, April 1973 to February 1975.

91. During this period, a few superintendent's wives took their roles so seriously that they resembled wives of high-ranking officers in the military or foreign service, requiring the attendance of ranger's wives, for example, at social functions.

92. M. G. McKibben, "NPS Women's Organization Annual Report," NPS *Courier* 24 (April 1976): 5; "NPS Women Draft Resolutions in D.C.," NPS *Courier* 23 (May 1976): 2; Thelma Warnock, ed.,

Living in National Parks; Stories by National Park Women—40th Anniversary, 1952–1992. In 1984 a logo competition for the National Park Women was won by Evelyn Janney, a cartographic technician in the Midwest regional office. "National Park Women's New Logo Now Available," NPS *Courier* 29 (March 1984): 25.

93. National Park Women scrapbook, National Park Women file.

Chapter Five

1. *Report of Committee on Interpretive Standards,* NPS, May 1962: 125, 130, NPS Library. Among sources for chapters 5 and 6 are taped interviews conducted by the author with 340 Park Service women employees in the ten NPS regions from 1985 to 1986, on file in the NPS library, and questionnaires received from 536 Park Service women (11 percent of the women employed) from 1985 to 1986, on file in The Schlesinger Library, Radcliffe College. The breakdown for the questionnaires approximated the percentage of women in an occupation (although fewer in the clerical field) and the percentage in a region (although more from the Western Region).

2. "Report on the Employment of Women as Guides at Independence National Historical Park," prepared by Dr. Dennis C. Kurjack, June, 1962, NPS Library; Charles B. Hosmer, Jr., "Verne E. Chatelain and the Development of the Branch of History of the National Park Service," *Public Historian* 16 (Winter 1994): 32–33.

3. To Chief, Division of Interpretation [Daniel B. Beard] from Staff Historian Appleman, 26 September 1968: 2, NPS Library. Thanks to Joan and David Dutcher for sharing the Appleman and Kurjack reports with me.

4. Ibid.: 2–5.

5. The first three women were recent college graduates Margaret Ciborowski and Ruth Friday, Pennsylvania State University, and Joan Riley, Immaculata College; the second two were also recent graduates: Judith Rhodes, College of William and Mary, and Elizabeth Brennan, Immaculata College. Kurjack report: 7.

6. Rogers W. Young, "Ladies Who Wear the Uniform of the National Park Service," *Planning and Civic Comment* (March 1962): 5; R. Bryce Workman, *To Uniform the Service,* Part 1, (draft), NPS, 1991: 10, 29, 60, 64, 65; Ruthanne Hariot, "A Personal Memoir on NPS Women's Uniforms," NPS *Courier* 29 (March 1984): 32–33. Thanks to Toni Dufficy, Women's Rights National Historical Park, for sharing information from her exhibit.

7. Jane and Jim Sullivan interview with author, 10 April 1986. See also Greiff, *Independence:* 178–82. In 1969 women employed at the Petrified Forest entrance were not allowed to take on such law enforcement activities as searching cars because, the superintendent wrote, "uniformed females do not command the respect or project an air of authority needed in handling law enforcement problems." He also said that the women performed "the boring, routine entrance station duties with more patience and good humor than men." Superintendent, Petrified Forest, to Regional Director, Southwest Region, 23 October 1969, courtesy of Ellen Britton.

8. Melvin J. Weig to Regional Director, 5 February 1963, enclosed in Ronald F. Lee to Director, 6 March 1963, NPS Library.

9. Luis Gastellum to Chief, Division of Interpretation, 13 October 1961; John Hennenberger to Regional Director, Region Two, 30 October 1961, Yellowstone National Park Archives; Ronald F. Lee to Director, 6 March 1963. For Meagher, see Margaret Mary Meagher, *Bison of Yellowstone National Park,* NPS Scientific Monograph Series, no. 1, 1973. The guides who served during World War II were: Ethel Meinzer at Scotts Bluff; Margaret Ness and Julia Arthur at Glacier; Nellie Wenande, Nancy Bowers, and Alice Hauber at Devils' Tower; Catherine Byrnes and Barbara Dickinson at Mount Rainier. John Hennenberger discovered Ester Cleveland Brazell, a ranger guide in the summer of 1914, at Wind Cave National Park, possibly making her the first women to hold the title of ranger. John Hennenberger to author, 11 June 1990. For Byrnes and Dickinson, see *Mountain Memories,* May 1978, Mount Rainier National Park.

10. Cynthia Harrison, *On Account of Sex: The Politics of Women's Issues, 1945–1968* (Berkeley: University of California Press, 1988): 142–46, 225–27.

11. *U.S. Park Ranger,* (New York: Arco Publishing, 1949); James Tobin interview with author, 12 April 1985.

12. Young, "Ladies Who Wear the Uniform."

13. Gale Belinky, formerly Zimmer, interview with Herbert Evison, 11 June 1973.

14. Kathleen Manscill interview with author, 17 June 1985.

15. Maude Crawford Harriott interview with author, 9 June 1988; Maude Crawford Harriott, "Breeding Behavior of the Anhinga," reprint from the *Florida Naturalist,* October 1970.

16. Among the ranger-nurses at Carlsbad Caverns in the 1930s were: Julia Dean, Jo Whitt Yardley, Viola Shannon, Nora Lee Hemler, Lucille White, and Rita Walker (names taken from annual photographs of seasonals from the park files). Olive M. Johnson interview with Dorothy Huyck, 18 October 1978; Dwight Pitcaithley interview with author, 5 March 1986; "Olive M. Johnson," USGSA CPR; Workman, "To Uniform the Service": 60, 64.

17. Letters to author from Barbara Erickson Bonds, 27 June 1986; Cindy Morey Hill, 29 August 1986; Kathleen Keenan Fox and Ann Keenan Beckett, 24 June 1986; Charles C. Sharp, 28 November 1988.

18. *Careers in the National Park Service,* 1965, 1967, 1968 editions, NPS Library.

19. Stewart Udall to Kathy, 9 May 1967, Yosemite National Park Library. A form letter from Personnel Officer Hugh M. Miller, dated 1946 stated: "Most of the out-of-door positions in the National Park Service are of such arduous nature that men are preferred for them. Permanent positions to which women are appointed most frequently are those of stenographer, clerk, typist, and telephone operator." Personnel file, NPS Record Group 79, National Archives.

20. Rachel Carson, *Silent Spring* (Boston: Houghton Mifflin, 1962); Sally Carrighar, *One Day on Beetle Rock* (New York: Curtis Publishing, 1944); Annie Dillard, *Pilgrim at Tinker Creek,* (New York: Harper & Row, 1974); Sue Consolo interview with author, 29 September 1985; Z-SW questionnaire, 23 October 1985.

21. Lisa D. Madsen, "Georgie! Woman of the River," *Wildwater* 7 (April/May 1986): 20–35; Georgie Clark and Deborah Whitford, "Tales from a River Woman," *Women's Sports and Fitness,* April 1987: 38–41. Clark retired in September 1991 and died in 1992. See also: Louise Teal, *Breaking into the Current: Boatwomen of the Grand Canyon* (Tucson: University of Arizona Press, 1994).

22. Herb and Jan Conn, *The Jewel Cave Adventure: Fifty Miles of Discovery under South Dakota* (St. Louis, MO: Cave Books, 1981); USDI, *Fiftieth Honor Awards Convocation,* 24 April 1984: 55; Jan Conn, "Manless Ascent of Devils Tower," *Appalachia* 9 (December 1952): 224–27.

23. "Saleswoman for the Olympics," *Seattle Times,* 9 October 1949, and "In Hoh, residents prefer the rain," *Boston Globe,* n.d. circa 1986, clippings in Olympic National Park library. Thanks to Susan Schultz for her assistance. James R. Hare, editor, *Hiking the Appalachian Trail* (Emmaus, PA: Rodale Press, Inc., 1975), v.1: 54–63; *Appalachian Trailway News* 51 (September/October 1990): 28.

24. "Grand Teton—A Rich History," *Jackson Hole News,* 6 August 1970, from Teton County Historical Center; Patricia Petzoldt, *On Top of the World* (New York: Thomas Y. Crowell, 1953): 206–14; Carroll Seghers, *The Peak Experience: Hiking and Climbing for Women* (New York: Bobbs-Merrill Company, 1979): 16–18; Sherry L. Smith, "A Woman's Life in the Teton Country: Geraldine L. Lucas," *Montana* (summer 1994): 18–33.

25. Barbara Washburn interview with author, 14 March 1989; Nan Elliot, "Shared Horizons," *We Alaskans,* 14 June 1987, M-8 to M-13; Alison Osius, "Washburn and Washburn," *Climbing,* no. 103 (August 1987): 58–61, courtesy Barbara Washburn. As a team, the Washburns mapped the Grand Canyon from 1970 to 1977 requiring seven hundred helicopter landings on remote sites.

26. Maynard M. Miller, "First American Ascent of Mount St. Elias," *National Geographic* 63 (February 1948): 229–48.

27. Arlene Blum, "Arctic Summit," *womenSports,* February 1975: 32–33, 52. See also, Ann E. Kruse, "Mountain Storms," in da Silva, *Leading Out:* 160–71. In 1993 Joni Phelps, a blind woman, climbed McKinley roped to her twin sons. AP news, 7 June 1993.

28. Jacqueline C. Warsaw, "The First Woman to Climb El Capitan Alone—Beverly Johnson," *Self Magazine,* February 1979, clipping in Yosemite Park Library. In 1984 Ellie Hawkins became the first woman to solo the face of Half Dome; a year later, she was the first woman to solo the "Never-Never Land" route of El Capitan. *Yosemite Sentinel,* November 1985. See also Jeanne Panek, "A Late Night on a High Wall," in da Silva, *Leading Out:* 172–77. Beverly Johnson was killed in 1994 in a heli-skiing crash in Nevada.

29. USDI, *Seventeenth Honor Awards Convocation,* 12 March 1956. Sarah L. Miller of Mineral, CA, received a valor citation in 1982 for saving a man from drowning. After Miller and her husband tied a rope to the victim's body, both she and the victim were swept through a culvert. She grabbed the rope and pulled him to safety. USDI, *Forty-eighth Honor Awards Convocation,* March 1982.

30. Elizabeth Titus interview with author, 21 April 1986; Bernard DeVoto, "Let's Close the National Parks," *Harper's Magazine* 207 (October 1953): 49–52; NPS *Courier* 34 (April 1989): 25.

31. Titus interview.

32. Ibid.; "Complete Report, 1957 Summer Trial Projects," SCA files, Charlestown, NH.

33. "Grand Teton National Park—Comments—SCP [SCA]—July 28, 1958," SCA files.

34. Frank Oberhansley to Ailene Kane, 27 September 1960; Peggy Thompson to Ailene Kane, July 1960; Management Assistant, Cedar Breaks, to Superintendent, Zion, 1 November 1960, *SCP Newsletter* 6 (fall–winter 1967); SCA files.

35. Titus interview; "Youth Finds a Way," *Garden Club of America Bulletin* 45 (January 1957): 77–78; 50 (January 1962): 67; 53 (March 1965): 61–62. Although the size of the program was reduced by the mid-1990s, the YCC continues to hire young women and men on an equal basis. In 1986, it placed 967 females and 714 males in 164 NPS locations for eight-week periods. Young women from the YCC at Yellowstone in 1984 cleared trails, rehabilitated backcountry cabins, and dug post holes. The Young Adult Conservation Corps (YACC) employed young women and men up to the age of twenty-three in nontraditional work in parks but was only funded between 1978 and 1982. See USDI, Youth Conservation Corps, FY 1986 and FY 1987 Programs, courtesy of Francis Gibson; NPS *Courier* 29 (January 1984): 9; 29 (September 1984): 18. See also: Gerald C. DiCerbo, "Legislative History of the Youth Conservation Corps," *Journal of Forest History* 32 (January 1988): 22–31.

36. Titus interview; NPS *Courier* 21 (May 1974): 3; 34 (July 1989): 25; USDI, *Fifty-first Honor Awards Convocation,* 26 September 1986. Former SCA volunteers who have held these positions cited SCA experience. Questionnaires from Kate Cannon, 27 November 1990; Shari Berg, 20 March 1985; Lois Winter, 27 September 1986; Janice Pauley, 8 November 1985; Jill Campbell, 3 December 1985; Pat Grediagin, 3 November 1985; Deborah Burge Neal, 12 March 1985; Dolly Chapman, 19 May 1987; Annie Barrett Boucher, 24 June 1987; interviews with author: Mary Meagher, 26 September 1985 and Edie Dillon, 16 March 1986. For women on the Yosemite trail crew, see Scott Weaver interview with author, 11 May 1987.

37. Harrison, *On Account of Sex:* 176–91; Janice Mendenhall, "Roots of the Federal Women's Program, *Civil Service Journal* 18 (July–September 1977), reprint from EO Office files, Harpers Ferry Center. The Grove City case suspended Title IX in 1984 until the Civil Rights Restoration Act in 1988. For an analysis of the impact of Title IX, see Mary A. Boutilier and Lucinda San Giovanni, *The Sporting Woman* (Champaign, Illinois: Human Kinetics Publishers, 1983): 170–81, and Andrew Szanton, "On Balance," *Brown Alumni Monthly* 94 (October 1993): 21–27.

38. Thanks to John Henneberger for sharing a letter sent to him by Frank Kowski dated 26 July 1965.

39. Interviews with author: Bill Clark, 24 June 1991; Larry Zollar, 13 August 1988; class lists supplied by the Albright Training Center; NPS *Courier* 10 (May 1964): 6; "Barbara A. Lund" and "Barbara A. Sorrill," USGSA CPR. Thanks to Ann Baugh for her help with the Albright study.

40. Interviews with author: Betty Gentry, 16 September 1985; Glennie Wall, 16 May 1985. Betty Gentry retired in 1988 as superintendent of Pea Ridge National Military Park and Glennie Wall in 1991 as chief of the Cultural Resources Unit at Golden Gate National Recreation Area. The FSEE was replaced by PACE (Professional and Administrative Career Examination), which was discontinued in 1982 after a court case determined it was culturally biased.

41. Cynthia Kryston interview with author, 20 March 1986. In 1987 she became the chief of interpretation for the North Atlantic region, at the time the only woman in that position in the then ten regions.

42. Interviews with author: Mary Bradley, 6 April 1985; Seymour Kotchek, 12 December 1985; Zollar; qualification standards for Park Ranger Series (453), December 1957, courtesy of Russ Olsen; Park Technician Series (GS-026) and Park Management Series (GS-025), August 1969, courtesy of Seymour Kotchek.

43. Interviews with author: Bradley and Tobin; Albright class lists.

44. Interviews with author: Martha Aikens, 10 December 1985; Celia Jackson-Suggs, 14 December 1985. J. T. Reynolds, chief of the Division of Ranger Activities, Rocky Mountain Region, was the only male African American in Aikens's class. The other female African Americans were Louise Driscoll, who became an Equal Opportunity specialist, and Lurrie Pope, a ranger in Rock Creek Park in Washington, D.C. Six months earlier, Geraldine Bell and Lillie Howse were the first two African-American women at Albright. Bell, the first African-American woman ranger at Independence, later became superintendent at Booker T. Washington National Monument. Bell interview with the author, 12 June 1985.

45. Interviews with author: Virginia Rousseau, 4 November 1985; Warren Hill, 12 September 1990. The second intake class was embroiled in controversy because a new NPS director, Ron Walker, disapproved of Hartzog's method of taking intake rangers directly from the FSEE lists. He interrupted the class, had the participants interviewed by personnel officers, and discharged some of them. No women were affected, but the members of the class, the fortieth ranger training class to be held, still call themselves The Fatal Fortieth. Interviews with author: Carol Kruse, 20 September 1985; Betty McSwain, 13 November 1985; Zollar.

46. Helen Lindsley McMullin to author, 3 March, 20 June, 22 August 1986, including copies of Richard Miller to Helen Lindsley, 1 April 1966 and 13 May 1966; "Courier profiles," NPS *Courier,* 22 (April 1975): 3.

47. Among other Mount Rainier telephone operators who performed the dispatch function were: Zelma Barnet, Elva Lewis Didio, Lil Towne, Marge Haggerty Halterman, and Mary Boyd. Ralph McFadden to author, 19 June 1986; Beatrice Hall to author, 9 February 1987.

48. FLETC class lists supplied by FLETC; total figures supplied by FLETC, 16 February 1995. My thanks to Carol Pfeifer.

49. Mary Bradley interview.

50. Confidential interview with author, 13 June 1985.

51. Gloria Skurzynski, "Janey McDowell: The Training of a Ranger," in *Safeguarding the Land: Women at Work in Parks, Forest, and Rangelands* (New York: Harcourt, Brace, Jovanovich, 1981): 5–54; Mary Jane McDowell interview with Dorothy Huyck, 24 July 1978; Margaret Short interview with author, 30 September 1985. McDowell left the service to join a religious sisterhood.

52. Interviews with author: Julia Kuncl 28 September 1985; Mona Divine, 29 September 1985; Rousseau. For a view of the life of a woman park ranger in law enforcement, see the mystery novels written by seasonal park ranger, Nevada Barr, published by G. P. Putnam's Sons: *Track of the Cat* (1993), *A Superior Death* (1994), and *Ill Wind* (1995).

53. Interviews with author: Patricia Baker Buccello, 20 May 1985; Janet Wilts, 17 May 1985; Carol Moses, 4 November 1985; Barbara Pettinger in National Geographic Society video, *The Grizzlies,* 1987. Another unusual example is used in FLETC training sessions on terrorism. A felon tried to throw a hand grenade at Alice Seebecker during what she thought was a routine vehicle stop. He blew up both himself and his vehicle. Alice Seebecker questionnaire, 23 June 1985.

54. Interviews with author: Cheryl Pagel, 13 June 1988; Lucy Eagen, 13 June 1988; Kathleen Loux, 2 September 1985.

55. NPS *Courier* 33 (December 1988): 23; Gail Minami, "Law Enforcement at Hawaii Volcanoes," NPS *Courier* 34 (April 1989): 23–25; USDI, *Fifty-Sixth Honor Awards Convocation,* October 1991.

56. For a report on the entire study, see Polly Welts Kaufman, "NPS Women: Benefits of the Al-

bright Ranger Training Program, 1964–1984," *Ranger* 6 (spring 1990): 14–16. Particular thanks to Loretta Schmidt for her work in tracing the women.

In 1991, the first new intake program in many years included 40 percent women of a total of fifty, chosen from park employees in lower grades or graduates of the Cooperative Education Program (college-linked NPS internships). Only half were already rangers. Vacancy announcement, NPS Intake Trainee Program, 6 March 1991.

57. Equal Rights Advocates, who represented McFarland, won a sex-bias class action suit against the U.S. Forest Service for Region 5 (California and Hawaii), affecting 1,500 women. Informal Resolution Agreement, Western Region, NPS, 23 September 1986; Press Release for Contempt Hearing Against U.S. Secretary of Agriculture in Landmark Sex-Bias Case, 9 May 1988, documents supplied by Equal Rights Advocates, San Francisco; Marybeth McFarland interview with author, 14 May 1985.

58. Barry Mackintosh, *The United States Park Police: A History* (Washington, D.C.: NPS, USDI, 1989): 58–59; list of Park Police women, 26 April 1974. The former requirements were five feet eight inches and 145 pounds. In 1972, Shirley Long challenged the requirement, saying that it eliminated 98 percent of U.S. women and only 50 percent of U.S. men. The park police chief, Grant Wright, contested her complaint. The park police tried to recruit tall Park Service women before the size requirement was lifted. USDI, "Height/Weight Requirements," *Reference Manual to Title VII Law for Compliance Personnel of the Equal Employment Opportunity Commission,* March 1984: 21–41; *Federal Women's Program Newsletter,* July 1972: 4. EO files, Harpers Ferry Center; Mary Bradford interview with author, 13 December 1985.

59. Jane Marshall interview with author, 20 April 1986. The male officer who was shot survived but retired soon afterwards. The three other women hired before Marshall were Paulette Tubbs, Judy Shuster Ferraro, and Janice Rzepechi. When Gretchen Merkle was a park technician at the Washington Monument, seeing Marshall as a Park Police officer inspired her to join the force in 1979. Gretchen Merkle interview with author, 21 February 1986.

60. Interviews with author: Valerie Fernandez, 8 February 1986; Gretchen Merkle; "First women horsemounted officers graduated," *Courier* 25 (April 1980): 10–11; USDI, *Forty-Sixth Honor Awards Convocation,* 10 October 1979. For Pepper Karansky, see "Priscilla Pepper Karansky, Mounted Police," in Elizabeth Simpson Smith, *Breakthrough: Women in Law Enforcement* (New York: Walker, 1982): 62–82. The first woman motorcycle officer was Kelcy Stefansson; Laura Beck was the first aviator. NPS *Courier* 35 (October 1990): 17; 36 (winter 1991): 42.

61. *Parade* Magazine, 30 September 1990; *Federal Times,* 29 October, 1990, clipping from EO Office, Harpers Ferry.

62. "Breakdown by Grade: WG and total," NPS, USDI, 31 March 1995. Thanks to Eleanor Pratt for providing this report. The two women chiefs of maintenance were Susan McGill at Great Smoky Mountains National Park and Cindy Cox at Rock Creek Park in Washington, D.C.

63. Interviews with author: Betty Smith, 16 April 1985; Tobin; Mary Ellen Snyder, 21 May 1985; Mary Cannarozzi questionnaire, 6 May 1985.

64. Interviews with author: Julie Doctor, 20 May 1985; Susan Bernotas, 18 September 1985.

65. Questionnaires: Tina Marie Levar, 26 March 1985; Patricia Haddad, 22 May 1985; Edith Roudebush, 14 April 1985. Kogl transferred to a law enforcement ranger position. Interviews with author: Sandy Kogl, 16 August 1985; Gina Muzinich, 19 May 1986; Kogl to author, 27 March 1987; Sandy Kogl, *Sled Dogs of Denali* (Alaska Natural History Association, 1981). As members of WOOF Search Dog Unit, Sequoia ranger Anne Walsten and her wilderness certified search-and-rescue dog Cody have participated in searches all over the country. NPS *Courier* 34 (March 1989): 33.

66. Lisa Lee Smith questionnaire, 8 May 1985; letter to author: Jim Snyder, 12 January 1987 (also filed in Yosemite library); Annie Barrett Boucher, 24 June 1987; Dolly Chapman, 19 May 1987. When Yosemite did not hire Dolly Chapman for a permanent position, she joined the Forest Service as wage supervisor for Inyo National Forest. All-women trail crews were used at Glacier in 1973, the Grand Tetons in 1974, and Rocky Mountain in 1977. *Courier* 1 (November 1977).

67. Sue McGill, "From Maintenance to Superintendent," *Women in Natural Resources* 13 (September 1991): 16–17; Sue McGill interview with author, 24 May 1995.

68. Interviews with author: Betty Diamond, 11 June 1985; Martha Ellis, 3 April 1991. See: Mary-anne Murillo, "Women in maintenance open doors for others," NPS *Courier* 29 (May 1984): 1–3. On a 1988 NPS roster, Diamond, Ellis, McGill, and Eleanor Chamberlain, maintenance foreman for Yosemite Valley, were the only women at the WS level (wage grade supervisor), compared with 450 men.

69. Interviews with author: Gentry; Sullivan; Betty Knight, 20 May 1985; Marion Durham, 26 February 1989; Marion J. Durham, "NPS Women and Their Uniforms," NPS *Courier* 34 (November 1989): 19–21; "Kiosk Kuties," NPS *Courier* 16 (January 1970): 1.

70. Knight interview.

71. Elaine Hounsell interview with author, 8 November 1985; "You Must Have Been a Beautiful Ranger," NPS *Newsletter* 5 (2 April 1970): 1–6; (9 July 1970): 3–4, 6; Eleni, "A New Look in the Parks," *Washington Sunday Star,* 11 October 1970, G-1, G-11. Carol Scanlon, a ranger at Independence, coordinated the new uniform task force. See also: Bryce Workman, *Breeches, Blouses, and Skirts: Women's Uniforms, 1918–1991* (Harpers Ferry, W.V.: NPS History Collection, 1995). For how even pants suits were controversial during this period, see Lindy Van Gelder, "The Truth About BraBurners," *MS* 11 (September/October 1992): 80–81.

72. "You Must Have Been a Beautiful Ranger;" Keith E. Miller to all Field Directors, 26 January 1971, enclosed in Peggy Wilson to Jeanetta Foreman, 29 January 1974, EO Files, Harpers Ferry. Marianne Gerbaukas noted that early women rangers were treated like park wives. Gerbaukas interview with author, 2 November 1985.

73. Gentry and Clark interviews with author; Ann Belkov to author with photograph, 11 September 1990.

74. Bill Clark interview.

75. Lyndel Meikle to Mary Maruca, 10 December 1989; William Hendrickson to Associate Director, Operations, WASO [John Cook], 2 January 1974, NPS Library.

76. John Cook to author, 21 June 1991. A cross tie was still available to women.

77. Interviews with author: Linda Balatti, 11 December 1985; Maria Burks, 16 May 1985; Elizabeth Snyder, 12 June 1985 (with enclosures); Mary Jenkins, 10 June 1985. Letters to author: Chloe Fisher, 26 February 1987; Joyce L. Grow, 5 June 1991.

78. Kruse interview; Grace Lichtenstein, "Women Park Rangers' Peril: Male Chauvinists Lurk Everywhere," *New York Times,* 15 March 1976: 38, Huyck Collection; Lana Creer Harris questionnaire, 3 September 1985.

79. "Breakdown by Grade Within Series: Series 025," 31 March 1995, NPS, USDI. Thanks to Eleanor Pratt for providing this report; 1970 statistics compiled by a hand count from Personnel Roster, 28 February 1970. Thanks to George Fischer for locating the 1970 NPS roster now in the NPS Library. The rapid increase of women rangers was partly due to the consolidation in 1985 of a park technician series (026), at the time made up of 37 percent women with the park ranger series (025), then 14 percent women. The minority women rangers in 1995 represented (as a percent of all women rangers): African American, 6 percent; Hispanic, 3 percent; Asian American and Pacific Islander, 2 percent; American Indian and Alaskan Native, 2 percent.

80. In "Ranger Careers," Director (Roger Kennedy) to Directorate, . . . all Park Superintendents, 14 June 1994; Eleanor Pratt, "Study of Ranger Futures Impacts in the North Atlantic Region," 10 June 1994; author interview with Tom Cherry, 23 January 1995.

81. Richard Cripe, "Work Profile of Women in the National Park Service," March 1991, prepared for NPS Women's Conference; Barbara Nelson interview, 11 April 1985; confidential interviews: 18 November 1985, 25 March 1985; *NPS Electronic Courier,* 1 (27 April 1995): 3.

82. 1985 Questionnaire Study; questionnaires: Jan Ryan, 23 September 1985; Patricia Haddad, 22 May 1985; Rowena Guzman, 29 May 1985; Debra Paschke, 12 May 1985; Greer Chesher, 10 May 1985. One woman kept her marriage a secret. Confidential interview, 14 May 1985. A particularly poignant example of the conflict some women felt between assuming the nontraditional career of ranger and having a family is illustrated in the suicide of a woman chief ranger in a remote park who killed herself with her service revolver on January 1, 1986. Two abortions, a divorce, a fast track to her

position combined with on-the-job frustration may have contributed to her action. Confidential letter to author, 23 January 1986; confidential interview with author, March 1986.

83. Betty and Robert Cunningham interview with author, 1 September 1985.

84. Interviews with author: Robert and Mary Sargent Martin, 3 November 1985; Marshall; Fernandez.

85. For an example of the differences between old-style male and new-style female (and male) interpretation, see video *Grand Canyon,* Readers' Digest and International Video Network, 1988. Constance Rudd gives an environmental message and natural history information; Stewart Fritts mimics a mule on a canyon trail.

86. *National Parks* 58 (November–December 1984): 32; 62 (January/February 1988): 8; 62 (November-December 1988): 9; Carol J. Spears, "Interpreting Biological Diversity," NPS *Courier* 34 (February 1989): 17–18; Sandy Dayhoff, "A Shared Learning Experience," NPS *Courier* 34 (June 1989): 20–21; *National Parks* 69 (January/February 1995): 20.

87. Lowell National Historical Park Junior Ranger Program file; letter to author from Marjorie Hicks, 25 October 1985; Mary O. Reinhart, "Urban park fosters neighborhood harmony," NPS *Courier* 29 (August 1984): 4–5.

88. Interviews with author: Gentry; Becky Lyons, 18 November 1985; Cynda Carpenter, 8 February 1996.

89. Patricia Lammers interview with author, 13 July 1985; Pat Lammers and Amy Boyce, "Alias Franklin Thompson: A Female in the Ranks," *Civil War Times* (January 1984): 24–30; Antietam living history file, Office of the Chief Historian, NPS. In 1991 Lauren Cook sued the Park Service because several Civil War parks would not let her portray a soldier in NPS reenactments, including the one at Antietam. *Boston Globe,* 25 February 1991.

90. Julia Parker interview with author, 15 October 1986; "Theo Dean Hugs," NPS *Courier* 36 (spring 1991): 43.

91. Althea Roberson, "Did You Know?" NPS *Courier* 33 (February 1988): 18–20; Barbara Tagger interview with author, 20 June 1985; Barbara A. Tagger, "The Beauty of Sweet Auburn," NPS *Courier* 32 (April 1987): 11; Rose Fujimori questionnaire, 28 June 1988.

92. Interviews with author: Erin Broadbent, 26 March 1985; Catherine Ingram, 3 April 1991; Ingram questionnaire, 10 April 1985; Jennifer Jacobs, "Deaf Services Program Prospers in Yosemite," NPS *Courier,* 35 (March 1990): 20–21. For Syd Jacobs and Lisa Riedel, NPS employees in wheelchairs, see: NPS *Courier* 4 (February 1981): 6 and 33 (May 1988): 20.

93. Barbara Consolo questionnaire, 10 July 1985; award letter to Lynne Dubiel, North Atlantic Region, 12 July 1991, courtesy EO office; Vivien Rose remarks, Lowell National Historical Park 31 May 1995.

94. Letters to author: Lucia Perillo, 13 August 1988; Jane Anderson, 3 December 1985; Elizabeth Knight, 15 November 1985.

95. Kathy and Bob Kerr interview with author, 22 September 1985; Lisa Lee Smith questionnaire.

96. Interviews with author: Wilts; Winter; Dillon; Dillon to author, 27 March 1987 with clippings: *Wenatchee World,* 31 December 1981; *Seattle Times,* 22 September 1982. For the inside story, see *Thunderbear: An Alternative NPS Newsletter,* July 1984: 7–9.

97. A woman superintendent said she was one of the few Jewish employees in the Park Service. Confidential interview, 15 October 1985.

98. David S. Boyer, "Yosemite Forever?" *National Geographic* 167 (January 1985): 79.

Chapter Six

Parts of this chapter were published in Polly Welts Kaufman, "Women Superintendents: A History," *Women in Natural Resources* 14 (March 1993): 4–7.

1. Carol Martin interview with the author, 21 June 1985; Charlie Boatner, "Meet Carol Martin," NPS *Courier* 18 (May 1971): 2.

2. Elaine D'Amico Hall interview with the author, 28 July 1985.

3. Martin interview. Martin became chief of the Western Archeological Laboratory in Tucson three years later. Mildred S. Gay, administrative officer at Manassas Battlefield, served as acting superintendent between April and June 1969. Clipping enclosed in Mildred S. Gay to author, 26 March 1986.

4. Larry Zollar interview with author, 13 August 1988; Director [George B. Hartzog] to All NPS Superintendents, 25 August 1969; EEO workshop schedule, January 17–19, 1971, NPS Archives.

5. Dates of superintendents' terms of office are taken from *Historic Listing of National Park Service Officials,* (Washington: NPS, USDI, 1 May 1986). Interviews with author: Kathleen Dilanardo, 13 June 1985; Elizabeth Disrude, 11 June 1985; Lorraine Mintzmyer, 7 May 1985; Claire St. Jacques, 28 March 1985.

6. Interviews with author: Margaret Wilson, 17 May 1985; Mike Hackett, 14 October 1986; NPS *Courier* 29 (July 1984): 22.

7. Superintendents' conference photographs, NPS Archives.

8. Isabelle F. Story, USGSA CPR; Marian E. Fadeley, "Isabelle's Story," *American Forests* 61 (April 1955): 37, 51-52, Huyck Collection; Isabelle F. Story, *The National Parks and Emergency Conservation* (Washington: USDI, 1933); Horace M. Albright, "Isabelle Story: talented writer-editor," NPS *Courier* 14 (December 1981): 21–22.

9. Isabelle Story to Ladies Auxiliary, Veterans of Foreign Wars, 28 July 1938; Isabelle Story to Mary Rolfe, 10 June 1946, National Archives, Record Group 79, no. 7, 252-S.

10. Fradeley, "Isabelle's Story;" Albright, "Isabelle Story." According to Albright, Story and Boss Pinkley, who was a widower, planned to marry, but Pinkley died suddenly in 1941.

11. Albright, "Isabelle Story;" Story to Rolfe, 10 June 1946; USDI, *Fifteenth Honor Awards Convocation,* 16 May 1955; NPS *Courier* 16 (January 1970): 8; interviews with author: Jean Matthews, 31 October 1988; Priscilla Baker, 11 December 1985.

12. Isabelle and Laurabel Story were apparently not related. Laurabel Story, USGSA CPR; "Laurabel Story," NPS *Courier* 15 (August 1969): 6; Dorothy Huyck interview with Naomi L. Hunt, 17 November 1978; "Editor Hunt completes 30-year Federal Career," NPS *Courier* 29 (September 1984): 21; Loretta Neumann, "The National Park Service at 75," NPS *Courier* 37 (February 1992): 12–14.

13. Sandra Alley interview with author, 26 March 1985; Joan Anzelmo to author, 23 April 1989.

14. Gertrude S. Cooper, USGSA CPR; "For New Job at Vanderbilt Site," clipping in Duane Pearson to author, 23 June 1986; Charles W. Snell, "Administrative History of Vanderbilt Mansion National Historic Site, Hyde Park, New York, 1939–1955," 9 June 1956, in office of NPS chief historian. Roosevelt's Campobello home is now an international park administered by the United States and Canada.

15. Wilhelmina Harris interview with author, 29 March 1985; Ross Holland, "'Super-woman' Wilhelmina Harris," NPS *Courier* 29 (March 1984): 16–17; Loretta DeLozier, "A Tour with Mrs. Harris," NPS *Courier* 17 (August 1971): 4–5; Thomas Boylston Adams, "A Tribute to Wilhelmina S. Harris," NPS *Courier* 32 (October 1987): 35; Wilhelmina Harris, *Adams National Historic Site: A Family's Legacy to America* (Washington, D.C.: USDI, 1983); Wilhelmina Harris, "The Brooks Adams I Knew," *Yale Review* 10 (autumn 1969): 50–78; USDI, *Thirty-Eighth Honor Awards Convocation,* 30 June 1970. See also Wilhelmina Harris file, Huyck Collection.

16. James I. Hill to author, 20 January 1988; James I. Hill interview with author, 9 June 1988; "Jim Hill, Liberty Island native," NPS *Courier* 29 (October 1984): 13–14.

17. Evelyn Frey interview with author, 19 September 1985; Ardis Hunter, "After half century Mrs. Frey closes shop," NPS *Courier* 24 (October 1979): 16–17 and Olga Curtis, "Evelyn Frey: She's 'Mrs. Frijoles'," *Empire Magazine,* 17 August 1975, Bandelier National Monument Archives. Evelyn Fry died in 1988.

18. Kay Riordan Steuerwald to author, 15 January 1988; Steuerwald interview with author, 21 June 1988; "Mount Rushmore concessioner receives award," NPS *Courier* 30 (March 1985): 12.

19. Women Superintendents' Study, 1994 (author's database combining interviews, questionnaires, EO studies). See also, Polly Welts Kaufman, "Women Superintendents."

20. In 1995 there were 368 parks in the National Park System, but only 276 had full superintendents. The three African-American women were: Martha Aikens, Independence; Audrey Calhoun,

George Washington National Parkway; and Diane Dayson, Roosevelt-Vanderbilt NHS; the Hispanic woman was Judith Cordova, Colorado National Monument. Equal Opportunity Manager [Magaly Green] to All Regional EO Managers, 1 June 1994; 20 April 1995.

21. Women Superintendents' Study.

22. Georgia Ellard interview with author, 27 March 1985. NPS leaders once supervised by Ellard were Joan Anzelmo, information chief; Meredith Belkov, manager of Ellis Island and Statue of Liberty; Lucia Bragan, deputy director of employee development.

23. "Historic Listing of National Park Service Officials" combined with Women Superintendents' Study; interviews with author: Disrude, Martin.

24. Connie Toops, "Crisis Strike Force," *National Parks* 64 (May–June 1990): 31–36; Anne Castellina, "Oil Spills and Parks Don't Mix," *Women in Natural Resources* 13 (September 1991): 34–36.

25. Ann Belkov interview with author, 5 April 1991; "Liberty Island official sees sticky situation," (Norfolk, VA) *Ledger Star,* 28 March 1991, courtesy North Atlantic Public Affairs Office.

26. Jim Robbins, "This tale, too, has two sides," *Boston Globe,* 25 June 1990. Gay Kingman, executive director of the National Congress of American Indians, testified for the name change. *Little Bighorn Battlefield,* Senate Hearing, National Parks Subcommittee, 102nd Cong., 1st sess. (25 July 1991): 98–101.

27. Jo Ann Kyral interview with author, 16 September 1985.

28. Women Superintendents' Study. Katherine Jope stated that the majority of women she has known "in top positions" in the Park Service were single. Vicki L. Berlin, "Katherine L. Jope," *Women in Natural Resources* 13 (September 1991): 40–41; *NPS Electric Courier* 1 (11 May 1995): 1.

29. Statistics are taken from the author's hand count of a 1970 NPS roster, now in NPS Archives, with thanks to George Fischer.

30. Imogene La Covey interview with Dorothy Huyck, 8 November 1978; USDI, *Forty-second Honor Award Convocation,* 27 June 1974.

31. "Mary Lou Grier named deputy director," NPS *Courier* 27 (February 1982): 14; Nancy Garrett interview with author, 11 December 1985.

32. Richard G. Cripe, "Work Force Profile of Women in the National Park Service," 3 April 1991; partly published in *Women in Natural Resources* 13 (September 1991): 20–23. In 1991, the GS-5 salary ranged from $16,973 to $22,067 and the GS-11 salary from $31,116 to $40,449, courtesy North Atlantic Personnel Office.

33. Interviews with author: Marie Rust, 19 March 1985; Barbara J. Griffin, 19 June 1985; Daina Dravnieks Apple, "Marie Rust," *Women in Natural Resources* 14 (March 1993): 26–31; Carol Anthony, "Griffin Named NPS Mid-Atlantic Regional Director," NPS *Courier* 38 (fall 1993): 35–36. The only woman superintendent of a systems support office in 1995 was Marcia Blaszak in Alaska.

34. Barry Mackintosh to author, 31 January 1995.

35. "Average Grade Breakdown by Patcob (GS/GM)," 31 March 1995, courtesy of Eleanor Pratt; USDI, *Fifty-second Honor Award Convocation,* 22 November 1994.

36. Cripe, "Work Force." A survey in 1992 identified a so-called glass ceiling for federal women, with women representing only one in four supervisors and only one in ten senior executives. Differences in education and length of government service did not totally explain the imbalance. Women were held back by failing to reach the GS-9 or GS-11 levels, which are necessary steps for advancement to top positions. U.S. Merit Systems Protection Board, *A Question of Equity: Women and the Glass Ceiling in the Federal Government* (Washington, D.C., 1992).

37. WG/WS Companion study by Eleanor Pratt based on "Breakdown by Grade: WG and total," NPS, USDI, 31 March 1995.

38. By 1990, twenty state governments had made pay equity adjustments in one or more female-dominated job areas and six states had implemented statewide plans. In July 1994, Representative Eleanor Holmes Norton introduced "The Fair Pay Act of 1994" to expand the 1963 Equal Pay Act to include "equal pay for equivalent jobs." National Committee on Pay Equity (NCPE), News Release, 20 July 1994. Under Constance Horner, OPM opposed the concept of comparable worth in the federal government in a study, *Comparable Worth for Federal Jobs: A Wrong Turn Off the Road toward Pay Equity and*

Women's Career Advancement (Washington, D.C., OPM, 1987), arguing that women's progress is based on two factors: the employer's guarantee of equal opportunity and women's personal investment in education and upward-mobility programs. NCPE disputed OPM's findings with "OPM Comparable Worth/ Pay Equity Study . . . ," NCPE, Washington, D.C., 3 November 1987.

39. Confidential questionnaires: 14 May 1985; 17 July 1985; 19 May 1985.

40. Interviews with author: Irma Buchholz, 19 May 1985; Barbara Teaster, 17 June 1985; USDI, *Forty-Ninth Honor Awards Convocation,* 20 September 1983; NPS *Courier* 37 (February 1992): 25. Among other superintendent's secretaries who held their posts between twenty-five and thirty years were June Campbell at Shenandoah and Mary Ruth Chiles at Great Smoky Mountains. NPS *Courier* 33 (February 1978): 11; 36 (December 1981): 20; Mary Ruth Chiles interview with author, 15 June 1985.

41. Terry Wood interview with author, 9 April 1986. The NPS *Courier,* started by the Employees & Alumni Association (E & AA) in 1956, became the E & AA *Newsletter* in 1994.

42. Alvina Zimmerman interview with author, 21 September 1985.

43. Information supplied by the NPS Office of Training, 22 April 1986, 2 April 1990, 30 November 1992.

44. Cecilia Matic interview with author, 23 September 1985.

45. 1985 Questionnaire study. Elaine Fitzmaurice expressed the problem: "Having to take boring, low level positions in order to follow my husband around in his career. Every time I reach a point of job satisfaction, my husband receives a transfer and I must quit my job. I went from a GS-7 in Yosemite to a GS-3 at Crater Lake." Elaine Fitzmaurice questionnaire, 7 May 1985.

46. 1985 questionnaire study.

47. Cripe, "Work Force;" 1970 roster. For the National Historic Preservation Act of 1966, see Barry Mackintosh, *The Historic Sites Survey and National Historic Landmarks Program: A History* (Washington, D.C.: USDI, NPS, 1985). See also: U.S. Conference of Mayors, *With Heritage So Rich* (New York: Random House, 1966); Gerda Lerner, "View from the Woman's Side," *Journal of American History* 76 (September 1989): 446–456.

48. Nan Rickey interview with author, 7 May 1985; Nan Rickey questionnaire, 1 August 1985.

49. Penelope Hartshorne Batchelder interview with author, 12 June 1985; Greiff, *Independence:* 112–60.

50. Carolyn Pitts interview with author, 9 December 1985; Daniel S. Levy, "Outracing the Bulldozers," *Time* 138 (6 August 1990): 80; Jeffrey Schmalz, "U.S. Historian Seeking New York Landmarks," *New York Times,* 13 May 1985: 12; Doug Stewart, "She can size up your old building in a heartbeat," *Smithsonian* 24 (April 1993): 126–39; Mary Culpin interview with author, 9 May 1985.

51. Melody Webb interview with author, 20 September 1985; Melody Webb, "Cultural Landscapes in the National Park Service," *Public Historian* 9 (spring 1987): 77–89. For her Alaskan findings, see *The Last Frontier: A History of the Yukon Basin of Canada and Alaska* (Albuquerque: University of New Mexico Press, 1985).

52. Culpin interview; Heather Huyck, "Beyond John Wayne: Using Historic Sites to Interpret Women's History," in Lillian Schlissel, Vicki Ruiz, Janice Monk, eds., *Western Women: Their Land, Their Lives* (Albuquerque: University of New Mexico Press, 1988): 303–30. Shirley Sargent pioneered women's history in Yosemite with *Pioneers in Petticoats: Yosemite's Early Women, 1856–1900* (Yosemite: Flying Spur Press, 1966).

53. For Sallie Harris as an Honorary Custodian Without Pay, see chapter 3. Sallie P. Harris, USGSA CPR; Sallie Harris interview with Dorothy Huyck, 11 October 1978; Sallie Harris to author, 5 March 1988; 18 April 1989; Sallie Van Valkenburgh (Harris), "Archaeological Site Survey at Walnut Canyon National Monument," *Plateau* 34 (July 1961): 3–17; "The Casa Grande of Arizona as a Landmark on the Desert, A Government Reservation, and a National Monument," *The Kiva* 27 (February 1962): 1–31. See also Sallie Harris file, Huyck Collection.

54. Jean Pinkley, USGSA CPR; Chester A. Thomas, "Jean McWhirt Pinkley, 1910–1969," *American Antiquity* 34 (October 1969): 471–73; Jean Pinkley interview with Herbert Evison; 5 December 1962; Wilfred Logan interview with author, 7 May 1985; Jean M. Pinkley, "The Pueblos and the Turkey:

Who Domesticated Whom?," *American Antiquity* 31 (October 1965): 70–72. See also Jean Pinkley file, Huyck Collection.

55. The other professional women archeologists were Florence Hawley Ellis and Emma Lou Davis. Carolyn M. Osborne, "The Preparation of Yucca Fibers: An Experimental Study," in Douglas Osborne and Bernard S. Katz, *Contributions of the Wetherill Mesa Archeological Project,* (Salt Lake City: Memoirs of the Society for American Archaeology, 1965):454–50; Carolyn Osborne to author, 29 October 1988.

56. Cynthia Irwin-Williams, "Women in the Field: The Role of Women in Archaeology Before 1860," unpublished manuscript: 58–65, courtesy of Irwin-Williams. For Southwestern women archeologists, see chapter 2 and Babcock and Parezo, *Daughters of the Desert.*

57. Carol A. Martin to author, 27 May 1988; Nancy Curriden, *Lewis-Weber Site: a Tucson Homestead* (Tucson, Western Archeological Center, March 1981).

58. George Fischer to author, 7 July 1988; Marion Riggs Durham to author, 6 September 1988; Marion Riggs Durham interview with author, 26 February 1989. Thanks to George Fischer for help on the chronology of the first women archeologists.

59. George Fischer to author, 5 June 1989; Toni Lynne Carrell questionnaire, 21 October 1985; Toni L. Carrell to author, 13 January 1993; Daniel J. Lenihan, Toni L. Carrell, Sandra L. Rayl, et al., *The Preliminary Report of the National Reservoir Inundation Study* (Washington, D.C.: USDI, 1977); Toni Carrell, editor; *Micronesia: Submerged Cultural Resources Assessment,* Southwest Cultural Resources Center Professional Papers, no. 36 (Santa Fe: NPS, 1991).

60. Michele Aubry questionnaire, 14 January 1986; Adrienne Anderson interview with Dorothy Huyck, 23 June 1978.

61. Ann Johnson interview with author, 10 May 1985; Leslie Davis, Stephen Aaberg, and Ann Johnson, "Archeological Fieldwork at Yellowstone's Obsidian Cliff," *Park Science* 12 (spring 1992): 26–27.

62. Janet R. Balsom, "The Challenge of Integration: How Cultural Resources are Natural Resources," paper for Council for American Indian Interpretation Conference, 26 September 1994, enclosed in Janet Balsom to author, 27 November 1994.

63. Some of the women who published reports while working on contract were Lynette Shenk, Patricia Parker Hickman, E. Jane Rosenthal, and Susan Wells. Kathleen Moffitt contracted as a "circuit rider" to assist six northern California parks that were undergoing construction projects with archeological surveys. Cripe, "Work Force"; Martin to author, 27 May 1988.

64. Cripe, "Work Force"; Mary Herber interview with author, 20 November 1985.

65. Ann Hitchcock interview with author, 9 December 1985; Jerry L. Rogers, "Strategic Directions for Cultural Resources Programs," NPS *Courier* 37 (November/December 1992): 4–5.

66. Vera Craig interview with Dorothy Huyck, 4 April 1978; "Vera B. Craig—a Tribute," NPS *Courier* 28 (April 1983): 22; Ralph Lewis interview with author, 20 November 1985; Ralph H. Lewis, *Museum Curatorship in the National Park Service, 1904–1982* (Washington: USDI, 1993): 119, 172, 190, 226–27, 236, 297–98.

67. Albro graduated from the University of Arizona and apprenticed at the Buffalo Museum of Science. Elizabeth Albro interview with Dorothy Huyck, July 1977; Lewis, *Museum Curatorship:* 297, 313.

68. Marilyn Wandrus interview with author, 19 November 1985.

69. Jean Swearingen interview with author, 3 September 1985; Lewis, *Museum Curatorship:* 145–46, 181, 314. Swearingen became superintendent of Florissant Fossil Beds in 1995.

70. Janet Stone interview with author, 20 March 1985; Lewis, *Museum Curatorship:* 346–49. When a man with less experience than she was chosen as an ethnographic curator at the Harpers Ferry Center, Janet Stone filed an equal opportunity complaint and left the Park Service for three years to teach conservation practices in Australia. After several appeals, the complaint was settled in her favor and she returned to the Park Service as a conservator at the North Atlantic Conservation Laboratory.

71. Virginia Salazar Robicheau interview with author, 19 September 1985; "International Partnership Program with Canada," *Southwest Storyteller* (Southwest Region) 2 (December 1992): 8–9. The Native American Graves Protection and Repatriation Act (1990) requires federal agencies and museums to return human remains and associated objects to "culturally affiliated tribes" on request. For a summary

of public laws associated with archeology, see: "Archeology and the Federal Government," *Cultural Resources Management* (NPS Bulletin), v. 17, no. 6, 1994.

72. Sarah Olson interview with author, 21 November 1985. See chapter 7 for the founding of Weir Farm National Historic Site.

73. Interviews with author: Diane Nicholson, 13 May 1985; Ann Hitchcock. Agnes Mullins, curator at Arlington House in Virginia, believes that women make the best curators for historic houses. "Men really don't seem to have a sensitivity for what a house needs," she said. "It is a rare man . . . who can visualize how a historic house operated even when they've got the historic facts." Agnes Mullins interview with author, 7 April 1986.

74. Cripe, "Work Force;" 1970 NPS roster.

75. Mary Meagher interview with author, 26 September 1985. Among her publications are: Margaret Mary Meagher, *The Bison of Yellowstone National Park* (Washington, D.C.: National Park Service, Scientific Monograph Series, Number One, 1973); E. Tom Thorne, Mary Meagher, and Robert Hillman, "Brucellosis in Free-Ranging Bison: Three Perspectives" in *The Greater Yellowstone Ecosystem: Redefining America's Wilderness Heritage,* Robert B. Keiter and Mark S. Boyce, eds. (New Haven: Yale University Press 1991): 275–87; Mary Meagher, William J. Quinn, and Larry Stackhouse, "Chlamydial-caused Infectious Keratoconjunctivitis in bighorn sheep of Yellowstone National Park," *Journal of Wildlife Diseases* 28 (2), 1992: 171–76; Mary Meagher, "Range Expansion by Bison of Yellowstone National Park," *Journal of Mammology* 70 (3), 1989: 670–75; Mary Meagher and Sandi Fowler, "The Consequences of Protecting Problem Grizzly Bears," *Proceedings of a Symposium on Management Strategies,* Northwest Territories Department of Renewable Resources, 1989: 141–44.

76. Meagher interview with author; Mary Meagher to author, 23 February 1989.

77. Interviews with author: Shirley Clark, 12 April 1985; Regina Rochefort, 12 April 1985; Shirley Clark questionnaire, 13 April 1985; Shirley Clark, "Smoke and Visibility in Washington State," *Park Science* 4 (fall 1983): 23; *National Parks* 67 (March/April 1993): 2; Susan Bratton questionnaire, 28 June 1985; Susan P. Bratton, "National Park Management and Values," *Environmental Ethics* 7 (summer 1985): 117–34; Susan P. Bratton, "Vegetation Management Course Emphasizes Field Projects," *Park Science* 6 (summer 1986): 3–5; Regina Rochefort, "Rare Plant Surveys in Mount Rainier NP," *Park Science* 9 (fall 1989): 13; Regina Rochefort and Stephen Gibbons, "Impact Monitoring and Restoration in Mount Rainier NP," *Park Science* 13 (winter 1993): 29–30.

78. Questionnaires: Ann Schaffer, 28 June 1988; Kate Kendall, 4 June 1985; Donna Shaver, 6 September 1988; Ann Schaffer, "Tackling the Non-Traditional and Loving It," NPS *Courier* 32 (April 1987): 36; Donna Shaver, "Kemp's Ridley Research Continues," *Park Science* 12 (fall 1992): 26.

79. "Ten Years of Training: The Natural Resources Management Trainee Program," in *Highlights of Natural Resources Management* (Washington, D.C.: National Park Service, 1991): 11–14; William H. Walker Jr., "The Natural Resource Specialist Trainee Program," *Trends* 23, no. 2, 1986: 39–42. See also: Karen Goodrich-Taylor, "Moving Up? Need a Plan?" *Women in Natural Resources* 13 (September 1991): 12–13.

80. Katherine L. Jope questionnaire, 27 August 1985; Vicki L. Berlin, "Katherine L. Jope," *Women in Natural Resources* 13 (September 1991): 40–41. Jope is seen with the bears in the National Geographic video, *The Grizzlies.*

81. Glen Mittlehauser and Judy Hazen, "Monitoring Harlequin Ducks at Acadia," *Park Science* 10 (winter 1990): 18; Sue Consolo, "Swift Fox Returns to Badlands NP," *Park Science* 8 (fall 1987): 22. For Renee Askins, a private citizen who founded the Wolf Fund to restore gray wolves to Yellowstone, see Nicholas Davidoff, "One for the Wolves," *Audubon* 94 (July–August 1992): 38–45; Todd Wilkinson, "Bringing Back the Pack," *National Parks* 67 (May/June 1993): 25–29. The first wolves were reintroduced in January 1995.

82. Nora Mitchell interview with author, 24 March 1986; Nora Mitchell to author, 15 March 1993; Nora J. Mitchell, "Conservation of English Heritage Landscapes: Programs with Potential Application to the U.S. National Parks," research report, NPS North Atlantic Region, April 1989; Lauren Meier and Nora Mitchell, "Principles for Preserving Historic Plant Material," (NPS) *Cultural Resources Management Bulletin,* 1990, no. 6: 17–24; *NPS Electric Courier,* 1 (18 May 1995): 4.

83. Matthews interview; Jean Matthews questionnaire, 1 September 1988; issues of *Park Science*.

84. Charisse Sydoriak worked on the Western Region's Fire Monitoring Handbook in 1990 and was chair of the natural fire monitoring task force. Interviews with author: Charisse Sydoriak, 2 October 1990; Rochefort.

85. "Study Finds Overhaul of Park Science Needed," *National Parks,* 66 (November/December 1992): 15. The 75th Anniversary Vail Agenda also called for a strengthening of science and resource management in the Park Service. For a response see F. Eugene Hester, "Highlights of the NPS Natural Resources Strategic Plan," NPS *Courier* 37 (November/December 1992): 4; interviews with author: Bill Walker, 27 June 1988, 27 October 1992; Sue Consolo; Matthews; Christine Baumann questionnaire, 24 October 1985; Christine Baumann to author, 10 March 1987.

86. Cripe, "Work Force."

87. Laura Wilson interview with author, 20 September 1985.

88. Kathryn Simons Cochrane interview with Dorothy Huyck, 12 December 1978; Kathryn S. Cochrane to author, 23 March, 31 May 1989 with clippings and photographs. See also Joseph Judge and James P. Blair, "New Grandeur for Flowering Washington," *National Geographic* 131 (April 1967): 500–12; 520–27. For the significance of Lady Bird Johnson's beautification movement, see Lewis L. Gould, *Lady Bird Johnson and the Environment* (Lawrence: University of Kansas Press, 1988): 51–135. Johnson was vice chair of the National Park Service Advisory Board from 1968–1974.

89. Darwina L. Neal to author, 21 March 1989 enclosing *ASLA Bulletin,* July 1973. Neal received the ASLA President's Medal in 1987 for her work with the Society; Cripe, "Work Force."

90. Darwina Neal interview with author, 19 January 1993; Darwina Neal to author, 21 February 1989; Darwina Neal interview with Dorothy Huyck, 7 November 1978; *The Lyndon Baines Johnson Memorial Grove on the Potomac* (Washington: Eastern National Park and Monument Association, 1977).

91. Eleanore Williams interviews with author, 29 September 1985; 24 January 1993. The seed bank was developed under an interagency agreement with the Soil Conservation Service.

92. Nancy Ward interview with author, 27 September 1985; Kim Titus interview with author, 22 January 1993.

93. Ibid.

94. Ibid.; Tammy Gorden Scholten interview with author, 22 January 1993. Titus felt the positive effects of the sex-bias class action suit which forced the Forest Service in 1988 to increase its hiring and promotion of women.

95. Tammy Gorden [Scholten] interview with author, 9 May 1985.

96. Kathleen Gavan interview with author, 21 March 1986; Kathleen Gavan to author, 29 September 1986.

97. USDI, *53rd Honor Awards Convocation,* 13 September 1988: 22. Up through 1994, the Interior Department had given only about one percent of the Distinguished Service Awards to women.

98. "The Directed Reassignments of John Mumma and L. Lorraine Mintzmyer," Hearing before the House Subcommittee on the Civil Service of the Committee on Post Office and Civil Service," 102nd Cong., 1st sess., 24 September 1991; "An Environmental Vision Thing," *Harper's Magazine* 285 (October 1992): 20–24; "Political Manipulation of NPS Investigated," *National Parks* 65 (November/ December 1991): 11–14; "New Evidence Out in Yellowstone Probe," *National Parks* 66 (September/ October 1992):8–9. A Congressional investigation found that Mintzmyer's claim was accurate and that her transfer was "in direct violation" of federal regulations. "Probe Finds Evidence NPS Was Manipulated," *National Parks* 67 (March/April 1993): 12–13.

99. Lorraine Mintzmyer, "The Keys to the Treasure Chest," remarks before the 1991 Annual Meeting of the Greater Yellowstone Coalition, West Yellowstone, Montana, 29 May 1992; "Chase to Mintzmeyer: That's fine, but what took so long to criticize?" *Star-Tribune* (Casper, WY), 2 June 1992; Karl Hess, "Former Park official's warning comes far too late," *Rocky Mountain News,* 12, October 1992, courtesy of Mary Kelly Black; Lorraine Mintzmyer, "Disservice to the Parks," *National Parks* 66 (November/December 1992: 24–25; NBC *Dateline,* 21 July 1992.

Chapter Seven

1. Carson, *Silent Spring*; Betty Friedan, *The Feminine Mystique* (New York: W. W. Norton, 1963); Jo Ann Gibson Robinson, *The Montgomery Bus Boycott and the Women Who Started It* (Nashville: University of Tennesee Press, 1987). Thanks to Laura Beatty for sharing the National Parks and Conservation Association's list of national park activists with me.

2. Wirth, *Parks, Politics, and the People:* 198–99; George B. Hartzog Jr., *Battling for the National Parks* (Mt. Kisco, NY: Moyer Bell, 1988): 88–89. The Land and Water Conservation Fund (1964) provides funds for acquiring lands for park and recreation areas. The income comes from park fees, off-shore oil leases, and the sale of surplus government real estate.

3. Park Service Director Wirth made the statement. *Our Vanishing Shoreline* (Washington, D.C.: NPS, USDI, circa 1956): 3.

4. U.S. Congress, House, Committee on Interior and Insular Affairs, Subcommittee on Public Lands, Hearings, *Cape Cod National Seashore Park,* 87th Cong., 1st sess. (16 December 1960): 148. See also Francis P. Burling, *The Birth of Cape Cod National Seashore* (Plymouth, MA: Lydon Press, 1979).

5. Miriam Hapgood DeWitt interview with author, 20 August 1988; petition dated June, 1959, in letter to author, 3 September 1988. DeWitt, who died in 1990, lived in Washington, D.C. in the winter until she became a year-round resident in Provincetown in 1978. A former writer/editor for the federal government, she ran an art program for the Park Service hiring artists to paint in national parks and organizing exhibits of their works. Thanks are due to Lois Rudnick for introducing me to Miriam De-Witt. Mrs. Walter P. Chrysler Jr. protested "the seizure of property" as "destruction of the inalienable rights of a citizen." She complained that Cape Cod was accessible to "one-third of the entire population of the United States," adding, "God help us if they all arrive at the same time with their hot dogs and bottles of pop." House Hearing, 16 December 1960: 176–78.

6. DeWitt interview with author; flyer, 13 March 1961; "Exhibit A," 28 December 1960; Mary Cecil Allen to Miriam DeWitt, 15 March 1961, in letter to author, 3 September 1988. DeWitt was also involved in the Peaked Hill Trust's successful effort to preserve the historic dune shacks used by such writers as Eugene O'Neill and Jack Kerouac that the NPS originally planned to tear down.

7. Murphy, who died in 1975, was married to naturalist Robert Cushman Murphy and wrote *There's Always Adventure* about their life. In 1961 the Federated Garden Clubs of New York awarded her their Marion B. Darrow Conservation Medal. A member of the Class of 1913 at Brown, she received an honorary degree from Brown for her work in conservation in 1967. Thanks to Martha Mitchell for the material on Murphy in the Brown University Archives.

8. For the full story of the complexities of the seashore, see Barry Mackintosh, *Assateague Island National Seashore: An Administrative History* (Washington, D.C.: NPS, USDI, 1982).

9. Judith Colt Johnson, "Assateague: Jewel of the East Coast," *National Parks & Conservation Magazine* 49 (January 1975): 4–9; Mrs. A. Reid Johnson, "What Assateague Means to Me," *Garden Club Bulletin* 63 (April 1975): 74–76.

10. Tom Horton, "Years in defense of Assateague have made her a master lobbyist," *Baltimore Sun,* 6 June 1982 and Judith Colt Johnson, "A Primer for Citizen Action," November 1976, in letter to author from Judy Johnson, 27 January 1988. For Johnson's testimony see: U.S. Congress, Senate, Committee on Interior and Insular Affairs, Subcommittee on Parks and Recreation, Hearings, *Assateague Island National Seashore,* 94th Cong., 1st sess. (12 May 1975): 128–29; U.S. Congress, Senate, Committee on Energy and Natural Resources, Subcommittee on Public Lands, National Parks and Forests, Hearings, *Miscellaneous National Park Legislation,* 102nd Cong., 1st sess. (25 July 1991): 69.

11. Committee to Preserve Assateague Island, 1987; William Jones, "Judith Johnson Fights to Save Assateague," *News American,* 20 June 1976; Horton, "Years in Defense of Assateague," in letter to author, 27 January 1988. The island also contains a Maryland State Park and a U.S. Fish and Wildlife preserve.

12. John McAllenan, "Art of conserving," *Floridian, St. Petersburg Times,* 8 February 1976: 18 (quote

in); Frank Peters, "Who's Minding the Shore?" *Floridian, St. Petersburgh Times,* 8 July 1979: 8–15; "Seashore Park protection top priority, *New Smyrna Beach News,* 13 February 1975, in letter to author, 27 June 1988; Doris Leeper interview with author, 12 August 1988.

13. Marjorie Stoneman Douglas, *The Everglades: River of Grass* (New York: Rinehart, 1947); Marjorie Stoneman Douglas with John Rothchild, *Voice of the River* (Englewood, Fla: Pineapple Press, 1987): 98–99, 136, 233.

14. Marjory Stoneman Douglas, "Wings," *Saturday Evening Post,* 14 March 1931: 10–11, 74–78; Douglas, *Voice of the River:* 224; "Fixing the Everglades," *Audubon* 94 (March/April 1992): 6.

15. Douglas, *Voice of the River:* 226–29. See also Steve Yates, "Marjorie Stoneman Douglas and the Glades Crusade," *Audubon* 85 (March 1983): 113–27.

16. Douglas, *Voice of the River:* 228–31.

17. NPS *Courier* 35 (June 1990): 30; *National Parks* 59 (July/August 1985): 38. For her tribute to Ernest Coe, see Marjory Stoneman Douglas, "The Forgotten Man Who Saved the Everglades," *Audubon* 73 (September 1971): 79–95.

18. Mark Derr, "Redeeming the Everglades," *Audubon* 95 (September/October 1993): 48–56, 128–31.

19. Maxine Johnston interviews with author, 14 August 1988; 28 July 1993; Pete A. Gunter, "The Big Thicket," *Living Wilderness* 31 (autumn 1967): 3–9.

20. Johnson interview, 14 August 1988; U.S. Congress, House, Committee on Interior and Insular Affairs, Subcommittee National Parks and Recreation, Hearings, *Big Thicket National Park,* 92nd Cong., 2nd sess. (10 June 1972): 242–46, 348–49; 93rd Cong., 1st sess. (16 and 17 July 1973): 28–31, 79–80, 138; Senate, 93rd Cong., 2nd sess. (5 and 6 February 1974): 135–49. See also: James Joseph Cozine Jr., "Assault on a Wilderness: The Big Thicket of East Texas," Ph.D. dissertation, Texas A & M University, August 1976; Pete A. Y. Gunter, *The Big Thicket: An Ecological Reevaluation* (Denton: University of North Texas Press, 1993).

21. Johnston letter to author, 27 July 1991; Johnston interview with author, 28 July 1993. Johnston, who started the *Big Thicket Reporter* in 1993, noted that the impact of Big Thicket on the local economy is about $5 million. The 1993 legislation included acquiring land from the U.S. Forest Service. Preservationists worked to include lands protecting the red cockaded woodpecker. *Big Thicket Reporter* 1 (May–June 1993); (July–August 1993).

22. Sharlon Willows to author, 14 January 1988, including *Canyon Coalition News Alert,* March 1987; Willows to author, 3 September 1993, including *Glacier Park Eco-Watch Alert,* April 1993.

23. Beatrice Willard talk, 20th Anniversary Celebration of Florissant Fossil Beds National Monument, 20 August 1989, audio recording. My thanks to Noel R. Poe for this recording.

24. Beatrice Willard interview with author, 29 June 1988; Estella Leopold, "Life with Father in Sand County," *Outdoors West* 7 (summer 1984): 4. For Willard's NPS career, see chapter 3.

25. Willard talk; Willard interview; "Senator Makes Helicopter Visit to County," *Gold Rush* (Cripple Creek), 17 May 1968; "Suit to Save Fossils Filed," *Denver Post,* 4 July 1969, Florissant Fossil Bed Archives, courtesy of Thomas C. Wylie. Both Willard and Leopold testified at the field hearings. U.S. Congress, Senate, Committee on Interior and Insular Affairs, Subcommittee on Parks and Recreation, Hearings, *Florissant Fossil Beds National Monument,* 91st Cong., 1st sess. (29 May 1969): 38–43.

26. Vim Crane Wright talk, 20th Anniversary Celebration, 20 August 1989, audio recording.

27. Ibid.; "Fossil Beds Given Last-Minute Reprieve," *Rocky Mountain News,* 30 July 1969; "Court Order Halts Construction at Monument Site," *Fort Collins Coloradean,* 30 July 1969, Florissant park archives. Noel Poe supplied an Oliphant cartoon from the *Denver Post* (11 August 1969) depicting a wicked bulldozer driver with his machine labeled "developers" poised to run over a little girl lying on the ground tied up in rope labeled Florissant. The operator says, "Curses! Very Well, Let's Talk Money."

28. Wright talk.

29. Letter to the author from Bob Belcher, 9 December 1989, enclosing Robert O. Belcher and Genevieve Gillette, "The Michigan Parks Association," *Planning and Civic Comment* 27 (1961): 32–35; *Our Fourth Shore: Great Lakes Shoreline Recreation Area Survey* (Washington, D.C.: NPS, USDI, 1959).

30. Among the state parks Gillette helped open were: Ludington, Hartwick, Porcupine Mountains, and P. J. Hoffmaster. The state dedicated the Genevieve Gillette Nature Center in Hoffmaster State Park in 1976. Claire V. Korn, "A Most Special Lady," *Michigan Natural Resources* (May–June 1985): 18–25, courtesy of Bob Belcher.

31. Belcher and Gillette, "The Michigan Parks Association."

32. Belcher letter, 9 December 1989; *Michigan Parks Association News* 2 (7 March 1963); Genevieve Gillette testimony for Sleeping Bear Dunes for Senate hearing, National Parks Subcommittee, 13 July 1965, Genevieve Gillette Collection, Bentley Historical Library, University of Michigan. Opponents included the Michigan State Federation of Women's Clubs, who resolved that the park proposal deprived private landowners of their constitutional rights. Michigan State Federation of Women's Clubs resolutions, 6 June 1963, Gillette papers. See also: Doug Fulton, *Ann Arbor News,* 16–18 September 1963, Gillette papers. Thanks to Deborah Herbert for her most helpful research in the Gillette papers.

33. Genevieve Gillette speech, Traverse City Commission meeting, 7 June 1962, Gillette papers. Gillette died in 1986.

34. U.S. Congress, Senate, Hearings, Committee on Public Works, Subcommittee on Flood Control—Rivers and Harbors, *Big South Fork National River and Recreation Area,* 92nd Cong., 2nd sess. (25 May and 5 June 1972): 94–97. The Wild and Scenic Rivers Act passed in 1968.

35. Lianne Russell interview with author, 18 August 1993.

36. In 1977, TCWP aided Tennessee in becoming the first state to pass a strip mining law. TCWP also opposed TVA's Tellico Dam, controversial because opponents stopped the dam in 1978 by using the Endangered Species Act to protect the snail darter.

37. See source cited in note 34 for the high quality of the expert volunteers' research and of Liane Russell's synthesis. The Corps also built a bridge and campgrounds. Interim management by the NPS was authorized in 1976 and full management in 1990.

38. Russell interview.

39. Ibid.; "Dam Plans Jeopardize Wild and Scenic River," *National Parks* 67 (May–June 1993): 12. Liane Russell received the Marjorie Stoneman Douglas Award in 1992. *National Parks* 67 (May–June 1993): 18.

40. Polly Dyer, "Preserving Washington Parklands and Wilderness," oral history by Susan Schrepfer and Ann Lage (1983), in *Pacific Northwest Conservationists,* Regional Oral History Office, The Bancroft Library, University of California, 1986: 23–27, 75.

41. Ibid.: 11–12; Brant, *Adventures in Conservation:* 312–13; Carsten Lien, *Olympic Battleground: The Power Politics of Timber Preservation* (San Francisco: Sierra Club Books, 1991): 274–77. Voting with the majority was the woman representing the Seattle General Federation of Women's Clubs.

42. Lien says that Eleanor Roosevelt responded by attacking Rayonier in *My Day.* Thanks to Mollie and David O'Kane for locating the advertisement in *Time,* 27 December 1954. Dyer oral history: 10; Lien, *Olympic Battleground:* 282–83.

43. Ibid.: 293–96; U.S. Congress, Senate, Committee on Interior and Insular Affairs, Subcommittee on Legislative Oversight with House, Committee on Government Operations, Subcommittee on Public Works and Resources, Joint Hearings, *Federal Timber Sales Policies,* 85th Cong., 1st sess. (23 November 1955): 1888–1890.

44. Douglas led a reunion walk in 1964. His more famous walk was in support of the Chesapeake and Ohio Canal in 1954. Dyer oral history: 1, 15–23; 128–33; Lien, *Olympic Battleground:* 303, 310–20, 365. Dyer also served as president of the Federation of Western Outdoor Clubs and became the Continuing Environmental Education Director for the Institute of Environmental Studies at the University of Washington. She received the Marjory Stoneman Douglas Award in 1989. Dyer oral history: 158; *National Parks* 63 (September/October 1989): 11.

45. U.S. Congress, House, Committee on Interior and Insular Affairs, Subcommittee on National Parks and Recreation, Hearings, *The North Cascades,* 91st Cong., 2nd sess. (19 April 1968): 272–73; Dyer oral history: 31–36. The papers of Emily Haig, who died in 1978, are at the University of Washington. See Allan Sommarstrom, "Wild Land Preservation Crisis: The North Cascades Controversy," Ph.D.

dissertation, University of Washington, 1970. Abigail and Stuart Avery funded David Brower's film, *The Wilderness Alps of Stehekin,* used in the campaign for the park. Abigail Avery was Jane McConnell's college roommate and became a summer resident at Stehekin. Her observation of the logging in Agnes Valley in 1956 turned her into an ardent environmentalist at the national level. Abigail Avery, "Nurturing the Earth: North Cascades, Alaska, New England . . . ", an oral history by Polly Kaufman (1988), Regional Oral History Office, The Bancroft Library, 1990: 5–10.

46. League of Women Voters, "Natural Resources," in *Impact on Issues, 1980–82: A Leader's Guide to National Program* (Washington, D.C.: League of Women Voters of the United States, n.d.): 30–41. Thanks to Linda Morrison for tracking down this guide.

47. Janet Hutchison interview with author, 4 August 1993; Ron Cockrell, *A Green Shrouded Miracle: The Administrative History of Cuyahoga Valley National Recreation Area* (Omaha, NE: NPS, USDI, 1992): 31–38.

48. Seiberling secured a seat on the House National Parks Subcommittee. Cockrell credits Loretta Neumann, Seiberling's legislative aide and former editor of the NPS *Courier* with the swift passage of the park bill. Seiberling published the league's brief, "The League of Women Voters Cuyahoga Valley Study," in the *Congressional Record.* Sue Klein from the Junior League, who edited *The Voice of the Cuyahoga Valley Association,* sponsored several park projects with her husband. Hutchison interview; Cockrell, *Green Shrouded Miracle*: v, 78–83, 95–111, 135–39.

49. Ibid.: 211–13; 171–188. The flyer is reproduced on page 183. Hutchison interview.

50. Ibid. Women continued to be active in the Cuyahoga Valley Association (CVA). Peg Bobel became executive director. Christine Freitag was president until 1992 when she became national president of the Garden Club of America. Sue Rogers succeeded her.

51. For Lady Bird Johnson's beautification work, see chapter 6.

52. William Whalen, nomination of Amy Meyer for the Mrs. Lyndon B. Johnson Award, 23 August 1979, NPS Western Regional Office; Amy Meyer, "Preserving Bay Area Parklands," an oral history by Galen R. Fisher, (6 February 1981), Regional Oral History Office, The Bancroft Library, 1983: 2. See also John Hart, *San Francisco's Wilderness Next Door* (San Rafael: Presidio Press, 1979).

53. Meyer oral history: 5; Whalen nomination; Mia Monroe Way interview with the author, 16 May 1985. Way, who became a park ranger in Muir Woods, led two hundred Sierra Club walks.

54. Polly Dyer, representing the Federation of Western Outdoor Clubs, and Geri Stewart from the Bay Area League of Women Voters also spoke for the bill. U.S. Congress, House, Committee on Interior and Insular Affairs, Subcommittee on National Parks and Recreation, Hearings, *Golden Gate National Recreation Area,* 92nd Cong., 1st sess. (9 August 1971): 57, 66–69, 320 (quote on p. 57); Senate, 92nd Cong., 2nd sess. (22 September 1972): 154.

55. Amy Meyer interview with the author, 9 August 1993; Jo-Ann Ordano, "Changing of the Guard," *National Parks* 67 (March–April 1993): 31–36. Amy Meyer received the Marjory Stoneman Douglas Award in 1993. In 1992 a movement led by Audrey Rust, executive director, Peninsula Open Space Trust, raised $14.5 million to buy the 1,250 redwood forest acres and high ridges of the Phleger estate in San Mateo County to add to Golden Gate NRA. U.S. Congress, Senate, Subcommittee on Public Lands, National Parks and Forests, Hearings, *Miscellaneous National Park Legislation,* 102nd Cong., 1st sess. (25 July 1991): 117–23. In 1994, California Representative Nancy Pelosi and Senator Barbara Boxer introduced legislation to establish the Presidio Trust to preserve the cultural and historic integrity of the site. Nancy Pelosi, "To the Editor," *New York Times,* 4 March 1995: 18.

56. J. Ronald Engel, *Sacred Sands: The Struggle for Community in the Indiana Dunes* (Middletown, CT: Wesleyan University Press, 1983): xv–xx, 11–28, 251–53, 261; Ron Cockrell, *A Signature of Time and Eternity: The Administrative History of Indiana Dunes National Lakeshore* (Omaha, NE: NPS, USDI, 1988): 19–31; Sheehan and Buell profiles in Kay Franklin and Norma Schaeffer, *Duel for the Dunes: Land Use Conflict on the Shores of Lake Michigan* (Urbana: University of Illinois Press, 1983): 85–87, 128–31.

57. Engel, *Sacred Sands*: 254–58; Cockrell, *Signature of Time*: 39–43.

58. Ibid.: 42–46; Engel, *Sacred Sands*: 260–61. Henry Cowles, a pioneer ecologist, used the dunes as the locus of his research. Opponents called Douglas the third senator from Indiana.

59. Ibid.: 261–62; Cockrell, *Signature of Time:* 46. Dunes Council member Earl H. Reed Jr. also served on the national park advisory board and convinced them to support Indiana Dunes.

60. Engle, *Sacred Sands:* 266–81; Cockrell, *Signature of Time:* 63–70, 82–85.

61. Franklin and Schaeffer, *Duel for the Dunes:* 218–221; 228–30; Engle, *Sacred Sands:* 282–89; Cockrell, *Signature of Time:* 238–45; letter to author from Sylvia Troy, 1 September 1989. The Department of the Interior awarded Troy a citation for conservation service in 1979. USDI, *Honors Awards Convocation,* 10 October 1979. For Troy's biography, see Franklin and Schaeffer, *Duel for the Dunes:* 213–17.

62. Ibid.: 93. Congress dedicated Indiana Dunes National Lakeshore to Senator Paul Douglas in 1980. Ibid.: 402.

63. Mike Davis, *City of Quartz: Excavating the Future in Los Angeles* (New York: Verso, 1990): 130–34.

64. Ibid.: 171–73; Carolyn Mann, "One Man's Romance with the Santa Monicas," *Sierra* 71 (July/August 1986): 89–95.

65. U.S. Congress, Senate, Committee on Energy and Natural Resources, Subcommittee on Parks and Recreation, *Santa Monica Mountains National Park and Seashore,* 93rd Cong., 2nd sess., (15 June 1974): 100.

66. Sue Nelson interview with author, with supporting clipping and newsletter file, 11 November 1988.

67. Jill Swift interview with author, 11 June 1988. Volunteer naturalist Sue Othmer conducted walks for inner-city children and trained docents. Sue Othmer interview with author, 13 June 1988.

68. Margot Feuer interview with author, 14 June 1988; Feuer letter to author, 6 September 1988.

69. Senate Hearing, 15 June 1974: 76–91, 99–100, 106–09. Several other women activists testified for the park, including Suzette Neiman, vice president of the Los Angeles Planning Commission; Betsy Laties, vice president of the Los Angeles Board of Environmental Quality; Louise L. Frankel, Los Angeles Board of Zoning Appeals; Dixie Mohan, Los Angeles Audubon Society. U.S. Congress, Senate Hearing, Subcommittee on Parks and Recreation, *Santa Monica Mountains National Park and Seashore,* 95th Cong., 2nd sess. (5 May 1978): 137–46.

70. Nelson interview; Jess Cook, "Los Angeles Lands a Huge New Park," *Smithsonian* 10 (July 1979): 27–34.

71. Mary Ellen Strote and Susan Nelson in *Los Angeles Times:* "L.A.'s Mountains, D.C.'s Plaything," 28 July 1985, IV: 5; "Santa Monica Mountains—Parkland Dream Dying on the Vine," 22 May 1988, V: 5; Susan B. Nelson and Ralph Stone, "Apocalypse Now: Why the Rains Hurt So," 24 February 1980, V: 1.

72. Feuer interview. By late 1993, Santa Monica NRA had acquired 20,400 acres of a goal of 35,000 acres and spent $142 million on land acquisition. Lands purchased from actor Bob Hope, an agreement hammered out over many years, added approximately eight thousand acres to the park, mostly in the Cheeseboro Canyon area, for $29.5 million in the early 1990s. At issue was Hope's request, eventually turned down, for access through park land for a development. Actress Barbra Streisand donated her 24-acre Malibu estate to the Santa Monica Mountains Conservancy in November 1993. Information on land acquisition from NPS San Francisco Land Resources Office, 12 October 1993. See also: "Final Santa Monica Mountains Deal Praised," *National Parks* 66 (January/February 1992): 11. Thanks to Roger Kaufman for clippings from the *Los Angeles Times,* 18 November 1993, 12 June 1994, describing the Streisand gift.

73. Robert Cahn, *The Fight to Save Wild Alaska* (New York: National Audubon Society, 1982): 8–12.

74. James and Regina Glover, "The Natural Magic of Olaus Murie," *Sierra* 72 (September/October 1987): 69–73; Margaret E. Murie, *Two in the Far North* (New York: Knopf, 1962; 2nd edition: Anchorage: Alaska Northwest Publishing Co. 1978): 75–142. The Arctic National Wildlife Range became a Refuge and the U.S. Biological Survey became the U.S. Fish and Wildlife Service.

75. Mardy Murie interview with author, 29 September 1985; quote in Margaret E. Murie address, Conference of Park Superintendents, 27 October 1977: 100, NPS Archives; Douglas W. Scott, "Securing the Wilderness," *Sierra* 69 (May/June 1984): 39; Cahn, *Fight to Save Wild Alaska* 5,9; Murie, *Two in the Far North*: 368–85; Frank Graham Jr., "Mardy Murie and Her Sunrise of Promise," *Audubon* 82 (May

1980): 106–27. In 1974 the Interior Department awarded Margaret Murie a citation for conservation service. USDI, *42nd Honors Award Convocation,* 27 June 1974.

76. Celia Hunter interview with author, 30 August 1985; Cahn, *Fight to Save Wild Alaska*: 10–11.

77. Ibid.: 8–11; Mark Ganopole Hickock interview with author, 9 October 1988.

78. Ibid.; Hunter interview; Cahn, *Fight to Save Wild Alaska*: 15. See Celia Hunter's columns in *Living Wilderness,* 1976–78. The only other woman president of the Wilderness Society was Karin Sheldon, an environmental lawyer, who served as an interim president in 1993.

79. U.S. Congress, House, Interior Subcommittee on . . . Alaska Lands, Hearings, *Inclusion of Alaska Lands in National Park, Forest, Wildlife Refuge, and Wild and Scenic River Systems,* held in Washington, D.C., Chicago, Atlanta, Denver, Seattle, and various places in Alaska, 95th Cong. 1st sess. (4 April through 21 September 1977). For a list of witnesses and abstracts of their testimony, see *Abstracts of Legislative Congressional Publications* (Washington, D.C.: Congressional Information Service, 1978): v. 9: 297–318; Cahn, *Fight to Save Wild Alaska*: 23.

80. Ibid.: 23–30; T. H. Watkins, "The Perils of Expedience," *Wilderness* 54 (winter 1990): 27–30.

81. Ibid.: 31–71, 78–80, 84; John Daniel, "The National Parks of Alaska: The Chance to Do It Right," *Wilderness* 56 (summer 1993): 11–25, 30–33.

82. Among women receiving awards for conservation service from the USDI were: the Junior League of Springfield, Illinois, for its work with the Lincoln Home National Historic Site and Anne Case Drummond for supporting research and education at Wilson's Creek National Battlefield. USDI, *56th Honor Awards Convocation,* 5 May 1992: 52; *51st Convocation,* 26 September 1986: 42.

83. Interviews with author: Glory Felder, 14 June 1988; Wanda Ford, 13 June 1988; San Antonio Conservation Society brochure; Ben Moffett, "Activating agreements signed at San Antonio Missions," NPS *Courier* 28 (April 1983): 4. For the complete history of the San Antonio Conservation Society, see Lewis F. Fisher, *Saving San Antonio: The Precarious Preservation of a Heritage* (Lubbock: Texas Tech University Press, 1996).

84. Greer Garson Fogelson, Pecos Visitor Center Groundbreaking, 7 August 1983, audio recording, courtesy of Pecos National Monument; Verna Hutchinson interview with author, 22 September 1985; "Congress Expands New Mexico Parks," *National Parks* 64 (July/August 1990): 8–9. In 1981 the USDI awarded the Fogelsons a citation for conservation service. USDI, *48th Honor Awards Convocation,* 2 December 1981.

85. Jane T. Merritt, *The Administrative History of Fort Vancouver National Historic Site* (Seattle, WN: NPS, USDI, 1993): 21–32. Quotation on page 32.

86. Ibid.: 32–35.

87. Hartzog, *Battling for the National Parks*: 139–45; USDI, *44th Honor Awards Convocation,* 7 December 1976.

88. Introduction to the Bernice Gibbs Anderson Collection, Golden Spike National Historic Site.

89. Bernice Gibbs Anderson to President Dwight D. Eisenhower, 6 April 1954; Eisenhower to Anderson, 10 May 1954; Anderson to Eisenhower, 29 May 1954, Anderson Collection.

90. Newton Drury to Utah Congressional delegation, April 1949; Robert M. Utley, *Golden Spike National Historic Site* (Santa Fe, NM: NPS, USDI, 1960); *A Bill to Establish Golden Spike National Monument,* S. 1191, (3 March 1961), Anderson Collection.

91. Anne D. Snyder to Ed Bearss, 11 April 1988, in Anne Snyder to author, 2 February 1989; Thomas A. Lewis, "Fighting for the Past," *Audubon* 91 (September 1989): 58–64.

92. Karl Rhodes, "The Third Battle of Manassas," *Virginia Business* (December 1988): 46–50, in Snyder to author.

93. Save the Battle Coalition Newsletter, 4 December 1988; "Warner surprises rally participants," *Potomac News,* 18 July 1988, in Snyder to author.

94. Ibid.; Jody Powell, "Battling Over Manassas," *National Parks* 62 (July/August 1988): 12–13.

95. "Manassas Preservationists Win a Last-Minute Hill Victory," *Washington Post,* 23 October 1988; "Reagan Signs Prince William Taking," *Journal Messenger,* 12 November 1988 (Rankin quote), in Snyder to author; Linda S. McCarthy to author, 6 February 1989. A new coalition defeated a Walt Disney

theme park near Manassas in 1994. Chris Fordney, "Embattled Ground," *National Parks* 68 (November/December 1994): 26–31.

96. Also included are: Carl Sandburg Home, Longfellow, Edgar Allen Poe, and Saint-Gaudens national historic sites. Although authorized in 1980, a Georgia O'Keeffe National Historic site planned for the artist's home in Abiquiu, NM, was withdrawn when she came to believe it would attract too much visitation.

97. Barry Mackintosh, *Wolf Trap Farm Park, An Administrative History* (Washington, D.C.: NPS, USDI, 1983): 1–4.

98. Ibid.: 5–12; Claire St. Jacques interview with author, 28 March 1985.

99. Mackintosh, *Wolf Trap Farm Park*: 23–31, 40–45.

100. Claire St. Jacques interview with author, 8 April 1986; Mackintosh, *Wolf Trap Farm Park:* 50–51; 62–68.

101. St. Jacques interview, 8 April 1986. Shouse died in 1994.

102. The 1982 board of directors included Linda Best, Travis Bogard, Lois Sizoo, Helen Kelly, H. L. Davisson, and Thalia Brewer. "History and Accomplishments of the Eugene O'Neill Foundation, Tao House," May 1982; U.S. Congress, Senate, Subcommittee on Parks and Recreation, Hearings, *Wilderness Areas and Historic Sites,* 94th Cong., 2nd sess. (24 March 1976): 48–58.

103. Ibid.: 39–43. *Tao* is pronounced *Dow* as in *now.*

104. Eugene O'Neill Foundation, Tao House, *Newsletter,* December 1985; Lois Sizoo interview with author, 14 November 1993.

105. U.S. Congress, Senate, Committee on Energy and Natural Resources, Subcommittee on Public Lands, National Parks and Forests, Hearings, *Miscellaneous National Park, National Historic Trails . . . ,* 101st Cong., 2nd sess. (28 March 1990): 37–40, 68–78, 120–26; Katherine Barnar interview with author, 3 June 1995.

106. Paula Giddings, *When and Where I Enter* (New York: William Morrow, 1984): 138.

107. Ibid.; Sharon Harley, *A Study of the Preservation and Administration of 'Cedar Hill': the Home of Frederick Douglass,* (Washington: NPS, USDI, 1988): 15–26.

108. Nannie Helen Burroughs was founder and president of the National Training School for Women and Girls. An agreement that 15 percent of NACW dues would be used for the upkeep of the home proved impossible to meet, but some state branches sent donations. Ibid.: 36–40, 57–64; Mary McLeod Bethune to Nannie Burroughs, 27 October 1938; Sallie W. Stewart to Miss (Nannie) Burroughs, 4 August 1941; Box 1, Frederick Douglass Memorial and Historical Association (FDMHA) Papers, Library of Congress.

109. Gladys Parham retired in 1972 but continued to work part time at the home until her death in 1983. Audio tape of video tape, *Gladys Parham,* n.d., courtesy, Public Affairs Office, National Capital Region, NPS; "Mrs. Gladys B. Parham," NPS *Courier* 27 (February 1984): 18.

110. Harley, *Cedar Hill:* 71–74; Deed Acceptance Ceremony program, 25 June 1964, Box 8; Mary Gregory in support of HR 568, 17 October 1969, Box 10, FDMHA Papers. The original ceiling for funding was $25,000.

111. Dorothy Benton interview with author, 26 March 1985; Mary B. Talbert to co-workers, 1 November 1921, Box 1, FDMHA papers.

112. Cheryl Brown Henderson interview with author, 30 October 1993.

113. Ibid.; Robert A. Pratt, "Segregation Overruled," *National Parks* 67 (September/October 1993): 34–39.

114. Henderson interview; Harry A. Butowsky, "Landmarks of Democracy," (NPS) *Cultural Resources Management Bulletin* 10 (April 1987): 1, 10–11. Cheryl Brown Henderson is a vocational equity coordinator and Linda Brown Buckner teaches Headstart.

115. Henderson interview; *Brown v. Board of Education of Topeka Management Alternatives Study* (Omaha, NE: NPS, USDI, March 1992).

116. Henderson interview.

117. U.S. Congress, Senate, National Parks Subcommittee, Hearings, *Brown v. Board of Education*

Site, 102nd Cong., 2nd sess. (6 August 1992): 76; Angela Bates, "New Promise for Nicodemus," *National Parks* 66 (July/August 1992): 39–46.

118. Sue Kunitomi Embrey interview with author, 27 October 1993; Linda M. Rancourt, "Remembering Manzanar," *National Parks* 67 (May/June 1993): 30–34. President George Bush signed the law on March 3, 1992. See also Robin Winks, "Sites of Shame," *National Parks* 68 (March/April 1994): 22–23.

119. Sue Embrey was a reporter and later managing editor for the *Manzanar Free Press.* Embrey interview; Manzanar Committee, "History of Manzanar," in Embrey to author, 11 December 1993.

120. The landmark designation resulted from the NPS theme study on World War II and the Pacific. Jerry Rogers, speech, "Vigilance," 27 April 1985, in Embrey to author; Embrey interview.

121. Ibid.; Rancourt, "Remembering Manzanar;" U.S. Congress, Senate, National Parks Subcommittee, *Manzanar National Historic Site,* 102nd Cong., 1st sess. (25 July 1991): 111–16. Each of the 79,000 of the 125,000 survivors were paid $20,000 in reparations.

122. Embrey interview; Embrey to author, 6 June 1994.

Chapter Eight

1. Hilda R. Watrous, *The County Between the Lakes: A Public History of Seneca County, New York, 1876–1982* (Seneca County, NY, Board of Supervisors, 1982): 339–43.

2. Ibid.: 349–53. The Sewall-Belmont House, meeting place of the National Woman's Party in Washington, D.C. since 1929, is owned by the Woman's Party Corporation and open to visitors, under a cooperative agreement with the Park Service. In 1974, when the house was in danger of removal, Congress designated the house as a national historic site. The Park Service offers technical assistance and is the conduit for grants from Congress for the rehabilitation, maintenance, and operation of the house. Mary Condon Gereau to author with supporting materials, 6 January 1994.

3. Watrous, *County Between:* 353. The refurbished tablet was placed in the Wesleyan Chapel surround wall at the 1993 opening. The League of Women Voters succeeded the National American Woman Suffrage Association after women achieved the right to vote.

4. Facts from National Women's Hall of Fame, 27 February 1995.

5. Interviews with author: Judy Hart, 17 October 1985; Nancy Dubner, 13 May 1986. At Houston, a resolution was passed to make the Wesleyan Chapel and the Stanton home national historic sites.

6. Other founding members of the Elizabeth Cady Stanton Foundation were Corinne Guntzel, Mary Curry, Marina Brown, Betsy Shultis (whose dramatization of the 1848 convention was presented at the 1982 park opening and the 1993 visitor center dedication), Pat Chiodo, Suzanne Cusick, and Myrna Pollino. Dr. August P. Sinicropi was chair of the Seneca Falls Downtown Revitalization Committee. "Former Superintendent Recalls Chronology," *The Reveille,* 29 July 1993: 25.

7. U.S. Congress, Senate, Committee on Energy and Natural Resources, Subcommittee on Parks, Recreation, and Renewable Resources, Hearing, *The Women's Rights National Historic Park,* 96th Cong., 2nd sess. (8 September 1980): 109–29, 204–09.

8. Interviews with author: Hart; Corinne Guntzel, 6 October 1985.

9. Ibid.; Martin Toombs, "A Village Discovers its History," National Women's Hall of Fame publication, (1985): 7. Members of the Advisory Commission were Marilyn Bero, Charlotte Conable, Suzanne Cusick, Nancy Dubner, Carrie George, August Sinicropi, Donna Carlson, and Dorothy Duke, chair. Judith Wellman was the park's first history consultant. See her "The Seneca Falls Women's Rights Convention: A Study in Social Networks," *Journal of Women's History* 3 (spring 1991): 9–35.

10. Judy Hart, editor, *A Vision Realized: The Design Competition for the Women's Rights National Historical Park* (Washington: NPS and National Endowment for the Arts, n.d.). Bonnie Campbell, planning team captain, suggested the design competition.

11. Interviews with author: Mary Ellen Snyder, 22 October 1992; Vivien Rose, 10 June 1994.

12. Interviews with author: Linda Canzanelli, 14 October 1992; Vivien Rose, 22 October 1992. The theater in the visitor center is named for the late Corinne Guntzel. The sculptor for the statues was Lloyd Lillie assisted by Vicki Guerina.

13. Nancy Dubner interview with author, 13 May 1986.

14. U.S. Congress, Senate, Committee on Interior and Insular Affairs, Subcommittee on National Parks and Recreation, Hearing, *Clara Barton National Historic Site* . . . , 93rd Cong., 2nd sess. (13 September 1974): 55–56, 70–71; Friends of Clara Barton, Inc., "Clara Barton House Preservation Project, 1963–1975," Clara Barton NHS Archives.

15. Clara Barton NHS, "Suffragist Lawn Party," 11 May 1980; "Sunday Afternoons," 16 December 1979 to 24 August 1980; Sandra Weber, "Core Mission Declaration," 1 December 1981, Barton archives; *Clara Barton* (Washington, D.C.: NPS, USDI, 1981): 8–13, 75.

16. Dubner interview.

17. Ibid.; Joyce Ghee and Joan Spence joint interview with author, 27 November 1985.

18. *Vision of Val-Kill,* 1 June 1976, audio tape, supplied by the Franklin Delano Roosevelt Library.

19. U.S. Congress, Senate, Committee on Energy and Natural Resources, Subcommittee on Parks and Recreation, Hearing, *Eleanor Roosevelt National Historic Site,* 95th Cong., 1st sess. (29 April 1977): 1–44.

20. Interviews with author: Ghee and Spence; Margaret Partridge, 2 February 1994; Pat Duane Lichtenberg, 2 February 1944.

21. Giddings, *When and Where I Enter:* 199–130.

22. Dorothy Benton interview with author, 26 March 1985; James R. Goode, *The Outdoor Sculpture of Washington* (Washington, D.C.: Smithsonian Institution Press, 1974): 87–88.

23. U.S. Congress, Senate, Calendar, no. 772, report no. 97–534, *Designating the Mary McLeod Bethune Council House as a National Historic Site,* 97th Cong, 2nd sess. (17 August 1982); Bethune Museum and Archives, *1993 Annual Report.* In 1994, the Department of the Interior awarded Bettye Collier-Thomas its conservation award for her service to the Bethune Archives. USDI, *Fifty-second Honor Award Convocation,* 22 November 1994.

24. U.S. Congress, Senate, Committee on Energy and Natural Resources, Subcommittee on Public Lands, National Parks, and Forests, Hearings, *Mary McLeod Bethune Council House National Historic Site,* 102nd Cong., 1st sess. (21 May 1991): 38–43, 85- 90; Dorothy Benton interview with author, 28 January 1994; "Dorothy Irene Height," Darlene Clark Hine, ed., *Black Women in America* (Brooklyn, NY: Carlson Publishing, 1993), v. 1: 552–54.

25. Celia Jackson-Suggs interviews with author, 14 December 1985, 3 February 1994; Maggie L. Walker Historical Foundation, 1974–1986, commemorative booklet. Officers of the foundation in 1986 were: President Mozelle Sallee Baxter, Dr. Edward D. McCreary, Muriel Miller Branch, Dorothy Rice, Gladys A. Shaw, Georgia S. Williams, William Carter, III. Special thanks to Celia Jackson-Suggs for providing me with information about the foundation.

26. Elsa Barkley Brown, "Womanist Consciousness: Maggie Lena Walker and the Independent Order of Saint Luke," *Signs* 14 (spring 1989): 610–33. Quote on page 617. Gertrude W. Marlowe is directing the NPS-funded Maggie L. Walker Biography Project.

27. U.S. Congress, Senate, Committee on Energy and Natural Resources, Subcommittee on Public Lands, National Parks and Forests, Hearing, *Vietnam Women's Memorial,* 100th Cong., 2nd sess. (23 February 1988): 83.

28. Page Putnam Miller, *Reclaiming the Past: Landmarks of Women's History* (Bloomington: Indiana University Press, 1992): 3.

29. Called the "driving force" behind Women Climbers Northwest, Kathy Phibbs died in 1991 while climbing in the North Cascades. Da Silva, *Leading Out:* 280–86, 292f (photograph), 356.

30. Vietnam Women's Memorial Project, *The Legacy,* (Fourth Quarter 1977): 1; (First Quarter 1988): 1–2; "The Proposed Vietnam Women's Memorial, Position Paper," n.d. In their call to action, the project quoted one of the commissioners as saying, "If we allow a statue of a woman, we'll have to add other statues such as one for the canine corps." Vietnam Women's Memorial Project, "Dear Friends," 23 October 1987. The Vietnam Veterans Memorial, designed by Maya Lin, was dedicated in 1980.

31. The other commissions are the National Capital Memorial Commission and the National Capital Planning Commission. Senate Hearings, 23 February 1988: 3–9, 13, 83, 89–91; *Vietnam Women's Memorial Project, Inc.,* "Brief Chronology of the Vietnam Women's Memorial Project," 1993.

32. Ibid.; AP news story, 12 November 1993; Adam Drzal to author with supporting documents, 18 January 1994. Ret. Air Force Brig. General Wilma Vaught directs the Women in the Military Service of America Memorial Foundation with plans to build a memorial at the entrance to Arlington National Cemetery to women who served in American wars. Out of 1,400 entries in a 1989 design competition, the final design was by Marion Gail Weiss and Michael Manfredi. It incorporates a museum and data bank of servicewomen. The project has Congressional approval and will cost at least $15 million. Robert Campbell, "Why Washington needs the Women's Memorial," *Boston Globe,* 2 January 1990.

33. Page Putnam Miller, "Women's History Landmark Project: Policy and Research," *The Public Historian* 15 (fall 1993): 82–88; Barry Mackintosh letter to the editor, *Public Historian* 16 Spring 1994): 6–9.

34. "Interior Secretary Designates 25 National Historic Landmarks," NPS News Release, Midwest Region, 4 September 1991; Page Putnam Miller, "Progress Report on the Women's History Landmark Project," *Bulletin of the Conference Group on Women's History* 22 (May–June 1991): 3–6.

35. Senate, Hearing, *Women's Rights,* 8 September 1980: 109.

36. Interviews with author: Peggy Lipson, 11 December 1985; Priscilla Baker, 11 December 1985.

37. Ibid.

38. Peggy Lipson, ed., National Park Service, *Women's Conference,* 13–16 November 1979, NPS Women's Conference Collection, NPS Archives, Harpers Ferry. During the conference, African-American women boycotted a session and caucused separately because they believed their needs were not being addressed. After Mary Whalen, the director's wife who was present as an observer, listened to their concerns, the women returned to the meetings.

39. Ibid.; Heather Huyck, "Since 1918: Women in the National Park Service," NPS *Courier* 3 (January 1980): 8–9.

40. NPS Women's Conference Recommendations Presented to Director Whalen, 15 November 1979, NPS Women's Conference Collection; "Participants outline their recommendations," NPS *Courier* 3 (January 1980): 3–4. Naomi Hunt, NPS *Courier* editor, produced a special issue on the conference.

41. NPS Women's Conference Program, 2–4 April 1991: 4. The NPS anniversary theme was: "Protecting the Past, Managing the Present, Investing in the Future."

42. NPS Women's Conference Program; Women's Conference Evaluation Summaries, 14 May 1991, in NPS Women's Conference Notebook, Office of Chief, NPS Employee Development Division. The top-level women were Christina Cameron, director general, National Historic Sites Directorate, Canadian Parks Service, and Constance Harriman, assistant secretary, Fish and Wildlife and Parks, USDI.

43. NPS Women's Conference, *Career Fair News,* 3 April 1991.

44. ANPR, *Dual Career Directory* (fall 1986); ANPR, Dual Career Newsletter, (March 1987); NPS personnel management letter no. 87–07 (300), Spouse Placement Assistance, 19 August 1987; "Working Couples at Carlsbad Caverns," NPS *Courier* 30 (May 1985): 18–21; "Dual Careers: Viewpoints and Policies," NPS *Courier* 32 (April 1987): 24–31; "Dual Careers Program," Director's Bulletin Board, 8 May 1995, NPS internal communications. The new NPS policy includes unmarried partners.

45. The enactment of the Family and Medical Leave Act in 1993 (P.L. 103–3, 103rd Congress, 5 February 1993), allowing twelve weeks of unpaid leave, has brought consistency to leave policies among Park Service units. Acting Director NPS, Special Directive 85–1, Day Care Facilities, 8 April 1985; "Yosemite Child Care Center," NPS *Courier* 32 (April 1987): 19; Richard Smith interview with author, 10 February 1993; Magaly M. Green to author, 29 April 1993. Thanks to Carol Aten for NPS policy statements.

46. Ivette Ruan interview with author, 10 February 1993.

47. Beryl Stella-Meszaros to author, 2 November 1992 with enclosures; North Atlantic Region Women, *Connections,* summer 1992; Michelle C. Pelletier to author, 12 May 1993.

48. Director Russell E. Dickenson to All National Park Service Employees, Policy Statement on Sexual Harassment, 8 July 1980 with enclosure from Robert L. Herbst, Sexual Harassment, 1 May 1980; William Penn Mott Jr., Policy Statement on Sexual Harassment, 7 November 1985; interviews with author: Carolyn Burrell, 13 December 1985; Magaly Green, 22 November 1985, 10 February 1994; Eleanor Pratt, 3 September 1985; 12 February 1994.

49. Don Henry, "On a New Policy Whose Time Has Come" and "Supporting Voices," NPS *Courier* 37 (September 1992): 36–38; Marie Rust to All Employees, North Atlantic Region, Equal Opportunity Policy Statement, 14 December 1992; Bruce Babbitt to All Employees, 26 January 1994, courtesy U.S. Representative Barney Frank.

50. Lipson interview, 11 December 1985.

Bibliographical Essay

An examination of women and national parks cuts across several different fields of study, notably the history of women in the United States, the history of conservation and environmentalism, and the history of national parks. Studies in women's history proved to be the most useful in helping me interpret this work. For each area, I will mention only the most significant.

For travel, exploration, and wilderness living as a liberating experience for women, often not available at home, see Bonnie Frederick and Susan H. McLeod, eds., *Women and the Journey: The Female Travel Experience* (Pullman: Washington State University Press, 1993); Rachel da Silva, ed., *Leading Out: Women Climbers Reaching for the Top* (Seattle: Seal Press, 1992); Anne LaBastille, *Women and Wilderness: Women in Wilderness Professions and Lifestyles* (San Francisco: Sierra Club, 1980); and Janet Robertson, *The Magnificent Mountain Women: Adventures in the Colorado Rockies* (Lincoln: University of Nebraska Press, 1990).

For the roots of nineteenth-century women's moral view of nature, see Estelle Jussim and Elizabeth Linquist-Cock, *Landscape as Photograph* (New Haven: Yale University Press, 1985); Barbara Novak, *Nature and Culture: American Landscape and Painting, 1825–1875* (New York: Oxford University Press, 1980); and John F. Sears, *Sacred Places: American Tourist Attractions in the Nineteenth Century* (New York: Oxford University Press, 1989).

For women's efforts to preserve the past, including their own, and guidebooks to women's history sites, see Page Putnam Miller, ed., *Reclaiming the Past: Landmarks of Women's History* (Bloomington: Indiana University Press, 1992); Barbara J. Howe, "Women in Historic Preservation: The Legacy of Ann Pamela Cunningham," *The Public Historian* 12 (winter 1990): 31–61; Marion Tinling, *Women Remembered: A Guide to Landmarks of Women's History in the United States* (New York: Greenwood Press, 1986); and Lynn Sherr and Jurate Kazickas: *Susan B. Anthony Slept Here: A Guide to American Women's Landmarks* (New York: Random House, 1994). Women's roles in historic preservation are documented in Charles B. Hosmer, Jr., *Presence of the Past: A History of the Preservation Movement in the United States before Williamsburg* (New York: G. P. Putnam's Sons, 1965) and *Preservation Comes of Age: From Williamsburg to the National Trust, 1926–1949* (Charlottesville: University Press of Virginia, 1981), 2 vols. Rescuing the history of women in Southwest archeology is Nancy J. Parezo, ed., *Hidden Scholars: Women Anthropologists and the Native American Southwest* (Albuquerque: University of New Mexico Press, 1993).

Discussions about the progress of women in professional positions include Margaret W. Rossiter, *Women Scientists in America: Struggles and Strategies to 1940* (Baltimore: Johns Hopkins University Press, 1982) and Nancy Cott, *The Grounding of Modern Feminism* (New Haven: Yale University Press, 1987), who both point out that scientists and other professionals welcomed superior women into new areas, but as fields became professionalized, women were excluded. Rossiter also demonstrates how prestige in a profession is linked to the concept of masculinity, as does Linda Kerber in "Separate Spheres, Female Worlds, Woman's Place," *Journal of American History* 75 (June 1988): 9–39. Rossiter states that the proportion of women who achieved distinction in the sciences continued to grow throughout the 1930s, particularly in federal employment, despite sexual stereotyping of positions. While Rossiter believes a "critical mass" of women keeps them from "being totally driven from the field" (page 152), Cott suggests that the entrance of large numbers of women into a profession limits their participation because it creates a backlash arising from the fear of feminization.

Several studies help explain how a Park Service wife would accept her role as a surrogate for her husband without seeing herself as possessing his authority. Laurel Ulrich defined the concept as "deputy husband" in her *Good Wives: Image and Reality in the Lives of Women in Northern New England, 1650–1750* (New York: Alfred A. Knopf, 1982): 36; and Sheila M. Rothman as "wife companion" in *Woman's Proper Place* (New York: Basic Books, 1978): 184–85. Both Rothman and Lois Rudnick in *Mabel Dodge Luhan: New Woman, New Worlds* (Albuquerque: University of New Mexico Press, 1984) explain how women achieved self-actualization by working through men. The desire of Park Service wives to domesticate national parks is comparable to the goals of pioneer women described in Annette Kolodny, *The Land Before Her* (Chapel Hill: University of North Carolina Press, 1984). For an insightful discussion of the broader significance of the portrayal in art in the 1930s of the "manly worker" and its corollary, "female dependence," see "Manly Work" in Barbara Melosh, *Engendering Culture: Manhood and Womanhood in New Deal Public Art and Theater* (Washington: Smithsonian Press, 1991): 83–109.

An explanation for why wives did not work or took low-paying clerical jobs was the belief that women worked only to supplement a male breadwinner's wages. Alice Kessler Harris in *A Woman's Wage: Historical Meanings and Social Consequences* (Lexington: University of Kentucky Press, 1990), explains how the demand by male workers for a "family wage," income enough to support a man and his family without a working wife, led to pay equity issues.

Issues of gender differences arise in studies of women who work in nontraditional occupations and wear male-identified uniforms. Discussions of dress as one of the most visible ways society can use to define and restrict women's roles are presented in the literature about women and cross-dressing, including Julie Wheelwright, *Amazons and Military Maids* (London: Pandora Press, 1989) and Martha

Vicinus, "Rational Dress or Social Disorder?" paper presented at the Berkshire Conference on the History of Women, Douglass College, 9 June 1990. For early examples of women dealing with dress while riding astride, see Grace Gallatin Seton-Thompson, *A Woman Tenderfoot* (New York: Doubleday, Page, 1901) and Agnes Morley Cleveland, *No Life for a Lady* (Boston: Houghton Mifflin, 1941). In *Gender Differences at Work: Women and Men in Nontraditional Occupations* (Berkeley: University of California Press, 1989), Christine L. Williams posits that if the definition of being masculine for men is not being female, no demonstration of women's competency will overcome job segregation, suggesting that women in nontraditional careers will be more successful if they identify themselves as women rather than if they try to be "one of the boys" (page 132). To compare Park Service women with women in the U.S. Forest Service, see Mary Albertson, "Progress of Women in the Forest Service," *Women in Natural Resources* 15 (September 1993): 4–5 and ongoing issues of that journal. To compare Park Service and U.S. Army women, see Carol Barkalow, *In the Men's House* (New York: Poseidon Press, 1990).

In "History and Difference," *Daedalus* 116 (fall 1987): 93–118, Joan Scott assesses the tension that surrounds the concept of *difference* as either honoring difference and using it to demand greater representation or of defining "the common interest" by rejecting difference "imposed" by others. Estelle Freedman's classic "Separatism as Strategy: Female Institution Building and American Feminism, 1870–1930," *Feminist Studies* 5 (fall 1979): 512–29, discussing women who gained "political leverage in the larger society" by using a "separatist political strategy," explains the women park advocates who chose to work through their own organizations.

Feminist scholars are in disagreement over the implications of the work of Carol Gilligan and Sara Ruddick, who emphasize gender differences and attribute value to traditional feminine behavior. Gilligan says that women place the highest value on relationships and men on abstract rights; Ruddick calls for the use of "maternal thinking" to end conflict: Carol Gilligan, *In a Different Voice* (Cambridge: Harvard University Press, 1982); Sara Ruddick, *Maternal Thinking: Toward a Politics of Peace* (New York: Ballantine, 1990). For one opposing view, see Cynthia Fuchs Epstein, *Deceptive Distinctions: Sex, Gender, and the Social Order* (New Haven: Yale University Press, 1988).

The growing literature on the contrast between women's holistic view of nature and men's domination of nature in the field of technology began with the publication of Carolyn Merchant's *Death of Nature: Women, Ecology, and the Scientific Revolution* (New York: Harper & Row, 1980), and Susan Griffin's *Woman and Nature: The Roaring Inside Her* (New York: Harper & Row, 1978). The ecofeminist movement connects the oppression of nature with the oppression of women. See Irene Diamond and Gloria Feman Orenstein, eds., *Reweaving the World: The Emergence of Ecofeminism* (San Francisco: Sierra Club Books, 1990) and Joni Seager, *Earth Follies: Coming to Feminist Terms with the Global Environmental Crisis* (New York: Routledge, 1993). For an essay setting studies of ecofeminism in a broad context, see Linda Vance, "Remapping the Terrain: Books on Ecofeminism," *Choice* 30 (June 1993): 1585–93.

For further reading on early women naturalists, see Vera Norwood, *Made From This Earth: American Women and Nature* (Chapel Hill: University of North Carolina Press, 1993); Paul Brooks, "Birds and Women" in *Speaking for Nature* (Boston: Houghton Mifflin, 1980): 165–80; Deborah Strom, ed., *Birdwatching with American Women* (New York: W. W. Norton, 1986); Marcia Myers Bonta, *Women in the Field: America's Pioneering Women Naturalists* (College Station: Texas A. & M. University Press, 1991).

Good discussions on the differences between "utilitarian conservationists," signifying the efficient use of natural resources, and "aesthetic conservationists," designating the preservation of natural scenery for personal inspiration, are included in Samuel P. Hays, *Conservation and the Gospel of Efficiency: The Progressive Conservation Movement, 1890–1920* (Cambridge: Harvard University Press, 1959) and Donald C. Swain, "The Passage of the National Park Service Act of 1916," *Wisconsin Magazine of History* 50 (Autumn 1966): 4–17. In *Beauty, Health, and Permanence: Environmental Politics in the United States, 1955–1985 (Cambridge, England: Cambridge University Press, 1987),* Hays argues that the postwar environmental movement was concerned with "amenities" associated with "home and leisure, with recreation and the 'good life'" (page 4). Carolyn Merchant reveals the turning point when women began to reject utilitarian conservation in "Women of the Progressive Conservation Movement, 1900–1916," *Environmental Review* 8 (spring 1984): 57–85.

The history of conservation and environmentalism is covered in Stephen Fox, *John Muir and His Legacy: The American Conservation Movement* (Boston: Little, Brown, 1981); Roderick Nash, *Wilderness and the American Mind* (New Haven: Yale University Press, 3rd ed., 1983), and Phillip Shabecoff, *Green Fire: The American Environmental Movement* (New York: Hill and Wang, 1993). Because these studies look at the major environmental organizations, they do not present the roles of women who most often worked at the grassroots level. Although Shabecoff states that environmental groups need to rebuild their ties to the "activist civil rights/peace/women's tradition of the 1960s" (page 281), he does not spell out women's contributions.

A debate about the history of national parks arises from Alfred Runte's suggestion that national parks were created out of "worthless lands" in *National Parks: the American Experience* (Lincoln: University of Nebraska Press, 1979). Although women preservationists did not use economic worth as an argument in selecting landscapes to preserve, they were far more likely to be successful when the landscapes they hoped to preserve had little economic value (like the Great Sand Dunes) than when they tried to preserve valuable resources (like timber in the Olympics). While several works present current threats to national parks, including Runte's *National Parks,* they neglect to mention the many positive examples of women advocates. They include Ronald A. Foresta, *America's National Parks and Their Keepers* (Washington, D.C.: Resources for the Future, Inc., 1984); John C. Freemuth, *Islands Under Siege: National Parks and the Politics of External Threats* (Lawrence: University Press of Kansas, 1991); and Michael Frome, *Regreening the National Parks* (Tucson, University of

Arizona Press, 1992). Hal Rothman, in *America's National Monuments: The Politics of Preservation* (Lawrence: University Press of Kansas, 1994), demonstrates the importance of the Antiquities Act of 1906 as a tool for preserving park lands.

For the use of history for the purposes of healing and reconciliation, see Michael Kammen, *Mystic Chords of Memory: The Transformation of Tradition in American Culture* (New York: Alfred A. Knopf, 1991), although he does not mention women's particular role in establishing historic sites or memorials to accomplish healing. For memorials, see Richard West Sellars, "Vigil of Silence: The Civil War Memorials," *History News,* July 1986.

For chronologies and bibliographies on national park history and policies, see Barry Mackintosh, *The National Parks: Shaping the System* (Washington, D.C.: NPS, USDI, 1991); Barry Mackintosh, "Park Administrative Histories: An Annotated Bibliography," (Washington, DC: NPS, USDI, rev. ed.); Harold P. Danz, compiler, "Historical Listing of National Park Service Officials (Washington, DC: NPS, USDI, 1 May 1986); William C. Everhart, *The National Park Service* (Boulder: Westview Press, 1983); Harlan D. Unrau and G. Frank Williss, "To Preserve the Nation's Past: The Growth of Historic Preservation in the National Park Service during the 1930's," *The Public Historian* 9 (spring 1987): 19–49; and Hazel Hunt Voth et al., *A Bibliography of National Parks and Monuments West of the Mississippi* (Washington, DC: USDI, 1941), 2 vols.

Specific sources for this study on women and national parks are spelled out in the notes for each chapter. Because my goal was to find women's voices, the most useful sources were women's articles about their park experiences (see Voth bibliography above); my 383 recorded interviews of Park Service women staff, wives, and park founders and 140 recorded interviews by Dorothy Boyle Huyck, filed in the Park Service Archives, Harpers Ferry; and 536 questionnaires from Park Service women filed in the Schlesinger Library, Radcliffe College. Other important sources were administrative histories of parks; Congressional hearings; Park Service publications and internal communications; Southwest Monument monthly reports from 1934 to 1940; official correspondence and clipping files in the Yosemite and Yellowstone archives and in Record Group 79, National Archives. The papers collected by Dorothy Boyle Huyck are housed in the Dorothy Boyle Huyck Collection, National Park Service Archives, Harpers Ferry, WV.

Index

Interpretation of Women's History in National Parks

West Coast, Southwest, Alaska, and Hawaii

National Park	Location	Description
Cabrillo NM	San Diego, CA	Wives of lighthouse keepers
Canyon de Chelly NM	Chinle, AZ	Spider Woman myth
Chiricahua NM	Wilcox, AZ	Lillian Erickson's Faraway Ranch
Fort Clatsop N Mem.	Astoria, OR	Sacagawea, Shoshone woman guide of Lewis and Clark Expedition
Fort Union NM	Watrous, NM	Women's daily life in frontier fort
Fort Vancouver NHS	Vancouver, WA	Native American women in fur trade
Glacier Bay NP & P	Gustavus, AK	Scidmore Glacier named for explorer Eliza Scidmore
Golden Gate NRA	San Francisco, CA	Women of the Presidio under three flags
Grand Canyon NP	Grand Canyon, AZ	Mary Jane Colter, architect; Georgie White Clark, Colorado River runner; Harvey girls
Hubbell Trading Post NHS	Ganado, AZ	Navajo women weavers; Dorothy Hubbell, trader
John Muir NHS	Martinez, CA	Orchard manager, wife Louie Strentzel Muir
Joshua Tree NP	Twentynine Palms, CA	Plaque to Minerva Hamilton Hoyt, park founder
Kalaupapa NHP	Molokai, HI	Mother Marianne Cope of Sisters of St. Francis, leader of nurses in leper colony
Klondike Gold Rush NHP	Seattle, WA/Skagway, AK	Women in gold rush
Lassen Volcanic NP	Mineral, CA	Lake Helen named for Helen Brodt, first woman climber of Lassen Peak

Mount Rainier NP	Ashford, WA	Fay Fuller, first woman climber of Mount Rainier
Nez Perce NHP	Spalding, ID	Nez Perce women's crafts and lives
Saguaro NM	Tucson, AZ	Tohono O'Odham Indian women's use of saguaro cactus
San Francisco Maritime NHP	San Francisco, CA	Captains' families on lady ships
Sitka NHP	Sitka, AK	Maria Maksutov, wife of Russian governor
Whiskeytown NRA	Whiskeytown, CA	Women in gold rush
Whitman Mission NHS	Walla Walla, WA	Narcissa Whitman, missionary to Cayuse

Midwest, Rocky Mountains, and Texas

National Park	Location	Description
Bent's Old Fort NHS	La Junta, CO	Diarist Susan Magoffin on Santa Fe Trail
Bighorn Canyon NRA	Fort Smith, MT	Writer Carolyn Lockhart's ranch
Brown v. Board of Education NHS	Topeka, KS	Women in Civil Rights Movement
Capitol Reef NP	Torrey, UT	Mormon women pioneers' lives
Cedar Breaks NM	Cedar City, UT	Mormon women pioneers' lives
Florissant Fossil Beds NM	Florissant, CO	Adeline Hornbeck, woman homesteader
Fort Laramie NHS	Fort Laramie, WY	Army officers' wives and laundresses in frontier fort; grave of pioneer Mary Homsley
Grand Portage MN	Grand Marais, MN	Native American women in fur trade
Grant-Kohrs Ranch NHS	Deer Lodge, MT	Women in cattle ranching
Harry S. Truman NHS	Independence, MO	Bess Truman, president's wife
Herbert Hoover NHS	West Branch, IA	Hulda Hoover, pioneer and president's mother; Mollie Brown, president's teacher
Homestead NM of America	Beatrice, NE	Pioneer family and frontier school
Jefferson National Expansion Mem.	St. Louis, MO	Pioneer and Native American women in Museum of Westward Expansion
Jewel Cave NM	Custer, SD	Cave explorers Jan and Herb Conn
Knife River Indian Villages NHS	Stanton, ND	Sacagawea, guide to Lewis and Clark; Hidatsa women
Lincoln Boyhood N Mem.	Lincoln City, IN	Nancy Hanks Lincoln, president's mother

Lyndon B. Johnson NHS	Johnson City, TX	President's mother Rebekah, wife Ladybird, teacher Kate Deadrich Loney
Pipe Spring NM	Moccasin, AZ	Mormon women pioneers' lives
Rocky Mountain NP	Estes Park, CO	Women mountaineers; Isabella Bird's 1873 ascent of Longs Peak
San Antonio Missions NHP	San Antonio, TX	Women's roles in Spanish mission
Scotts Bluff NM	Gering, NE	Women on the overland trail
Voyageurs NP	International Falls, MN	Artist Frances Ann Hopkins' paintings of fur trade

Northeast

National Park	Location	Description
Adams NHS	Quincy, MA	Four generations of Adams women including wives of two presidents
Boston African American NHS	Boston, MA	African American women abolitionists: Maria Stewart, Susan Paul, and Ellen Craft
Boston NHP	Boston, MA	Women shipbuilders during World War II
Cape Cod Nat. Seashore	Eastham, MA	Penniman House, home of Augusta Penniman, whaling ship captain's wife
Edison NHS	West Orange, NJ	Women of Glenmont, Thomas Edison's mansion: wife Mina and women servants
Eleanor Roosevelt NHS	Hyde Park, NY	Val-Kill, home of "first lady of the world"
Ellis Island NM	New York, NY	Immigrant women
Fire Island NS	Patchogue, NY	Display on Margaret Fuller, women's rights leader drowned in shipwreck
Gateway NRA	Brooklyn, NY	Women aviators at Floyd Bennett Field
John Fitzgerald Kennedy NHS	Brookline, MA	Life of Rose Fitzgerald Kennedy, president's mother
Longfellow NHS	Cambridge, MA	Lives of Fanny and Alice Longfellow, poet's wife and daughter
Lowell NHP	Lowell, MA	Mill girls' boarding houses and work places
Martin Van Buren NHS	Kinderhook, NY	Women servants in Lindenwald mansion; Angelica Singleton, White House hostess

Minute Man NHP	Concord, MA	Wayside: home of authors Louisa May Alcott and Margaret Sidney; women in Revolution
Morristown NHP	Morristown, NJ	Women in Revolutionary War
Sagamore Hill NHS	Oyster Bay, NY	Lives of women associated with President Theodore Roosevelt
Salem Maritime NHS	Salem, MA	Salem witchcraft hysteria
Springfield Armory NHS	Springfield, MA	Women gun makers in World War II
Women's Rights NHP	Seneca Falls, NY	Home of Elizabeth Cady Stanton, women's rights leader; Wesleyan Chapel, site in 1848 of first women's rights convention

Mid–Atlantic and Washington, D.C.

National Park	Location	Description
Antietam N Battlefield	Sharpsburg, MD	Women in Civil War; Clara Barton memorial
Appomattox Court House NHP	Appomattox, VA	Role of Confederate women in Civil War
Arlington National Cemetery	Arlington, VA	Memorials: Army nurses Jane Delano and Anita McGee; Challenger crew: Christa McAuliffe and Judy Resnik; Women in Military Service for America
Arlington House, The Robert E. Lee Memorial	Arlington, VA	Lee family women during the Civil War
Booker T. Washington NM	Hardy, VA	Roles of plantation mistresses and enslaved women
Chesapeake & Ohio Canal NHP	Sharpsburg, MD	Wives steering canal boats
Clara Barton NHS	Glen Echo, MD	Home of American Red Cross founder
Colonial NHP	York Town, VA	Women in Revolutionary War
Edgar Allan Poe NHS	Philadelphia, PA	Influence of poet's wife Virginia and mother-in-law Maria Clemm
Eisenhower NHS	Gettysburg, PA	Role of president's wife, Mamie
Frederick Douglass NHS	Washington, DC	Leader of civil rights and women's rights movements
Fredericksburg & Spotsylvania County Battlefields Mem. NP	Fredericksburg, VA	Civil war women, in medicine: Clara Barton and Dr. Mary Walker; in disguise as soldier: Sarah Edmonds

George Washington Birthplace NM	Washington's Birthplace, VA	Home of Mary Ball Washington, president's mother
Hampton NHS	Towson, MD	Plantation women
Harpers Ferry NHP	Harpers Ferry, WV	Civil War women
Hopewell Furnace NHS	Elverson, PA	Women workers in cast iron industry
Independence NHP	Philadelphia, PA	Todd House, home of Dolley Todd [Madison], future president's wife; women printers
Johnstown Flood N Mem.	St. Michael, PA	Disaster relief effort led by Clara Barton and American Red Cross
Maggie Walker NHS	Richmond, VA	African-American community leader
Mary McLeod Bethune Council House NHS	Washington, DC	Home and office of founder of National Council of Negro Women; NCNW archives
Petersburg N Battlefield	Petersburg, VA	Civil War women: U.S. Sanitary Commission
Richmond N Battlefield	Richmond, VA	Confederate women nurses at Chimborazo Hospital
Sewall-Belmont House NHS	Washington, DC	National Woman's Party headquarters
Steamtown NHS	Scranton, PA	Women railroaders during World War II
U.S. Capitol Building	Washington, DC	Suffrage monument; statues of Maria Sanford, Frances Willard, Florence Sabin, Esther Morris, Mother Joseph
Valley Forge NHP	Valley Forge, PA	Women in Revolutionary War encampment
Vietnam Women's Memorial	Washington, DC	Monument to military women in Vietnam War

Southeast

National Park	Location	Description
Abraham Lincoln Birthplace NHS	Hodgenville, KY	Nancy Hanks Lincoln, president's mother
Andersonville NHS	Andersonville, GA	Clara Barton memorial sundial
Blue Ridge Pkwy	Asheville, NC	Cabin of midwife Orelena Puckett
Carl Sandburg Home NHS	Flat Rock, NC	Dairy of Paula Sandburg, goat breeder

Castillo de San Marcos NM	St. Augustine, FL	Women teachers in Native American school
Charles Pinckney NHS	Mt. Pleasant, SC	Eliza Lucas Pinckney, horticulturist
Chickamauga and Chattanooga NMP	Fort Oglethorpe, GA	Women in Civil War: nurses and soldiers; Dr. Mary Walker
Fort Frederica NM	St. Simons Island, GA	Women's lives in 18th century Georgia
Fort Pulaski NM	Savannah, GA	Florence Martus, "waving girl of Savannah"; lighthouse resident
Fort Smith NHS	Fort Smith, AR	Anna Dawes's campaign to improve conditions in frontier jail
Great Smoky Mountains NP	Gatlinburg, TN	Women's roles in mountain communities; women teachers in Greenbrier School
Hot Springs NP	Hot Springs, AR	Ladies' bathhouse, beauty shop, hydrotherapy rooms
Jean Lafitte NHP & Pres.	New Orleans, LA	Women in Civil War; Cajun and historic New Orleans women
Jimmy Carter NHS	Plains, GA	Lillian and Rosalynn Carter, president's mother and wife; Julia Coleman, teacher
Kennesaw Mountain N Battlefield Pk	Kennesaw, GA	Civil War women
Martin Luther King, Jr. NHS	Atlanta, GA	Queens of Sweet Auburn: business women leaders on Auburn Avenue
Moores Creek N Battlefield	Currie, NC	Statue of Polly Slocumb, tribute to Revolutionary War heroines
Timucuan Ecol. & Hist. Pres.	Jacksonville, FL	Anna Madgigine Jai Kingsley: former slave then wife of plantation owner
Tuskegee Institute NHS	Tuskegee Inst., AL	Olivia Davidson Washington and Margaret Murray Washington, Women's Normal School principals and second and third wives of Booker T. Washington
Vicksburg NMP	Vicksburg, MS	Women soldiers in Civil War: Jennie Hodgers disguised as Pvt. Albert Cashier